Common Spoken English Errors in Hong Kong

Joseph and Linda Boyle

Longman朗文

Published by
Longman Hong Kong
A division of Longman Asia Limited
18th Floor, Cornwall House
Taikoo Place
979 King's Road
Hong Kong
Tel: (852) 811 8168
and Associated Companies throughout the world

First published 1991
Reprinted 1994

Produced by Longman Asia Limited
Printed in Hong Kong
NPC/05

ISBN 962 359 494 1

The Publishers welcome any comments from readers.
Please contact the School Publishing Department on 811 8168.

Preface

Good spoken English is becoming more and more important nowadays. People travel more frequently and deal with each other face to face. They also use the telephone more. For international communication we need accurate spoken English.

Errors in spoken English can cause misunderstanding and annoyance. Often the speaker is unaware of the error. This book aims at helping Chinese speakers of English to avoid some of the common errors in their spoken English.

Some of the errors are mistakes of grammar or vocabulary. Sometimes the influence of the Cantonese language on the error can be detected and this is pointed out where appropriate.

Others are more a matter of inappropriate language. It would be considered very impolite, for example, to say 'Wait!' to someone on the phone, or 'Hey, waiter!' in a restaurant, instead of the more polite forms, 'Would you mind holding on?' and 'Excuse me, waiter!' But it is not easy for a non-native English speaker to know when a form is impolite and what the correct expression should be.

The examples have been gathered over many years and represent commonly heard errors in spoken English among Chinese speakers. Explanations of the errors are deliberately kept very simple and non-technical. The purpose of the book is practical — to help Chinese speakers of English recognise their mistakes and correct them.

The errors are listed alphabetically within sections covering different topic areas such as on the telephone, job interviews, banking, shopping, etc. At the end of each section there are two types of exercise. The first exercise is in multiple-choice form. Help is given by underlining three possible places where the error may lie.

The second type of exercise is more difficult. The texts of two conversations are given containing ten errors each. These have to be located and corrected. This type of exercise may prove challenging even for quite advanced speakers of English.

The examples used in the exercises recycle the errors listed in the first part of each section. The exercises thus reinforce the learning of the correct version.

Thanks are owed to several people: to the many teachers and students who have helped with collecting errors over the years; to Denise Suen Lai Kuen, Annie Wong Pui Yee, Wendy Chan Sau Wing and others, who advised on the influence of the Cantonese language on certain errors; to the Longman team, especially Sue Falkingham who saw in the authors the potential for a book of this kind, to Chris Knott who gave encouragement and advice throughout the writing and production stage, to the Longman readers who offered suggestions for improvement, especially David Bunton, the author of the first very successful book in this series, to Grace Pow for high-quality editing and to Justin Rae for the amusing cartoons.

Joseph and Linda Boyle
June 1991

CONTENTS

For Fiona and Teresa

Chapter **1**   *In a Restaurant*

Balanced food

x   *You should eat **balanced food** with plenty of vegetables.*

√   *You should eat **a balanced diet** with plenty of vegetables.*

Your 'diet', not your 'food' is balanced.

Beef-steak

x   *I want to order a **beef-steak**.*

√   *I want to order a **steak**.*

Normally you do not have to specify that it is a 'beef' steak that you want.

Calculated

x   *I think the bill **is calculated wrongly**.*

√   *I think the bill **is wrong**.*

√   *I think there **is a mistake in the bill**.*

The use of the word 'calculated' is inappropriate and is influenced by the Cantonese 計錯數.

Call

x   *Can I **call dishes** now?*

√   *Can I **order** now?*

In different contexts the Cantonese 叫 can mean 'call', 'tell' or 'order'. This explains the choice of the word 'call'. In

English we say 'order' when we make a request for food in a restaurant.

Certain times

x *I used to eat at any time, but now I have my meals at **certain times**.*

√ *I used to eat at any time, but now I have my meals at **fixed times/definite times/ regular times**.*

'Certain times' would mean that you only have a meal occasionally. The speaker wishes to say that she has her meals at definite times of the day.

Choices

x *What's the **choices** of salad **dressing**?*

√ *What's the **choice** of salad **dressings**?*

There is one choice (singular) of many salad dressings (plural).

Check for / on

1 x *I think my bill's wrong. Would you **check for** it?*

√ *I think my bill's wrong. Would you **check** it?*

When 'check' is used with 'bill', no preposition is used.

2 x *Please **have a check on** the bill?*

√ *Would you please **check** the bill?*

Cup

x *One **cup** of Coke, please.*

√ *One **glass** of Coke, please.*

The Cantonese 一杯 can be used for a cup or a glass. In English you use 'cup' for tea, coffee, etc, but 'glass' for Coke, beer, etc.

Dinner

1   x   *May I have the pleasure **to have dinner with you** tonight?*

√   *May I **have dinner with you** tonight?*

The speaker means to invite someone to dinner. But 'to have dinner with you' sounds like you are asking to join other people at their dinner, to be their guest. Another wrong way of inviting someone is:

2   x   *May I **enjoy dinner with you** tonight?*

This again seems to be asking to join other people at their dinner. A good formula to use when inviting someone to dinner is:

√   ***Would you like to join me for dinner** tonight?*

Do

x   ***Do** you like a drink?*

√   ***Would** you like a drink?*

'Do' means 'do you like to drink regularly?'. 'Would' is used when offering someone a drink on a particular occasion.

Don't

x   ***Don't** you have breakfast today?*

√   ***Didn't** you have breakfast today?*

The past tense is required here. 'Don't' can be used to ask about habitual action:

√   ***Don't** you have breakfast at seven every morning?*

√   ***Don't** you have breakfast with your wife?*

DON'T YOU HAVE BREAKFAST TODAY !!

Easy

x   *We can **easy** eat six dishes between us.*
√   *We can **easily** eat six dishes between us.*
The correct adverbial usage here is 'easily'.
'Easy' is correctly used as an adjective in the
following sentence:
√   *It is **easy** to eat too much at a buffet
dinner.*

Enjoy

x   *I **enjoy** the meal very much.*
√   *I **enjoyed** the meal very much.*
This may be an error of grammar (present for
past) or an error of pronunciation (not
sounding the final syllable -ed).

Fifty per cent

x   *I'd like my steak **fifty per cent**, please.*
√   *I'd like my steak **medium**, please.*
This is simply a direct translation from the
Cantonese 五成熟 . If you want the meat to
be well cooked, you should say 'well-done'.

Five

x   *The bill comes to two hundred and twenty-
seven dollars and **five** (227.50).*
√   *The bill comes to two hundred and twenty-
seven dollars and **fifty cents**.*
√   *The bill comes to two hundred and twenty-
seven **fifty**.*
The shorter last form is the most common.

Give

x   *Excuse me. Can you **give** me the fish I
ordered?*
√   *Excuse me. Can you **bring** me the fish I
ordered?*
When a service is expected (as in a
restaurant), the Cantonese 拎 is translated as
'bring', not 'give'.

Had bought

x   *Today I **had bought** two ice creams.*
√   *Today I **bought** two ice creams.*
The simple past tense, not the past perfect, is
what is required here. You could say:
√   *I **had bought** two ice creams before an
hour had gone by.*

Hardly	x	*The waiters are working very **hardly**.*
	√	*The waiters are working very **hard**.*

The correct form of the adverb is **hard**. The word 'hardly' is used in other ways:

√ *We had **hardly** finished eating when the plates were collected.*

Here 'hardly finished' means 'only just that moment.'

√ *We can **hardly** expect to get a good table.*

Here 'hardly expect' means 'to a very limited extent'.

Have/Having	1	x	*There will **have** plenty of food for four of us.*
		√	*There will **be** plenty of food for four of us.*
	2	x	*Can we get a table **having** a sea view?*
		√	*Can we get a table **with** a sea view?*

This error comes from the Cantonese use of 有.

Hey	x	***Hey!** Waiter.*
	√	***Excuse me**, waiter.*

'Hey' in English is impolite.

Holding you	x	*Sorry for **holding you**.*
	√	*Sorry for **holding you up**.*
	√	*Sorry for **keeping you**.*

'Holding you' would mean 'holding on to you'. If you want to apologise for keeping someone waiting, you use 'holding you up' = 'delaying you', or 'keeping you' = 'keeping you waiting'.

It	x	*You ate bad seafood. **It** is why you are sick.*
	√	*You ate bad seafood. **That** is why you are sick.*

You cannot use 'it' in this way. The more definite demonstrative word 'that' is required.

Lately

x *Let's dine early. I don't like to eat **lately**.*
√ *Let's dine early. I don't like to eat **late**.*
The adverb used to express 'at a late hour' is
'late'. 'Lately' means 'recently', 'over the past
few days', as in:
√ *I have lost my appetite **lately**.*

Meal of breakfast

x *A **meal of breakfast** gives you energy for
the day.*
√ *A **good breakfast** gives you energy for
the day.*
You cannot say 'a meal of breakfast', though
you can say 'a meal of porridge', meaning
that the meal consisted of nothing but
porridge. There are many alternative
idiomatic expressions in English for 'a good
breakfast': 'a big/hearty/substantial/proper
breakfast'.

Mind to check

1 x *Would you **mind to check** the bill?*
√ *Would you **mind checking** the bill?*
After 'mind' use the gerund (-ing form), not
the infinitive.

2 x *Would you **mind coming** to my home for
dinner tonight?*
√ *Would you **like to come** to my home for
dinner tonight?*
'Mind coming' is grammatically correct. But
'would you mind' means 'would it be
troublesome', which is not appropriate when
giving a dinner invitation, unless, for example,
you had previously arranged to go out for
dinner. In this case 'home' would be stressed.

Nearby

x *Could we have a table **nearby** the
window?*
√ *Could we have a table **near** the window?*
'Nearby' is an adverb and cannot be used
before a noun like 'the window'. A preposition
is needed such as 'near', 'beside', or 'by'.

Of course not

x   *Does the restaurant serve meals all day?*
    (Reply) ***Of course not****! Lunch is 11-2,*
    and dinner 7-11.

√   *Does the restaurant serve meals all day?*
    (Reply) ***Sorry, I'm afraid not****. Lunch is*
    11-2, and dinner 7-11.

'Of course not' is a rude answer. It gives the impression that the person has asked a foolish question.

One of

x   ***One of the suggestion*** *made seemed*
    good to all the diners.

√   ***One of the suggestions*** *made seemed*
    good to all the diners.

'One of' is followed by a plural noun.

Opened

x   *We are not* ***opened*** *till six o'clock.*

√   *We are not* ***open*** *till six o'clock.*

Although we do say 'closed', we use 'open', not 'opened', for a restaurant or shop. In some cases 'opened' can be used:

√   *The doors will not be* ***opened*** *till the film*
    has ended.

Order

1 x *I **haven't made such an order**.*
  √ ***This wasn't my order**.*
  √ *I **didn't order this**.*
The present perfect is wrong here. Also 'this' would be used, not 'such an order'.

2 x *I **make an order** later, thank you.*
  √ *I'll **make my order** later, thank you.*
We have to use the future tense here.

Pieces of

x *I ate only two **pieces of sandwich** for lunch.*
√ *I ate only two **sandwiches** for lunch.*
We do not use 'piece of' (like a classifier in Cantonese) with 'sandwich' which is a countable noun. But we do use it with some other food terms which need to be cut up or divided: 'pieces of cake/bread/shortbread/chocolate'.

Prefer

x *I **prefer** rice **than** potatoes.*
√ *I **prefer** rice **to** potatoes.*
You prefer one thing 'to' another, not 'than' another. You could, however, say:
√ *I **prefer to** eat rice **rather than** potatoes.*

Reservation

x *Do you have **reservation**?*
√ *Do you have **a reservation**?*
When it means a booking for a particular meal, the indefinite article is needed. But 'reservation' is sometimes found without an article when it is used in a more general sense.
√ ***Reservations** are necessary on Saturdays and Sundays.*

Right

x *You're now ready to order, **right**?*
√ ***Excuse me, are you** ready to order now?*
√ ***Would you like** to order now?*
'Right' is too abrupt and impolite.

Seat

x *I telephoned earlier and booked a **seat** near the window.*
√ *I telephoned earlier and booked a **table** near the window.*

You would say a 'seat' in a theatre, but a 'table' in a restaurant.

Selling

x   *The food **selling** by hawkers can make you ill.*

√   *The food **sold by** hawkers can make you ill.*

The passive 'sold by' ('which is being sold by') is correct. You can also say:

√   *The hawkers **are selling** the food at the corner of the street.*

Several times

x   *I invited him to lunch **for several times**.*

√   *I invited him to lunch **several times**.*

Words like 'several' or 'many' do not take 'for' with 'times'. The error may be influenced by the correct common expression 'for several reasons'.

Show

x   *Waiter, **show** me the menu.*

√   *Waiter, **please bring** me the menu.*

√   *Waiter, **could I please have/see** the menu?*

'Show' is too abrupt and impolite.

Suggest to

x   *I suggest to eat early.*
√   *I suggest eating early.*
√   *I suggest that we should eat early.*
√   *I suggest that we eat early.*
√   *I suggest we eat early.*

Not 'suggest to eat'. There are many correct ways of saying this.

Taste

x   *You have **a good taste** in the decoration of your dining room.*
√   *You have **good taste** in the decoration of your dining room.*

The omission of the article is important in this idiom. 'Have a good taste' means someone is eating you.

They

x   *The dishes, **they** are all very tasty.*
√   *The dishes **are** all very tasty.*

The pronoun is redundant here.

Used to

x   *I **used to** eat at McDonald's.*
√   *I **usually** eat at McDonald's.*

When you want to say, 'My custom/habit is to ...', you do not say 'used to', which is an auxiliary verb denoting the past tense. 'I used to eat' would mean 'My practice in the past was to eat'.

Vegetable

x   *You should eat more* **vegetable**.
√   *You should eat more **vegetables**.*

Though 'meat' is an uncountable noun (you cannot say 'meats'), with 'vegetable' the correct plural form is 'vegetables', not 'vegetable'.

Very delicious

x   *The dinner was **very delicious**.*
√   *The dinner was **delicious**.*
Since 'delicious' already implies 'very tasty/ very enjoyable', another 'very' with 'delicious' should not be used, though this is a very common usage among Hong Kong speakers of English.

Want

x   *I **want** a sandwich.*
√   *I **would like** a sandwich.*
We must use 'would like' in polite English.

Yes

x   *Do you mind sitting over here? (Reply)*
    ***Yes**.*
√   *Do you mind sitting over here? (Reply)*
    ***Not at all**.*
'Yes' as a reply can give the impression you do mind sitting over there, that is, you are unwilling to.

Exercises

A   There is an error in each question. Decide whether the error is in the underlined section A, B or C by circling the appropriate letter. Then give the correct answers in the space provided.

1   We <u>had better</u> <u>call the dishes</u> now
         A   B
or <u>we'll be late back</u> for work.   _____
         C

2   They ordered two <u>cups of coffee,</u>
                           A
one <u>cup of orange juice</u> and a
         B
<u>half-pint of beer</u>.   _____
         C

3   I suggest t<u>o leave</u> <u>as soon as</u> we
           A   B

    <u>finish</u> eating.
     C
                                    _____

4   Waiter, it's <u>rather cold</u>. Do you mind
                A

    <u>turning down</u> the fan. (*Waiter replies*):
       B

    <u>Yes</u>.
     C
                                      _____

5   The cook works so <u>hardly</u> that he
                   A

    <u>seldom</u> <u>gets enough</u> time to eat his
      B   C

    own lunch.
                                      _____

6   Sorry <u>for holding you</u>. You should
           A

    <u>just have started</u> and <u>not waited</u> for
       B   C

    me.
                                      _____

7   <u>One of the reason</u> tourists <u>enjoy</u>
        A   B

    Hong Kong is <u>the number of choices</u>.
                    C
                                    _____

8   <u>In addition to</u> to chicken and pork,
      A

    <u>would you like</u> to order <u>vegetable</u>?
      B   C
                                    _____

9   Alan eats <u>fast</u>. He can <u>easy</u> finish his
           A   B

    food in <u>no time at all</u>.
            C
                                    _____

10 I think <u>there will have</u> problems
           A

    <u>if we choose</u> the Diplomat hotel <u>for</u>
      B   C

    our annual ball.
                                      _____

B(i) There are ten errors in the dialogue below. Read carefully and underline the errors. Then, rewrite the dialogue in the space provided. (Please note that errors are not found in every line.)

Francis : What restaurant do you go to most often?

Margaret : I used to eat at Sun Sui Wah. The dishes they are very delicious there.

Francis : Can we go early, say six o'clock? I get indigestion if I eat lately.

Margaret : But the restaurant is not opened till seven. Don't you have lunch today?

Margaret : Well, I had bought two pieces of sandwich from a hawker this morning.

Francis : But the food selling by hawkers is not clean.

Margaret : Maybe it is why I am not feeling so well just now.

_____

_____

_____

_____

_____

_____

_____

_____

_____

_____

_____

_____

_____

_____

_____

_____

_____

_____

_____

_____

_____

B(ii) Underline the ten errors and rewrite the dialogue in the space provided. (Please note that errors are not found in every line.)

Waiter : Do you have reservation?

Mr Ng : Yes, my name is Ng. I asked for a seat near the window.

Waiter : This way, sir. (*He pulls out a chair for Mr Ng*). Do you like something to drink?

Mr Ng : No thanks. Show me the menu. I make an order now. (*Pause*). I want a beef-steak.

Waiter : How would you like it done?

Mr Ng : Fifty per cent. (*He finishes and gets the bill*). Hey! Waiter. Would you mind to check the bill? This looks too much.

Waiter : Sorry, you are right. It is calculated wrongly.

Mr Ng : Be more careful in future or you will lose a customer.

Chapter 2   Telephone Manners

Able

x   *I will be **able** on any date.*
√   *I will be **available** on any date.*
In Cantonese, 可以 means that you are able to or can do something. The words also imply that you have time for an appointment. In English, 'able' means that you have the knowledge, power or skill to do something. If you want to say that you have time for an appointment, either 'able to come' or 'available' should be used.

Afraid

x   *I **afraid** you have the wrong number.*
√   *I'm **afraid** you have the wrong number.*
'Afraid' cannot be used as a verb.

Back

x   *Sorry she's not **back** yet.*
√   *Sorry she's not **in** yet.*
'Not back yet' means the person has been in but has gone out. Some speakers wrongly use 'not back yet' even when a person has not been in that day.

Before

x   *I called you half an hour **before**.*
√   *I called you half an hour **ago**.*
The Cantonese 之前 can mean 'before' and 'ago'. In English 'before' is normally followed by something else, e.g. 'I called you before I left.'

Business trip

x   *He's gone to Bangkok for **business trip**.*
√   *He's gone to Bangkok for **a business trip**.*
'Trip' is a countable noun and needs an article. Other correct ways of saying this would be:
√   *He's gone to Bangkok **on business**.*
√   *He's gone to Bangkok **for business reasons**.*

Busy

x   ***My work is so busy** I haven't time for sports.*
√   ***I'm so busy at work** I haven't time for sports.*
The expression 'work is so busy' follows the

Cantonese 我工作好忙. In English you cannot say 'work is busy'. A person is busy because of the work.

Call at

x *May I know who you are **calling at**?*
√ *May I know who you are **calling for**?*
Note the preposition should be 'for'.

Cut-off

x *Sorry **we had a cut-off of the telephone***.
√ *Sorry **our call was cut off**.*
√ *Sorry **we were cut off**.*
In Cantonese 電話 can refer to the telephone or the call. 'Our call' is used in English since the conversation over the telephone, not the telephone itself, is cut off.

Dial

x *I think you **dial** the wrong number.*
√ *I think you**'ve dialled** the wrong number.*
The person has finished dialling the number but is still on the line, so the present perfect tense is required.

Died

x *Sorry my telephone **died**.*
√ *Sorry my telephone **went dead**.*
The correct idiomatic usage is 'went

dead'. 'Died' can be correctly used as follows:

√ *The noise suddenly **died down/out** (became less strong/disappeared).*

Do

x ***Do** you like to leave a message?*
√ ***Would** you like to leave a message?*
'Do' means as a matter of habit. 'Would' is used as a matter of courtesy.

Engaged in

x *He's **engaged in** another line.*
√ *He's **engaged on** another line.*
He could be engaged 'in' another room or engaged 'in' conversation. But you say engaged 'on', not 'in', the telephone.

Expect

x ***I'm expecting** your call for an hour.*
√ ***I've been expecting** your call for an hour.*
The present perfect is the correct tense here.

Find time

x *Sorry I can't **find time** to see you.*
√ *Sorry I can't **seem to find time** to see you.*
We need to add extra words 'seem to' so as to be more polite. The wrong example is a bit too blunt.

Goes

x *I'm sorry he's not in. He **goes** to lunch.*
√ *I'm sorry he's not in. He**'s gone** to lunch.*
The wrong tense has been used. 'Goes' would be correct in:

√   *He **goes** to lunch at twelve every day.*

Got

x   *You **got** the wrong number. This is 6351740.*

√   *You**'ve got** the wrong number. This is 6351740.*

Since the caller is still on the line, 'you've got' is appropriate. If someone wants to say he got the wrong number on a call that is now over, he could say:

√   *I **got** the wrong number.*

Hanged

x   *I had dialled the wrong number, so I **hanged** up.*

√   *I had dialled the wrong number, so I **hung** up.*

'Hanged' is the correct past tense for the act of hanging a criminal with a rope. But you do not say 'hanged up' for a telephone.

Here

x   *Is that 3360769? (Reply) No. **Here** is 3360768.*

√   *Is that 3360769? (Reply) No. **This** is 3360768.*

There is no distinction between 'this' and 'here' in Cantonese. 呢度 refers to the place; and associates a telephone number with the location of the telephone. In English, 'this' refers to the number.

I'm

x   *Hello. **I'm** David.*
√   *Hello. **It's** David.*
√   *Hello. **This is** David.*
Cantonese says: 我係 . But English says: 'it's'
or 'this is'.

In

x   *Sorry he's **in** the other line right now.*
√   *Sorry he's **on** the other line right now.*
The correct preposition should be 'on'.

Is it

x   *Can you tell me who **is it** calling?*
√   *Can you tell me who **it is** calling?*
√   *Can you tell me who **is** calling?*
In direct speech we say: 'who is it calling?',
but when the question starts with 'can you tell
me who ...', we must use 'it is' or 'is'.

Isn't it

x   *You called me this morning, **isn't it**?*
√   *You called me this morning, **didn't you**?*
Cantonese has the general question tag
係唔係. In English the tag refers back to the
subject of the main clause and the auxiliary
verb varies. After the past tense 'called', we
use 'didn't'.

It

x   *Is **it** Wing Hung Co.?*
√   *Is **that** Wing Hung Co.?*
x   *Is **it** Mr Lee?*
√   *Is **that** Mr Lee?*
In both cases, 'that' is used in the question.

Just doesn't

x   *Has he really gone out or **just doesn't**
     want to speak to me?*
√   *Has he really gone out or **is it just that**
     he doesn't want to speak to me?*
Cantonese verbs don't have a third person
singular inflexion 只係唔想 . The correct
English construction here is a little
complicated. 'Just don't' can be used as a
strong command:
√   ***Just don't** do that again.*

Keep

x *Sorry for **keep** you waiting.*
√ *Sorry for **keeping** you waiting.*
√ *Sorry **to keep** you waiting.*
The wrong version combines the two correct ones.

Leave ... to

x *Can I **leave** my number **to** him?*
√ *Can I **leave** my number **for** him?*
Note the preposition should be 'for'.

May

x ***May** you tell Eva to ring me back?*
√ ***Can** you tell Eva to ring me back?*
The correct usage here is 'can', 'could' or 'will'.

Maybe I

x ***Maybe I leave** my office number with you.*
√ ***Maybe I could leave** my office number with you.*
In Cantonese both 留 and 可以留 are correct, but in English only the second version is acceptable.

Message

x *I will **tell the message** to Mr Wong.*
√ *I will **give the message** to Mr Wong.*
√ *I will **tell** Mr Wong.*
You 'give the message' to someone, not 'tell the message'.

Mind that

x *Would you **mind that** we cancel the appointment?*
√ *Would you **mind if** we cancel the appointment?*
A polite question beginning with 'would you mind' is followed by 'if'.

Never mind

x *You are a week behind with your project report. (Reply) **Never mind**. It will be in soon.*
√ *You are a week behind with your project report. (Reply) **I'm very sorry**. It will be in soon.*

The Cantonese 唔緊要 cannot be used in English in many cases, especially when you have done something wrong. To say 'Never mind' sounds as if you don't care.

Nice for

x   It's **nice for** you to call back.
√   It's **nice of** you to call back.
'Nice for you' means it is pleasant for you. What the speaker wishes to say is:
√   It is **good of** you to call back.

Next

x   I'll call you **on next** Tuesday.
√   I'll call you **next** Tuesday.
No preposition is required.

Occupied

x   Sorry the line is **occupied**.
√   Sorry the line is **engaged**.
√   Sorry the line is **busy**.
'Occupied' is the appropriate word in some contexts.
√   The seat is **occupied**.
√   The toilet is **occupied**.
But not 'the line is occupied'.

Repair

x   My phone is **in need of repair**.
√   My phone is **out of order**.
You use 'in need or repair' for some things

e.g. a car, a house. But for a phone the usual expression is 'out of order' or 'not working'.

Return a call

x *Please ask him to **return me a call**.*
√ *Please ask him to **return my call**.*
The direct object of 'return' is the call, not the caller. Other correct idioms are:
√ *Please ask him to **call me back**.*
√ *Please ask him to **ring me back**.*

Speaking

x ***John's** speaking.*
√ ***John** speaking.*
'John speaking' is the correct short idiomatic form. Often the name is not repeated. So if the caller says: 'Could I speak to John please?', and John himself is answering, he simply says:
√ ***Speaking**.*

This

x *Hello. Is **this** Edward?*
√ *Hello. Is **that** Edward?*
'This' is felt to be the person who is speaking at 'this' end of the phone, not 'that' end.

Totally

x *There **are totally** six pages of Chengs in the telephone directory.*
√ *There **are altogether** six pages of Chengs in the telephone directory.*
√ *There **are a total of** six pages of Chengs in the telephone directory.*

'Totally' can be used with an adjective to mean completely.

√ I am **totally** exhausted.

Wait

x May I talk to Mr Ho please?(Reply) **Wait.**

√ May I talk to Mr Ho please?(Reply) **Hold on, please.**

√ May I talk to Mr Ho please?(Reply) **Could you please hold on.**

Simply to say 'wait' is much too abrupt and impolite.

Who

x May I know **who is this?**

√ May I know **who this is?**

√ May I know **who is calling?**

In direct speech we say 'who is this?', but when the question starts with 'may I know who...', we must say 'this is' or 'is'.

Would

x Do you know when she **would** come back?

√ Do you know when she **will** come back?

The conditional is wrong here.

Wrong dial

x Sorry **you must get the wrong dial.**

√ Sorry **you've got the wrong number.**

Cantonese says 搭錯線 while correct English should be 'you've got the wrong number'.

Exercises

A   *There is an error in each question. Decide whether the error is in the underlined section A, B or C by circling the appropriate letter. Then give the correct answers in the space provided.*

1   Sorry, **the telephone had a cut-off**.
        A

I'm here **on the line** again. What was it
            B

you were saying?   _____
        C

2   **I've told you** three times already that
        A

you got the wrong number. Please
    B

check again **that you have** the right
                    C

number.   _____

3   He **should call** the telephone company
        A

because his phone **has been giving**
                        B

him a lot of trouble. I think his phone is

in need of repair.   _____
        C

4   I'm sorry **for keep** you waiting.
                A

It took me a long time to find the
    B

particular number you **were looking for**.   _____
                        C

5   Miss Chan is in a hurry and **can't talk** to
                            A

you right now. **May you** please **ring back**
                B   C

in an hour's time?   _____

6   Peter was talking to the sales agent

   <u>on the phone</u> <u>when suddenly</u> the phone
      A   B

   <u>died</u>.
    C   _____

7   <u>With the help of</u> ten other companies,
       A

   we <u>are opening</u> our first business
         B

   machine exhibition <u>on next</u> Thursday.
                      C   _____

8   I <u>phoned</u> you many times yesterday but
      A

   <u>your line</u> was always <u>occupied</u>.
     B   C   _____

9   <u>Could you</u> please <u>tell my message</u>
     A   B

   <u>to Miss Cheung</u> as soon as possible.
       C   _____

10 The caller <u>had hanged up</u> <u>by the time</u>
                A   B

   Mr Leung <u>came to</u> the phone.
             C   _____

B(i)   There are ten errors in the dialogue below. Read carefully and underline the errors. Then rewrite the dialogue in the space provided. (Please note that errors are not found in every line.)

William   :   Hello, is it Wing Sun Company? Can I speak to Jenny Ho, please?

Receptionist :   Sorry, she's not back yet. Do you like to leave a message?

William   :   Yes, can I leave my number to her? It's 4836397.

Receptionist :   May I know who is it calling?

William	:	William Cheung.
Receptionist	:	Thank you, Mr Cheung. I would tell her. *(One hour later Jenny rings back.)*
Jenny	:	Hello, is that William? Jenny's speaking. You called me an hour ago, isn't it? Sorry I was out.
William	:	Hello, Jenny. Yes, I'm expecting your call for an hour. I have a long story to tell you and …
Jenny	:	Oh William, I'm sorry. My work is so busy that I can't talk now. Let's meet this evening at six.
William	:	Good. See you then. Bye bye.

_____

_____

_____

_____

_____

_____

B(ii) Underline the ten errors and rewrite the dialogue in the space provided. (Please note that errors are not found in every line.)

Caller : Hello, can I speak to Danny Wong, please?

Reply : Wait. *(After a pause.)* He's engaged in another phone. Would you like to ring back or wait?

Caller : I'll wait, thanks. *(After a minute or two.)*

Reply : Hello, I am Danny Wong.

Caller : Is this Danny Wong, the manager of Green Jade Company?

Reply : No, sorry. I afraid you dial the wrong number. There are totally eight Danny Wongs in the telephone directory. Here is Wade's Construction Company. Try 5379741 for Danny Wong of Green Jade.

Caller : Thank you and sorry for the trouble. *(Rings that number.)* Hello, Green Jade Company? Danny Wong, please.

Reply : Sorry, he's not in. He goes to Taiwan for business trip. He'll be back on Tuesday.

Caller : Thank you. I'll call on Tuesday.

Chapter 3   Job Interviews

Advantage	x *My previous experience will be **the advantage of me** in this new job.* √ *My previous experience will be **to my advantage** in this new job.* Note how the correct phrase is used.
Apply ... for	x *I want to **apply** the position **for** sales manager.* √ *I want to **apply for** the position **of** sales manager.* You 'apply for' a job. And you say 'the position of sales manager'.
At last	x *I have now given four reasons for my application. **At last** I want to work for an American company.* √ *I have now given four reasons for my application. **Finally**, I want to work for an American company* When giving a list of reasons, 'at last' cannot be used to mean 'as a final reason'. 'At last' means 'finally in time'. √ *She took a long time to find the right job. **At last** she found one that suited her well.*
Attend to	x *I **attended to** four interviews last week.* √ *I **attended** four interviews last week.* 'Attend' means 'be present at'. 'Attend to' means 'give attention to'. √ *The clerk **attended to** her work.*

Care	x *What salary do you expect? (Reply)*
	    I don't care about it.
	√ *What salary do you expect? (Reply)*
	    I don't really mind too much about salary.
	√ *What salary do you expect? (Reply)*
	    Salary is not the most important thing for me.
	The Cantonese 唔緊要 is meant as an expression of humility. In English, however, 'don't care about' indicates a lack of

seriousness and concern, and it would not give a good impression in an interview.

Confidence	1	x *I have **confidence to be able** to handle the job.*
		√ *I have **confidence that I will be able** to handle the job.*

Sometimes, the same word can be used as an abstract noun or an adjective in Cantonese, such as 信心 can mean confidence or confident. English makes a distinction between an abstract noun and an adjective.

	2	x *I am **confidence** that I will be able to handle the job.*
		√ *I am **confident** that I will be able to handle the job.*

Course	x *I took a **course of computer** last year.*
	√ *I took a **computer course** last year.*
	√ *I took a **course in computers** last year.*

Either 'a computer course' or 'a course in computers' is correct.

Curriculums	x *I learnt bookkeeping at University. It was **one of the curriculums**.*
	√ *I learnt bookkeeping at University. It was **one of the courses on the curriculum**.*

The 'curriculum' at a University is a set of courses, not an individual course.

Deal

x   *I can **deal** the emergency problems efficiently.*

√   *I can **deal with** the emergency problems efficiently.*

You 'deal with' problems. No article is needed here.

Distant

x   *Among my hobbies are badminton and **distant** running.*

√   *Among my hobbies are badminton and **distance** running.*

The correct idiom is 'distance (the noun) running'. However, the adjective 'distant' is correctly used, for example, in:

√   *He could see the **distant** object.*

Edition

x   *I am **in charge of the edition** of the company newsletter.*

√   *I am **in charge of the editing** of the company newsletter.*

√   *I am **the editor** of the company newsletter.*

If the speaker means that he edits the newsletter on a regular basis, he should use 'editing' or 'editor'. 'Edition' means the newsletter as it comes out on one particular occasion.

√   *That **edition** is one of the best.*

Enlarge my sight on

x   *I want to **enlarge my sight on** the world.*

√   *I want to **broaden my vision of** the world.*

The wrong version comes from the Cantonese 大開眼界 .

Escort

x   *I had a job as an **escort** for a few months.*

√   *I had a job as a **tour guide** for a few months.*

In Hong Kong 'escort' usually means 妓女 when describing the job, so it is best to avoid using it.

Even

x   ***Even** you do excellent work for that company, no one recognises it.*

√   ***Even if** you do excellent work for that company, no one recognises it.*

'If' is always required with 'even' in this kind of example.

Expect ... be

x   *How much would you **expect** your salary **be**?*

√   *How much would you **expect** your salary **to be**?*

After 'expect' we need 'to be', not 'be'.

Expose myself

x   *I would like to **expose myself** in another field.*

√   *I would like to **gain experience** in another field.*

'Expose myself' usually means 暴露自己 . The expression should be avoided.

Find out

x   *I hope to **find out** many challenges in this job.*

√   *I hope to **find** many challenges in this job.*

√   *I hope to **meet** many challenges in this job.*

The phrasal verb 'find out' is incorrectly used with 'challenge'.

First time

x   *Is this the **first time** you **go** to interview?*

√   *Is this the **first time** you **have been** to an interview?*

Usually, after 'first time' you use the present perfect.

Had been

x   *I know you **had been** working for ABC Company for a long time.*

√   *I know you **have been** working for ABC Company for a long time.*

The present perfect, not past perfect, is required here.

How

x   *__How__ do you think about our company's public image?*

√   *__What__ do you think about our company's public image?*

The wrong version is influenced by the Cantonese 點樣 .

Informations

x   *Please provide more __informations__ about your previous job.*

√   *Please provide more __information__ about your previous job.*

'Information' is an uncountable noun.

Initiative

x   *I think I __am quite initiative__.*

√   *I think I __have a good deal of initiative__.*

The abstract noun 'initiative' cannot be used like this. In English there is no adjective for 'initiative', so you must use the verb 'have' and the noun 'initiative'.

Interesting

x   *I have always been __interesting__ in working with people.*

√   *I have always been __interested__ in working with people.*

The second sentence is correct because 'interested' means that someone 'is showing an interest' or 'has interest' in doing something, while 'interesting', indicates that something is 'holding' or 'keeping' someone's interest.

Makes me learn

x   *Working in the stock exchange __makes me learn__ a lot about money.*

√   *Working in the stock exchange __has helped me to learn__ a lot about money.*

√   *Working in the stock exchange __has given me the chance__ to learn a lot about money.*

√   *Working in the stock exchange __has given me the opportunity__ to learn a lot about money.*

The error comes from the Cantonese expression 令我學到 .

Many experience

x   *I have **many experience** in marketing.*
√   *I have **a lot of experience** in marketing.*
'Experience' means 'knowledge gained through practical work' and is an uncountable noun. You use 'a lot of' with it. With a negative verb you can also use 'much'.
√   *I haven't **much experience** in marketing.*
'Experience' can also be a countable noun when it means 'something that happens to you'. In this case 'experiences' could be used with 'many'.
√   *He has had **many** interesting **experiences** while working abroad.*

Monthly

x   *My present salary is **monthly $8,000**.*
√   *My present salary is $8,000 **a month**.*
The correct expression is 'a month'. You could say:
√   *My **monthly** salary is $8,000.*

Notice

x   *We will **notice you of** the result soon.*
√   *We will **notify you of** the result soon.*
√   *We will **send you notice of** the result soon.*
The noun 'notice' often means something posted on a board, such as 'a notice board'. 'Notice' can be used with 'send' as here in 'send you notice' to mean 'notify'. 'Notice' as a verb means 'see'.
√   *He didn't **notice** the step and tripped over it.*

On the other hand

x   *I worked as a clerk in the shipping office. **On the other hand**, the company went bankrupt.*
√   *I worked as a clerk in the shipping office. **However**, the company went bankrupt.*
Cantonese has some expressions like 但係 which express a link between what has gone before and after. 'On the other hand' is used in English in direct contrast to 'on the one hand'.

√ *On the one hand he enjoys the responsibility, but on the other hand he hates the travelling.*

Promote

x *I hope I will promote next year.*
√ *I hope I will be promoted next year.*
When 'promote' is used in the context of career advancement you must use the passive form, 'be promoted'. 'Promote' can be used as an active verb with the meaning 'help to advertise goods'.
√ *We should hire Jackie Chan to promote our product.*
Another common meaning of 'promote' used actively is 'help to produce'.
√ *Regular exercise promotes good health.*

Prospect

x *Working as a salesman I may get a better prospect.*
√ *Working as a salesman I may have better prospects.*
You must use the plural 'prospects' when the idea is 'chances of advancement in one's career'. 'Prospect' in the singular can be used to mean 'chance', 'likelihood', as in:
√ *He had no prospect of getting housing benefits.*

Quite

x *I don't quite care about the working hours, provided there is job satisfaction.*
√ *I don't really care about the working hours, provided there is job satisfaction.*
√ *I don't care very much about the working hours, provided there is job satisfaction.*
'Quite' cannot be used with 'care about', as in the wrong example. 'Quite' can be used idiomatically with the verb 'like', as in:
√ *I don't quite like the way this job's going.*

Reach

x *If you give me the opportunity, I think I can reach your requirements.*
√ *If you give me the opportunity, I think I can meet your requirements.*

In English you say 'reach a goal/target', but 'meet/fulfil requirements'.

Refer

x *You can **refer all this information to my CV**.*
√ *You can **refer to my CV for all this information**.*
'Refer to' something (my CV) 'for' something (this information) or 'refer' someone 'to' someone else, as in:
√ *I'll **refer you to my secretary**. She'll be able to help you.*

Right man

x *You seem to be the **right man we're looking for**.*
√ *You seem to be the **right man for the job**.*
√ *You seem to be the **man we're looking for**.*
There is redundancy in the wrong example. It includes parts of both the correct expressions.

Shift

x *I've been long enough in this job and I'm going to **shift** a new one.*
√ *I've been long enough in this job and I'm going to **shift to** a new one.*
There is no preposition to go with 轉 in Cantonese, whereas we need to use 'shift to' in English.

Sociable

x *Sociable is another of my good qualities.*

√ *Sociability is another of my good qualities.*

善於交際 means 'sociable' as well as 'sociability'. In Cantonese the same words apply to both the adjective and abstract noun, whereas in English they do not.

So long if

x *I don't mind a low starting salary, so long if I have good promotion prospects.*

√ *I don't mind a low starting salary, so long as I have good promotion prospects.*

You could also say 'as long as', or more simply 'if'. The wrong example 'so long if' combines two correct usages.

Success

x *It is important to success this project.*

√ *It is important to succeed in this project.*

'Success' is the abstract noun and we have to use the verb 'succeed' here.

The

x *I read your advertisement in South China Morning Post.*

√ *I read you advertisement in the South China Morning Post.*

We need the article 'the' with the name of a newspaper.

Well planned

x *You are a well planned person.*

√ *You are a person who plans things well.*

The Cantonese expression 有計劃嘅人 can refer to a person, but in English you cannot say 'a well planned person'. You can say:

√   Your life seems **well planned**.
√   The project was **well planned**.

Wrongly

x   If I've **done wrongly**, I will try to correct it.
√   If I've **done something wrong**, I will try to correct it.
√   If I've **made a mistake**, I will try to correct it.

The wrong version is a direct translation of 做錯.

Exercises

A   *There is an error in each question. Decide whether the error is in the underlined section A, B or C by circling the appropriate letter. Then give the correct answers in the space provided.*

1   I can **deal the challenges** of
              A

the new job with great confidence.
      B   C   _____

2   **Even you want** to enter the **banking field,**
      A   B

you are not **going to be** able to.
                  C   _____

3 <u>Last</u> summer, I <u>worked</u> as <u>an escort</u>.
    A   B   C

  It was a very enjoyable job.   _____

4 The first time I <u>attend to</u> a
               A

  <u>job interview</u>, I <u>was shaking</u> all over.   _____
     B   C

5 <u>I'm sure</u> the practical experience
    A

  <u>I've gained</u> will be useful <u>to success</u>
     B   C

  in the post.   _____

6 <u>If I work</u> as a tourist guide, I can
     A

  <u>enlarge my sight</u> <u>of the world</u>.   _____
       B   C

7 My good <u>academic record</u> will be
            A

  <u>the advantage of me</u> when I
        B

  <u>apply for</u> that job.   _____
    C

8 <u>Having taken</u> a secretarial course, I'm
      A

  <u>certain</u> I can <u>reach</u> your requirements.   _____
    B   C

9 I <u>would like</u> <u>to expose myself</u> in the
     A   B

  business field <u>by working</u> as a part-
            C

  time accountant.   _____

10 My <u>chances</u> of getting a job <u>are good</u> because
      A   B

   I have just completed a <u>course of computer</u>.   _____
                         C

B(i) *There are ten errors in the dialogue below. Read carefully and underline the errors. Then rewrite the dialogue in the space provided. (Please note that errors are not found in every line.)*

Interviewer : Why do you want to apply the position of accountant in our company?

Candidate : I have always been interesting in working with figures. And I think I can find out more challenges in a company like yours.

Interviewer : I see you had been working for Telecom for two years. Did your job involve any bookkeeping?

Candidate : Yes, I had many experience there in bookkeeping. Also I did a course in the Polytechnic in bookkeeping. It was one of the curriculums.

Interviewer : What about your other activities when you were a student?

Candidate : I was responsible for the edition of the student newspaper. And one of my hobbies was distant running.

Interviewer : Well, you seem to be the right man we're looking for. What problems do you think you might find with the job?

Candidate : Not very many, I hope. I have confidence to be a good accountant.

_____

_____

_____

_____

_____

_____

B(ii) Underline the ten errors and rewrite the dialogue in the space provided. (Please note that errors are not found in every line.)

Interviewer : How did you find out about this job?

Candidate : I read your advertisement in _South China Morning Post._

Interviewer : Can you give me some informations about your previous jobs?

Candidate : I have worked in very many different jobs. You can refer all the details to my curriculum vitae.

Interviewer : Why do you wish to leave your present job?

Candidate : I find it unchallenging, and also it is difficult to be promote to a higher position. So I want to shift a new job. With your company I think I may get a better prospect.

Interviewer : How much would you expect your salary be?

Candidate : I don't quite care about the salary. I would be satisfied to start with a low salary, so long if I could learn on the job.

Interviewer : Thank you. We will notice you of the result in a week's time.

Chapter **4** Banking

A good advice

x   *I got **a good advice** on when to sell my stocks.*

√   *I got **good advice** on when to sell my stocks.*

√   *I got **a good piece of advice** on when to sell my stocks.*

'Advice' is uncountable and therefore does not need an article.

Afraid

x   *You need not **afraid** of using an ETC machine.*

√   *You need not **be afraid** of using an ETC machine.*

'Afraid' cannot be used as a verb.

After

x   ***After finished** the transfer, I sent the cheque.*

√   ***After finishing** the transfer, I sent the cheque.*

√   ***After having finished** the transfer, I sent the cheque.*

The gerund (-ing) is used following 'after'.

Although ... but

x   ***Although** I sold my bonds at once, **but** the price has already gone down.*

√   *I sold my bonds at once, **but** the price had already gone down.*

√   ***Although** I sold my bonds at once, the price had already gone down.*

Unlike Cantonese 雖然 ... 但係 , you use either 'although' or 'but' in English.

Amazed

x   *I amazed at the continuing rise of the US dollar.*

√   *I was amazed at the continuing rise of the US dollar.*

√   *The continuing rise of the US dollar amazed me.*

Are

x   *One hundred dollars are only a small amount.*

√   *One hundred dollars is only a small amount.*

The subject 'one hundred dollars' is taken as a singular noun.

As ... so

x   *As my checking account was low, so I had to transfer some money into it.*

√   *As my checking account was low, I had to transfer money into it.*

√   *My checking account was low, so I had to transfer money into it.*

In English you use either 'as' or 'so', not both.

At last

x   *He keeps on borrowing more and more and at last he is unable to pay.*

√   *He keeps on borrowing more and more and in the end he is unable to pay.*

'In the end' is the correct idiom in this context.

Before

x   *I withdrew all my money two months before.*

√   *I withdrew all my money two months ago.*

Cantonese uses 之前 for 'ago' and 'before'. In English, 'before' is normally followed by something else.

√   *I withdrew all my money two months before the bank collapsed.*

Borrow ... to

x   *I will borrow $100 to my friend.*

√   *I will lend $100 to my friend.*

Both 'borrow' and 'lend' are expressed by 借 and no preposition is required in Cantonese. In English, however, you say 'borrow ... from' and 'lend ... to'.

Change me for

x *Can you **change me for this ten dollars**?*

√ *Can you **change this ten dollars for me**?*

'Change me for' means 將我換.

√ *Can you **give me change** for this ten dollars?*

'Change' in this sense, meaning 'money back', is an uncountable noun.

Concern

x *I do **concern** about Hong Kong's rising inflation.*

√ *I **am concerned** about Hong Kong's rising inflation.*

'Concerned' is an adjective meaning 'worried' or 'anxious'.

Convenient

x *A credit card will **make you more convenient**.*

√ *A credit card will **be more convenient for you**.*

The Cantonese expression 令你更方便 cannot be translated directly into English.

Dollar

x *Do you want the traveller's cheques in sterling or in Hong Kong **dollar**?*

√ *Do you want the traveller's cheques in sterling or in Hong Kong **dollars**?*

'Dollar' is a countable noun and the plural is

'dollars'. You do, however, say:
√   A Hong Kong **dollar** account.
√   The US **dollar** is going up.

Enough

x   You **are not enough experience** for such a job.
√   You **are not experienced enough** for such a job.
√   You **don't have enough experience** for such a job.

The wrong version is a combination of the two correct ones.

Even

x   **Even** the pound rises, I wouldn't advise buying it.
√   **Even if** the pound rises, I wouldn't advise buying it.

'If' follows 'even' in this context.

Except

x   You may not become overdrawn in your account **except** you arrange it beforehand.
√   You may not become overdrawn in your account **except if** you arrange it beforehand.
√   You may not become overdrawn in your account **unless** you arrange it beforehand.

You have to use either 'except if' or 'unless' as the linking words.

Expected

x   Customers **are being expected** to look after their cheque books carefully.
√   Customers **are expected** to look after their cheque books carefully.

The correct passive form is 'are expected'.

Feel sorrow

x   He has gone bankrupt. I **feel sorrow** for him.
√   He has gone bankrupt. I **feel sorry** for him.

The adjective, not the noun, is required.

Few

    x *I have too **few** money to open a checking account.*

    √ *I have too **little** money to open a checking account.*

    √ *There are very **few** poor bankers.*

'Few' is used with plural countable nouns, while 'little' is used with uncountable nouns.

Find

    x *Everyone must **find** the receipt which is missing.*

    √ *Everyone must **look for** the receipt which is missing.*

'Look for' is used in this context because it implies 'search for' something.

Hard

    x *I am **hard** to get a loan since my salary is very low.*

    √ *It **is hard for me** to get a loan since my salary is very low.*

The impersonal construction is used here: 'It' + verb + adjective + 'for'.

Has

    x *There **has** a machine outside the bank.*

    √ *There **is** a machine outside the bank.*

In Cantonese, 有 means 'to be' or 'to have'. In English the verb 'to be' follows 'there'.

Here

    x *Could I have a bank draft form please? (Reply) **Here**.*

    √ *Could I have a bank draft form please? (Reply) **Here you are**.*

√ *Could I have a bank draft form please? (Reply)* **Certainly**.

'Here' alone is impolite. 'Here you are' or 'certainly' sound less abrupt.

Hesitated

x *I am* **hesitated** *about buying shares in that company.*

√ *I am* **hesitant** *about buying shares in that company.*

The verb 'hesitate' has no passive form. The adjective 'hesitant' must be used.

Hour

x *Banks have shorter working* **hour** *than most other places.*

√ *Bank have shorter working* **hours** *than most other places.*

'Hour' is a countable noun, with plural 'hours'.

How ... supposed

x *The US dollar is strengthening.* **How** *am I* **supposed** *to do about it?*

√ *The US dollar is strengthening.* **What** *am I* **supposed** *to do about it?*

With 'do about it', you must say 'what' not 'how'. With other verbs, 'how' can be used as in:

√ **How** *am I* **supposed to deal** *with it?*

√ **How** *am I* **supposed to react** *to it?*

√ **How** *am I* **supposed to handle** *it?*

Include

x **Is** *that include commission?*

√ **Does** *that include commission?*

'Does' is the correct word to ask a question in this context. However:

√ *Is that including commission?*

It

x *My cheque book, it is finished.*
√ *My cheque book is finished.*

The 'it' is redundant here.

Later

x *I won't come today. I'll come two days later.*
√ *I won't come today. I'll come in two days' time.*

When stating a time in the future when we will come, we say 'in X days' time', not 'X days later'!

Locate

x *The cash point locate outside the bank.*
√ *The cash point is located outside the bank.*

The passive form is used here.

Make a decision

x *When I have made up my decision, I will come back.*
√ *When I have made up my mind, I will come back.*
√ *When I have made my decision, I will come back.*

The wrong version confuses the two correct examples.

Necessary

x *I am necessary to ask for an overdraft.*
√ *It is necessary for me to ask for an overdraft.*

Cantonese uses a personal construction whereas English uses the impersonal construction.

Never

x *With my Visa card, it's been years I've never carried much cash with me.*
√ *With my Visa card, it's been years since I've carried much cash with me.*

After expressions like 'it's been years', 'it's been a long time', you use 'since'.

Nowaday

x *Nowaday, people use credit cards more and more.*

√ *Nowadays, people use credit cards more and more.*

The mistake could be caused by confusing 'nowaday' with 'today'. 'Nowadays' is the correct idiom, like 'these days'.

On the other hand

x *You can open a current account tomorrow. On the other hand, I will give you a cheque book.*

√ *You can open a current tomorrow. And I will give you a cheque book.*

另一方面 , which is a general linking word in Cantonese, is often translated into English as 'on the other hand' or 'besides'. Neither of these would be suitable here. (See also Chapter 3.)

One month

x *One month I'll put in $1,000.*

√ *I'll put in $1,000 a month.*

The correct sentence means 'per month' or 'each month'. The incorrect sentence suggests the payment will be made only once, at some unspecified month in the future.

Open

x *You open till when?*

√ *When are you open till?*

你開到幾點 should be translated as 'When are you open till?'

Pound sterlings

x *I transferred my Hong Kong dollars into pound sterlings.*

√ *I transferred my Hong Kong dollars into pounds sterling.*

The unit of currency should in this case be plural. Similarly, Hong Kong dollars, Swiss francs, etc. (Note that 's' is added to 'pound', not 'sterling'.

Saving

x *Do you want to open a saving account?*

√ *Do you want to open a savings account?*

However, you do say 'a checking account'.

See

x   *I **see** the Banking Journal every week.*
√   *I **read** the Banking Journal every week.*
The Cantonese word 睇 can mean 'see' or 'read'. In English, you say 'to read' a magazine, newspaper, book, etc., and 'to see' someone or something.

Through

x   *You can let your capital increase **through** two ways.*
√   *You can let your capital increase **in** two ways.*
The preposition 'in' should be used.

Traveller cheques

x   *When travelling abroad, it is safer to have **traveller cheques**.*
√   *When travelling abroad, it is safer to have **traveller's cheques**.*
This means, cheques of the traveller.

When do you

x   *Just let me know **when do you** want the fixed deposit to end.*
√   *Just let me know **when you** want the fixed deposit to end.*
The words of the direct speech 'do you want' have wrongly been kept in the indirect question.

Exercises

A   *There is an error in each question. Decide whether the error is in the underlined section A, B or C by circling the appropriate letter. Then give the correct answers in the space provided.*

1   <u>It is easy</u> to withdraw money nowadays.
      A

   <u>There has</u> lots of <u>teller machines</u>
        B   C

   outside the banks.   _____

2   <u>Can</u> you <u>borrow</u> me $100? I don't think
      A   B

   I have enough money <u>with me</u>.   _____
                              C

3   <u>After finished</u> listing the <u>exchange rates</u>
        A   B

   for the day, I decided to <u>take a break</u>.   _____
                                    C

4   <u>In nowaday</u>, it is <u>much harder</u> to save
      A   B

   money because everything <u>seems</u> to
                                  C

   have gone up.   _____

5   Mrs Man <u>lost</u> all her money on the
              A

   <u>stock market</u>. I really <u>feel sorrow</u>
      B   C

   for her.   _____

6   I <u>do concern</u> about the <u>link</u>
        A

   <u>between</u> the Hong Kong <u>dollar</u> and
      B   C

   the American dollar.   _____

7   I'm <u>**planning to**</u> get a Visa card. <u>**How**</u>
             A   B

do you <u>**think of**</u> that?   _____
           C

8   You <u>**can tell**</u> Miss Cheung she
         A

<u>**need not afraid**</u> to <u>**put her money on**</u>
    B   C

bonds.   _____

9   He quickly <u>**made up his decision**</u>
                     A

to buy Japanese yen <u>**instead of**</u>
                       B

Australian dollars <u>**as soon as**</u> he heard
                    C

the news.   _____

10 Mr Mok neglected <u>**to keep**</u> a careful
                  A

account of his money. <u>**At last**</u>, he
                     B

<u>**was unable**</u> to pay his debts.   _____
    C

B(i) There are ten errors in the dialogue below. Read carefully and underline the errors. Then rewrite the dialogue in the space provided. (Please note that errors are not found in every line.)

Amy   :   I'm travelling abroad in the summer and I usually take traveller cheque. But as I'm going on a long trip this time, so I've been advised to get a Visa card.

Florence :   That's a good advice.

Amy   :   But I am very hesitated about getting a Visa. I think I have too few money to bother about it.

Florence :   You should get one. A Visa card will make you more convenience. With my ETC card it's been months I've never been into a bank.

Amy : In other countries are there cash points for Visa cards?

Florence : Yes. They usually locate outside the bank. But you'd better take some cash too.

Amy : Yes. I'll need some pound sterlings and dollar.

_____

_____

_____

_____

B(ii) Underline the ten errors and rewrite the dialogue in the space provided. (Please note that errors are not found in every line.)

Bank Manager : Mr Leung, your current account it is overdrawn.

Mr Leung : Well, I amazed at that. By how much?

Bank Manager : Six hundred dollars.

Mr Leung : But six hundred dollars are only a small amount. Can't it be taken out of my saving account?

Bank Manager : Yes, but you must make the transfer.

Mr Leung : You open till when?

Bank Manager : The bank's working hour are nine to four.

Mr Leung : But I am hard to get to the bank before four.

Bank Manager : Then you can make the transfer with your ETC card.

Mr Leung : Good. And I'll come to make a deposit sometime.

Bank Manager : Will you come today?

Mr Leung : No, I'll come three days later. Oh, there's something else. I've changed my address. Do you need the new one?

Bank Manager : Yes. Clients are being expected to inform us of a new address. It's hard to keep records correct except you inform us.

Chapter **5**   *Good Health*

Abundant

x *You should have **an abundant** meal.*
√ *You should have **a large** meal.*
In English, 'abundant' is not a suitable word
for a meal. Apart from 'large', the idea can be
expressed by 'hearty/good/good solid/
substantial'.

Appetite

1 x *Do you have **appetite**?*
√ *Do you have **an appetite**?*
In many cultures (e.g. French — *Bon
appetit!*) we wish the eaters 'Good appetite!'
as they begin a meal. However, in English a
determiner (a/any) normally needs to be
used with 'appetite'.

2 x *I don't have **appetite** for dinner.*
√ *I don't have **any appetite** for dinner.*

**As many as
possible**

x *You must eat **vegetables as many
as possible**.*
√ *You must eat **as many vegetables as
possible**.*
Note the position of the noun in English.

Balance

x *An important thing is **the balance of** your
lunch and dinner.*
√ *An important thing is **a balance between**
your lunch and dinner.*
In English, we say a balance 'between' two
things, not 'of' two things.

Because of

x   I was admitted to hospital before **because of this reason**.

√   I was admitted to hospital before **for this reason**.

√   **Because of this** I was admitted to hospital before.

The wrong example combines and confuses the two correct examples. 'Because of this reason' comes from the Cantonese expression 因為呢個原因. There is no distinction between 'because of' and 'for' in Cantonese.

Be ill

x   She's not used to **be ill**.

√   She's not used to **being ill**.

After 'used to' and 'accustomed to', the gerund form (-ing) is used, not the infinitive.

Catch a cold

x   I have **caught a cold** for ten days.

√   I have **had a cold** for ten days.

√   I **caught a cold** ten days **ago**.

The wrong version combines the two correct examples.

Collided

x   I was injured when my car **was collided with** a van.

√   I was injured when my car **collided with** a van.

√   I was injured when my car **was in collision with** a van.

'Collide' has no passive form.

Covering

x   I got a cold because I slept without **covering a blanket**.

√   I got a cold because I slept without **covering myself with a blanket**.

'Covering a blanket' means putting a covering on the blanket.

Depending

x   **Too depending** on drugs can make you addicted.

√   **Depending too much** on drugs can make you addicted.

√   **Becoming too dependent** on drugs can make you addicted.

'Too depending on' comes from the Cantonese expression 太倚賴.

Difficult

x   *I am difficult to bend down.*
√   *It is difficult for me to bend down.*
The impersonal construction is used here: 'It'
+ verb + adjective + 'for'.

IT'S NO GOOD WE CAN'T BEND HIM OVER

Disturb

x   *Is your blood pressure still disturbing you?*
√   *Is your blood pressure still troubling you?*
'Disturbing' which signifies mild annoyance is an inappropriate word to use for an illness.

Do/Don't

1   x   *Do you have any vomiting before?*
    √   *Did you have any vomiting before?*
When you ask a question with 'before', you need the past tense of the auxiliary verb.

2   x   *Why you don't see a doctor?*
    √   *Why don't you see a doctor?*
You must reverse the subject and verb in a 'why' question.

Do aerobics

x   *During my lunch hour, I go to a health club do aerobics.*
√   *During my lunch hour, I go to a health club to do aerobics.*
Usually when you have two verbs in a sentence, you need to use a 'to' infinitive for the second verb.

Drug

x *You need to get some **drug** in the drugstore.*

√ *You need to get some **drugs** in the drugstore.*

'Drug' is a countable noun and the plural is needed here.

Evenly

x *You must eat meat and vegetables **evenly**.*

√ *You must eat meat and vegetables **in a balanced way**.*

'Evenly' conveys the general idea, but is not the correct idiom.

Exercise

x *I need to **practise exercise**.*

√ *I need to **do exercise**.*

√ *I need to **take exercise**.*

You 'do/take' exercise. You 'practise' individual forms of exercise.

√ *I **practise** yoga/basketball/squash, etc.*

Fat

x *You are becoming **fat and fat**.*

√ *You are becoming **fatter and fatter**.*

The comparative form of the adjective is used. You can also say:

√ *You are **putting on a lot of weight**.*

The two examples given (√) are grammatically correct, but normally we would not make statements like this to people.

Feel a headache

x   *When I woke up this morning, I **felt a** serious **headache**.*

√   *When I woke up this morning, I **had a** serious **headache**.*

In Cantonese, you say 覺得. In English, you use 'felt' only with words like 'sick' or 'unwell'. But you talk of 'having a headache', not 'feeling a headache'.

Go swim

x   *I **go swim** for half an hour each day.*

√   *I **go swimming** for half an hour each day.*

In Cantonese, you can have two verbs together 去游水. In English, however, either you have a verb + a 'to' infinitive or a verb + a gerund. In this case we use verb + gerund.

Having

x   *I **am having** a sore throat.*

√   *I **have** a sore throat.*

Even though you continue to have it, the present continuous is not correct. The simple present 'have' is what is needed.

Health

x   *You have **a very good health**.*

√   *You have **very good health**.*

√   *You have **a very good constitution**.*

No article is needed before the word 'health' but you can say 'a very good constitution'.

Improvement

x   *In time you will **get improvement on** your health.*

√   *In time you will **see an improvement in** your health.*

'Improvement' is a noun meaning 'a getting better'. It therefore cannot be used with the verb 'get'. Also 'improvement' requires an article because it is a countable noun. Finally you 'improve in' health, not 'on'. However, 'improve on' is usually used when two things are compared.

√   *You will **improve on** your previous score.*

Infected

x   *My wife says I might have **infected those virus** in India.*

√ *My wife says I might have **got infected with that virus** in India.*

The wrong example sounds as if the person has given a disease to the virus instead of getting a disease from the virus. 'Virus' is singular.

Injection

x *You will need to **have injection***
√ *You will need to **have an injection**.*

The article 'an' is required, because injection is a countable noun.

Is being

x *You can get sick by swimming in sea water which is **being polluted**.*
√ *You can get sick by swimming in sea water which **is polluted**.*

You need to use the past participle here.

Look

x *Why **are you look** so exhausted?*
√ *Why **are you looking** so exhausted?*
√ *Why **do you look** so exhausted?*

The wrong version combines the two correct models.

Medicine

1   x *I've got to **eat** my medicine every night.*
    √ *I've got to **take** my medicine every night.*

Unlike Cantonese 食 , we say 'take', not 'eat' in English.

2   x *The doctor gave me some **medicines** to help me sleep.*
    √ *The doctor gave me some **medicine** to help me sleep.*

'Medicine' is usually an uncountable noun.

YUMMIE YUMMIE MORE PILLS

Overweighted	x *An **overweighted** person is liable to get heart attacks.*
	√ *An **overweight** person is liable to get heart attacks.*
	'Overweight' is the adjective.

Painful	x *I **am painful** in my stomach.*
	√ *I **have a pain** in my stomach.*
	You can either say some part of your body is 'painful' or that you 'have a pain' in some part of your body.

Proved	x *The doctor has **proved** that she has cancer.*
	√ *The doctor has **diagnosed** that she has cancer.*
	You can say 證實 . But 'proved' sounds as if the doctor is proud of himself to have discovered the nature of the disease. 'Diagnosed' is the correct word for discovering what the illness is.

Put off	x ***Put off** your shirt, please.*
	√ ***Take off** your shirt, please.*
	You 'take off', not 'put off' your clothes.

Put on	x ***My weight has put on** for the last six months.*
	√ ***I have been putting on weight** for the last six months.*
	You have been gaining weight. The weight has not been put on to you.

Regular time	x *You must have your meals **in a regular time**.* √ *You must have your meals **at regular times**.* The correct idiom uses the plural.
Seek	x *Have you **seeked** a second opinion on your illness?* √ *Have you **got** a second opinion on your illness?* The past tense of the verb 'seek' is 'sought'. But 'sought' is rarely used in modern English. The normal word is, 'got/asked for a second opinion'.
Sign	x *Could you please **sign up** a letter for my sick leave?* √ *Could you please **give me** a letter for my sick leave?* Some doctors may have a standard form which they simply sign (hence 'sign up'), rather than writing a separate letter for every patient who is off work.
Since	x *The girl **coughs since two weeks ago**.* √ *The girl **has been coughing for two weeks**.* The present perfect continuous tense should be used.
Sleep early/ late	x *It's been a long day, so I think I'll **sleep** early.* √ *It's been a long day, so I think I'll **go to bed** early.* x *I **slept** late last night, so I'm tired today.* √ *I **went to bed** late last night, so I'm tired today.* In English we distinguish 'sleep' and 'go to bed'. Cantonese uses 瞓覺 for both 'going to bed' (i.e. beginning one's sleep) and 'sleeping'.
Suggest ... to	x *I **suggest you to take** a day off.* √ *I **suggest you take** a day off.* After suggest you do not use 'to'.

Suspects of

x *My doctor **suspects me of** diabetes.*
√ *My doctor **suspects I have** diabetes.*
'Suspects ... of' is used most frequently of a crime, and is not the way to talk of your doctor's opinion about your illness.

Temporal

x *The doctor says the illness is only **temporal**.*
√ *The doctor says the illness is only **temporary**.*
'Temporal' means 'within time', 'belonging to this world' as opposed to 'eternal'.
'Temporary' is the word required.

Therefore

x *I had a headache, **therefore** I didn't go to school.*
√ *I had a headache, **so** I didn't go to school.*
'Therefore' might be used in written English.
'So' would be used in spoken English.

Tiny food

x *She lost her appetite and couldn't eat even **a tiny food**.*
√ *She lost her appetite and couldn't eat even **a tiny amount of food**.*
'Food' is an uncountable noun. You cannot say 'a food' but can say 'an amount of food'.

You'd better	x	***You are better to see** a kidney specialist.*
	√	***You'd better see** a kidney specialist.*
	x	*I think **you'll better to stop** smoking.*
	√	*I think **you'd better stop** smoking.*

'You'd better' is followed by the verb without 'to' (bare infinitive).

Uncomfortable	x	*I had to stay off work because I felt so **uncomfortable**.*
	√	*I had to stay off work because I felt so **unwell**.*

'Uncomfortable' is too weak a word to use for feeling so ill that you have to stay off work. 'Unwell', 'ill', or 'sick' would be better.

Exercises

A   *There is an error in each question. Decide whether the error is in the underlined section A, B or C by circling the appropriate letter. Then give the correct answers in the space provided.*

1 Victor <u>recovered from</u> his illness very
             A

slowly because he <u>always forgot</u> to
                     B

<u>eat his medicine</u>.   _____
      C

2 You <u>look</u> pale. Why <u>you don't</u> <u>see</u>
        A   B   C

a doctor?   _____

3 <u>Too depending</u> on drugs <u>can cause</u>
      A   B

all <u>sorts of</u> problems.   _____
    C

4 Viola <u>didn't like</u> the idea <u>of being sick.</u>
        A   B

She's not <u>used to be</u> ill at all. _____
        C

5 <u>Had Anita seeked</u> medical advice
        A

   sooner, she <u>would have been</u> better
                B

   <u>by now</u>.
    C   _____

6 <u>If you have</u> a <u>balanced diet</u>,
     A   B

   <u>you will no doubt get improvement on</u>
                    C

   your health.   _____

7 <u>Every Saturday</u> I <u>go to</u> a child
       A   B

   centre <u>take care of</u> the children there.   _____
            C

8 <u>Do you have</u> <u>an</u> X-ray <u>before</u>?   _____
       A   B   C

9 I <u>don't like it</u> when people tell me
       A

   <u>I'm becoming</u> <u>fat and fat</u>.
       B   C   _____

10 Sunny <u>is now</u> <u>in the hospital</u>. His
         A   B

   car <u>was collided by</u> a van.   _____
        C

B(i) *There are ten errors in the dialogue below. Read carefully*
      and underline the errors. Then rewrite the dialogue in the
      space provided. (Please note that errors are not found in
      every line.)

Patient : Good morning, doctor. I feel painful in my back.

Doctor : Put off your shirt, please, and I will examine you.
           (After the examination.) You have strained a muscle.
           It is why you have the pain.

Patient : Do I need injection?

Doctor : No. But I will give you some medicines to relieve the pain. I suggest you to rest your back for a few days. Also, you are too heavy. It is more common for an overweighted person to have back trouble.

Patient : Yes, my weight has put on in the past few months.

Doctor : Then you must practise exercise more often and watch your diet.

Patient : Thank you, doctor. Could you please sign up a letter for my sick leave?

B(ii) Underline the ten errors and rewrite the dialogue in the space provided. (Please note that errors are not found in every line.)

John : Why are you look so pale?

William : I have caught a bad cold for two weeks.

John : And is it still disturbing you?

William : Yes. I am having a sore throat and am very difficult to breathe. I bought some drug in the drug store, but I'm still feeling uncomfortable.

John : Do you have appetite?

William I can't even swallow a tiny food.

John : I think you are better go and see a doctor. Go to Doctor Chan. He is a famous doctor in Hong Kong.

Chapter **6** Hotel Management

Accompany

x *The porter **accompanied with me** to the lift.*

√ *The porter **accompanied me** to the lift.*

'Accompany' means 'come with', so another 'with' is not needed.

Arrive

x *The plane was late so we **arrived** the hotel after midnight.*

√ *The plane was late so we **arrived at** the hotel after midnight.*

A preposition is needed with 'arrived'. You arrive 'at' a hotel. However, you arrive 'in' a city or a country.

√ *He **arrived in** Hong Kong today.*

No preposition is used with 'home'.

√ *He **arrived home** today.*

At least

x *I **at least** will stay **for one week**.*

√ *I will stay **for one week at least**.*

√ *I will stay **for at least one week**.*

The word order is wrong. In Cantonese the adverb 'at least' comes before the verb 'will stay'. In English, 'at least' comes after.

Boring

x *I get very **boring** with my job as a chambermaid.*

√ *I get very **bored** with my job as a chambermaid.*

The person is 'bored', the job is 'boring'. Cantonese uses 悶 for both.

Clothes washed

x   *Does the hotel have **a place where I can get my clothes washed**?*

√   *Does the hotel have **a laundry service**?*

Though 'clothes washed' gives the desired meaning well enough, you would use it for washing clothes, for example, in a river. In a hotel, 'laundry service' is the correct expression.

Depend

x   *The price of the room will **be depend on** which floor you want.*

√   *The price of the room will **be dependent on** which floor you want.*

√   *The price of the room will **depend on** which floor you want.*

Either the adjective or the active form of the verb can be used.

Each day

x   *How much **each** day?*

√   *How much **per** day?*

When you are charging a daily rate, you say 'per day', not 'each day'.

Else

x   *What luggage **else** do you have?*

√   *What **other** luggage do you have?*

√   *What **other** rooms are available?*

'Else' is not used after a noun but must be replaced by 'other' before the noun. You can use 'else' after 'something/anything'.

√   *Do you have something/anything **else**?*

Emphasis

x   *Some hotels **emphasis on** the quality of service.*

√   *Some hotels **put emphasis on** the quality of service.*

√   *Some hotels **emphasise** the quality of service.*

In the wrong example, the noun is used instead of the verb. The noun can be used correctly in the expression 'put/place emphasis on'.

Enough	x *Single rooms and double rooms are **all not enough**.*
	√ ***There are no** single or double rooms available.*
	√ ***There are neither** single nor double rooms available.*

The wrong expression 'all not enough' comes from the Cantonese 全部都唔夠 .

Except	x ***Except** going on a package tour, I have never stayed in a hotel.*
	√ ***Except for** going on a package tour, I have never stayed in a hotel.*
	√ ***Apart from** going on a package tour, I have never stayed in a hotel.*

English uses 'except for' or 'apart from' with a gerund (-ing). We can also use 'besides'. It does not require any preposition.

√ ***Besides** going on package tours, I often go on holiday on my own.*

Facing	x *I would like a room **face to** the harbour.*
	√ *I would like a room **facing** the harbour.*
	√ *I would like a room **overlooking** the harbour.*

With buildings, rooms, etc., we say 'facing'.

Famous	x *The Peninsula hotel in Hong Kong is **a famous hotel in the world**.*
	√ *The Peninsula hotel in Hong Kong is **one of the most famous hotels in the world**.*

It is wrong to translate directly from the Cantonese 係世界出名嘅酒店 .

Gather	x *If there is a fire, we should all **gather around** in the lobby.*
	√ *If there is a fire, we should all **gather** in the lobby.*

'Gather around' gives the impression of a

casual gathering which is not appropriate if there is a fire.

Go

x   *If you want **to go to climbing**, there are some lovely hills nearby.*
√   *If you want **to go climbing**, there are some lovely hills nearby.*
A gerund is used after the infinitive 'to go', such as 'to go shopping'.

Hear

x   *I can **hear** Japanese.*
√   *I can **understand** Japanese.*
'Hear' means 'to listen' whereas 'understand' refers to 'comprehend' or 'know'. In this context, 'understand' is the correct word. In Cantonese 聽 implies 'understand' as well as 'hear'.

Hold

x   *I'll **hold** your luggage at the desk for an hour.*
√   *I'll **keep** your luggage at the desk for an hour.*
√   *I'll **look after** your luggage at the desk for an hour.*

'Hold' means 'hold in my hand' which is not correct here.

In

x *Can I have a room **in** the sixth floor?*
√ *Can I have a room **on** the sixth floor?*
You say a room 'in' the Regent hotel, but 'on' the third floor.

Is

x *There **is** still a few single rooms available.*
√ *There **are** still a few single rooms available.*
Though 'a few' looks like a singular subject, it is really plural and is used with a plural verb.

Lead

x *Can someone **lead** me to my room?*
√ *Can someone **take** me to my room?*
The Cantonese uses 帶 which is translated 'lead' or 'take' depending on the context. In English you 'take' someone to his or her room. You use 'lead' only for a blind person.

Lift not working

x ***Lift not working** today.*
√ ***The lift is not working** today.*
You need to have the article 'the' and the verb 'is' to make the sentence complete.

Live

x   *I want to **live** in this hotel for three nights.*
√   *I want to **stay** in this hotel for three nights.*
Usually you 'live at home', but 'stay at a hotel' because 'to stay' implies that you are in a place only for a short while. Cantonese 住 can mean 'live' and 'stay'.

Look after

x   *My clock is not working. Could you send someone to **look after** it?*
√   *My clock is not working. Could you send someone to **look at** it?*
'Look after' means 'take care of'. 'Look at' means 'to examine and see what is wrong and mend it'.

Miss

x   *Did you **miss** your key?*
√   *Did you **lose** your key?*
'Lose' means 'fail to find something' while 'miss' suggests either 'to feel pain at the absence of something or someone' or 'to lose a good chance often by being too slow', as in 'miss an opportunity'.

Occupied

x   *Sorry, our hotel **has been** fully **occupied**.*
√   *Sorry, our hotel **is** fully **booked**.*
'Has been occupied' sounds as if a group of soldiers has 'occupied' 霸佔 the hotel.

Opposite	x *Please go to the **opposite** Information Centre.*
	√ *Please go to the Information Centre **opposite**.*

'Opposite' used as an adjective means 'totally different from' as 'in the opposite direction'. When 'opposite' means 'facing', 'over there', it comes after the noun:

√   *The buildings **opposite** were destroyed.*

Peoples	x *Many **peoples** come to Hong Kong during the Chinese New Year.*
	√ *Many **people** come to Hong Kong during the Chinese New Year.*

When used as a general term, 'people' is already plural and does not take a final 's'. You use 'peoples' when you mean different nations or races.

Problem of	x *Is there any **problem of** my booking?*
	√ *Is there any **problem with** my booking?*

'Of' cannot be used after 'any problem' in a sentence like this. But in a sentence beginning with 'The problem ...', both 'of' and 'with' can be used.

√   *The **problem of** booking a room during the high season is acute.*

√   *The **problem with** leaving your luggage in the lobby is that it might get stolen.*

Record	x *Let me have your **record**, please.*
	√ *Let me have your **particulars**, please.*

When a receptionist wants to greet a visitor in a hotel, the expression 'particulars' is used for the details in a form, like age, profession, length of stay, etc.

Rent	x *What's the **rent** for a room?*
	√ *What's the **price** of a room?*
	√ *What's the **cost** of a room?*

You could ask an estate agent or a landlord the 'rent' of a room. But in a hotel, 'rent' is not used.

Responsible

x *In my job as security officer, **responsible** is a must.*

√ *In my job as a security officer, **a sense of responsibility** is a must.*

√ *In my job as a security officer, **I must be responsible**.*

'Responsible' is an adjective and cannot be the subject of the sentence. The noun 'responsibility' alone does not express the idea well enough. You need to say: 'a sense of responsibility'.

Situate

x *Where is the hotel **situate**?*

√ *Where is the hotel **situated**?*

The passive is 'situated', just like 'located'.

Sleep late

x *I like to work at night and **sleep** late.*

√ *I like to work at night and **go to bed** late.*

You 'go to bed' late, not 'sleep late'. In English we say 'sleep in', or 'have a long lie in' when we mean getting up late in the morning. In Cantonese 夜瞓 means to go to bed late, although a direct translation is to 'sleep late'.

Speak

x *How many languages **are you speaking**?*

√ *How many languages **do you speak**?*

√ *How many languages **can you speak**?*

The present continuous would mean the person is speaking all the languages at this moment.

Sports	x *Do you have any **sports** in the hotel?* √ *Do you have any **sports facilities** in the hotel?* 'Sports' on its own means games like football, tennis, etc. But the questioner means: 'Are there any rooms/facilities provided by the hotel for sports?' e.g. squash court and table tennis room.
Straight forward	x *You go **straight forward** to the end of the corridor.* √ *You go **straight** to the end of the corridor.* When giving directions and using 'straight' you do not need to add 'forward'. You can use 'straightforward' as one word, meaning 'simple', 'easy to follow'. √ *It's perfectly **straightforward**.*
Suggest	x *Can you **suggest me another hotel**?* √ *Can you **suggest another hotel to me**?* √ *Can you **suggest another hotel for me**?* Note the prepositions used.
Surrounding	x *I like a room with quiet **surrounding**.* √ *I like a room with quiet **surroundings**.* When the general immediate environment is meant, the plural 'surroundings' is used. 'Surrounding' is an adjective as in: √ *The **surrounding** countryside is very peaceful.*
Take	x *Please **take** this way.* √ *Please **come** this way.* When the meaning is 'follow me', you use 'come this way'.
Taste	x *This hotel is decorated **in high taste**.* √ *This hotel is decorated **tastefully**.* √ *This hotel is decorated **in good taste**.* We can say 'high fashion' but not 'high taste'. 'Good taste' is correct.

That	x	***As you know that*** *empty rooms are the last thing a hotel wants.*
	√	***As you know****, empty rooms are the last thing a hotel wants.*

Either omit 'that' and say: 'As you know ...' or omit 'as' and say: 'You know that ...'.

The	x	*I'm staying in Ambassador hotel.*
	√	*I'm staying in* ***the*** *Ambassador hotel.*

When giving the name of your hotel (a proper name), you use the definite article.

Well-tempered	x	*Even with people who always complain, you have to be* ***well-tempered****.*
	√	*Even with people who always complain, you have to be* ***good-tempered****.*

Though we call a person who has good behaviour/manners 'well-behaved' or 'well-mannered', we cannot say 'well-tempered'. We must use 'good-tempered'.

When	x	***When*** *there is a fire, don't use the lift.*
	√	***If*** *there is a fire, don't use the lift.*

'When' sounds as if there is certain to be a fire. Hotel guests would no doubt prefer the more accurate 'if'.

Write	x	*What is your name? (Reply)* ***I write*** *it down for you.*
	√	*What is your name? (Reply)* ***I'll write*** *it down for you.*

You 'are going to' write it down so future tense is required.

Exercises

A   *There is an error in each question. Decide whether the error is in the underlined section A, B or C by circling the appropriate letter. Then give the correct answers in the space provided.*

1   My hotel is **too far from** the shopping
           A

    areas. **Can you** **suggest me another?**   _____
           B   C

2   If I could afford it, **I'd stay** in a hotel
                          A

    where there are **sports**.   _____
     B   C

3   There's a toilet **on this floor**. Just
                      A

    walk straight forward **to the end**   _____
           B   C

    of this corridor and turn right.

4   The dinner buffet in our hotel **is** very
                                   A

    popular. Many **peoples** from different
                   B

    countries **come** here regularly.   _____
               C

5   If you want **to go to swimming**,
                A

    there is a huge swimming pool
     B

    on the top floor. It's open all day.   _____
     C

6   My TV set **is not working**. Can you
        A

    please **send someone to look after**
                B   C

    it right away?   _____

7   **Although** our hotel is small, we
        A

    emphasis courtesy and **quality** of
        B   C

    service.   _____

8   **As you know that** this hotel has been
        A

    renovated **recently**, so the prices of the
                B

    rooms **have also been increased.**
                        C   _____

9   **Is there** any problem **of** my booking?
        A   B

    I confirmed it three days **ago**.
                                C   _____

10 Sorry, **lift not working** today.
                A

    Can you use the other one **opposite**
        B   C

    the reception desk?   _____

B(i) There are ten errors in the dialogue below. Read carefully and
underline the errors. Then rewrite the dialogue in the space
provided. (Please note that errors are not found in every line.)

Guest   :   Good evening. I would like to live here for two
                    nights. What's the rent for a single room?

Receptionist   :   That will be depend on which floor you would like.

Guest	:	I'd like a room at the top floor, with quiet surrounding, and if possible face to the harbour.
Receptionist	:	Yes. We have a room like that. It's $600 a night.
Guest	:	Thank you. I'll take it.
Receptionist	:	Could you sign here, please. Here is your key. The porter will lead you to your room.
Porter	:	Please take this way. *(They go into the lift.)*
Guest	:	You know, I'm afraid of lifts.
Porter	:	There's no need to be, but when there's a fire, please don't use the lift. All guests should use the stairs and gather around in the lobby.

B(ii) Underline the ten errors and rewrite the dialogue in the space provided. (Please note that errors are not found in every line.)

Guest : I'd like a call tomorrow morning.

Receptionist : Certainly. What is your name, please?

Guest : I write it down for you. _(Writes his name.)_ Is the hotel door open all night? I won't be back before midnight. I sleep late.

Receptionist : Yes, there is someone on the desk all night.

Guest : Thanks. If you don't mind my asking, how do you like your job?

Receptionist : I get a bit boring all day at the desk. And with rude guests, it's difficult sometimes to be well-tempered. But it's a nice hotel.

Guest : Yes, this lobby is decorated in high taste, don't you think?

Receptionist : Yes, I like it.

Guest : You must be good at languages. How many are you speaking? Apart from Chinese and English, what language else do you know?

Receptionist : Well, I can hear Japanese, but not really speak it.

Guest : Oh, by the way, can I get my clothes washed?

Receptionist : Yes, just leave them in the laundry bag in your room.

Guest : I have to check out by twelve tomorrow. Could I leave my bags with you here tomorrow for a couple of hours while I go shopping?

Receptionist : Certainly. I'll hold them for you until you come back.

Chapter **7**   Business Meetings

Abrupt

    x   *I must apologise for **my abrupt saying** at this morning's meeting.*

    √   *I must apologise for **being abrupt** at this morning's meeting.*

There are several correct idiomatic expressions: 'rudeness/impoliteness/sharp words/being so short'. 'Abrupt saying' cannot be used.

According to

    x   ***According to** my opinion, the problem lies in the sales department.*

    √   ***In** my opinion, the problem lies in the sales department.*

We can say 'according to a person' other than the speaker: 'According to you/him/her/them'.

Acquaint

    x   *Newcomers must **acquaint with** the methods our company use.*

    √   *Newcomers must **acquaint themselves with** the methods our company uses.*

    √   *Newcomers must **get acquainted with** the methods our company uses.*

You 'acquaint' yourself or someone 'with' something but you 'get acquainted with' something or someone.

After then

    x   *First he will see how the whole department runs. **After then**, he will be appointed to a particular section.*

    √   *First he will see how the whole department runs. **After that**, he will be appointed to a particular section.*

You can use 'then' or 'after that', but not 'after then'.

Agree

    x   ***I am agree** with him on this matter.*

    √   ***I agree** with him on this matter.*

    √   ***I am in agreement** with him on this matter.*

The wrong example confuses the two correct versions.

Are

    x   *If the quality of our products **are** poor, please tell us.*

√ *If the quality of our products **is** poor, please tell us.*

The subject is not 'products' but 'quality' which is singular and requires the singular verb 'is'.

Because ... so

x ***Because** inflation is very high, **so** we have to limit pay rises this year.*

√ ***Because** inflation is very high, we have to limit pay rises this year.*

√ *Inflation is very high, **so** we have to limit pay rises this year.*

In Cantonese, we say 因為 ... 所以. In English, we say either 'because' or 'so', not both.

Be last

x *The special sale should **be last** for only two days.*

√ *The special sale should **last** for only two days.*

When 'last' is used as a verb, you do not need 'be'. You can use 'be' with 'last' when 'last' is an adverb, as in:

√ *The question of vacation leave should **be last** on the agenda.*

Best offer

x *That is the **best offer** I can **do for** you.*

√ *That is the **best offer** I can **make** you.*

√ *That is the **best offer** I can **give** you.*

You 'make' someone a good offer, not 'do' someone a good offer. The mistake may be influenced by the following sentence:

√ *That is the best **thing I can do for** you.*

Care

x *Modern machines are sensitive. You need to **care them well**.*

√ *Modern machines are sensitive. You need to **care for them well**.*

√ *Modern machines are sensitive. You need to **take good care of them**.*

You cannot simply say 'care them'. The preposition 'for' is needed.

Confidence

x   *This year's profits should gain confidence from our customers.*

√   *This year's profits should gain our customers' confidence.*

√   *This year's profits should win our customers' confidence.*

You can 'gain confidence from something'. But here the intended meaning is 'make our customers grow in confidence' and we use 'gain/win our customers' confidence'.

Creative mind

x   *She is full of creative mind.*

√   *She is full of creative ideas.*

√   *She is full of creativity.*

√   *She has a creative mind.*

The wrong version sounds as if you have more than one 'mind'.

Demand

x   *Building up my new business demands me to work at weekends.*

√   *Building up my new business requires me to work at weekends.*

'Requires' is the correct verb. The adjective 'demanding' could be used as in:

√   *My new business is very demanding.*

Don't

x   *Will they only look around and **don't** buy anything?*

√   *Will they only look around and **not** buy anything?*

You cannot say: 'Will they don't ...' but rather 'Will they not ...'

Enjoy

x   ***She very enjoy** her work despite the tough challenge.*

√   ***She really enjoys** her work despite the tough challenge.*

√   ***She enjoys her work very much** despite the tough challenge.*

'Very' is an adjective and you cannot describe a verb (enjoy) with an adjective; you need to have an adverb (really). Do not translate directly from Cantonese 好鐘意.

Equipments

x   *We need more modern **equipments**.*

√   *We need more modern **equipment**.*

'Equipment' is an uncountable noun.

Focus

x   *The survey **will be focus on** higher productivity.*

√   *The survey **will be focussed on** higher productivity.*

The passive of the verb 'focus' is 'be focussed' and this passive form is sometimes heard. But the active form of the verb is more common.

√   *The survey **will focus on** higher productivity.*

The noun can also be used as in:

√   *The **focus** of the survey **will be on** higher productivity.*

Give out

x   *We encourage our members to **give out their opinion** whenever they like.*

√   *We encourage our members to **give their opinion** whenever they like.*

√   *We encourage our members to **speak out** whenever they like.*

In English you do not 'give out' an opinion. However, we can use 'give out' as follows:

√   *Please **give out** the copies of the report.*

Here 'give out' means 'distribute'.

Good pay

x   *I will stay in sales as long as **it is good pay**.*

√   *I will stay in sales as long as **the pay is good**.*

'It is' is unclear. The sentence becomes clearer when 'the pay' is made the subject.

How to	1	x	*How to* address the letter to Mr Siu's company?
		√	*How do I* address the letter to Mr Siu's company?

Do not translate directly from Cantonese 點樣.

	2	x	*How* are we supposed to do about our losses?
		√	*What* are we supposed to do about our losses?

If the verb were 'deal with', then 'how' could be used, but you cannot use 'how' with 'do about'.

Initiative

x   The new staff *are not initiative enough*.
√   The new staff *do not have enough initiative*.

'Initiative' is a noun, not an adjective.

Interest

x   The pricing system will be *the interest of* most people.
√   The pricing system will be *of interest to* most people.
√   The pricing system will be *a point of interest to* most people.

Let

x   If I were in charge, I would ask *to let me* do a pilot survey first.
√   If I were in charge, I would ask *to be allowed to* do a pilot survey first.
√   If I were in charge, I would ask *if I could* do a pilot survey first.

'Ask to let' is redundant.

Much

x   I have so *much* files to deal with that life is just impossible.
√   I have so *many* files to deal with that life is just impossible.

'Much' is used with uncountable nouns, as in 'not much hope'. 'Many' is used with countable nouns.

One

x   *I really hope to become **one** member of the planning division.*

√   *I really hope to become **a** member of the planning division.*

The Cantonese 一個 can be translated by both 'one' and 'a'. But English does not use 'one' as an equivalent to 'a'.

Point of view

x   ***To my point of view**, it is a waste of money to hire a consultant.*

√   ***From my point of view**, it is a waste of money to hire a consultant.*

√   ***In my view**, it is a waste of money to hire a consultant.*

Note the correct idioms here.

Quite

x   *He gave us **a quite good** report.*

√   *He gave us **quite a good** report.*

'Quite' comes before the article 'a'.

Save up

x   *To **save up** expenses, the members were asked to fly economy class.*

√   *To **save on** expenses, the members were asked to fly economy class.*

'Save up' means 'to accumulate money/ supplies for future use'.

√   *The clerks **saved up** to buy their boss a present.*

When 'save' means 'economise', you use 'save on':

√   *To **save on** electricity, please turn off the lights.*

Say

x   *I can understand Mandarin but I can't **say** it.*

√   *I can understand Mandarin but I can't **speak** it.*

Cantonese 講 means 'say' and 'speak'. In English you use 'speak' when you mean to talk in a language.

Spend time

x   *We have **spent a long time to discuss** this problem.*

√   *We have **spent a long time discussing** this problem.*

The gerund form (-ing) is used, not the infinitive (to).

Staffs

x   *The boss gave every **staffs** a rise.*

√   *The boss gave every **member of staff** a rise.*

'Staff' is an uncountable noun.

That

x   *The problem is **that how to** attract customers.*

√   *The problem is **how to** attract customers.*

No 'that' is necessary. It probably arises from expressions like:

√   *The problem is **that** we have no customers.*

Think it

x   *I haven't **thought it** before.*

√   *I haven't **thought about it** before.*

The phrasal verb 'think about' is needed. A

stronger expression of the same idea, using the noun, is:

√ *I haven't **given it a thought** before.*

Together

x *There are **together** six points on today's agenda.*
√ *There are **altogether** six points on today's agenda.*

The meaning required here is 'in total', so 'altogether' should be used. 'Together' is used for 'in company with' as in:

√ *They went **together** to the party.*
√ ***Together with** two others he was given the sack.*

To me, I

1 x ***To me, I** think we should cut costs.*
√ *I think we should cut costs.*
2 x ***To me, I** find job satisfaction.*
√ *I find job satisfaction.*

Omit the redundant 'To me'. If you begin with 'To me', you must use an impersonal verb, as in:

√ ***To me it seems a good idea** to cut costs.*
√ ***To me it looks good**.*

Too many ... that

x *Have we **too many** plans **that** we cannot concentrate on any one of them?*
√ *Have we **too many** plans **so that** we cannot concentrate on any one of them?*
√ *Have we **so many** plans **that** we cannot concentrate on any one of them?*

If you use 'too many' you need 'so that' not just 'that'. If you use 'so many' you need 'that'.

Wording

x *I didn't catch your **wording** clearly.*
√ *I didn't catch your **words** clearly.*

'Wording' is used in an example like:

√ *The **wording** of the letter had to be altered.*

This means the precise form and order of words. When we simply mean 'what you said', we use 'catch your words'.

Exercises

A   *There is an error in each question. Decide whether the error is in the underlined section A, B or C by circling the appropriate letter. Then give the correct answers in the space provided.*

1   <u>For the good of</u> our company, we
        A

   should not hesitate <u>to give out</u> our
                  B

   views <u>when asked</u>.   _____
        C

2   The store manager <u>was of the opinion</u>
                     A

   that the trial period <u>should be last</u>
                 B

   for a <u>little longer</u>.   _____
         C

3   It's incredible <u>but</u> my friend <u>very enjoy</u>
              A   B

   the daily <u>challenge of</u> her new job.   _____
          C

4   Thomas <u>asked for</u> a 20% discount but
         A

   the shopowner <u>insisted that</u> 10% was
              B

   the best offer he could <u>do for</u> him.   _____
                C

5   <u>To cut costs</u>, the operations manager
     A

   decided <u>to save up on</u> electricity and
         B

   <u>shut off</u> the machines.   _____
   C

6 <u>Getting these plans</u> ready on time
     A

  <u>demands me</u> <u>to spend</u> a lot of extra
    B   C

  time in the office.   _____

7 The PR man <u>successfully avoided</u>
             A

  the employees' question <u>by saying</u>,
                  B

  'I haven't <u>thought it</u> before.'   _____
          C

8 Our sales representatives must

  <u>acquaint with</u> the strategies <u>used by</u>
    A   B

  our <u>rival companies</u>.   _____
       C

9 I'm sorry but I didn't <u>catch your wording</u>
                  A

  clearly <u>when</u> you <u>raised that objection</u>
       B   C

  at the meeting.   _____

10 The new <u>bonus scheme</u> will be
        A

  <u>the interest of</u> all <u>dissatisfied employees</u>.   _____
    B   C

B(i) There are ten errors in the dialogue below. Read carefully and underline the errors. Then rewrite the dialogue in the space provided. (Please note that errors are not found in every line.)

Chairman : There are together three problems to be discussed in connection with our department store. First, variety of products. Have we too many products that customers don't know where to start buying? Second, comfort and attractiveness of our store. If we make it too comfortable and attractive, will customers only walk around and don't buy anything? Third, price range. If the price of our products are too high, will people go elsewhere?

Mr Chan : We have spent a long time to discuss all these issues before. According to my opinion, it's just a waste of time.

Mr Lo : No, I don't think so. I am agree with the Chairman. To me, I would prefer to discuss these important matters. They're certainly not a waste of time.

Mr Chan : Sorry for my abrupt saying.

Chairman : Right. Let's get back to the problems. How are we supposed to do about them?

B(ii) Underline the ten errors and rewrite the dialogue in the space provided. (Please note that errors are not found in every line.)

Emma : The boss wants to conduct a survey of our office
procedures. It will be focus on better efficiency.

Diana : It's because of that visiting consultant we had. I thought he
would give us a quite good report.

Emma : Apparently he said our staff were not initiative enough and
that young people like us should be full of creative mind.

Diana : To my point of view, the problem is we are too busy. There
are so much files to update.

Emma : We should have more computers in the office. After all,
because we live in an advanced technological society in
Hong Kong, so it would gain confidence from our
customers if they see that we have modern equipments.

Diana : But don't computers break down a lot?

Emma : Yes. You need to care them well.

Chapter 8   Travel

A	x *How much is one-way ticket?* √ *How much is **a** one-way ticket?* The article 'a' is needed here.
Any	x *There are three flights **any** day.* √ *There are three flights **a** day.* √ *There are three flights **per** day.* 'A' and 'per' means 'each'.
Anyone	x ***Have anyone** of you been to Europe?* √ ***Has anyone** of you been to Europe?* 'Anyone' is singular and needs a singular verb 'has'.
Arrive	x *I **arrived** Hong Kong very late.* √ *I **arrived in** Hong Kong very late.* The preposition 'in' is needed.
As many as possible	x *You must visit countries **as many as possible**.* √ *You must visit **as many** countries **as possible**.* 'Countries' should come between 'as many' and 'as possible'.
Be begun	x *When will the film **be begun**?* √ *When will the film **begin**?* The active verb 'begin' is correct here.
Better	x *You'd **better to** take out travel insurance.* √ *You'd **better** take out travel insurance.* √ *You'd **be better to** take out travel insurance.* When 'be' is omitted ('you'd better'), 'to' is not used. When 'be' is included ('you'd be better'), then 'to' is used.
Close	x *I can't **close** the tap in the toilet.* √ *I can't **turn off** the tap in the toilet.* In Cantonese both 'close' and 'turn off' are expressed by 閂 . In English, we say 'close the door/window/curtain' but use 'turn off the tap/TV/radio', etc.

Double of

x *Is the round-trip ticket **double of** the single trip?*
√ *Is the round-trip ticket **double** the single trip?*
When used as an adverb, 'double' does not take the preposition 'of'. When used as a noun, it does.
√ *He's **the double of** his brother.*
'Double' can also be used as an adjective.
√ *I don't like the idea of a **double** journey.*
And it can be used as a verb.
√ *Going via Malaysia will **double** the time you take.*

Dull

x *On a long journey I usually feel **dull**.*
√ *On a long journey I usually feel **bored**.*
'Bored' is used when your spirits are low because you have nothing to keep you occupied. 'Dull' in English is commonly used for 'not very intelligent'.
√ *He's a nice boy but a bit **dull**.*

Easy

x *In October, visitors in Hong Kong **are not easy** to get accommodation.*
√ *In October, visitors in Hong Kong **do not find it easy** to get accommodation.*
√ *In October, **it is not easy for** visitors in Hong Kong to get accommodation.*
The wrong version comes from the Chinese expression 唔容易 .

Economic

    x   *Are you flying business or economic class?*

    √   *Are you flying business or economy class?*

There are three forms of the adjective from the noun 'economy':

1 economic

    √   *The economic condition of Hong Kong will benefit airlines.*

2 economical

    √   *Some planes use fuel in an economical manner.*

3 economy

    √   *An economy class ticket is cheaper than a first-class ticket.*

Number 3 is the correct one to use for airline tickets.

Good

    x   *He speaks English very good.*

    √   *He speaks English very well.*

    √   *He speaks very good English.*

Either use the adverb 'well' after 'English', or the adjective 'good' before 'English'.

Has/Have

1 x   *On which day of the week has flight to London?*

    √   *On which day of the week is there a flight to London?*

    √   *On which day of the week do you have a flight to London?*

English says this either in a personal way, 'Do you have', or in an impersonal way, 'Is there'.

2 x   *Was the journey OK? (Reply) No. Have some problems on the way back.*

    √   *Was the journey OK? (Reply) No. I had some problems on the way back.*

    √   *Was the journey OK? (Reply) No. There were some problems on the way back.*

Again, English uses either the personal 'I had' or the impersonal 'there were'.

He/She

    *The stewardess is very helpful. **He** got me a drink.*

√ *The stewardess is very helpful. **She** got me a drink.*

In Catonese the pronoun 佢 refers to both 'he' and 'she'.

How

x ***How to** pronounce this word?*

√ ***How do you** pronounce this word?*

The correct way to ask a question using 'how' is 'how do you ...'.

In addition

x *I have travelled to many parts of the world. **In addition**, I like flying.*

√ *I have travelled to many parts of the world. I like flying.*

English would not use 'In addition' in the example above. You can use 'in addition' as follows:

√ *I booked this flight two months ago. I reconfirmed it last week. **In addition**, I checked the reconfirmation yesterday.*

Interest

x *All of us are very **interest to go** abroad.*

√ *All of us are very **interested in going** abroad.*

'Interest' is a noun. The past form of the verb must be used. Also, after 'interested', we use 'in' plus the gerund (-ing form), not the infinitive 'to go'.

In the

x   *The hostel closes at eleven **in the** night.*
√   *The hostel closes at eleven **at** night.*
We say 'at' not 'in the'. But you can say:
√   *The flight leaves **in the** morning.*
And you can use 'in the night' in a sentence like:
√   *He heard noises **in the night**.*
Here 'in the night' means in the dark.

Is

x   *It **is** raining when we reached Singapore.*
√   *It **was** raining when we reached Singapore.*
There must be agreement between the tenses: 'reached' and 'was'.

It

x   ***In** Hong Kong **it** is a beautiful place.*
√   *Hong Kong **is** a beautiful place.*
√   *In Hong Kong **it is** beautiful.*
The wrong version combines the two correct ones.

Load

x   *My **load** is rather heavy.*
√   *My **luggage** is rather heavy.*
When you go for a trip, you carry 'luggage' or 'baggage', but not 'a load'.

Maybe

x   ***Maybe I reserve** a seat on another flight for you.*
√   ***Maybe I could reserve** a seat on another flight for you.*

'Could' is required in this kind of polite idiom.

√ **Maybe you could try again** later.

Necessary

x **I am necessary to** take a sleeping pill before a long flight.

√ **It is necessary for me to** take a sleeping pill before a long flight.

The impersonal construction should be used.

Need

x How long **do we need** to travel to Singapore?

√ How long **does it take** to travel to Singapore?

The personal 'do we need' is not used with 'to travel'. The impersonal 'does it take' is the correct usage. However, 'do we need' can often be correctly used as follows:

√ How long **do we need** to keep our safety belts fastened?

√ How long **do we need** to allow for the stopover in Tokyo?

No

x You can't speak Japanese, can you? (Reply) **No, I can.**

√ You can't speak Japanese, can you? (Reply) **No, I can't.**

√ You can't speak Japanese, can you? (Reply) **Yes, I can.**

In Cantonese, 'No' 唔識 answers the whole question. In English, you have to say 'No, I can't (speak Japanese).' or 'Yes, I can (speak Japanese).'

Non-smoking

x I'd like the **non-smoking class.**

√ I'd like the **non-smoking section/area.**

We talk of the 'economy/business class', but the 'smoking/non-smoking section/area' or more simply 'non-smoking' with 'section/area' understood.

√ I'd like **non-smoking.**

On

1 x We should land **on** London Airport soon.

√ We should land **in/at** London Airport soon.

Land 'on' sounds as if the plane will land on top of London airport. We say land 'at' or 'in' an airport. But you can say:

√   *We landed **on** the runway.*

2   x   *I'd like **a seat on the aisle**.*
√   *I'd like **an aisle seat**.*

To say 'on the aisle' sounds as if the person will be sitting down on the aisle/corridor. The prepositions 'by/beside/near' the aisle can all be used, or most commonly 'aisle seat', like 'window seat'.

Play

x   *I'm going to Penang to **play**.*
√   *I'm going to Penang to **have a good time**.*
√   *I'm going to Penang to **enjoy myself**.*

The Cantonese expression 玩 means 'to play' or 'have a good time'. 'To play' would usually mean to play some game, which is not the meaning intended in this context.

Rate

x   *What is the **rate** of a round-rip ticket to Sydney?*
√   *What is the **price** of a round-trip ticket to Sydney?*

You use 'price' or 'cost' not 'rate' for a ticket. You can use 'rate/price' in:

√   *Is there a special **rate** for children?*
√   *Is there a special **price** for children?*

Ready

x   *They will **ready the dinner** soon after takeoff.*

√   *They will **get the dinner ready** soon after takeoff.*

In the wrong example, the adjective is wrongly used as if it were a verb.

Refund

x   *If I cancel the trip, can I **refund**?*

√   *If I cancel the trip, can I **get a refund**?*

√   *If I cancel the trip, can I **be refunded**?*

Either we use a noun with 'get' or the passive form.

Risk

x   *We can't **risk to travel** without insurance.*

√   *We can't **risk travelling** without insurance.*

When 'risk' is used as a verb, it is followed by the gerund (-ing form), not by the infinitive 'to travel'. If 'risk' is used as a noun, it can be followed by both:

√   *It's **a risk to allow** only an hour for check in.*

√   *It's **a risk allowing** only an hour for check in.*

Sceneries

x   *In Japan we saw **many beautiful sceneries**.*

√   *In Japan we saw **a lot of beautiful scenery**.*

'Scenery' is an uncountable noun.

Staffs

x   *The **staffs** are very efficient.*

√   *The **staff** are very efficient.*

'Staff' is an uncountable noun. Since it has a collective sense (a number of people), 'staff' can be used with a plural verb.

Take

x   *The taxi fare **takes** about $20.*

√   *The taxi fare **costs** about $20.*

'Cost' is the correct verb to use in answer to the question 'How much?' 'Take' is the correct verb in answer to 'How long?'

√   *The taxi **takes** about 20 minutes to the airport.*

Take best care of

x   *I always **take best care of** my belongings.*

√   *I always **take very good care of** my belongings.*

You say 'very good', not 'best' when 'care' is used without an article. However, you can use 'best' in phrases like 'the best care possible' and 'the best care I can'.

√   *I take the **best care possible** of my belongings.*

√   *I always take the **best care I can** of my wallet.*

The

x   *I'll go by **the** Korean Airlines.*

√   *I'll go by Korean Airlines.*

The article is not used with the name of an airline company.

√   *I usually fly by Cathay Pacific.*

Tie

x   *How do I **tie** my seat belt?*

√   *How do I **fasten** my seat belt?*

Because a seat belt has a buckle, you use 'fasten', not 'tie'.

To

x   *He is leaving us **to** America tomorrow.*

√   *He is leaving us **for** America tomorrow.*

√   *He is leaving us **to go to** America tomorrow.*

The Cantonese 去 means 'to go to' and 'to', and this influences the wrong English usage.

Travel	1	x	*What a long **travel**!*

Travel   1   x   *What a long **travel**!*
                      √   *What a long **journey**!*

Journey' is used when you mean the time spent and distance covered. 'Travel' is used more in a general sense.

You cannot say 'a travel'. But a plural form of 'travel' can be used.

      √   *I saw many wonderful things on my **travels**.*

2   x   *He **has been travelled** all over the world.*

      √   *He **has travelled** all over the world.*

You cannot use the passive of the verb 'travel' when the subject is a person. You can say, however:

      √   *This route **has been travelled** by many people.*

And you can talk of a 'far-travelled' person.

3   x   *Is this the first time you **travel** by boat?*

      √   *Is this the first time you **have travelled** by boat?*

Avoid this very common error of tenses.

Two three   x   *I've been **two three** times to Taiwan.*

                      √   *I've been **two or three** times to Taiwan.*

The wrong version is translated directly from 兩三次 .

Will   x   *I don't like England as it **will often rain** there.*

                    √   *I don't like England as it **often rains** there.*

The simple present tense should be used because of the word 'often'.

Exercises

A *There is an error in each question. Decide whether the error is in the underlined section A, B or C by circling the appropriate letter. Then give the correct answers in the space provided.*

1 The air stewardess **remained** cheerful
                      A

  although **he** was busy **the whole night.** _____
         B   C

2 If you **get a chance** to travel, you
         A

  should **go to** Thailand. **In Thailand it**
       B   C

  is a beautiful place. _____

3 Most youth hostels **abroad** stay open
             A

  until eleven **in the night**. _____
  B   C

4 **None of** my friends **has been travelled**
  A   B

  to Europe **before**. _____
        C

5 Although Mr Walsh **has only been** to
               A

  Hong Kong **for a year**, he speaks
          B

  Cantonese **very good**. _____
         C

6 **Did you have** a nice journey **back**?
  A   B

  (Reply) No. **Have** some problems with my
          C

  air ticket. _____

7 The taxi fare **from** the airport **to** your
             A   B

   hotel **takes** about $70.   _____
        C

8 **Since** the economy class is **fully**
     A   B

   booked, **maybe I book** a business
            C

   class for you.   _____

9 You **should use** that travel agency.
          A

   The **staffs** are **most helpful**. _____
       B   C

10 I think we'd better **to take out** an
                      A

    insurance policy **before** we **leave for**
                  B   C

    Canada.   _____

B(i) There are ten errors in the dialogue below. Read carefully and underline the errors. Then rewrite the dialogue in the space provided. (Please note that errors are not found in every line.)

Traveller : Is this the counter of the Thai Airlines? I'd like some information about the rate of a ticket to Bangkok. How much is one-way ticket?

Salesgirl : Do you want Business class?

Traveller : No, thank you. Economic class.

Salesgirl : That costs $3,900.

Traveller : And is a round-trip ticket the double of a single trip?

Salesgirl : No, a round-trip ticket is $7,200.

Traveller : How often do flights go to Bangkok?

Salesgirl : There are two flights any day. One is at morning and the other is at noon.

Traveller : Does the plane have a non-smoking class?

Salesgirl : Yes, a large number of seats are reserved for non-smokers.

Traveller : Can I have a seat on the aisle, as I have long legs?

Salesgirl : If you book early, I'm sure there will be no problem.

Traveller : But if I cancel the ticket, will I be refund?

Salesgirl : Sorry, I'm afraid not.

_____

_____

_____

_____

_____

_____

_____

_____

_____

_____

_____

_____

_____

_____

_____

_____

_____

_____

_____

B(ii) Underline the ten errors and rewrite the dialogue in the space provided. (Please note that errors are not found in every line.)

Mary : Excuse me. Can you show me how to tie my seat belt?

Mr Ho : Certainly. Like this. *(He shows her.)* Is this the first time you travel by air?

Mary : Yes, it is.

Mr Ho : Is it a business trip?

Mary : No, I'm just going to play. Tell me, how long do we need to fly to Japan?

Mr Ho : We should land on Tokyo in about three hours.

Mary : Oh, what a long travel! I am sure I will begin to feel dull.

Mr Ho : Don't worry. The film will be begun soon. By the way, is that your passport on the floor?

Mary : Yes it is. I am necessary to find a safe place for it.

Mr Ho : You must take best care of your passport when you are travelling.

Chapter 9 Socialising

Almost think	x	*I **almost think you have** given up visiting me.*
	√	*I **almost thought you had** given up visiting me.*

You have to use the past tense of the verb, 'thought', in this idiom. The idea is: 'Until you came, I almost thought ...'.

Already	x	*We haven't seen each other for **already four months**.*
	√	*We haven't seen each other for **four months now**.*
	√	***It's already four months since we've seen** each other.*
	√	***It's four months now since we've seen** each other.*

Compare the use of 'already' in the following example:

√ *I've been hoping to see him for **four months already**.*

This means that 'I've been hoping to see him for the past four months and I'm still hoping to see him'.

As ... therefore	x	***As** I enjoy meeting people, **therefore** I like coming to parties.*
	√	*I enjoy meeting people, **and so** I like coming to parties.*
	√	***As** I enjoy meeting people, I like coming to parties.*

Cantonese uses 由於⋯所以 . English uses either one or the other.

Aren't you	x	***Are you** William, **aren't you**?*
	√	***You're** William, **aren't you**?*
	√	***Aren't you** William?*

You cannot use a positive question 'Are you William?' followed by a negative question tag 'aren't you?' Either use a positive statement 'You're William' and a negative question tag 'aren't you?', or a question in the negative, 'Aren't you William?'

Available

x   *It's my birthday party on Thursday.* **Do you available?**

√   *It's my birthday party on Thursday.* **Are you available?**

With 'available' we use 'are', not 'do'.

Been

x   **We've been** *there last year.*

√   **We went** *there last year.*

When you state a definite time 'last year' you use the simple past tense. When the time is indefinite, you use the present perfect.

√   **We've been** *there before.*

Confidence

x   *I would like to* **be more confidence** *on social occasions.*

√   *I would like to* **be more confident** *on social occasions.*

√   *I would like to* **have more confidence** *on social occasions.*

Cantonese uses 信心 for the adjective and the abstract noun. In English 'confident' is the adjective and 'confidence' is the noun.

Difficult

x   **You are very difficult** *to find your way in Hong Kong if you don't know the city.*

√   **It is very difficult for you** *to find your way in Hong Kong if you don't know the city.*

The impersonal construction is used.

Does ... hold

x   *When **does** the party **hold**?*
√   *When **will** the party **be held**?*
The passive is required. You 'hold' a party; a party 'is held' by you. Also, since the party is in the future, the future tense is used. However, in colloquial usage you can use the present tense of the verb 'to be' to express the future.
√   *When **is** the party?*

Doesn't matter

x   *I've just lost my job. (Reply) **It doesn't matter**.*
√   *I've just lost my job. (Reply) **I'm sorry to hear that**.*
The Cantonese 唔緊要 translated as 'it doesn't matter' is very inappropriate in some cases. Here it does matter very much to the man that he has lost his job.

Enjoy

x   *I **enjoy to live** in the New Territories.*
√   *I **enjoy living** in the New Territories.*
'Enjoy' takes the gerund (-ing), not the infinitive (to).

Excited

x   *My friend is coming from Canada today and I'm so **exciting**.*
√   *My friend is coming from Canada today and I'm so **excited**.*
You feel 'excited' about something 'exciting'.

Fiction

x   *I read a very good **fiction** last week.*
√   *I read a very good **novel** last week.*
'Fiction' is the word for imaginitive prose writing in general. A particular work of fiction is a 'novel'. Cantonese usage 小說 means both.

First time

x   *Is this the **first time you come** to Hong Kong?*
√   *Is this the **first time you've come** to Hong Kong?*
The present perfect is the correct tense here.

For a moment

x   *Sorry I'm late. (Reply) Don't worry. I've only **come here for a moment** myself.*
√   *Sorry I'm late. (Reply) Don't worry. I've only **been here for a moment** myself.*
√   *Sorry I'm late. (Reply) Don't worry. I've only **came here a moment ago** myself.*
'I've only come here for a moment' sounds as if you intend to stay only for a very brief visit. What the speaker means to say is that he has come only a short time before.

Frog

x   *I am not a very good swimmer. I can only do the **frog**.*
√   *I am not a very good swimmer. I can only do the **breast stroke**.*
Cantonese 蛙式 cannot be translated as 'frog' when you refer to this kind of stroke in swimming.

Glad	x *How **glad that I can see** you!*
	√ *How **glad** I **am to see** you!*
	√ *How **nice to see** you!*

If you begin 'I'm glad ...' then you can use 'that'.

√   *I'm **glad that** I've had the chance to see you.*

Greet	x *I want you to **greet** my mother.*
	√ *I want you to **meet** my mother.*

When introducing someone, you say 'meet' not 'greet'. 'Greet' is used correctly in the following:

√   *He always **greets** you in a friendly way.*
√   *She **greeted** him with a big smile.*

Hair	x *You've got **a lovely hair**.*
	√ *You've got **lovely hair**.*
	√ *You've got **a lovely hairstyle**.*
	√ ***Your hair is lovely**.*

'A lovely hair' sounds as if the person has only got one hair!

I and my wife	x ***I and my wife** are delighted you could come.*
	√ ***My wife and I** are delighted you could come.*

In English it is good manners to mention the other person first.

It

x   *Is **it** the first visit you've made to Hong Kong?*

√   *Is **this** the first visit you've made to Hong Kong?*

You need the stronger demonstrative 'this'.

Just come back

x   ***I've just come back for** two months.*

√   *I **came back just** two months **ago**.*

√   ***I've been back for only** two months.*

The speaker wants to say she came back two months ago, but the words in the wrong version would mean: 'I have come back and will only remain for two months'.

Lady

x   *Joyce became 21 last week. She's now **a lady**.*

√   *Joyce became 21 last week. She's now **an adult**.*

'Lady' is not used in this way to mean a mature female person.

Last

x   *It's been three years since we **met last time**.*

√   *It's been three years since we **last met**.*

When 'last' is used as an adverb, 'time' is not added to the sentence. But when 'last' is used as an adjective, it can be used with 'time'.

√   *The **last time** we met was three years ago.*

Like

x   *I **am very like** Hong Kong.*

√   *I **like** Hong Kong **very much**.*

鐘意 cannot be translated as 'I am very like'. 'I am like' in English means 'I look like', 'I resemble'. In this context, 'like' means 'fond of'.

Long time	x *It's **a long time I've never seen you**.*
	√ *It's **been a long time since I've seen you**.*
	√ ***I haven't seen you for a long time**.*
	Note these correct ways to use 'a long time'.

Lovers	x *Many of my fellow students have **lovers**.*
	√ *Many of my fellow students have **boyfriends/girlfriends**.*
	In English 'lovers' is a very strong word which implies a deep and intimate relationship.

Marry	x *We're going to **get marry** soon.*
	√ *We're going to **get married** soon.*
	√ *We're going to **marry** soon.*
	Note how the verb 'marry' is used.

Mind	x *Would you **mind to come** back tomorrow?*
	√ *Would you **mind coming** back tomorrow?*
	'Would you mind' is followed by the gerund (-ing form) of the verb. For future time 'would you mind' is preferable. For present time 'do you mind' and 'would you mind' are both quite acceptable.
	√ ***Do you mind** waiting?*
	√ ***Would you mind** waiting?*

Most	x *What do you dislike most about your job? (Reply) The long hours **most**.*
	√ *What do you dislike most about your job? (Reply) The long hours **mostly**.*
	In the question, 'most' as an adverb, going with 'dislike', is correct. But in the reply, 'most' cannot be used on its own and 'mostly' is needed.

Nearly	x *I **nearly can't** recognise you.*
	√ *I **can hardly** recognise you.*
	'Nearly' meaning 'not quite', 'not yet completely', is negative in meaning and should not be used with another negative 'can't'. We use 'hardly' meaning 'almost not',

'with difficulty' following the positive verb 'can'.

Never mind

x   *My car was in a terrible mess when you returned it. (Reply)* **Never mind.**

√   *My car was in a terrible mess when you returned it. (Reply)* **I'm very/awfully sorry.**

The speaker is expecting an apology, but the wrong version indicates a reply which means, 'it doesn't really matter', 'it's not important', 'don't bother about it'.

Nightgown

x   *She was wearing a beautiful* **nightgown** *to the ball.*

√   *She was wearing a beautiful* **evening dress** *to the ball.*

A nightgown is used as a sleeping garment in bed.

MAYBE THAT'S THE FASHION

No matter

x   **No matter** *you forbid it, I'm going to the karaoke tonight.*

√   **No matter whether** *you forbid it or not, I'm going to the karaoke tonight.*

√   **Even if** *you forbid it, I'm going to the karaoke tonight.*

Either you use the phrase 'No matter whether' or 'even if'.

Of	1	x	*My jewellery is kept in **the safe of** Mr Lau.*
		√	*My jewellery is kept in **Mr Lau's safe**.*

Note the correct possessive forms used.

	2	x	*When to hold the party is the problem **of them**.*
		√	*When to hold the party is the problem **for them**.*
		√	*When to hold the party is **their** problem.*

OK	x	*Thank you for coming to the party.* (Reply) **It's OK.**
	√	*Thank you for coming to the party.* (Reply) **Not at all. Thank you for asking me.**

'It's OK' is not an appropriate response. It is too casual, as if you have done the person a favour by coming to the party. There are occasions when 'it's OK' is appropriate in colloquial usage.

√ *Sorry my car will be blocking you if I park here.* (Reply) **It's OK.** *We'll be leaving together anyway.*

On	x	*Can you come to a barbecue **on** this Friday?*
	√	*Can you come to a barbecue this Friday?*

No preposition is needed.

One	x	*This is Mr Lee. This is Mr Ho. And **this one** is Miss Cheung.*
	√	*This is Mr Lee. This is Mr Ho. And **this is** Miss Cheung.*

We use 'this is' to introduce a person.

Only	1	x	***Only** by boat **you can** get there.*
		√	***Only** by boat **can you** get there.*

When a limiting expression like 'only' is at the beginning of a sentence, the order of subject and auxiliary verb is reversed. Also note:

√ ***Not** very often **have I seen** such a beautiful sunset.*

You use the normal subject-verb order when the limiting expression follows the verb.

√   **You can** get there **only** by boat.

2   x   For a formal dinner a man should wear **only a black tie**.

√   For a formal dinner a black tie **is essential**.

The first example sounds as if the man should wear nothing but a black tie, i.e. go naked.

Play

x   **Play** basketball is very energetic.

√   **Playing** basketball is very energetic.

A gerund is needed here.

Prefer

x   I prefer tennis **than** swimming.

√   I prefer tennis **to** swimming.

If 'prefer' is used, you need to have 'to' followed by a gerund.

Quite

x   It's not **quite** easy to meet every week.

√   It's not **very** easy to meet every week.

In a negative statement in English 'very' should be used. If the statement is positive, both 'quite' and 'very' can be used.

√   It's **quite** easy to meet every week.

√   It's **very** easy to meet every week.

Recall

x   I'll try to **recall my memory on** her name.

√   I'll try to **recall** her name.

√   I'll try to **refresh my memory on** her name.

The wrong version confuses the two correct ones.

Send

x   Let me **send** you to the door.

√   Let me **see** you to the door.

√   Let me **take** you to the door.

'See' and 'take' are the correct verbs to use.

She	x	*She was an only child and **he** missed her mother very much.*
	√	*She was an only child and **she** missed her mother very much.*

'She' is the feminine form, the second pronoun needs to be consistent.

Slangs	x	*He uses a lot of **slangs**.*
	√	*He uses a lot of **slang**.*

'Slang' is an uncountable noun.

The case	x	*I gave up my job. (Reply) Why's that **the case?***
	√	*I gave up my job. (Reply) **Why was that?***

'... the case' is not necessary here. You would use 'the case' in:

	√	*He thought she was a film star, but it was not really **the case**.*

Try	x	*If I get away from work early, I'll **try if I** can make it.*
	√	*If I get away from work early, I'll **see if I** can make it.*
	√	*If I get away from work early, I'll **try to see if** I can make it.*

Either you use the verb 'see' or 'try to see'. 'Try' alone will not do.

Waste your time	x	*Thank you for **wasting your time with me**.*
	√	*Thank you for **spending your time with me**.*
	√	*Thank you for **giving me your time**.*

The person may indeed have been wasting his time 浪費佢嘅時間 with you, but there is no need to tell him so.

What	x	*Excuse me. Can you tell me how to get to the Cultural Centre? (Reply) **What?***
	√	*Excuse me. Can you tell me how to get to the Cultural Centre? (Reply) **Pardon?***
	√	*Excuse me. Can you tell me how to get to the Cultural Centre? (Reply) **I beg your pardon?***

'What?' in response to a question you didn't hear or didn't understand is too abrupt and impolite.

Yes

1 x *Do you mind helping me to give out these cups? (Reply)* **Yes.**

√ *Do you mind helping me to give out these cups? (Reply)* **Not at all.**

'Yes' in English would be interpreted as 'Yes, I do mind'.

2 x *You haven't any children, have you? (Reply)* **Yes.**

√ *You haven't any children, have you? (Reply)* **No.**

In the mind of the Cantonese speaker, 'Yes', means 'Yes, you are right. I haven't any children'. However, simply to say 'Yes' would confuse a native English speaker.

Yet

x *Have you got married yet?*
√ *Are you married?*

The Cantonese 結咗婚未 cannot be translated directly into English. Some people might resent the assumption that they are going to get married.

Exercises

A *There is an error in each question. Decide whether the error is in the underlined section A, B or C by circling the appropriate letter. Then give the correct answers in the space provided.*

1 I'm sure my parents **wouldn't mind**
A

if I have a **lover** as long as I don't
B   C

neglect my studies.

2   Excuse me, can you tell me <u>**If this is**</u>
                                          A

the <u>**way to**</u> Harbour City? *(Reply)*
       B

<u>**What**</u>? _____
     C

3   <u>**I'm afraid**</u> there is <u>**no other form of**</u>
        A   B

transport available. Only by ferry

<u>**you can**</u> get there. _____
     C

4   <u>**Normally**</u> I prefer squash <u>**than**</u>
        A   B

badminton. But today I don't mind

<u>**playing**</u> badminton. _____
     C

5   <u>**Unless**</u> you're <u>**familiar with**</u> the local
       A   B

customs, <u>**you are very difficult**</u> to
                        C

know the right thing to do. _____

6   <u>**Do you think play chess**</u> is
           A   B

intellectually more challenging and

exciting than <u>**doing puzzles**</u>? _____
                C

7   Excuse me, but <u>**do you realise**</u>
                       A

that's my umbrella <u>**you've taken**</u>?
                        B

(Reply) <u>**Never mind**</u>. _____
               C

8   I am very **exciting** because I just
          A

    received **an invitation to** Leslie's
                    B

    party. I thought **he'd forgotten me**.
                           C
                                                    _____

9   **A lot of** people don't believe
        A

    in living with someone before they
           B

    get marry.
        C
                                                    _____

10 **What** do you like most **about** your new
       A   B

    flat? *(Reply)* The size **most**.
                               C
                                                    _____

*B(i) There are ten errors in the dialogue below. Read carefully and
      underline the errors. Then rewrite the dialogue in the space
      provided. (Please note that errors are not found in every line.)*

Wendy   :   As you are an old friend, Alan, therefore I want you to
            come to my party on Saturday. Do you available?

Alan   :   I'm very busy, thanks, but I'll try if I could make it. What
            time does the party hold?

Wendy   :   Six o'clock at my home. No matter you are busy, I'll
            expect to see you.

            (At the party).

Wendy   :   I'm glad you could come. Do you remember Gloria, our
            classmate?

Alan   :   Yes of course. How glad that I can see you, Gloria.
            Sorry I'm late.

Gloria :   Don't worry. I just come here for a moment myself.

Alan   :   We haven't seen each other for already three years.

Gloria : No, it's been four years since we met last time. I almost think you have emigrated.

Alan : Yes, time flies.

_____

_____

_____

_____

_____

_____

_____

_____

_____

_____

_____

_____

_____

_____

_____

_____

_____

_____

_____

_____

B(ii) Underline the ten errors and rewrite the dialogue in the space provided. (Please note that errors are not found in every line.)

Mrs So : Please come in. I and my husband are happy you could visit us.

Thomas : It's OK.

Mrs So : Is it the first time you come to Hong Kong?

Thomas : Yes. I'm really enjoying to see around.

Mrs So : I would like you to greet my son, Vincent.

Vincent : Hello, I think we've met before. Are you Thomas Mok, aren't you?

Thomas : Yes, I am. Where did we meet? Help me to recall my memory.

Vincent : Wasn't it in Singapore on this July at the conference?

Thomas : Yes, now I remember. You look different somehow. I nearly can't recognise you.

_____

_____

_____

_____

_____

_____

_____

_____

Chapter *10* Shopping

Bought

   x   *Sorry, the last one of that model was*
        bought out *yesterday.*
   √   *Sorry, the last one of that model was*
        bought *yesterday.*

The wrong use of 'out' comes partly from the influence of the Cantonese expression 賣出.

Budget

   x   *I think the price of your computer is* ***out***
        of my budget.
   √   *I think the price of your computer is*
        beyond my budget.
   √   *I think the price of your computer is* ***out***
        of my range.

'Out of' and 'beyond' can both be used in some cases, e.g. 'out of my control' and 'beyond my control'; 'out of my reach' and 'beyond my reach'. But only 'beyond' is correct with 'budget'.

Change

1 x   *This radio is not working. Can you*
        change?
   √   *This radio is not working. Can you*
        change it?

'Change' in this example needs an object 'it'.

2 x   *There is something wrong with this. Can I*
        change *another one?*
   √   *There is something wrong with this. Can I*
        change it for *another one?*

In Cantonese, we would use simply 換. We need to add 'it' and 'for' in English.

Colour

   x   *We have a wide selection of* ***colour*** —
        red, green, blue ...
   √   *We have a wide selection of* ***colours*** —
        red, green, blue ...

When you say 'a wide selection/choice of ...', you must use the plural form 'colours'.

Cost

   x   *How much* ***it cost?***
   √   *How much* ***does it cost?***

You use the 'does' form in a question.

Dangerous

   x   *Children going into big shops alone **are dangerous.***

   √   ***It is dangerous to allow** children **to go** alone into big shops.*

It is not the children who are dangerous; it is allowing them to go alone into shops that is dangerous.

Discount

   x   *Can I have a **10% off discount**?*

   √   *Can I have **10% off**?*

   √   *Can I have a **discount of 10%**?*

The wrong version combines the two correct ones.

Elegance

   x   *This dress is beautiful and **elegance**.*

   √   *This dress is beautiful and **elegant**.*

'Elegance' is a noun while 'elegant' is the correct adjective.

Exchange

   x   *Can I **exchange it back** for another?*

   √   *Can I **exchange it** for another?*

You can say 'give back' or 'exchange', but not 'exchange back'.

Few

   x   ***Few** days ago I bought this lamp.*

   √   ***A few** days ago I bought this lamp.*

The speaker means to say 'some, but not very many days ago' and must therefore use 'a few'. 'Few' is more negative in meaning than 'a few'.

√ **Few** shops open before eight o'clock in the morning.

Furnitures

x We have different kinds of **furnitures** on sale.

√ We have different kinds of **furniture** on sale.

'Furniture' is an uncountable noun.

Good

x You have to pay for the **good** before we send **it** to you.

√ You have to pay for the **goods** before we send **them** to you.

'Goods' is an uncountable noun. The error arises because 'goods' looks like a plural form, which should be able to have a singular form 'good'.

Guarantee

x How long is this watch **in the guarantee**?

√ How long is this watch **on guarantee**?

√ How long is **the guarantee period for** this watch?

Not 'in the' but 'on', or a phrase like 'the guarantee period'.

Happen

x Something **was happened** to the switch on this hair-drier.

√ Something **has happened** to the switch on this hair-drier.

With the verb 'happen', do not confuse the past continuous 'was happening' with the past perfect 'has happened'.

Help

1 x **What can I help** you?

√ **What can I do to help** you?

In English we must say 'do to help'. In Cantonese we say 我點幫你 .

2 x Is there anything I can **help** you?

√ Is there anything I can **do to help** you?

How much

x *This handbag, how much?*
√ *How much is this handbag, please?*
The wrong version sounds impolite and a proper question form must be used.

Instruction

x *Is there any **instruction** to show how it works?*
√ ***Are** there any **instructions** to show how it works?*
√ *Is there **any book of instructions** to show how it works?*
'Instructions' is used in the plural when it refers to a series of orders or method of operation.

Liked

x *The two bracelets are very **liked** each other in appearance.*
√ *The two bracelets are very **like** each other in appearance.*
√ *The two bracelets are very **alike** in appearance.*
'Liked' is a verb. The adjective 'like/alike' is needed.

Make

1 x *What **does it make** of?*
√ *What **is it made** of?*
The correct passive form is 'is made of'.
2 x *The top is **made by** plastic material.*
√ *The top is **made of** plastic material.*
Things are 'made of' some material — wood, metal, plastic, etc. They are 'made by' a person — a carpenter, metalworker, etc.

Measure

x *Can I **help you measure your body**?*
√ *Can I **take your measurements for you**?*
The wrong version comes from the Cantonese expression 幫你度身.

Middle-size	x *I would like a **middle-size** yellow shirt.*
	√ *I would like a **medium-size** yellow shirt.*

Cantonese says 中碼 but English uses 'medium' for clothes.

More cheaper	x *This T-shirt is much **more cheaper** than that one.*
	√ *This T-shirt is much **cheaper** than that one.*

If the adjective has already a comparative form, as in 'cheaper', you do not add 'more'. You use 'more' with words which do not have a comparative form:

√ *This T-shirt is much **more expensive** than that one.*

One	x *Shopper: I would like a pair of shoes, please.*
	*Salesman: What about **this one**?*
	√ *Shopper: I would like a pair of shoes, please.*
	*Salesman: What about **this pair**?*
	√ *Shopper: I would like a pair of shoes, please.*
	*Salesman: What about **these**?*

'This one' is incorrect because it could be misunderstood to mean only one shoe.

Open

   x   *It's too hot to work. Could we **open** the air-conditioner?*
   √   *It's too hot to work. Could we **turn on** the air-conditioner?*

The Cantonese word 開 means 'open' and 'put on'. In English, we say 'open the window/door' and 'turn on the air-conditioner'.

Pack

   x   *I'll take this silk scarf. Can you **pack it** for me?*
   √   *I'll take this silk scarf. Can you **wrap it up** for me?*

You use 'pack' for something like a suitcase, or some big article which is going to be sent abroad. You would use 'wrap up' for a small article which was being taken home.

Price

1 x   **How much is the price of** *this car?*
   √   **How much is** *this car?*
   √   **What is the price of** *this car?*

Either use 'how much is' or 'what is the price of'.

2 x   *We have a **one price** policy.*
   √   *We have a **fixed price** policy.*

'One price' in English would mean that all the articles are the same price. 'Fixed price' means that no bargaining is allowed, and no reduction will be given.

Profit for	x *Sorry, no discount. The **profit for** this item is **too little now**.*
	√ *Sorry, no discount. The **profit on** this item is **already very slight/small**.*

The profit 'on', not 'for'. 'Too little now' is understandable, but the correct idiomatic expression is 'already very slight/small'.

Put on	x *The leather of the shoes will stretch after you have **put them on** for a few days.*
	√ *The leather of the shoes will stretch after you have **worn them** for a few days.*

'Put on' means the act of putting on whereas 'worn' indicates having them on and wearing them.

Refunding	x *Can I **give** this broken toy **for refunding**?*
	√ *Can I **return** this broken toy **for a refund**?*

Not 'give' but 'give back' or better, 'return'. The gerund (-ing form) can be used correctly with 'for' in some cases.

√ *The plane landed **for refuelling**.*

But 'for refunding' in this example is wrong; 'for a refund' is the correct expression. The most idiomatic way of asking for a refund is:

√ *Can I **get a refund on** this broken toy?*

Return	x *Can I **return back** this umbrella?*
	√ *Can I **return** this umbrella?*

'Return' already means 'bring back', so you do not say 'return back'.

Sale	x *This week we **are on sale**.*
	√ *This week we **have a sale on**.*

'We are on sale' would mean the people who work in the shop are for sale.

Satisfy

x *If I am not **satisfy** with this video, can I return it?*

√ *If I am not **satisfied** with this video, can I return it?*

√ *If this video **does not satisfy me**, can I return it?*

'Satisfy' can be used in two ways.

√ *This does not **satisfy** me.*

√ *I am not **satisfied** with this.*

Sell out

x *They **sold out** a lot of tickets on the first day.*

√ *They **sold** a lot of tickets on the first day.*

Cantonese says 賣出. In English you use 'out' with 'sold' only when you mean that all the tickets have gone and there are none left.

√ *All the tickets have been **sold out**.*

If the tickets are selling well, but there are still some left, you cannot say 'sold out'.

Selling price

x *What is the **selling price** of this kettle?*

√ *What is the **price** of this kettle?*

You do not normally use 'selling' with 'price', except in a few special cases.

√ *The **selling price** of gold was $370.*

Here you are contrasting the 'selling price' with the 'buying price'.

Some wrong

x *There is **some wrong** with this. Can I change it?*

√ *There is **something** wrong with this. Can I change it?*

'Some wrong' can be used in an expression like:

√ *He has **done some wrong**.*

But when you are returning an article which has a fault and you are not sure what the fault is, you must say there is 'something wrong' with it.

Suit

x *Is this one **suit** me?*

√ *Does this one **suit** me?*

'Suit' is a verb. The correct question word should be 'does'.

Wait

x *Sorry you **wait** a long time.*
√ *Sorry you **have been waiting** a long time.*
√ *Sorry **to keep you waiting** a long time.*
'You wait' is grammatically wrong. English says 'you have been waiting'. But the most correct expression of apology is 'sorry to keep you waiting'.

Want

x **What do you want?**
√ **Is there anything you would like?**
√ **What can I do for you?**
√ **Can I help you?**
The first wrong expression is impolite, especially if it is said in an unfriendly tone.

Worth

x *This tennis racket certainly **worths** $300.*
√ *This tennis racket **is certainly worth** $300.*
The verb is 'to be worth', not 'to worth'.

Wrong

x *What is **wrong** with **my** product?*
√ *What is the **problem** with **the** product?*
The wrong version, though grammatically correct, is too aggressive and takes the complaint personally. The correct version is more pleasant and polite.

Exercises

A   There is an error in each question. Decide whether the error is in the underlined section A, B or C by circling the appropriate letter. Then give the correct answers in the space provided.

1   This ring **certainly worths** a lot of
                     A

money. **I'll have to** think hard **before**
        B   C

I buy it.

                                                _____

2   **Is** the style of this shirt **suit your taste**?
    A   B   C

3   Would this **middle-size** green pullover
                      A

look better on me?
   B   C

                                                  _____

4   This book **seems interesting**.
                      A

Unfortunately, the price is
    B

out of my budget.
     C

                                                  _____

5   **If you buy** casual clothes in Mong Kok,
      A

you'll find them **more cheaper** than
   B   C

in Tsim Sha Tsui.

                                                _____

6   What is the **selling price** of this
                    A

computer? It's the model **I've been trying**
                              B

to find **for weeks**.
       C

                                                _____

7   We <u>were glad</u> to donate our old
        A

 <u>furnitures</u> to the <u>children's home</u>.   _____
        B   C

8   You can always <u>exchange back</u> the
                          A

 microwave oven <u>within</u> three days
                      B

 <u>of purchase</u>.   _____
        C

9   <u>Would you like</u> me to <u>pack</u> the
        A   B

 necklace <u>for you</u>?   _____
                C

10 <u>Despite</u> the humid weather, the <u>good</u>
        A   B

 we ordered <u>from</u> China arrived in
                  C

 excellent condition.   _____

B(i) There are ten errors in the dialogue below. Read carefully and
       underline the errors. Then rewrite the dialogue in the space
       provided. (Please note that errors are not found in every line.)

Buyer   : Good morning.

Seller : Good morning. Sorry you wait a long time. What can I help
           you?

Buyer   : I would like to buy a pair of rubber shoes. This pair how
           much?

Seller : Those are $350. They are usually $480, but they are
           cheaper today because we are on sale.

Buyer   : The sole feels very hard. What does it make of?

Seller : The sole is made by rubber, but the upper part is leather.

Buyer : What about this one? How much it cost?

Seller : Those are $700. Would you like to try them on? *(The buyer tries them on.)*

Buyer : They are a bit tight.

Seller : Don't worry. They will stretch after you have put them on for a few days.

Buyer : I like them, but they are quite dear. Can I have a 10% off discount?

Seller : Yes, if you pay in cash.

Buyer : Then I'll buy them. Here's $700.

Seller : Thank you. I'll get your change.

_____

_____

_____

_____

_____

_____

_____

_____

_____

B(ii) Underline the ten errors and rewrite the dialogue in the space provided. (Please note that errors are not found in every line.)

Buyer : Good afternoon.

Seller : Good afternoon. What do you want?

Buyer : I bought this radio in your shop and I am not satisfy with it. I want to return it back. Can you change another one?

Seller : Let me see. *(He tries the radio.)* It seems to be working well enough.

Buyer : No. There is some wrong with the volume. Something was happened to the volume control switch.

Seller : When did you buy it?

Buyer : I bought it few days ago. It is still in the guarantee.

Seller : I am sorry, there are no more of that model left. It has been completely sold.

Buyer : In that case can I give this one for refunding?

Seller : Certainly. I'm sorry for the trouble we've caused you.

ANSWER KEY

Unit 1   In a Restaurant

A
1   [B order the dishes]
2   [B glass of orange juice]
3   [A leaving]
4   [C Not at all]
5   [A hard]
6   [A for holding you up]
7   [A One of the reasons]
8   [C vegetables]
9   [B easily]
10   [A there will be]

B(i)

Francis   :   What restaurant do you go to most often?
Margaret   :   I [usually] eat at Sun Sui Wah. The [food is] [delicious] there.
Francis   :   Can we go early, say six o'clock? I get indigestion if I eat [late.]
Margaret   :   But the restaurant is not [open] till seven. [Didn't] you have
                lunch today?
Francis   :   Well, I [bought] two [sandwiches] from a hawker this morning.
Margaret   :   But the food [sold by] hawkers is not clean.
Francis   :   Maybe [that's] why I am not feeling so well just now.

B(ii)

Waiter :   Do you have [a] reservation?
Mr Ng :   Yes, my name is Ng. I asked for a [table] near the window.
Waiter :   This way, sir. *(He pulls out a chair for Mr Ng.)* [Would] you like
            something to drink?
Mr Ng :   No thanks. [Please bring] me the menu. [I'll make] an order now.
            (Pause). I want a [steak.]
Waiter :   How would you like it done?
Mr Ng :   [Medium.] *(He finishes and gets the bill)* [Excuse me, waiter.]
            Would you [mind checking] the bill? This looks too much.
Waiter :   Sorry, you are right. [It has been added up] wrongly.
Mr Ng :   Be more careful in future or you will lose a customer.

Unit 2   Telephone Manners

A
1   [A we were cut off]
2   [B you've got]
3   [C out of order]
4   [A for keeping]

174

5 [B Would you]
6 [C went dead]
7 [C next]
8 [C engaged]
9 [B give my message]
10 [A had hung up]

B(i)

William	:	Hello, is [that] Wing Sun Company? Can I speak to Jenny Ho, please?
Receptionist	:	Sorry, she's not [in] yet. [Would] you like to leave a message?
William	:	Yes, can I leave my number [for] her? It's 4836397.
Receptionist	:	May I know who [it is/is] calling?
William	:	William Cheung.
Receptionist	:	Thank you, Mr Cheung. I [will] tell her. *(One hour later Jenny rings back.)*
Jenny	:	Hello, is that William? [Jenny] speaking. You called me an hour ago, [didn't you?] Sorry I was out.
William	:	Hello, Jenny. Yes, [I've been expecting] your call for an hour. I have a long story to tell you and ...
Jenny	:	Oh William, I'm sorry. [I'm so busy at work] that I can't talk now. Let's meet this evening at six.
William	:	Good. See you then. Bye bye.

B(ii)

Caller	:	Hello, can I speak to Danny Wong, please?
Reply	:	[Hold on, please.] *(After a pause.)* He's engaged [on] another phone. Would you like to ring back or wait?
Caller	:	I'll wait, thanks. *(After a minute or two.)*
Reply	:	Hello, [this is] Danny Wong.
Caller	:	Is [that] Danny Wong, the manager of Green Jade Company?
Reply	:	No, sorry. [I'm afraid] [you've dialled] the wrong number. There are [altogether] eight Danny Wongs in the telephone directory. [This] is Wade's Construction Company. Try 5379741 for Danny Wong of Green Jade.
Caller	:	Thank you and sorry for the trouble. *(Rings that number.)* Hello, Green Jade Company? Danny Wong, please.
Reply	:	Sorry, he's not in. He [has gone] to Taiwan for [a] business trip. He'll be back on Tuesday.
Caller	:	Thank you. I'll call on Tuesday.

Unit 3   Job Interviews

A
1 [A deal with the challenges]
2 [A Even if you want]

3   [C a tour guide]
4   [A attended]
5   [C to succeed]
6   [B broaden my vision]
7   [B to my advantage]
8   [C meet/fulfil]
9   [B to gain some experience]
10 [C a computer course/a course in computers]

B(i)

Interviewer	:	Why do you want to [apply for] the position of accountant in our company?
Candidate	:	I have always been [interested] in working with figures. And I think I can [discover] more challenges in a company like yours.
Interviewer	:	I see you [have] been working for Telecom for two years. Did your job involve any bookkeeping?
Candidate	:	Yes. I had [a lot of] experience there in bookkeeping. Also I did a course in the Polytechnic in bookkeeping. It was [one of the subjects on the curriculum.]
Interviewer	:	What about your other activities when you were a student?
Candidate	:	I was responsible for the [editing] of the student newspaper. And one of my hobbies was [distance] running.
Interviewer	:	Well, you seem to be [the man] we're looking for. What problems do you think you might find with the job?
Candidate	:	Not very many, I hope. I have [confidence that I can be] a good accountant.

B(ii)

Interviewer	:	How did you find out about this job?
Candidate	:	I read your advertisement in [the] *South China Morning Post.*
Interviewer	:	Can you give me some [information] about your previous jobs?
Candidate	:	I have worked in very many different jobs. You can [refer to my curriculum vitae for all the details.]
Interviewer	:	Why do you wish to leave your present job?
Candidate	:	I find it unchallenging, and also it is difficult to be [promoted] to a higher position. So I want to shift [to] a new job. With your company I think I may [have better prospects.]
Interviewer	:	How much would you expect your salary [to] be?
Candidate	:	[The salary is not the most important thing for me.] I would be satisfied to start with a low salary, [so long as] I could learn on the job.
Interviewer	:	Thank you. We will [notify] you of the result in a week's time.

Unit 4   Banking

A
1   [B There are]
2   [B lend]
3   [A After finishing/after having finished]
4   [A Nowadays]
5   [C feel sorry]
6   [A am concerned]
7   [B What]
8   [B need not be afraid]
9   [A made up his mind]
10 [B In the end]

B(i)
Amy   :   I'm travelling abroad in the summer and I usually take
              [traveller's cheques.] But as I'm going on a long trip this
              time, [X] I've been advised to get a Visa card.
Florence :   That's [a good piece of advice.]
Amy   :   But I am very [hesitant] about getting a Visa. I think I have
              too [little] money to bother about it.
Florence :   You should get one. A Visa card will [be more convenient
              for you.] With my ETC card it's been months [since I've
              been] into a bank.
Amy   :   In other countries are there cash points for Visa cards?
Florence :   Yes. They [are usually located] outside the bank. But
              you'd better take some cash too.
Amy   :   Yes. I'll need some [pounds sterling] and [dollars.]

B(ii)
Bank Manager : Mr Leung, your current account [X] is overdrawn.
Mr Leung   : Well, [I am amazed] at that. By how much?
Bank Manager : Six hundred dollars.
Mr Leung   : But six hundred dollars [is] only a small amount.
                 Can't it be taken out of my [savings] account?
Bank Manager : Yes, but you must make the transfer.
Mr Leung   : [Till when do you stay open?]
Bank Manager : The bank's working [hours] are nine to four.
Mr Leung   : But [it is hard for me] to get to the bank before four.
Bank Manager : Then you can make the transfer with your ETC
                 card.
Mr Leung   : Good. And I'll come to make a deposit sometime.
Bank Manager : Will you come today?
Mr Leung   : No, I'll come [in three days' time.] Oh, there's
                 something else. I've changed my address. Do you
                 need the new one?
Bank Manager : Yes. Clients [are expected] to inform us of a new
                 address. It's hard to keep records correct [unless]
                 you inform us.

Unit 5   Good Health

A
1   [C take his medicine]
2   [B don't you]
3   [A Depending too much/Becoming too dependent]
4   [C used to being]
5   [A Had Anita got]
6   [C you will see an improvement in]
7   [C to take care of]
8   [A Did you have]
9   [C fatter and fatter]
10   [C was in collision with]

B(i)
Patient : Good morning, doctor. I feel [a pain] in my back.
Doctor   : [Take off] your shirt, please, and I will examine you. *(After the examination.)* You have strained a muscle. [That] is why you have the pain.
Patient : Do I need [an] injection?
Doctor   : No. But I will give you some [medicine] to relieve the pain. I suggest you [X] rest your back for a few days. Also, you are too heavy. It is more common for an [overweight] person to have back trouble.
Patient : Yes, [I have put on weight] in the past few months.
Doctor   : Then you must [take] exercise more often and watch your diet.
Patient : Thank you, doctor. Could you please [give me] a letter for my sick leave?

B(ii)
John   : Why are you [looking] so pale?
William : I have [had] a bad cold for two weeks.
John   : And is it still [troubling] you?
William : Yes. I [have] a sore throat and [it is very difficult for me] to breathe. I bought some [drugs] in the drug store, but I'm still feeling [ill].
John   : Do you have [any] appetite?
William : I can't even swallow a tiny [amount of food.]
John   : I think [you'd better] go and see a doctor. Go to Doctor Chan. He is a famous doctor in Hong Kong.

Unit 6   Hotel Management

A
1   [C suggest another to me]
2   [C sports facilities]
3   [B walk straight]

4   [B people]
5   [A to go swimming]
6   [C to look at]
7   [B emphasise]
8   [A As you know]
9   [B with]
10 [A the lift is not working]

B(i)
Guest	:	Good evening. I would like to [stay] here for two nights. What's the [price of] a single room?
Receptionist	:	That will [X] depend on which floor you would like.
Guest	:	I'd like a room [on] the top floor, with quiet [surroundings], and if possible [facing] the harbour.
Receptionist	:	Yes. We have a room like that. It's $600 a night.
Guest	:	Thank you. I'll take it.
Receptionist	:	Could you sign here, please. Here is your key. The porter will [take] you to your room.
Porter	:	Please [come] this way. *(They go into the lift.)*
Guest	:	You know, I'm afraid of lifts.
Porter	:	There's no need to be, but [if] there's a fire, please don't use the lift. All guests should use the stairs and gather in the lobby.

B(ii)
Guest	:	I'd like a call tomorrow morning.
Receptionist	:	Certainly. What is your name, please?
Guest	:	[I'll write] it down for you. *(Writes his name.)* Is the hotel door open all night? I won't be back before midnight. I [go to bed late.]
Receptionist	:	Yes, there is someone on the desk all night.
Guest	:	Thanks. If you don't mind my asking, how do you like your job?
Receptionist	:	I get a bit [bored] all day at the desk. And with rude guests, it's difficult sometimes to be [good-tempered.] But it's a nice hotel.
Guest	:	Yes, this lobby is decorated [in good taste], don't you think?
Receptionist	:	Yes, I like it.
Guest	:	You must be good at languages. How many [do you speak]? Apart from Chinese and English, what [other languages] do you know?
Receptionist	:	Well, I can [understand] Japanese, but not really speak it.
Guest	:	Oh, by the way, [is there a laundry service]?
Receptionist	:	Yes, just leave them in the laundry bag in your room.
Guest	:	I have to check out by twelve tomorrow. Could I leave my bags with you here tomorrow for a couple of hours while I go shopping?
Receptionist	:	Certainly. I'll [look after] them for you until you come back.

Unit 7   Business Meetings

A
1 [B to give]
2 [B should last]
3 [B enjoys very much]
4 [C make]
5 [B to save on]
6 [B requires me]
7 [C thought of it]
8 [A acquaint themselves with]
9 [A catch your words]
10 [B of interest to]

B(i)
Chairman : There are [altogether] three problems to be discussed in
connection with our department store. First, variety of
products. Have we [too many/so many] products [so that/that]
customers don't know where to start buying? Second, comfort
and attractiveness of our store. If we make it too comfortable
and attractive, will customers only walk around and [not] buy
anything? Third, price range. If the price of our products [is]
too high, will people go elsewhere?

Mr Chan : We have spent a long time [discussing] all these issues
before. [In my opinion,] it's just a waste of time.

Mr Lo : No, I don't think so. [I agree] with the Chairman. [X] I would
prefer to discuss these important matters. They're certainly
not a waste of time.

Mr Chan : Sorry for my [rudeness.]

Chairman : Right. Let's get back to the problems. [What] are we supposed
to do about them?

B(ii)
Emma : The boss wants to conduct a survey of our office procedures. It
will [focus on] better efficiency.

Diana : It's because of that visiting consultant we had. I thought he would
give us [quite a good] report.

Emma : Apparently he said our staff [had not enough initiative] and that
young people like us should be full of [creativity.]

Diana : [From] my point of view, the problem is we are too busy. There
are so [many] files to update.

Emma : We should have more computers in the office. After all, [X] we
live in an advanced technological society in Hong Kong, so it
would [gain our customers' confidence] if they see that we have
modern [equipment.]

Diana : But don't computers break down a lot?

Emma : Yes. You need to [care for them.]

Unit 8   Travel

A
1   [B she]
2   [C It]
3   [C at night]
4   [B had travelled]
5   [C very well]
6   [C There were]
7   [C costs]
8   [C maybe I could book]
9   [B staff]
10   [A take out]

B(i)
Traveller :   Is this the counter of [X] Thai Airlines? I'd like some information
               about the [price] of a ticket to Bangkok. How much is [a] one-
               way ticket?
Salesgirl :   Do you want Business class?
Traveller :   No, thank you. [Economy] class.
Salesgirl :   That costs $3,900.
Traveller :   And is a round-trip ticket [double] a single trip?
Salesgirl :   No, a round-trip ticket is $7,200.
Traveller :   How often do flights go to Bangkok?
Salesgirl :   There are two flights [every] day. One is [in the] morning and
               the other is at noon.
Traveller :   Does the plane have a non-smoking [section]?
Salesgirl :   Yes, a large number of seats are reserved for non-smokers.
Traveller :   Can I have [an aisle seat], as I have long legs?
Salesgirl :   If you book early, I'm sure there will be no problem.
Traveller :   But if I cancel the ticket, will I be [refunded]?
Salegirl   :   Sorry, I'm afraid not.

B(ii)
Mary   :   Excuse me. Can you show me how to [fasten] my seat belt?
Mr Ho :   Certainly. Like this. *(He shows her.)* Is this the first time [you've
           travelled] by air?
Mary   :   Yes, it is.
Mr Ho :   Is it a business trip?
Mary   :   No, I'm just going to [enjoy myself.] Tell me, how long [does it
           take] to fly to Japan?
Mr Ho :   We should land [in] Tokyo in about three hours.
Mary   :   Oh, what a long [journey]! I am sure I will begin to feel [bored].
Mr Ho :   Don't worry. The film will [begin] soon. By the way, is that your
           passport on the floor?
Mary   :   Yes it is. [It is necessary for me] to find a safe place for it.
Mr Ho :   You must take [very good care] of your passport when you are
           travelling.

Unit 9   Socialising

A
1 [C boyfriend/girlfriend]
2 [C I beg your pardon?/Pardon?]
3 [C can you]
4 [B to]
5 [C it is very difficult for you]
6 [B playing chess]
7 [C Oh, I'm very sorry]
8 [A excited]
9 [C get married]
10 [C mostly]

B(i)

Wendy	:	As you are an old friend, Alan, [X] I want you to come to my party on Saturday. [Are] you available?
Alan	:	I'm very busy, thanks, but I'll [try to see if] I could make it. What time [is the party being held]?
Wendy	:	Six o'clock at my home. No matter [whether you are busy or not], I'll expect to see you. *(At the party.)*
Wendy	:	I'm glad you could come. Do you remember Gloria, our classmate?
Alan	:	Yes of course. How glad [I am to see you], Gloria. Sorry I'm late.
Gloria	:	Don't worry. I [only came here a moment ago/have only been here for a moment] myself.
Alan	:	We haven't seen each other [for three years now].
Gloria	:	No, it's been four years since we last [met]. I [almost thought you had] emigrated.
Alan	:	Yes, time flies.

B(ii)

Mrs So	:	Please come in [My husband and I] are happy you could visit us.
Thomas	:	[Not at all].
Mrs So	:	Is [this] the first time [you've come] to Hong Kong?
Thomas	:	Yes. I'm really enjoying [seeing] around.
Mrs So	:	I would like you to [meet] my son, Vincent.
Vincent	:	Hello, I think we've met before. [You are] Thomas Mok, aren't you?
Thomas	:	Yes, I am. Where did we meet? Help me to [refresh] my memory.
Vincent	:	Wasn't it in Singapore [X] this July at the conference?
Thomas	:	Yes, now I remember. You look different somehow. I [almost didn't] recognise you.

Unit 10   Shopping

A
1   [A is certainly worth]
2   [A Does]
3   [A medium-size]
4   [C beyond my budget]
5   [C cheaper]
6   [A price]
7   [B furniture]
8   [A exchange]
9   [B wrap up]
10 [B goods]

B(i)
Buyer : Good morning.
Seller : Good morning. Sorry [you've been waiting] a long time. What can I [do to help] you?
Buyer : I would like to buy a pair of rubber shoes. [How much is this pair, please]?
Seller : Those are $350. They are usually $480, but they are cheaper today because we [have a sale on].
Buyer : The sole feels very hard. What [is it made of]?
Seller : The sole is [made of] rubber, but the upper part is leather.
Buyer : What about this [pair]? How much [does it cost]?
Seller : Those are $700. Would you like to try them on? *(The buyer tries them on.)*
Buyer : They are a bit tight.
Seller : Don't worry. They will stretch after you have [worn them] for a few days.
Buyer : I like them, but they are quite dear. Can I have [a discount of 10%]?
Seller : Yes, if you pay in cash.
Buyer : Then I'll buy them. Here's $700.
Seller : Thank you. I'll get your change.

B(ii)
Buyer : Good afternoon.
Seller : Good afternoon. [Can I help you]?
Buyer : I bought this radio in your shop and I am not [satisfied] with it. I want to return it [X]. Can you [change it for another]?
Seller : Let me see. *(He tries the radio.)* It seems to be working well enough.
Buyer : No. There is [something] wrong with the volume. Something [has] happened to the volume control switch.
Seller : When did you buy it?
Buyer : I bought it [a few] days ago. It is still [on guarantee].

Seller : I am sorry, there are no more of that model left. It has been completely [sold out].

Buyer : In that case can I [get a refund on this one]?

Seller : Certainly. I'm sorry for the trouble we've caused you.

DID YOU KNOW?

That if your baby is born between March 21 and April 20, he is destined to be a dynamic leader? A complete horoscope for your baby is just one of the many unique features contained in NAME YOUR BABY.

DID YOU KNOW?

That every name has a special meaning? For example: Agnes means "good," Emily means "flattering," Alan means "handsome." You can find the meanings of all the different names in NAME YOUR BABY.

DID YOU KNOW?

That there are over 20 separate nicknames for Elizabeth? Nicknames are another of the many special features in NAME YOUR BABY.

NAME YOUR BABY

THE MOST COMPLETE BOOK
OF ITS KIND
AND
THE WORLD'S BESTSELLER

NAME
YOUR BABY
LAREINA RULE

BANTAM BOOKS
TORONTO • NEW YORK • LONDON • SYDNEY • AUCKLAND

NAME YOUR BABY
A Bantam Book / June 1963
46 printings through August 1984

Library of Congress Catalog Card Number: 63-14178

ISBN 0-553-23407-2

Published simultaneously in the United States and Canada

Bantam Books are published by Bantam Books, Inc. Its trade-
mark, consisting of the words "Bantam Books" and the por-
trayal of a rooster, is Registered in U.S. Patent and Trademark
Office and in other countries. Marca Registrada. Bantam
Books, Inc., 666 Fifth Avenue, New York, New York 10103.

PRINTED IN THE UNITED STATES OF AMERICA

H   55 54 53 52 51 50 49 48

CONTENTS

NAME YOUR BABY

THE ARIES CHILD

for those born between March 21 and April 20.

The birthstone is the diamond.
The flower is the daisy.
The color is deep red.

April was the second month of the old Roman calendar and was named from the Latin word "aperire" meaning "to open," because it ushers in the astrological new year, since the zodiac commences with this sign.

The symbol of the Sign of Aries is the Ram. The ruling planet of Aries is Mars.

Personality characteristics:

If your child was born under the Sign of Aries, he was born with the qualities that make a leader. It is a positive sign, giving much force and active energy. Those born in Aries are the pioneer people of the zodiac and they adventure into many new enterprises. These people love to lead as well as to govern others. They are aggressive and enthusiastic, yet inclined to be impulsive and quick in action. The persons born in this sign are extremely impatient and inclined to be very headstrong and self-willed. Aries children attract many people and admirers. Aries children dislike to work for others; they have a great tendency to like changes in occupation, home location and friends. The changes, however, are from a desire to progress in life, as well as to eliminate monotony. This sign is one of great strength of character. When challenged, the Aries person is a formidable opponent, for he is bold and firm.

One of the lessons for the Aries child to learn is to curb his determination to have his own way. He must learn to yield to the inevitable and to give in, and to admit when he is wrong. He must learn that wanting to do a thing is not always the best for him. His pioneer instincts and attributes should not be discouraged. His dreams and plans for the future should be given attention and understanding. Physically this child has a strong constitution, with good recuperative powers. He suffers most when he is frustrated in obtaining his objectives.

Talents and attributes:

The Aries child is always thinking up new enterprises, new schemes and ideas. Some of his remarkable ideas are so far advanced over those of the ordinary individual that he is often misunderstood and laughed at. However, the Aries person is noted for his unusual ability to plan and map out the future. He works better in a position of authority, for he is not at his best with others over him. He can achieve great things if he can direct others to carry out his original ideas. In his life's work he does best managing large enterprises, businesses, or corporations. He does well in exploring new or unknown fields.

Types of persons for whom your child will have an affinity in friendship, marriage, partnership, and business:

The Aries child will usually find Sagittarius and Leo, and to a lesser degree Aquarius and Gemini people the most compatible.

Among great political leaders born in the Sign of Aries are:

John Tyler, 10th U. S. President, March 29.

Thomas Jefferson, 3rd U. S. President, April 2.

Robert the Bruce, King of Scotland, March 21.

Henry Clay, American statesman, April 12.

Roger Sherman, American statesman, April 19.

Other internationally known persons born in the Sign of Aries are:

General William C. Westmore-land, U. S. Army, March 26.

William Wordsworth, poet, April 7.

Booker T. Washington, educator, April 18.

Walter Winchell, columnist, April 7.

Emile Zola, author, April 2.

Outstanding entertainment personalities:

Joan Crawford, March 23.	Herb Alpert, April 2.
Steve McQueen, March 24.	Jack Webb, April 2.
Gregory Peck, April 3.	Doris Day, April 3.
William Holden, April 17.	Omar Sharif, April 9.
Warren Beatty, March 30.	Hari Rhodes, April 10.

Pearl Bailey, March 29.

THE TAURUS CHILD

for those born between April 21 and May 20.

The birthstone is the emerald.

The flower is the lily-of-the-valley.

The color is deep yellow.

May was the third month of the old Roman calendar. Its name source was the Roman goddess Maia, the wife of Vulcan.

The symbol of the Sign of Taurus which rules May is the Bull. The ruling planet of Taurus is Venus.

Personality characteristics:

If your child is born in Taurus he is resolute, practical, matter-of-fact, obstinate, patient, and overly conservative. He is reliable and is careful in speech and action. The Taurus child has reserve energies and desires, often hidden and held in check until provocation of some sort releases them. Then the pent-up energy and emotion of Taurus erupts like water pouring over a broken dam. The child's apparently good nature loses its complacency and he is transfixed with rage. Then like a mad bull he is generally ungovernable while the anger lasts. The Taurus child can also be peaceful, forgiving, and loving. Thought and feeling are very much interblended in this child. His desires are often hard to understand.

The Taurus children who are mentally and morally developed are sensitive, intuitive persons, seeking to control their wrong instincts and to better themselves. The unrestrained Taurus-born who do not understand themselves or their desires cannot progress if they are not helped to control their emotional storms.

The Taurus child is a lover of beauty and harmony, and dislikes discord. He generally has a happy mien unless he becomes a martyr seeking sympathy. He is generous, kindhearted, and trustworthy, intensely strong-willed, dogmatic, and forceful. He can be molded by the ones he loves. He is usually sensible and prudent until he is crossed. Taurus children have excellent memories, are well-informed, energetic, artistic, and musical. They are usually affable and pleasant but tend to be too fixed and opinionated without reason. Their strong likes, dislikes, and prejudices often offend others. These children will act from preconceived motives, either for good or selfish purposes. They are fond of luxury; never overexpressive in speech.

Taurus children are usually strong and have great physical endurance, but they are liable to suffer from stubborn overexertion and overindulgence in physical pleasures such as eating. Ruled by Venus, they take great pride in their looks, body, and general appearance and in their environment.

The Taurus child is inclined to fits of jealousy, envy, and hatred, and should be left alone at the time he makes a scene, then made to understand why he was doing wrong. This child should be given responsibility.

Talents and attributes:

This child's wish is for personal success and attainment and he will be gifted with many talents. He will be good in executive work where he has charge of others. Things to do with the earth, such as real estate, mining, and oil fields will be his metier. He will be competent in positions where trust and confidence are placed in him. This child can qualify as a doctor, lawyer, electrician, or contractor. Many artists and designers are found in Taurus, working with colors, happy and satisfied with their beautiful creations. Even though this practical ability is there and can always be utilized, they can become the most eccentric of artists. The girl in this sign can become a nurse, interior decorator, model, or actress. She personifies the Venus attributes. A Taurus man excels as a financier or director of companies.

Types of persons for whom your child will have an affinity in friendship, marriage, partnership, and business:

The Taurus child will usually find Capicorn and Virgo, and to a lesser degree Pisces and Cancer people the most compatible.

Among great political leaders born in the Sign of Taurus are:

James Monroe, 5th U. S. President, April 28.
Queen Elizabeth II of England, April 21.
Harry S. Truman, 33rd U. S. President, May 8.
Emperor Hirohito of Japan, April 29.
James Buchanan, 15th U. S. President, April 23.

Other internationally known persons born in the Sign of Taurus are:

William Shakespeare, April 23.
Robert Browning, poet, May 7.
Moshe Dayan, Israeli statesman and general, May 20.
Willie Mays, baseball, May 6.
Irving Berlin, composer, May 11.

Outstanding entertainment personalities:

Bing Crosby, May 2.	Ella Fitzgerald, April 25.
Fred Astaire, May 10.	Duke Ellington, April 30.
Eddie Albert, April 22.	Carol Burnett, April 26.
Barbra Streisand, April 24.	Samantha Eggar, May 3.
Shirley MacLaine, April 24.	Fernandel, May 8.

THE GEMINI CHILD

for those born between May 21 and June 20.

The birthstone is the pearl.

The flower is the rose.

The color is violet.

June was the fourth month of the old Roman calendar. Its name source was the Latin word Junius.

The symbol of the Sign of Gemini which rules June is the Twins. The ruling planet of Gemini is Mercury.

Personality characteristics:

If your child is born in Gemini he will be inclined toward intellectual pursuits. He will live more in the mental world of thoughts than in feelings, emotions, or the material. He will seldom finish one thing before commencing another, causing him to appear unreliable and indecisive. Actually it seems that his active mind and thoughts race along too fast for his body to keep up. He will be quick-witted, often very clever, expressing more in words than in emotions.

This child will be kind, willing, loving, and expressive in disposition. He will exhibit curiosity and a desire to learn about everything and everybody. He can follow two occupations at the same time. His nature is sympathetic and sensitive as well as imaginative. He is very idealistic, fond of mental study and research. The Gemini child will enjoy adventure and travel. Although somewhat high-strung and excitable, he makes friends easily. He loves change and must keep continually busy to be happy.

The June child will stand and walk very erect, with quick, energetic, firm steps. Although he may not seem overly strong, he has much stamina and endurance unless he exhausts himself nervously.

The Gemini child's restlessness, high-strung, impatient, indecisive nature must be stabilized and channeled into conclusive accomplishments. He will argue but needs to be convinced that there is a future state of existence. He needs to understand the order and harmony of the universe, and the relativity of all things. His indecision needs help to be overcome.

Talents and attributes:

Your Gemini child is inclined toward scientific, intellectual work as well as to education and national betterment. He will have many dual experiences, two courses of action or two subjects of study often entering his life, in which he will have to learn to make a choice. His whole life will advance through educational progression. The Gemini person's associates and friends must be his intellectual equals or he will be unhappy. He has inventive abilities that may be of great help to him. Those born in Gemini make fine bookkeepers, accountants, clerks, secretaries, editors, reporters, teachers, lawyers, translators, lecturers, and foreign diplomats. They generally succeed by following more than one occupation. They possess literary ability. Educational work is, however, one of their best outlets.

Types of persons for whom your child will have an affinity in friendship, marriage, partnership and business:

The Gemini child will usually find Aquarius, Libra, and to a lesser degree Aries and Leo people the most compatible.

Among great political leaders born in the Sign of Gemini are:

Queen Victoria of England, May 24.

John F. Kennedy, 35th U. S. President, May 29.

Tito, Yugoslavian statesman, May 25.

Prince Philip of England, June 10.

Hubert H. Humphrey, U. S. Vice President, May 27.

Other internationally known persons born in the Sign of Gemini are:

Richard Wagner, composer, May 22.

Brigham Young, Mormon leader, June 1.

Duchess of Windsor, June 19.

Walt Whitman, poet, May 31.

Ralph Waldo Emerson, poet, May 25.

Outstanding entertainment personalities:

Rosalind Russell, June 2.	James Arness, May 26.
John Wayne, May 26.	Bob Hope, May 29.
Dean Martin, June 7.	Andy Griffith, June 1.
Raymond Burr, May 21.	Maurice Evans, June 3.
Richard Benjamin, May 22.	Jim Nabors, June 12.

THE CANCER CHILD

for those born between June 21 and July 22.

The birthstone is the ruby.

The flower is the water lily.

The color is light green.

July was the fifth month of the old Roman calendar. Its name source was Julius, used in honor of Julius Caesar who was born in this month.

The symbol of the Sign of Cancer is the Crab. The ruling planet of Cancer is the Moon.

Personality characteristics:

If your child is born in Cancer he has a sentimental and versatile nature and a constructive imagination. He is sympathetic, talkative, loves home and family, and has a tenacious memory, especially for details and historical events. The Cancer child appreciates praise and is encouraged by kindness. This child will delight in beautiful scenery, romantic settings, and new adventures. He is very conscientious but somewhat skeptical of new ideas until he understands them. However he can adapt himself to different people and environments easily.

Cancer children appear retiring, but are really positive and tenacious and love to be noticed while appearing to be unassum-

ing and not anxious to attain the limelight. They are not adverse
to fame, should recognition come.

Your Cancer child will be fond of older persons, ancient customs, and things connected with the past that have sentimental
value. It seems that his fate is bound up with domestic ties and
family interests, the home and home-improvement. The Cancer
individual has a tendency to have a bright, alert, oval, or round
face. He often worries over things others don't worry about and
as a result may have slight indigestion or suffer from nervousness.

The Cancer child must learn to think and say, "I can," instead
of "I can't." He must recognize and control moodiness, wavering
and inconsistency, and by no means should self-condemnation be
tolerated. Your Moon child may have a fear of ridicule and criticism and need help in being relaxed while meeting new people.
He needs to be taught to avoid spending much time analyzing
himself and worrying over what people think of him. He can
overstress the importance of people who do not agree with him.
He should be encouraged to try for new horizons, leaving out-
moded customs of the past behind.

Talents and attributes:

This imaginative, impressionable child may make many changes
in his life until he finds the position or occupation where he feels
self-assured, well integrated, and appreciated. This person can succeed as a manager of a large corporation, a manufacturer, a public
employee, or utility worker, a job where there is much responsibility and a duty to perform. Women in this sign make good
nurses and managers in business, but their greatest attribute is
their love of home. They can turn a cave into a paradise. Men
born in Cancer like the sea, employment with shipping lines and
sea travel.

Types of persons for whom your child will have an affinity in
friendship, marriage, partnership, and business:

The Cancer child will usually find Pisces and Scorpio, and to a
lesser degree Taurus and Virgo people the most compatible.

Among great political leaders born in the Sign of Cancer are:

    John Quincy Adams, 6th U. S. President, July 11.

    Julius Caesar, Roman emperor, July 12.

    Calvin Coolidge, 30th U. S. President, July 4.

    King Constantine II of Greece, July 2.

    Haile Selassie, Emperor of Ethiopia, July 17.

Other internationally known persons born in the Sign of Cancer are:

    David Brinkley, commentator, July 10.

Pearl Buck, author, June 26.
Roald Amundsen, explorer, July 16.
John Paul Jones, U. S. Navy hero, July 6.
Helen Keller, blind educator, June 27.

Outstanding entertainment personalities:

Red Skelton, July 18.   Vittorio De Sica, July 7.
Art Linkletter, July 17.   Ringo Starr, July 7.
Martin Landau, June 30.   Yul Brynner, July 11.
Susan Hayward, June 30.   Van Cliburn, July 12.
Louis Armstrong, July 4.   Phyllis Diller, July 17.

THE LEO CHILD

for those born between July 23 and August 22.

The birthstone is the sardonyx.
The flower is the gladiolus.
The color is light orange.
August was the sixth month of the old Roman calendar, and
was formerly called "Sextilis."
Its name source was the Roman Emperor Augustus Caesar.
The symbol of the Sign of Leo is the Lion. The ruling planet
of Leo is the Sun.

Personality characteristics:

If your child is born in Leo he is usually a happy extrovert. He
loves power, not as a leader of others, but as the one completely
in charge of others. A child of the Sun is sincere, honorable, and
magnanimous, proud and impatient with those who would dare
to question their intentions or motives. As adults they are generally dignified and positive.

The Leo child is philosophical, forceful, and demonstrative.
Because he is assured, he demonstrates faith, hope, and fortitude.
This child is apt to be overly energetic and lavish in expenditure
of energy and money when his sympathy or interest is aroused. He
is usually a popular person socially, even-tempered but quick to
anger if his Leo pride is hurt. Ever facing the Sun as he does, he
is sometimes superoptimistic. The Leo person is powerful, commanding, and kinglike in his determination and ambitions. Although deeply emotional, he can triumph over his wrong desires.
He trusts those who believe in him, until he is betrayed or de-
ceived. He always aims for the stars and with his determination
and self-confidence, the Leo child usually gets there. He is rarely
if ever deceptive or secretive.

Leos can resist illness and recuperate from fatigue quickly. They have a superabundance of vitality and wonderful physiques.

The Leo child is daring, unflinching, and unafraid, and must be taught to somewhat curb his exuberance. This child does tend to have too much false pride and may be boastful and snobbish. The Leo person needs direction and control as a child. Since he always wants to be at the head of things, he must be made to realize that others like to be leaders too.

Talents and attributes:

Leo's great organizing ability and commanding power usually brings success to these persons. They are charming and have the power to make people like them. Used beneficially this is a God-given gift; used selfishly it is disastrous, to them as well as to their victims. These individuals make good managers, organizers, and military leaders. They seem more adapted to a career or professional life before the public than anywhere else. They excel as artists, actors, and musicians, succeeding best where they have authority or where they hold a high, responsible and trusted position as executives.

Types of persons for whom your child will have an affinity in friendship, marriage, partnership, and business:

The Leo child will usually find Sagittarius, Aries, and to a lesser degree Gemini and Libra people the most compatible.

Among great political leaders born in the Sign of Leo are:

Simón Bolívar, South American liberator, July 24.

Herbert Hoover, 31st U. S. President, August 10.

Napoleon I, Emperor of France, August 15.

Benjamin Harrison, 23rd U. S. President, August 20.

Alexander the Great, Macedonian Greek world conqueror, July 23.

Other internationally known persons born in the Sign of Leo are:

St. Francis de Sales, August 21.

Aldous Huxley, author, July 26.

Bernard Baruch, financier, August 18.

Princess Margaret Rose of England, August 21.

Outstanding entertainment personalities:

Walter Brennan, July 25.	Lucille Ball, August 6.
Don Galloway, July 27.	Andy Williams, August 9.
Shelley Winters, August 18.	Eddie Fisher, August 10.
Peter O'Toole, August 2.	George Hamilton, August 12.
Alfred Hitchcock, August 11.	Hayley Mills, August 18.

THE VIRGO CHILD

for those born between August 23 and September 23.

The birthstone is the sapphire.
The flower is the aster.
The color is dark violet.

September was the seventh month of the old Roman calendar. Its name source was "Septem" meaning "seven."

The symbol of the Sign of Virgo is the Virgin. The ruling planet of Virgo is Mercury.

Personality characteristics:

If your child is born in Virgo he is cautious, discreet, and not only contemplative but industrious. He will have ardor for the things money can buy and will gladly work for it. Self-assured this child is, not easily content with the commonplace. He will learn to memorize quickly; he may worry and have an overanxiety to succeed. He will be sensitive to his surroundings, and have a thirst for knowledge. He will be very careful of details as he enters mental ventures. He can be impudent and very critical at times, leaving those he cares for astounded at his cruelty. This Virgo child is methodical and wastes no time speculating on the unknown.

Virgoans want facts for their everyday world; they are self-possessed and discreet. In business they work for greater improvements, unobserved and sometimes unappreciated. These individuals are greatly affected by marriage and expect purity and constancy in their mates.

The Virgo-born is persevering and ingenious, very intelligent, but rarely controls his own life or makes changes unaided. There is a tendency to let the less-developed mentally give them orders. They earn money but often spend it for pleasure and education instead of for material things. In emergencies, they may think of themselves before others.

The Virgo child can absorb and learn anything he is determined to learn. He must correct selfishness and the continual criticism he usually practices. He must learn that his overanxiety only dissipates his mental and physical energy.

Talents and attributes:

This aspirant can succeed in life as an agent or intermediary for a large company, or can be the trusted executive secretary for a public or political figure. He excels in general commercial lines, imports and exports by land or air, and matters connected with the good earth and its products bring him success. Virgo persons generally rise in life through their own merits, but can fail if they use the wrong judgment of others. Writing, bookkeeping, record-keeping, research, and the instruction of others lure this person.

Types of persons for whom your child will have an affinity in friendship, marriage, partnership, and business:

The Virgo child will usually find Taurus, Capricorn, and to a lesser degree Cancer and Scorpio people the most compatible.

Among great political leaders born in the Sign of Virgo are:

William Howard Taft, 27th U. S. President, September 15.
Elizabeth I, Queen of England, September 7.
Lyndon B. Johnson, 36th U. S. President, August 27.
Marquis de La Fayette, French statesman, September 6.
Nguyen Ky, South Vietnamese statesman, September 8.

Other internationally known persons born in the Sign of Virgo are:

Leonard Bernstein, composer, August 25.

Eugene Field, poet, September 2.

Upton Sinclair, author, September 20.

Jane Addams, social worker, September 6.

O. Henry, writer, September 11.

Outstanding entertainment personalities:

Maurice Chevalier, September 12.

Sean Connery, August 25.

Sid Caesar, September 8.

Ben Gazzara, August 28.

Fred MacMurray, August 30.

Shirley Booth, August 30.

Michael Rennie, August 25.

Bob Newhart, September 5.

Adam West, September 19.

David McCallum, September 19.

THE LIBRA CHILD

for those born between September 24 and October 23.
The birthstone is the opal.
The flower is the cosmos.
The color is yellow.

October was the eighth month of the old Roman calendar. Its name source was "Octo" meaning "eight."

The symbol of the Sign of Libra is the Balances. The ruling planet of Libra is Venus.

Personality characteristics:

If your child is born in Libra he loves justice and hates injustice. He is an extremely sensitive individual and likes to be shielded from the unhappy side of life. He has a tendency to cling to his happy illusions, especially those about people he likes, usually to his detriment. Because he is a happy, sincere, honest child, it is difficult for him to believe that all others do not see life as he does. Your Libra child loves beauty, such as colors, music, and the artistic. If not talented in the arts, he will deeply appreciate them. His great sense of sympathy toward people whom he feels have been dealt with unkindly by fate often deludes him into mistaking sympathy for love.

Libra children often have difficulty in learning from others or in learning through logic and reason. They seem to learn from experience and intuition, which is amazingly developed.

These children are usually handsome or beautiful and well-formed. It is as if their innate soul beauty finds expression in the physical.

Be prepared to give your Libra child artistic surroundings and an education in the arts. Help him to face things as they are and to learn that the reality of things is often different from their appearance. He must learn the law of cause and effect, that all life has an interrelationship. This is the lesson of the Balances, as symbolized by the Sign of Libra. He must learn self-control and that uncontrolled emotions or rampant impulses can never exalt one's soul or mind. Libra children will need help in making everyday decisions. They must not be allowed to avoid responsibility by justifying their procrastination. They need to understand more about their vacillating nature.

Talents and attributes:

Libra's predominating talents are in the artistic and the beautiful. They may like work with beautiful fabrics, perfumes, clothing, jewelry designing, interior decorating, ceramics, stage designing, landscape architecture, drawing, painting, cartooning, flower gardening, music, singing and acting. They can be successful leaders in any of these professions by cultivating their talents along these lines. They love peace and harmony and are often outspoken exponents of these virtues.

Types of persons for whom your child will have an affinity in friendship, marriage, partnership, and business:

The Libra child will usually find Aquarius, Gemini, and to a lesser degree Aries and Leo people the most compatible.

Among great political leaders born in the Sign of Libra are:

John Adams, 2nd U. S. President, October 19.

Pope Paul VI, September 26.

Dwight D. Eisenhower, 34th U. S. President, October 14.

Mahatma Gandhi, leader in India, October 2.

Cordell Hull, U. S. statesman, October 2.

Other internationally known persons born in the Sign of Libra are:

Hiram L. Fong, senator, October 1.
Truman Capote, author, September 30.
Art Buchwald, columnist, October 20.
Sam Yorty, mayor, October 1.
Gore Vidal, author, October 23.

Outstanding entertainment personalities:

Julie London, September 26.   Angela Lansbury, October 16.
Greg Morris, September 26.   Melina Mercouri, October 18.
Johnny Mathis, September 30.   Diana Dors, October 23.
John Lennon, October 9.   Johnny Carson, October 23.
Yves Montand, October 13.   Julie Andrews, October 1.

THE SCORPIO CHILD

for those born between October 24 and November 22.

The birthstone is the topaz.
The flower is the chrysanthemum.
The color is red.

November was the ninth month of the old Roman calendar. Its name source was "Novem" meaning "Nine."

The symbol of the Sign of Scorpio which rules November is the Scorpion. The ruling planet of Scorpio is the fiery planet Mars.

Personality characteristics:

If your child is born in Scorpio he likes truth and dislikes falsities. A Scorpio child likes to visualize the completion and realization of his mental and physical efforts. He has an inner vision of the soul that can see beyond illusion. He tends to be secretive. Parents must earn his trust. This child has a tendency to go to extremes. There is also a tendency to let himself be diverted from his goals. Scorpios do not easily comply with the wishes and dictates of others. If they do, it is often unwillingly. This child is the most magnetic of all the children of the zodiac, always attracting the admiration, attention, and often the jealousy of the opposite sex.

Scorpio children are noted for their effervescent humor and their attractiveness. Whether they are tall or short, dark or light, they still attract people. They are quick and restless, and tireless workers.

The Scorpio child, because of his great energy and force, should be taught the difference between constructive and destructive power. He should be taught self-mastery and be given careful direction so that his tremendous energy and drive is channeled into creative activity. This child should also be taught early in life that as he shows understanding, so will understanding and compassion be shown to him. The study of psychology will help him to better understand himself and others. Another important lesson for the Scorpio child to learn is to curb his feelings of jealousy and envy. One of his weaknesses will be procrastination. The time to do his work is "now" and not tomorrow. Never listen to his many excuses for putting things off. Another lesson to be learned is the difference between impetuous physical attraction and deep, enduring affection. His outbreaks, moods, and tempers should be traced to their motivating causes and these corrected. The Scorpio child should always remember the Bible quotation, "To him that overcometh, will I give to eat of the hidden manna."

Talents and attributes:

The Scorpio child's talents are many and varied. He is unusually talented in promotional activities. The boy will make a good engineer, electrician, contractor, surgeon, scientist, or chemist. He will be excellent at research as well as a forceful leader. The Scorpio daughter can write, design, and become a successful model or actress, but the role she will like to play best in life is that of a loving wife, for she wants to love and be loved.

Types of persons for whom your child will have an affinity in friendship, marriage, partnership, and business:

The Scorpio child will usually find Cancer, Pisces, and to a lesser degree Virgo and Capricorn people the most compatible.

Among great political leaders born in the sign of Scorpio are:

Theodore Roosevelt, 26th U. S. President, October 27.

Indira Gandhi, leader of India, November 19.

Robert F. Kennedy, senator, November 20.

Gen. Charles de Gaulle, French statesman, November 22.

Warren G. Harding, 29th U. S. President, November 2.

Other internationally known pesrons born in the Sign of Scorpio are:

Martin Luther, religious leader, November 10.

Robert Louis Stevenson, author, November 13.

Pablo Picasso, painter, October 25.

Billy Graham, religious leader, November 7.

Jim Bishop, columnist, November 21.

Outstanding entertainment personalities:

Rock Hudson, November 17.

Mahalia Jackson, October 26.

Burt Lancaster, November 2.   Richard Burton, November 10.
Art Carney, November 4.   Brian Keith, November 14.
Roy Rogers, November 5.   Marcello Mastroianni,
Katharine Hepburn,   November 18.
    November 8.   Dick Smothers, November 20.

THE SAGITTARIUS CHILD

for those born between November 23 and December 22.

The birthstone is the turquoise.

The flower is the narcissus.

The color, light shades of purple.

December was the tenth month of the old Roman calendar and is named from the Latin word "Decem" meaning "ten."

The symbol of the sign of Sagittarius is the Archer. The ruling planet of Sagittarius is Jupiter.

Personality characteristics:

If your child is born in Sagittarius he is intelligent, generous, and often possessive, especially of those he loves. A child with this sun sign is hopeful and impressionable. He is quick and enterprising, demonstrative in affection, and loyal. This individual loves liberty and will vie with anyone to obtain it. Because of his firm belief in freedom of speech and expression, he is often opinionated and decidedly independent in his thinking and reasoning. If twenty-five people in a room agree on one point, the Sagittarius person would disagree and challenge them, and would express himself vehemently. These children are often rebellious against governmental restrictions, with a tendency to be indifferent to law and order, especially if it affects their individual freedom. Their blunt characteristics often cause the people of this sign to lose friends. The Sagittarius child has a religious, philosophical, and psychological outlook on life. He loves people and tries to understand them. His sympathetic and methodical nature is well developed. He is inquisitive, witty, and has a penetrating mind.

Constitutionally this child is strong but when his health is afflicted it usually comes from overactivity, excessive worry, and frustration over inability to solve problems. The Sagittarius child is a lover of beauty, but the beauty of knowledge predominates. These children take short cuts in almost everything they do. Often they get lost in petty details or the unimportant things of life, and forego the big things. This child is noble, sentimental, and impulsive, tactless and undiplomatic, but he loves deeply and is usually artistic and refined.

The Sagittarius child needs help in learning discrimination in choosing his friends, companions, and later, his mate. He must learn to evaluate people and learn that all people are not honest or dishonest, and that they do not have the same motives and reactions. This child will have a desire to help humanity, especially the ones he feels are unfortunate, but with his lack of discrimination he may find himself helping and sympathizing with those who seek only to take advantage of him. Sagittarians cannot judge people by themselves, for in them there is no guile as a criterion. The Sagittarius child will love nature and the great outdoors. By understanding himself, his talents, weaknesses, and rebellions, his life can be so directed that he can accomplish anything that he wants to do, and emerge like Joseph in the Bible, as the conqueror.

Talents and attributes:

Sagittarians' talents expand best where they come in contact with others, such as in instructing classes in art, education, dancing, and in the ministry. They may enter into large business deals, or be in any one of many professions such as the law.

Among great political leaders born in the Sign of Sagittarius are:

Sir Winston Churchill, English statesman, November 30.
Mary, Queen of Scots, December 7.
Martin Van Bureau, 8th U. S. President, December 5.
Zachary Taylor, 12th U. S. President, November 24.
Franklin Pierce, 14th U. S. President, November 23.

Other internationally known persons born in the Sign of Sagittarius are:

Rudolf Friml, composer, December 7.

Jane Austen, novelist, December 16.

William F. Buckley, Jr., author, November 24.

Drew Pearson, columnist, December 13.

Eli Whitney, inventor, December 8.

Outstanding entertainment personalities:

Lynn Fontanne, December 6.

Sammy Davis, Jr., December 8.

Walt Disney, December 5.

Kirk Douglas, December 9.

Robert Goulet, November 26.

David Susskind, December 19.

Andy Williams, December 3.

Jane Fonda, December 21.

Marshall Thompson, November 26.

THE CAPRICORN CHILD
for those born between December 23 and January 20.
The birthstone is the garnet which gives its wearer the virtue of constancy.
The flower is the carnation.

The color is deep blue.

January was the eleventh month of the old Roman calendar. Its name came from the ancient Roman deity Janus, the god of gates and doors, interpreted as the beginning of all things.

The symbol of the sign of Capricorn is the Goat. The ruling planet of Capricorn is Saturn.

Personality characteristics:

If your child is born in Capricorn he will have a quiet, somber, meditative nature ruled by reason instead of impulse. Such children are thrifty, reserved, diplomatic, deep thinkers, and determined. They are painstaking; unusually slow and cautious in what they do. They give the appearance of self-confidence, yet they are not really too independent of others. They are often too cautious for their own rapid progression, often suspecting the innocent of ulterior motives in business dealings.

Capricornians are like the tortoise in the old fable, which kept plodding and persisting until belatedly he reached his desired goal. The Capricorn child is receptive to down-to-earth activities. His tendency is to receive, but not give, to utilize others' work, abilities, and learning to his own advantage.

A Capricorn child must be taught unselfishness and the joy of sharing and giving. The law is that he who gives not, receives not, and he who gives, receives. Capricorn children must learn to master trials and hardships and not blame others for their misfortunes. They must be helped to decide early in life that their achievements not only depend upon their faithful performance of duties, but upon their exchange of ideas and trust in others. This child must be taught that to carry out mental and creative work the body must have good food, necessary rest, and exercise. This child may find himself too interested in mundane, earthly affairs, which is good if he does not forget the soul needs of beauty and spiritual things also. This child can be obstinate, jealous, and inclined to envy. Often life has to deal severely with him before he realizes the lesson it is trying to teach. Children ruled by Capricorn limit themselves by their static nature and their reluctance to make changes or to transcend their self-imposed limitations.

Talents and attributes:

Capricorn girls are industrious and ambitious. They often love wealth for the power and prestige it brings them. The Capricorn child is talented in mechanics, engineering, and in politics. Literary and religious things interest them. They like positions and occupations that influence and impress others. They make good executives and love power in any field they enter, whether scientific, artistic, or the world of law. They are good managers of large businesses and are excellent in real estate. A Capricornian person often delays marriage until late in life, vacillating in his choice of a mate. Once married however, they become faithful, devoted mates.

Types of persons for whom your child will have an affinity in friendship, marriage, partnership, and business:

The Capricorn child will usually find Virgo and Taurus, and to a lesser degree Pisces and Scorpio people the most compatible.

Among great political leaders born in the Sign of Capricorn are:

Woodrow Wilson, 28th U. S. President, December 28.

Benjamin Franklin, American diplomat, January 17.

Richard M. Nixon, U. S. statesman, January 9.

General Robert E. Lee, January 19.

Daniel Webster, American statesman, January 18.

Other internationally known persons born in the Sign of Capricorn are:

J. Edgar Hoover, head, F.B.I., January 1.

Sir Isaac Newton, scientist, December 25.

Louis Pasteur, chemist, December 27.

Martin Luther King, Jr., January 15.

Johannes Kepler, astronomer, December 27.

Outstanding entertainment personalities:

Marlene Dietrich, December 27.	Elvis Presley, January 8.
Richard Widmark,	Ray Bolger, January 10.
December 26.	Cary Grant, January 18.
Tony Martin, December 25.	Danny Kaye, January 18.
Steve Allen, December 26.	Patricia Neal, January 20.

Jose Ferrer, January 8.

THE AQUARIUS CHILD

for those born between January 21 and February 19.

The birthstone is the amethyst, which bequeaths its wearer the gift of sincerity.

The flower is the violet.

The color is light blue.

February was the twelfth month of the old Roman calendar and was named from "Februa," the Roman festival of purification.

The symbol of the sign of Aquarius is the Water Bearer or the Sage. The ruling planet of Aquarius is Uranus.

Personality characteristics:

If your child is born under the Sign of Aquarius, he has a faithful and dependent nature and at times may be difficult to understand. He is patient, unobtrusive, faithful, kind, and inoffensive. The Aquarian child will not always defend himself against injustice. He is quiet when it would be better for him to speak up. Rather than argue with a person who is wrong, he is apt to say, "Why should I argue or point out his errors? Let him find out his own mistakes." Thus Aquarians are often guilty of the sin of omission. Many of this sign are interested in exploring the mysteries of nature. The Aquarian child is intuitive and honest. He is more mental than emotional. Love plays a part in his life, but love does not dominate it. He is too obsessed with learning, too curious about life and its mysteries to be possessed. The Aquarian child likes people and wants people to like him. He is attracted to persons of intelligence and refinement. He may be tempted at times to let his idealism and dreams interfere or make him dissatisfied with reality.

The Aquarian child must be taught early in life that his plans do no materialize overnight. One has to visualize and work to accomplish objectives. Aquarians may want to start at the top instead of the bottom in anything they go into. The Aquarian child can learn and retain whatever knowledge he desires if he uses persistence and studies. He is capable of directing his interests to whatever he desires, and succeeding in it. He must learn the necessity of establishing a state of equilibrium between his higher consciousness and his lower self. When this is accomplished he becomes a guiding earth-angel or a sage that can help his fellow men to higher understanding.

Talents and attributes:

Aquarius' talents are numerous. He can succeed in scientific research or as an executive or writer. He can sell anything to anyone. Consequently he is at his best when associated with large corporations, large promotional or pioneering activities. This child will be interested in international progress and reform. He may also find himself interested in archaeology, geology, physics, astronomy, or studies of the evolution of life.

Among great political leaders born in the Sign of Aquarius are:

Abraham Lincoln, 16th U. S. President, February 12.

Dean Rusk, U. S. Secretary of State, February 9.

Franklin D. Roosevelt, 31st U. S. President, January 30.

William Henry Harrison, 9th U. S. President, February 9.

Other internationally known persons born in the Sign of Aquarius are:

John D. Rockefeller, Jr., industrialist, January 29.
Charles A. Lindbergh, aviation pioneer, February 4.
General Omar N. Bradley, U. S. Army, February 12.
Johnny Longden, jockey, February 14.
Thomas A. Edison, inventor, February 11.

Outstanding entertainment personalities:

Dame Judith Anderson, February 9.
Paul Newman, January 26.
Vanessa Redgrave, January 30.
Suzanne Pleshette, January 31.
Tom Smothers, February 2.
Jack Lemmon, February 8.
Leontyne Price, February 10.
Claire Bloom, February 15.
Lee Marvin, February 19.
Carol Channing, January 31.

THE PISCES CHILD

for those born between February 20 and March 20.

The birthstone is the bloodstone.

The flower is the daffodil.

The color is dark purple.

March was the first month of the Old Roman calendar. Its name source was Mars, the Roman god of war.

The symbol of the Sign of Pisces is the Fishes. The ruling planet of Pisces is Neptune.

Personality characteristics:

If you child is born in Pisces he is affectionate, sympathetic, loyal, idealistic, kind, and forgiving, especially if he understands what the Great Teacher meant when He said, "Love your enemies and do good to those who persecute you." The Pisces child is the mystic and the seeker after the hidden truths of the zodiac. Pisces is considered a dual sign, one fish battling odds and swimming upstream, and the other fish being nonresistant and drifting along with the current.

The Pisces child loves peace, almost at any price. He cannot stand a discordant, inharmonious atmosphere. Loud noises, discordant voices and arguments fill him with despair and make him very nervous. This child is sincere and truthful and because of these qualities he is not always able to see the "man behind the mask," so he may cultivate many wrong friends.

The March child can enjoy a happy married life if he chooses with conscious awareness of his marital partner. If he is not careful in choosing friends and the marriage partner, his life can be one of sacrifice and service to those who are not appreciative of him.

The Piscean child often devotes his life to the cause of truth and justice. This is good if it is for a just cause and if he is not loyal to the wrong individual or cause. March children should cultivate the spiritual and beautiful part of their natures. They must learn to search for facts. They should be told to learn to make decisions and conclusions without help. They should guard against jealousy and possessiveness and not let them interfere with happiness and with friendship with others. They must learn to trust their hunches and premonitions. Their lives should not be ruled by emotions and idealism.

It is important for the Pisces child to develop confidence and self-assurance. If he does, he can attain his ultimate happiness. "For he who can master himself can master the world."

Talents and attributes:

This sign claims writers, poets, idealists, religious leaders, doctors, nurses, lawyers, all with the divine motivation of helping humanity as their objective. Pisceans like lovely gowns, beautiful fabrics, poetry, and music. If they could materialize the beautiful dreams that they perceive in their minds and souls, they could bring about an earthly paradise.

Types of persons for whom your child will have an affinity in friendship, marriage, partnership, and business:

The Pisces child will usually find Cancer and Scorpio, and to a lesser degree Capricorn and Taurus people the most compatible.

Among great political leaders born in the Sign of Pisces are:

George Washington, 1st U. S. President, February 22.
José de San Martín, South America liberator, February 25.
Andrew Jackson, 7th U. S. President, March 15.
Grover Cleveland, 22nd U. S. President, March 18.
Harold Wilson, British Prime Minister, March 11.

Other internationally known persons born in the Sign of Pisces are:

Edna St. Vincent Millay, poet, February 22.
Victor Hugo, novelist, February 26.
Luther Burbank, agriculturist, March 7.
Amerigo Vespucci, explorer, March 9.
Johann Strauss, composer, March 14.

Outstanding entertainment personalities:

Marian Anderson, February 20.	Rex Harrison, March 5.
Elizabeth Taylor, February 27.	Ed McMahon, March 6.
Sidney Poitier, February 20.	Lawrence Welk, March 11.
Harry Belafonte, March 1.	Liza Minelli, March 12.
Jerry Lewis, March 16.	Peter Graves, March 18.

INTRODUCTION

In America today we find given names gleaned from all over the world. Our nomenclature is not of any single people. Even though we are an English-speaking nation, we are an amalgamation of many races whose names, with the exception of those of the American Indians, have their roots in other parts of the world.

Names are fascinating. Their meanings and interpretations take us back into the archives of world history. From names we learn about our forefathers' occupations, environment, and geographical location. Some were idealized heroes and their names were words of praise for their merits. Our given names are derived from the root words of our present spoken languages, English, German, French, Dutch, Hebrew, and others.

People throughout the world adopted or were given names describing their attributes, such as beauty and handsomeness, their coloring, their bravery, strength, or their deitylike virtues and accomplishments. Vine and fern, tree and flower names are word pictures of where our ancestors lived, and often they were used in commemoration of pastoral scenes. People were often named for animals, the fleet deer, gentle rabbit or the couragous wolf. Legendary gods and goddesses played a prominent part in name evolvement, as well as colors, light and dark. Abstract and almost uninterpretable names, especially in the case of some girls' names, were used in our present and past cultures and societies.

Names evolve gradually and their popularity often diminishes as other names take the ascendant. Many names used in the sixteenth and seventeenth centuries or in A.D. 100 are seldom heard today. Biblical names are the exception. Frequently the titles or heroines and heroes of popular novels have been widely used as baptismal names during the past century.

Surnames were once unknown, and many time-honored given names were not in use until the thirteenth century surname-adoption period. The usage of surnames as given names has advanced with the centuries, until at present a large percentage of boys' names owe their origin to family names, and a few girls' names as well. Included among the boys' given names in this book are many English, Irish, and Scottish family names which during the past fifty years have been increasingly used in our country as given names. These surnames usually represent the mother's maiden name, or are from her side of the family, but they are becoming more frequent, and are often picked at random without relation to family background. The author feels that the inclusion of these interesting, dignified surnames provides an inspiration and a variety for those who wish to give their sons distinctive names.

Written history began when individuals were personified by name, especially so when they were identified by two names. The unnamed person was never recorded; consequently he was a nonentity and was forgotten.

Names once identified a person as belonging to a country, district, clan, stock, or tribe. They often identified the person's religion and beliefs.

In writing this book, the material which I researched and interpreted has been used to give the name meanings in intelligent, modern phraseology. In the root words used for English, German, and French origin names I have used a variety of early source spellings to demonstrate name spelling evolution from the earliest times. For that reason name roots termed "Old English" are not necessarily the primitive "Anglo-Saxon" English spelling in all cases.

Some nicknames that are widely used as independent given names are listed alphabetically among the given names. Otherwise they are only included below the given name from which they are derived.

The root words and their meanings are as accurate as possible. However, authorities do dispute the meanings in a few instances. Where there are several sources and meanings I have included them.

In writing the extended and explanatory lines, not in quotes, that are included with some names, I drew upon my many years of study of historical, philosophical, genealogical, psychological, and religious studies of mankind. The historical encompasses the records of mankind, the genealogical takes in the history of families, tribes, or clans; the philosophical and religious studies open a stored wealth of information on man's beliefs and cultures. Here I found the wonderful Hebraic Biblical names with their inspirational, divine meanings. The old legendary gods and goddesses of long-forgotten races still exist in names we sometimes give our children today. In early times men and women were psychologically characterized by name in the same way they are analyzed and psychoanalyzed today, but we now have different words to express the analysis today. My constant question in my research was why were these comparison names, hero names, and deity names used, and why were men designated as "Gift of God," or "Justice of the Lord." The answer, I hope, will be revealed by my explanatory lines.

Since this book was written primarily to help mothers to find a name for their children, I would like to offer a few suggestions:

1. The name you give your child will be one of your most important gifts to him. It is therefore necessary to give your baby a pleasant-sounding name.

2. A short given name coupled with a short surname often sounds harsh or insignificant. A short given name is more euphonious and harmonious with a two- or three-syllable family name. If you like a longer, two- or three-syllable first name, such as Bradley or Meredith, it will sound better with a short, one-syllable last name, for example Bradley Jones or Meredith Brown.

3. Two given names make identification easier in our expanded population. May I also suggest that you check name combinations for the initials they form, discarding names that form the initial letters of words that might prove embarrassing to your child.

4. Repeat the name you select over for sound and rhythm.

5. Names can be a source of unhappiness or happiness. A West Virginia Wesleyan College study found that persons who disliked their first names tended to dislike themselves; also that male students felt less dissatisfied with their names than girl students. When you name your child for relatives or ancestors the name should sound well with your surname. If you feel obligated to give your child a name you think he may not like, make it his middle name. Persons with unusual or freakish first names have more difficulty as children in getting along with other children. If your child calls himself by another name than his own, it is time you found out why.

6. You will also want to see that the given name is clearly defined from the last name, so that the same-sounding syllables or letters do not run together when spoken, as in Martin Newcomb or Ralph Forbes. If these names are spoken rapidly the distinctive sounds of the separate names disappear.

7. Be certain that the name you give your child designates his sex clearly. Do not give a girl a boy's name or vice versa. This will cause tremendous trouble for the child and will eventually reflect upon you.

8. Nicknames are widely prevalent as distinct given names today, and they are spelled in varying ways, with "I" often

used instead of "Y" or "IE," in the endings of such names as Toni, Teri, Joni.

9. You can proclaim your child's heritage too, if you wish, by his name. If you have a boy you may name him, for instance, Stuart or MacLean, designating his Scottish ancestry. Stanford or Alden may refer to English forebears. Inger designates Scandinavian roots, while Hildegarde gives an old German background. Colleen infers Irish ancestors, and Moira, Scottish ones. Greece can be designated by the lovely old name Helen. Ruth, Naomi, and the favorite John can designate devout religious backgrounds. These designations of our religious or ancestral heritage are not a definite rule today, however.

In the past one hundred years we Americans, as well as the people of other countries of the world, have borrowed names profusely from each other, and in the Space Age of the future we will continue to widen our horizons for names to be used by the generations to come.

NAMES FOR GIRLS

A

ABIGAIL—Hebrew: Abigayil. "Father of joy" or "My father is joy." Abigail Adams, wife of U.S. President John Adams, 1744-1818.
English nicknames: Abbey, Abbie, Gail, Gale.
Foreign variations: Abaigeal (Irish).

ABRA—Hebrew: Abraham. "Mother of multitudes." A woman who personified the eternal mother of the world. Abra was a favorite of Solomon in the Bible, and the heroine of the 16th-century European romance, *Amadis of Gaul*.

ACACIA—Greek: Akakia. "Thorny." The acacia symbolized immortality and resurrection.

ACANTHA—Greek: Akantha. "Sharp pointed; thorned." Acanthus leaves were used as a decorative design in Greek architecture, honoring Acantha, legendary mother of Apollo.

ADA—Old English: Eada. "Prosperous, happy." St. Ada, 7th-century French abbess.
English variations: Adda, Aida.

ADAH—Hebrew: Adah. "Tiara, crown or ornament." A woman considered as precious as a jewel. Adah Isaacs Menken, famous 19th-century American actress.

ADALIA—Old German: Adal. "Noble one."

ADAMINA—Latin: Adamina. "Of the red earth." A feminine form of Adam.
English nicknames: Ada, Addie, Mina.

ADAR—Hebrew: Adar. "High eminent," or "Fire." Adar, the sixth month of the Jewish year, was introduced in the Babylonian calendar before 3500 B.C.

ADDA—See Ada.

ADELA—See Adelle, Adelaide.

ADELAIDE—Old German: Adal-heit. "Of noble rank." Old German: Adal-heida. "Noble-cheerful." A hereditary princess of the land. St. Adelaide, of Burgundy, 10th century, called "Mother of kingdoms."
English nicknames: Addie, Addy, Adela, Adel, Della.
Foreign variations: Adelheid (German), Adelaida (Italian, Spanish).

ADELINE—See Adelle.

ADELLE—Old German: Adal. "Noble." Adela Rogers St. Johns, American writer; Adele Mara, film actress; Adelina Patti, famous 19th-century singer.
English nicknames: Addie, Addy, Del, Della.
English variations: Adela, Adaline, Adelina, Adeline, Aline, Edeline.
Foreign variations: Adela, Adelina (Spanish), Adele, Adelina (French), Adelina (Italian).

ADELPHA—Greek: Adelph. "Sisterly." Exponent of culture and beauty, a sister to all men.

ADINA—Hebrew: Adin. "Voluptuous." A woman esteemed for her beautiful figure.
English nickname: Dina.
English variation: Adine, Adena.

ADOLPHA—Old German: Adal-wolf. "Noble wolf." A brave defender of her home and children. Feminine of Adolf.

ADONIA—Greek: Adonis. "Beautiful or godlike." A Greek beauty, a goddess come to life.

ADORA—Latin: Adoria. "Gift, glory, renown." A beloved lady, highly honored.

ADORABELLE—Latin-French: Adora-belle. "Beautiful gift."

ADOREE—French: Adorée "Adored one."

ADORNA—Latin: Adorna. "Adorned one." One bejeweled by nature with great beauty.

ADRIA—Latin: Adria, Hadria. "Dark one." A girl whose black eyes danced with the mystery and witchery of love. Adrienne Allen, actress.
English variations: Adriana, Adrea
Foreign variations: Adrienne (French), Adriana (Italian), Adriane (German).

ADRIANA—See Adria.

AGATHA—Greek: Agathe. "Good, kind." St. Agatha, 3rd-century Sicilian martyr; Agatha Christie, noted English novelist.
English nicknames: Ag, Aggie, Aggy.
Foreign variations: Agathe (French, German), Agata (Italian), Agueda (Spanish), Agata (Irish).

AGAVE—Greek: Agaue. "Illustrious, noble." Agave was a daughter of Cadmus in Greek legends.

AGNES—Greek: Hagne. "Pure one." Like a polished diamond, this woman reflected all the colors of the spectrum. St. Agnes, 4th-century Roman virgin martyr; Agnes De Mille, choreographer; Agnes Moorehead, actress.
English nicknames: Aggie, Annis, Nessa, Nessi, Nessie, Nesta, Neysa.

Foreign variations: Agnes (French), Agnese (Italian), Ines, Inez, Ynes, Ynez (Spanish), Aigneis (Irish), Agneta (Swedish, Danish).

AIDA—See Ada.

AIDAN—Irish Gaelic: Aid-an. "Little fire." In ancient Ireland fire symbolized purity and refinement. St. Aidan, 7th-century Irish bishop.
English variation: Adan.

AILEEN—Anglo-Irish: Aileen. "Light bearer." One who brought spiritual truth and knowledge to the world. An Irish form of Helen.
English variations: Aleen, Alene, Eleen, Elene, Eileen, Ilene, Ileana.

AIMEE—See Amy. Aimee Semple MacPherson, American religious leader.

AISLINN—Irish Gaelic: Aislinn. "Vision or dream."
English variation: Isleen.

ALANNA—Irish Gaelic: Alain. "Bright, fair, beautiful." A feminine form of Alan, Allen. Alanna Ladd, actress.
English variations: Lana, Lanna, Alaine, Alayne, Allene, Allyn, Alina.

ALARICE—Old German: Alhric. "Ruler of all." The feminine form of Alaric.
English variation: Alarica.

ALBERTA—Old English: Adalbeorht. "Noble, brilliant." St. Alberta, 3rd-century Christian martyr; Albertina Rasch, choreographer.
English nicknames: Allie, Berta, Bertie.
English variations: Albertina, Albertine, Elberta, Elbertine.

ALBINIA—Latin: Albinia. "White or blonde." A winsome woman, beautiful and fair.

English variations: **Albina, Alvina.**
Foreign variations: **Aubine** (French), **Albinia** (Italian).

ALCINA—Greek: Alkinoe. "Strong-minded." One who could turn stardust into gold by her persuasive power.

ALDA—Old German: Alda; Eada. "Old, wise, rich." St. Alda of Siena, Italy, 1249-1309.

ALDORA—Old English: Aeldra. "Of superior rank."

ALERIA—Middle Latin: Alario. "Eaglelike." A girl named for the bird that teased the clouds and spanned the peaks.

ALETHEA—Greek: Aletheia. "Truthful one." She who knows truth has wisdom. See Alice.
English variations: **Aleta, Aletta.**
Foreign variations: **Aletea** (Spanish, Italian).

ALEXANDRA—Greek: Alexandros. "Helper and defender of mankind." Princess Alexandra of Kent (England), cousin of Queen Elizabeth II; Alexandra, wife of England's King Edward VII; Alexandra Danilova, ballerina.
English nicknames: **Alex, Alexa, Alexine, Alexis, Alla, Lexie, Lexine, Sandi, Sandie, Sandy, Sandra, Zandra.**
Foreign variations: **Alexandrine** (French), **Alessandra** (Italian), **Alejandra** (Spanish).

ALEXIS—See Alexandra.

ALFONSINE—Old German: Adal-funs. "Noble and ready." The feminine of Alfonso.
English variations: **Alphonsine, Alonza.**

ALFREDA—Old English: Aelfraed. "Elf-counselor, good counselor." With wisdom and diplomacy this woman counselled others.

English nicknames: **Alfie, Freda.**
English variations: **Elfreda, Elfrieda, Elfrida, Elva.**

ALICE—Greek: Alethia. "Truthful one." A Grecian who knew neither lie nor deception. Alice is also a version of Adelaide. Princess Alice (died 1878), daughter of England's Queen Victoria; Alice Marble, tennis champion; Alice Cary, American poet; Alicia Markova, ballerina.
English nicknames: **Allie, Ellie, Elsie, Elsa.**
English variations: **Alicea, Alicia, Alissa, Alithia, Allys, Alyce, Alys.**
Foreign variations: **Alicia** (Italian, Spanish, Swedish), **Ailis** (Irish).

ALIDA—Late Latin: Ala-ida. "Little winged one." A woman compared to a bird in the air. Alida was also a city in ancient Asia Minor. Alida Valli, Italian actress, born 1921.
English variations: **Aleda, Aleta, Alita, Leda, Lita.**
Foreign variations: **Aletta** (Italian), **Aleta** (Spanish), **Alette** (French).

ALIMA—Arabic: 'Alimah. "Learned in dancing and music." Music is the common language that unites all nations in harmony and rhythm.

ALINA—See Alanna.

ALINE—See Adelle. Aline Mac-Mahon, actress.
English variations: **Alena, Alene, Alina.**

ALISON—Irish Gaelic: Allsun. "Little truthful one." A Gaelic form of Alice and Louise. Alison Skipworth, noted actress (1870-1952).
English nicknames: **Alie, Allie, Lissie, Lissy.**
English variation: **Allison.**
Foreign variation: **Allsun** (Irish Gaelic).

ALLA—See Alexandra. Alla Nazimova, famous actress (1879-1945).

ALLEGRA—Italian: Allegra. "Cheerful, gay." Heartbreaks are often healed by joyousness and love. Allegra Kent, actress.

ALLENE—See Alanna.

ALLIE—See Alison, Alice, Alberta.

ALLISON—See Alison.

ALMA—Spanish; Italian: Alma. "Soul or spirit." A spritelike girl, a spark of God's celestial light. Alternate: Latin: Alma. "Nourishing." Alma Gluck, famous opera singer (1884-1938).

ALMIRA—Arabic: Almira. "Fulfillment of the Word" or "Truth without question."
English variation: Elmira.

ALOHA—Hawaiian: Aloha. "Greetings or farewell." Aloha is the greeting and farewell from that fair state, Hawaii.

ALONZA—See Alfonsine.

ALOYSIA—See Louise.

ALPHA—Greek: Alpha. "First one." Alpha is the first letter of the Greek alphabet. "In the beginning God created the heaven and the earth."—Genesis 1:1. This was the Alpha.
English variation: Alfa.

ALTA—Latin: Altus. "High or lofty." Tall in spirit, a lady whose face was always turned toward the sky.

ALTHEA—Greek: Althaia. "Healer." Love makes all things right, for it heals the sorrows of the heart. Althea Gibson, tennis champion.
English nickname: Thea.

ALULA—Late Latin: Alula. "Winged one," or Arabic: Al-ula. "The first."

ALURA—Old English: Alh-raed. "Divine counselor." A seer who gave advice, helping people to help themselves.

ALVA—Latin: Alba. "Blonde one." One who seemed related to the yellow daffodil. Alva Belmont, American philanthropist.

ALVINA—Old English: Aethelwine. "Noble friend." A lady strong of heart, loyal and wise. Alternate origin, Old English: Aelf-wine. "Elf-friend."

ALYCE—See Alice.

ALYSSA—Greek: Alysson. "Sane one." A wise Grecian who thinks and reasons for herself. The sweet alyssum flower.

ALZENA—Arabic-Persian: Alzan. "The woman." A feminine woman who personifies beauty, love and fidelity.

AMABEL—Latin: Amabilis. "Loveable one." Sweet, soft, and beautiful was this fair lady.
English variation: Amabelle.

AMADEA—Middle Latin: Amadeus. "Loved of God." God gave his splendor to this exquisite woman.

AMANDA—Latin: Amanda. "Worthy of love." Virtuous in thought and deed, was this bride-to-be. Amanda Sewell, American painter (1859-1926).
English nicknames: Manda, Mandy.

AMARIS—Hebrew: Amaryah. "God has promised." A promise of God fulfilled by a daughter.

AMARYLLIS—Latin: Amaryllis. "The amaryllis lily."

AMBER—Old French: Ambre. "The amber jewel." Red amber, ancient tree sap solidified by that great chemist, Nature. Usage famed from the novel and motion picture *Forever Amber* by Kathleen Winsor.

AMBROSINE—Greek: Ambrotos. "Divine, immortal one." The feminine of Ambrose.

AMELIA—Gothic: Amala. "Industrious one." Also traced to Latin: Aemilia. "Flattering, winning one." Amelia Earhart, famous aviatrix (1898-1937); Amelita Galli-Curci, operatic singer.
English nicknames: Amy, Em, Emmie, Emmy.
English variations: Amalea, Amalia, Amilia, Emilia, Ameline, Emelina, Emeline, Amelita, Emelita, Emmeline, Emelie, Amalie.
Foreign variations: Amélie (French), Amalia (German, Spanish, Dutch) Amelia (Italian, Portuguese).

AMELINDA—Latin-Spanish: Ami-linda. "Beloved and pretty."

AMETHYST—Greek: Amethystos. "Wine-color or not-intoxicated." The amethyst was accredited with the power of preventing intoxication in ancient Greece. A girl with eyes like the purple amethyst.

AMI—See Amy.

AMINTA—Latin: Amyntas. "Protector." Amynta was a shepherdess in Greek myths.

AMITY—Old French: Amiste. "Friendship."

AMY—French: Aimée; Latin: Amare. "Beloved." Amy Lowell, American poet, Pulitzer Prize winner (1874-1925); St. Amata, niece of St. Clare of Assisi, died 1250.
English nickname: Ame.
English variations: Aimee, Amie.

Foreign variations: Aimée (French), Amata (Italian, Swedish, Spanish).

ANASTASIA—Greek: Anastasios. "Of the Resurrection." Spring, when all nature is renewed, reveals the soul's immortality. Famous from the Russian Grand Duchess Anastasia, believed by some to have escaped death in 1918 when the Czar's family were assassinated.
English nicknames: Stacie, Stacia, Stacey, Stacy.
English variation: Anstice.
Foreign variation: Anastasie (French).

ANATOLA—Greek. Anatolios. "From the East; from Anatolia."

ANDREA—Latin: Andrea. "Womanly." Beauty, love and grace are in that dream called "woman." Andrea is a feminine form of Andreas or Andrew.
English variations: Andria, Andreana, Andriana.
Foreign variation: Aindrea. (Irish).

ANDRIA—Latin: Andria. "Maiden of Andros, a Greek island." The woman from Andros was like sunshine after rain. See Andrea.

ANEMONE—Greek: Anemone. "Wind-flower." A flower that enticed the wind's caresses. A legendary Greek nymph pursued by the wind was changed into the beautiful anemone flower.

ANGELA—Old French: Angele. "Angel or messenger." St. Angela of Foligno, Italy (1248-1309), great religious mystic; Angela Lansbury, actress.
English nicknames: Angie, Angy.
English variations: Angelina, Angeline, Angel, Angelita.
Foreign variations: Aingeal (Irish), Angèle (French).

ANGELICA—Latin: Angelicus.
"Angelic one." An idealistic con-
cept of the perfect woman. Angelica Catalini, 19th-century Italian singer; Angelique Arnauld,
17th-century French abbess.
Foreign variations: Angelika
(German), Angelique (French).

ANGELINE—See Angela.

ANITA—See Anne. Anita Loos,
novelist.

ANNABELLE—Hebrew-Latin:
Hannah-bella. "Graceful-beauti-
ful.
English nicknames: Annie, Belle.
English variation: Annabella.
Foreign variation: Annabla
(Irish).

ANNE—Hebrew. Hannah.
"Graceful one." A magic name
for beauty walking. Mother of
the prophet Samuel. St. Anne was
the mother of the Virgin Mary.
Famous in history: Anne Boleyn
and Anne of Cleves, wives of
England's King Henry VIII;
Queen Anne of England, 1664-
1714; entertainers: Anna Pavlova,
ballet dancer; Anna Maria Al-
berghetti, actress; Anne Bancroft,
actress.
English nicknames: Annie, Anny,
Nan, Nancy, Nita.
English variations: Anna, Ana,
Anette, Anita, Nina, Ninon.
Foreign variations: Ana, Anita,
Nita (Spanish), Annette, Nan-
ette (French), Anna (German,
Italian, Dutch, Swedish, Danish).

ANNETTE—See Anne.

ANNIS—See Agnes.

ANNUNCIATA—Latin: An-
nuntiatio. "Bearer of news." A
bearer of news to the Virgin that
Christ would incarnate through
her. Used for a daughter born in
March, the month of the Annunciation.

Foreign variations: Annunziata
(Italian), Anunciacion (Spanish).

ANONA—Latin: Annona.
"Yearly crops." Spring breathed
upon the meadows and gave
them warmth and life. Annona
was the Roman goddess of crops.

ANORA—English: Ann-nora.
Combination of Anne and Nora.

ANSELMA—Old Norse: Ans-
helm. "Divinely protected." A
feminine form of Anselm.
English nicknames: Selma, Zelma.

ANSTICE—See Anastasia.

ANTHEA—Greek: Antheia.
"Flower." Antheia was a name
for Aphrodite as the Greek goddess of flowers.

ANTOINETTE—See Antonia.

ANTONIA—Latin: Antonia.
"Inestimable; priceless." The
priceless jewel of kindness is en-
cased within our hearts. A femi-
nine form of Anthony. Famous
from Queen Marie Antoinette of
France and Willa Cather's novel
My Antonia.
English nicknames: Tonie, Toni,
Tony, Tonia, Netta, Nettie,
Netty.
Foreign variations: Antoinette
(French), Antonietta (Italian),
Antonie (German), Antonetta
(Swedish, Slavic).

APOLLINE—Greek: Apollon.
"Sun or sunlight." St. Apolline of
Alexandria, martyred. A.D. 249.

APRIL—Latin: Aprilis. "Open-
ing; born in April." April was
the beginning of spring in the
old Roman and Greek calendars.

ARA—Greek: Ara. "An altar."
Ara was the Greek goddess of
vengeance and destruction.

ARABELLA—Latin: Ara-bella. "Beautiful altar."
English nicknames: Bella, Belle.
Foreign variations: Arabella (Italian, Dutch), Arabelle (French, German), Arabela (Spanish).

ARDATH—Hebrew: Aridatha. "A flowering field." Character in a novel by Marie Corelli.

ARDELLE—Latin: Ardere. "Warmth, enthusiasm."
English variations: Arda, Ardelia, Ardis, Ardine, Ardene, Ardeen, Ardella.

ARDIS—See Ardelle.

ARETA—Greek: Arete. "Excellence, virtue, valor." Moral excellence, unsurpassed by any maid.
English variation: Aretta.
Foreign variation: Arette (French).

ARGENTA—Latin: Argentum. "Silvery one." A lady with gray hair.

ARIA—Italian: Aria. "A melody." A donna of Italy whose voice was like a melody of love.

ARIANA—Latin: Ariadna. "Very holy or very pleasing one." Ariadne, daughter of a king of ancient Crete, extricated the hero Theseus from the labyrinth.

ARIELLA—Hebrew: Ariel. "Lioness of God." Beauty, strength and courage made this woman celebrated.

ARLEEN—See Arlene.

ARLENE—Irish Gaelic: Airleas. "A pledge." The feminine of Arlen. Arlene Francis and Arlene Dahl, actresses.
English nicknames: Arlie, Lene, Lena.
English variations: Arleen, Arlena, Arleta, Arlette, Arline, Arlyne.

ARMIDA—Latin: Armida. "Little armed one." A name used by Tasso for a famous beauty in his 16th-century work, *Jerusalem Delivered*.

ARMILLA—Latin: Armilla. "Bracelet." A daughter with an ancestral talisman.

ARMINA—Old German: Harimann. "Warrior-maid."
English variations: Armine, Arminie, Erminie.

ARNALDA—Old German: Arnwald. "Eagle-ruler" or "Eagle-strong." A feminine form of Arnold.

ARVA—Latin: Arvus. "Pasture-land or seashore."

ASELMA—Old Norse: As-helm. "Divine helmet or protection."

ASTA—Greek: Aster. "Star; star-like." A woman who imbued men with high resolutions.
English variation: Astra.

ASTRID—Old Norse. As-tryd. "Divine strength." The name of many Scandinavian queens and princesses.

ATALANTA—Greek: Atalante. "Mighty bearer." Feminine of Atlas, the hero who carried the world on his shoulders. Atalanta was a huntress in Greek myths.
English variation: Atlanta.

ATALAYA—Spanish: Atalaya. "Guardian."

ATHALIA—Hebrew: Athaleyah. "God is exalted." God is exalted by the purity of one's mind and deeds.
English variation: Atalia.

ATHENA—Greek: Athene. "Wisdom." Athena, Greek goddess, one who taught that knowledge and experience result in wisdom.
English nicknames: Athie, Attie.

ATLANTA—See Atalanta.

AUDREY—Old English: Aethelthryth. "Noble strength." Strength to overcome life's difficulties. St. Audrey, died A.D. 679, famous English abbess; Audrey Hepburn, actress.
English variations: **Audrie, Audry.**

AUGUSTA—Latin: Augusta. "Majestic one." Kaiserin Augusta, wife of Wilhelm II, the German Emperor during World War I.
Foreign variations: **Auguste** (German, French, Dutch, Danish).

AURA—Latin: Aura. "Gentle breeze." A lady with an air of sublime culture.
English variations: **Aurea, Auria.**

AURELIA—Latin: Aurelia. "Golden." Roman goddess of the dawn. Gold was the symbol of refinement and purity. St. Aurelia, 11th-century French princess; Aurelia Reinhart, noted American educator.
English variations: **Oralia, Orelia.**
Foreign variation: **Aurélie** (French).

AURORA—Latin: Aurora. "Daybreak." The rosy dawn of morning that heralds each new day.
Foreign variation: **Aurore** (French).

AUSTINE—Latin: Augustinus. "Majestic little ones." Feminine form of Augustine and Austin.

AVA—Latin: Avis. "Birdlike." A subtle, graceful maid whose heart was filled with song. Ava Gardner, actress.

AVELINE—See Evelyn.

AVENA—Latin: Avena. "Oats or oatfield." A blonde daughter compared to a yellow-ripe oatfield.

AVERA—Hebrew: Aberah. "Transgressor." A woman who outgrew old precepts.

AVERIL—Old English: Averil. "Born in the month of April," or Old English: Efer-hild. "Boar warrior-maid."
English variations: **Averyl, Avril.**

AVICE—Old French: Avice. "Warlike." A sensitive girl who was quick to anger.

AVIS—See Avice.

AZALEA—Latin: Azalea. "Dry earth." The azalea flower thrives in dry earth.

AZELIA—Hebrew: Aziel. "Helped by God." A woman God helped to conquer sorrow.

AZURA—Old French from Persian: Azur. "Blue sky." When friends spoke of her sky-blue eyes, the maiden blushed.

B

BAB—Arabic: Bab. "From the gateway." See Barbara.

BABETTE—See Barbara.

BALBINA—Latin-Italian: Balbina. "Little stammerer." Words are poor expressions of a wise one's nimble thoughts.

BAMBI—Italian: Bambino. "Child." A beautiful expression of God's greatest miracle.

BAPTISTA—Latin: Baptista. "Baptizer." A symbol of freedom from all the baser thoughts that trouble man.

Foreign variations: Batista (Italian), Baptiste (French), Bautista (Spanish).

BARBARA—Latin: Barbara. "Stranger." Beautiful, but a stranger to the land. St. Barbara, early Christian martyr; Barbara Hutton, American heiress; actresses Barbara Stanwyck, Barbara Britton, Barbara Hale.
English nicknames: Bab, Babb, Babs, Barbie, Barby.
English variations: Babette, Barbette, Babita.
Foreign variations: Barbe (French), Bárbara (Spanish), Varvara, Varina (Slavic).

BASILIA—Greek: Basileus. "Queenly, regal." A feminine form of Basil.

BATHILDA—Old German: Badu-hildi. "Commanding battle-maiden." A maid who fought for honor and truth.
Foreign variation: Bathilde (French).

BATHSHEBA—Hebrew: Bathsheba. "Daughter of the oath; seventh daughter." A pledge to God that she would follow His precepts. Bathsheba was the wife of the Biblical King David.

BATISTA—See Baptista.

BEATA—Latin: Beata. "Blessed, happy one."

BEATRICE—Latin: Beatrix. "She who makes others happy." Beatrice was the famous heroine of Dante's 13th century *Divine Comedy*. Entertainers include Beatrice Lillie.
English nicknames: Bea, Bee, Trixie, Trixy.
Foreign variations: Béatrice (French), Beatrix (German, Spanish), Beitris (Scotch).

BEDA—Old English: Beadu. "Warrior maiden."

BELINDA—Old Spanish: Bellalinda. "Beautiful, pretty." Belinda Lee, actress.
English nicknames: Belle, Linda.

BELLANCA—Italian: Bellanca. "Blonde one."
Foreign variation: Blanca (Spanish).

BELLE—French: Belle. "Beautiful one." See also Belinda, Isabelle.
English variations: Bell, Bella, Belva, Belvia.

BELVA—See Belle.

BENEDICTA—Latin: Benedicta. "Blessed one." One numbered among the blessed who practiced righteousness. The feminine of Benedict.
English nicknames: Bennie, Benita, Binnie, Dixie.
Foreign variations: Benoite (French), Benedikta (German), Benedetta (Italian), Benita (Spanish).

BENIGNA—Latin: Benigna. "Kind, gentle, gracious." The perfect woman for a wife.

BENITA—See Benedicta.
Benita Hume, English actress.

BERDINE—Old German-French: Berd-ine. "Glorious one." An inner radiance made this girl seem ethereal.

BERENGARIA—Old English: Beran-gari. "Bear-spear maid." Berengaria was the queen of England's famous King Richard the Lion-Hearted, 1157-1199.

BERNADETTE—French: Bernard-ette. "Brave as a bear." The feminine of Bernard. Famed from St. Bernadette of Lourdes, 1844-1879.
English nicknames: Bernie, Berny.
English variations: Bernadine, Bernadene, Bernita.
Foreign variation: Bernardina (Italian, Spanish).

BERNIA—Old Anglo-Latin: Beornia. "Battle maid." An angel in armor.

BERNICE—Greek: Berenike. "Harbinger of victory."
English nicknames: Bernie, Berny, Bunny, Nixie.
English variations: Berenice, Veronica.
Foreign variations: Berenice, Veronique (French), Veronike (German).

BERTHA—Old German: Perahta. "Shining, glorious one." Bertha was the old German fertility goddess.
English nicknames: Berta, Bertie, Berty.
Foreign variations: Berthe (French), Berta, Berthe (German), Berta (Italian, Spanish).

BERTILDE—Old English: Beorht-hilde "Shining battle maid."

BERTRADE—Old English: Beorht-raed. "Shining counselor."

BERYL—Greek: Beryllos. "The sea-green jewel." The beryl was an emblem of good fortune.

BETHEL—Hebrew: Bethel. "House of God."
English variation: Beth.

BETHSEDA—Hebrew: Bethesda. "House of mercy."

BEULAH—Hebrew: Beulah. "The married one." Beulah Bondi, noted American actress.
English variation: Beula.

BEVERLY—Old English: Beofor-leah. "Dweller at the beaver-meadow." Beverly Garland, American actress.

BEVIN—Irish Gaelic: Bebhinn. "Melodious lady." A singer with a voice so sweet that wild birds stopped to listen. Bebhinn or Bevin was the daughter of Brian Boru, most famous of all Irish kings, 11th century.

BILLIE—Old English: Willa. "Resolution; will-power." See also Wilhelmina. Billie Burke, noted American actress.
English variation: Billy.

BINGA—Old German: Binge. "From the kettle-shaped hollow."

BIRDIE—English: Birdie. "Little birdlike one."

BLANCA—See Bellanca, Blanche.

BLANCHE—Old French: Blanch. "White, fair one." A female who reminded one of a white lily. Blanche of Castile, Queen of France, 1187-1252; Blanche Thebom, noted opera singer.
Foreign variations: Bianca (Italian), Blanka (German), Blanca (Spanish), Blinnie, Bluinse (Irish).

BLASIA—Latin: Blasius. "Stammerer." When thoughts are rapid and speech is slow, one often stammers. Alternate origin, Old German: Blas. "Firebrand."
Blasia is the feminine form of Blasius or Blaze.

BLESSING—Old English: Bletsüng. "Consecrated one."

BLISS—Old English: Bliths. "Gladness, joy." A delightful, bonny lass who brought happiness to others.

BLITHE—See Blythe.

BLOSSOM—Old English: Blostm. "Fresh, lovely." A daughter fragrant and sweet as a snowflower. Blossom Seeley, American vaudeville actress, singer.

BLYTHE—Old English: Blithe. "Joyful, cheerful one." A girl who saw no shadows, for the sun seemed always bright.
English variation: Blithe.

BONITA—Spanish: Bonita. "Pretty." Bonita Granville, American actress.
English nicknames: Bonnie, Nita.

BONNIE—Middle English: Bonie. "Good one." Little girl, pink and sweet as an angel. See also Bonita.
English variations: Bonny, Bunni, Bunnie, Bunny.

BRENDA—Irish Gaelic: Breandan. "Little raven," or Old English: Brand. "Firebrand." A dark beauty who kindled a flame of love in every heart. American actresses include Brenda Frazier and Brenda Bruce.

BRENNA—Irish Gaelic: Brann. "Raven."

BRIDGET—Irish Gaelic: Brighid. "Strength." The strength to accept or the strength to resist. St. Brigid of Kildare, patroness of Ireland; St. Brigitta of Sweden; actresses Brigitte Bardot, Brigid Bazlen
English nicknames: Biddie, Biddy, Bridie, Brita, Brydie.
Foreign variations: Brigitte (French, German), Brigida (Italian, Spanish).

BRITA—See Bridget.

BRONWEN—Old Welsh: Brangwen. "White bosomed." Girl with black hair like the raven, but with skin as white as the dove. In ancient Welsh lore Bronwen was the daughter of Llyr, the sea god, and sister of Bran, King of Ireland.

BRUCIE—Old French: Bruis. "From the thicket." A forest sprite, an elfin queen of great charm. The feminine of Bruce.

BRUELLA—See Brunella.

BRUNELLA—Old French: Brunelle. "Brown-haired one."

BRUNETTA—Italian: Brunetta. "Brunette." Dark-haired.

BRUNHILDA—Old German: Bruni-hilde. "Armored warrior maiden." A maid who fought beside the warriors of her day. Brunhilda was a queen in the old Germanic Siegfried legend.

BRYNA—Irish Gaelic: Brian. "Strength, virtue, honor." The feminine of Brian.

BUENA—Spanish: Buena. "The good one."

BUNNY—See Bernice, Bonnie.

C

CADENA—See Cadence.

CADENCE—Late Latin: "Rhythmic."
English variation: Cadena.
Foreign variations: Cadenza (Italian), Cadence (French).

CALANDRA—Greek: Kalandros. "Lark."
English nicknames: Cal, Callie, Cally.
Foreign variations: Calandre (French), Calandria (Spanish).

CALANTHA—Greek: Kalanthe. "Beautiful blossom." A child of flowerlike beauty.
English nicknames: Cal, Callie, Cally.
Foreign variation: Calanthe (French).

CALEDONIA—Latin: Caledonia. "From Scotland." An ancient name for Scotland.

CALIDA—Spanish: Calida. "Warm, ardent." Ever-loving and ardent little one.

CALISTA—Greek: Kallisto. "Most beautiful one." "A daughter of the gods, divinely tall, and most divinely fair."—Tennyson.

CALLA—Greek: Kalos. "Beautiful."

CALLULA—Latin: Callula. "Little beautiful one."

CALTHA—Latin: Caltha. "Yellow flower." A reminder of yellow marigolds and buttercups.

CALVINA—Latin: Calvina. "Bald." The feminine of Calvin. White, soft down where hair should be.

CALYPSO—Greek: Kalypso. "Concealer." Behind a calm countenance surged a woman's emotions. Calypso was a sea nymph who kept Odysseus captive seven years in the Homeric Odyssey.

CAMEO—Italian: Cammeo. "A sculptured jewel." A daughter who is like pink, carved carnelian.

CAMILLE—Latin: Camilla. "Young ceremonial attendant." A beautiful maiden who assisted in ancient pagan ceremonies. Camilla was a Volscian queen in Virgil's Aeneid; Camille was the heroine of a novel by Dumas.
English nicknames: Cam, Cammie, Cammy, Millie, Milly.
Foreign variations: Camille (French), Camilla (Italian), Camila (Spanish).

CANACE—Greek: Kanake. "Daughter of the wind." In Greek myths Canace was the daughter of Aeolus, god of the winds.

CANDACE—Greek: Kandake. "Glittering, glowing white." Unblemished mind and character is often described as white.
English nicknames: Candee, Candie, Candy.
English variation: Candice.

CANDIDA—Latin: Candide. "Bright-white." See Candace. St. Candida of Naples, died A.D. 78, was said to have welcomed St. Peter to Italy; Candida is the heroine of the play by that name by Bernard Shaw.
Foreign variation: Candide (French).

CAPRICE—Italian: Capriccio. "Fanciful." A changeable maiden.

CARA—Italian: Cara. "Dear, beloved one," or Irish Gaelic: Caraid. "Friend."
English variations: Carina, Carine, Kara.

CARESSE—French: Caresse. "Endearing one." A maid who won both hearts and flowers.

CARISSA—Latin: Carissa. "Dear or artful one." Ingenious coquette, but still a lovely lady.

CARITA—Latin: Caritia. "Beloved, dear one."

CARLA—See Caroline, Charlotte.

CARLINE—See Caroline, Charlotte.

CARLITA—See Caroline, Charlotte.

CARLOTTA—See Charlotte.

CARMA—Sanskrit: Karma. "Fate or destiny." The cosmic operation of retributive justice, according to Hinduism and Buddhism; the Law of Cause and Effect.

CARMEL—Hebrew: Karmel. "Garden," or "God's vineyard." God's garden of creative thoughts and deeds. Mount Carmel in Palestine is famed in the Bible.
English nicknames: Carma, Carmie, Carmy, Lita.
Foreign variations: Carmela (Italian, Spanish), Carmelita (Spanish), Carmelina, Melina (Italian).

CARMEN—Latin: Carmen. "A song." A voice that was like soft music. Carmen is the heroine of Bizet's opera and Prosper Merimee's story. Usage is from Santa Maria del Carmen in honor of St. Mary. Additional French and Spanish meaning: "Crimson."
English nicknames: **Carma, Carmia.**
English variations: **Carmina, Carmine, Carmita, Charmaine.**
Foreign variation: **Carmencita** (Spanish).

CARNATION—French: Carnation. "Flesh color."

CAROL—Latin: Carola. "Strong and womanly." The feminine of Charles and Carl. Alternate origin, Old French: Carole. "A song of joy." See Caroline. Carol Heiss, American skater; actresses Carroll Baker, Carol Channing.
English nicknames: **Carrie, Caro.**
English variations: **Carel, Caryl.**

CAROLINE—Latin-French: Caroline. "Little, womanly one." "A perfect woman, nobly planned; sworn to comfort and command." —Wordsworth. Queen Caroline, wife of England's King George II; Carrie Jacobs Bond, composer; Carrie Nation, American reformer; Caroline Herschel, German-English astronomer, died 1848; Princess Caroline of Monaco.
English nicknames: **Carrie, Caro, Carol, Lina, Line.**
English variations: **Carline, Charleen, Charlene, Charline, Sharleen, Sharlene, Sharline.**
Foreign variations: **Carolina** (Italian, Spanish), **Karoline, Karla** (German).

CASSANDRA—Greek: Kassandra. "Helper of men" or "Disbelieved by men." Cassandra in Greek legend was a Trojan princess whose prophetic warnings went unheeded; also a character in Shakespeare's play, *Troilus and Cressida.*

English nicknames: **Cassie, Sandy.**
Foreign variations: **Cassandre** (French), **Casandra** (Spanish).

CASTA—Latin: Caste. "Pure, pious, modest one."

CATHERINE—Greek: Katharos. "Pure one." St. Catherine of Alexandria, 4th century, escaped martyrdom on a spiked wheel known later as a "Catherine wheel." Other famous Catherines: Catherine the Great, Empress of Russia, died 1796; Catherine of Aragon, first wife of England's King Henry VIII; Catherine Macauley, Irish founder of Sisters of Mercy; St. Catherine of Siena, 14th century; Katharine Cornell, American actress.
English nicknames: **Cathie, Cathy, Kate, Kathy, Katie, Katy, Kit, Kitty, Kay, Kaye.**
English variations: **Catharine, Katharine, Katherine, Cathleen, Kathleen, Kathlene, Kathline.**
Foreign variations: **Katerine, Katrina, Katti, Ketti** (German), **Catalina** (Spanish), **Catarina, Caterina** (Italian), **Katinka, Kassia** (Slavic), **Caitlin, Caitrin** (Irish), **Catriona** (Scotch).

CATHLEEN—See Catherine.

CEARA—Irish Gaelic: Ceara. "Spear." A woman who wielded a spear.

CECILIA—Latin: Caecilia. "Dim-sighted one." St. Cecilia, 3rd-century martyr, patron of music; Cecile Chaminade, French composer; Cecile Dionne of the famous quintuplets.
English nicknames: **Cele, Celia, Celie, Ciel, Cissie, Sissie.**
Foreign variations: **Cäcilia, Cäcilie** (German), **Cecile, Celie** (French), **Celia** (Swedish), **Cecilia** (Spanish, Italian), **Sisile, Sile** (Irish), **Sileas** (Scotch).

CELANDINE—Greek: Cheladon. "The swallow." Named for the swallow with its dark wings and white breast.

CELENE—See Selene.

CELESTE—Latin: Caelestis. "Heavenly." A terrestrial beauty compared to the divine. Celeste Holm, actress.
English nicknames: Cele, Celia.
English variations: Celesta, Celestina, Celestine.

CELESTINE—See Celeste.

CELIA—See Cecilia, Celeste.

CELOSIA—Greek: Keleos. "Flaming, burning." An ardent, faithful woman.

CERELIA—Latin: Cerealia. "Of the spring." A young lady, fresh and fragrant as spring flowers.

CERYL—See Cheryl.

CHANDRA—Sanskrit: Candra. "Moon; moonlike." "That orbed maiden with white fire layden, whom mortals call the moon."—Shelley, *The Cloud.*

CHARISSA—Greek: Charis. "Loving." See Charity.

CHARITY—Latin: Caritas. "Benevolent, charitable." Introduced as a given name to America by the Pilgrim Fathers.
English nicknames: Charissa, Charita, Charry, Cherry.

CHARLA—See Carla.

CHARLEEN—See Caroline, Charlotte.

CHARLENE—See Caroline, Charlotte.

CHARLOTTE—French: Charlotte. "Little womanly one." The epitome of femininity. A feminine form of Charles. Charlotte, queen of England's George III; Charlotte Corday, heroine of French Revolution; Charlotte Brontë, English author; Carlotta, 19th-century Mexican empress; Lola Montez, 19th-century actress; Charlotte Greenwood, actress-comedienne.
English nicknames: Carla, Charyl, Cheryl, Sheryl, Sheree, Sherrill, Sherry, Karla, Lotta, Lottie, Lotty, Lola, Loleta, Lolita.
English variations: Carlotta, Carlene, Carline, Charleen, Charlene, Charline, Karline, Sharleen, Sharlene.
Foreign variations: Carlota (Spanish), Carlotta (Italian), Charlotta (Swedish), Karlotte (German).

CHARMAINE—Latin: Carmen. "Singer." A singer who made people happy. See Carmen. Made popular by the song of the 1920s, written by Rapee and Pollack, and as heroine of the play and film *What Price Glory.*
English variations: Charmain, Charmian, Charmion.

CHARYL—See Charlotte.

CHERIE—French: Cher. "Dear, beloved one."
English variations: Cheri, Chery.

CHERRY—Old North French: Cherise. "Cherrylike." Lips the color of red cherries. See Charity.

CHERYL—See Charlotte.

CHIQUITA—Spanish: Chiquita. "Little one."

CHLOE—Greek: Chloe. "Young; verdant." "Chloe, thou fliest me like a fawn."—Horace. The shepherdess heroine of Longus' romance *Daphnis and Chloe.* Popularized from a song by George Gershwin; Chloe was the Greek deity of green grain.

CHRISELDA—See Griselda.

CHRISTABELLE—Latin-French: Christe-belle. "Beautiful Christian." A radiant-faced one who believed in Christian precepts.
English variation: Cristabel.

CHRISTINE—French: Christine. "Christian." Christina, 17th-century Swedish queen; Christine Nilsson, Swedish singer; Kirsten Flagstad, Norwegian opera singer; Christina Rossetti, 19th-century English poet.
English nicknames: Chris, Chrissie, Chrissy, Christie, Tina, Tine, Tiny.
English variations: Christina, Christiana, Christiane, Cristina.
Foreign variations: Cristina (Italian, Spanish), Kirsten, Kirstin, Kristin (Scandinavian), Christiane, Kristel (German), Cristiona, Cristin (Irish), Cairistiona (Scotch).

CHRYSEIS—Latin: Chryseis. "Daughter of the golden one." In the Greek *Iliad* she was a beautiful maiden captured by the Greeks and given to the hero Agamemnon.

CINDERELLA—French: Cendrillon. "Little one of the ashes." From the fairy tale of the hearth drudge, miraculously found by, and married to a prince.
English nicknames: Cindie, Cindy, Ella.

CINDY—See Lucinda, Cinderella.

CLAIRE—See Clara.

CLARA—Latin: Clara. "Brilliant, bright, illustrious." St. Clara of Assisi, born A.D. 1193, follower and aide of St. Francis, known in Italy as Santa Chiara; Clara Barton, founder of the Red Cross, died 1912; Klara Schumann, 19th-century German composer; Clare Booth Luce, American writer, diplomat; Claire Bloom, actress.

English nicknames: Clarey, Clari, Clarie, Clary.
English variations: Claire, Clare, Clarette, Clarinda, Clarine, Clarita.
Foreign variations: Claire (French), Chiara (Italian), Klara (German), Clara, Clareta, Clarita (Spanish), Sorcha (Scotch).

CLARABELLE—French: Clarebelle. "Brilliant, beautiful."

CLARAMAE—English: Claramay. Modern compound of Clara and May. Claramae Turner, opera singer.

CLARESTA—English: Clar-esta. "Most brilliant one."

CLARETTE—See Clara.

CLARICE—French: Clarice. "Little brilliant one."
English variations: Clarissa, Clarisse, Clarrisse, Clerissa.

CLARIMOND—Latin-German: Clari-mond. "Brilliant protector."

CLARINDA—Spanish: Claralinda. "Brilliant, beautiful."

CLARISSA—Latin: Clarissima. "Most brilliant one." See Clarice.

CLAUDETTE—See Claudia.

CLAUDIA—Latin: Claudia. "The lame one." Feminine form of Claudius, a famous Roman family and imperial name. Claudia Muzio, famous singer; Claudette Colbert, noted actress.
English nicknames: Claudie.
English variations: Claudette, Claudina, Claudine.
Foreign variations: Claude, Claudette, Claudine (French), Gladys, Gwladys (Welsh), Claudia (German, Italian, Spanish).

CLEMATIS—Greek: Klematis. "Vine or brushwood." From the sweet-smelling clematis flower.

CLEMENCY—See Clementia.

CLEMENTIA—Latin: Clementia. "Mild, calm, merciful." A wonderful characterization of a good woman. Popularized by the song, "Oh, My Darling Clementine."
English nicknames: Clem, Clemmie, Clemmy.
Foreign variations: Clemence (French), Klementine (German).

CLEMENTINE—See Clementia.

CLEO—Greek: Cleo. "Glory, fame." See Cleopatra. Cleo Moore, film actress.

CLEOPATRA—Greek: Cleopatra. "Father's glory or fame." A father's pride and joy. Cleopatra, B.C. 69-30, Queen of Egypt; heroine of Shakespeare's play, *Antony and Cleopatra*.

CLEVA—Middle English: Cleve. "Dweller at the Cliff." Feminine of Cleve and Clive.

CLIANTHA—Greek: Kleianthe. "Glory-flower." This child has the splendor and beauty of a flower from heaven.
English variation: Cleantha.
Foreign variation: Cleanthe (French).

CLIO—Greek: Kleio. "The proclaimer." A woman who made known her opinion. Clio was the ancient Greek Muse of History.

CLORINDA—Latin: Clorinda. Fictional name formed by Tasso, 16th-century, for a character in *Jerusalem Delivered*. Possible meanings: "Renowned," or "Verdant, beautiful."

CLOTILDA—German: Chlodhilde. "Famous battle-maid." A girl who fought beside the man she loved. St. Clotilda, 6th century, was the wife of Clovis I, King of France.
Foreign variations: Clothilde (French), Klothilde (German), Clotilda (Italian, Spanish).

CLOVER—Old English: Claefer. "Clover blossom." A daughter sweet and fragrant as a field of blooming clover.

CLYMENE—Greek: Klymene. "Renowned, famed one." Clymene in Greek myths was the daughter of Oceanus and the mother of Atlas and Prometheus.

CLYTIE—Greek: Klytai. "Splendid or beautiful one." Clytie, a nymph, daughter of Oceanus in Greek legends, was changed into a heliotrope flower because she loved the sun and could then always turn her face toward it.

COLETTE—Greek-French: Colette. "Victorious army." A French nickname form of Nicolette, from Nicholas. Collette, French novelist.
Foreign variation: Collette (French).

COLLEEN—Irish Gaelic: Cailin. "Girl, maiden."

COLUMBA—Latin: Columba. "The dove." An ancient symbol of peace in all nations. St. Columba, born in Ireland, became the greatest religious benefactor of Scotland, 6th century. His name is used by both men and women.
English nicknames: Collie, Colly.
English variations: Coline, Columbia, Columbine.
Foreign variations: Colombe, Coulombe (French).

COMFORT—French: Confort. "Strengthening aid and comfort." A Puritan name first popularized in the 18th century.

CONCEPTION—Latin: Conceptio. "Beginning." Used in Spain and Latin America in

honor of Santa Maria de la Concepcion.
Foreign variations: Concepcion, Concha, Conchita (Spanish).

CONCHA—See Conception.

CONCHITA—See Conception.

CONCORDIA—Latin: Concordia. "Harmony." At peace with man and nature. Concordia was a Roman goddess representing peace after war.

CONRADINE—Old German: Kuon-rad. "Bold, wise counselor." The feminine of Conrad.
English nicknames: Connie, Conny.

CONSOLATA—Italian: Consolata. "Consolation." Used in honor of St. Mary.

CONSTANCE—Latin: Constantia. "Firmness, constancy." St. Constance, 2nd-century Roman martyr; Constance Collier, noted actress.
English nicknames: Connie, Conny.
English variations: Constancy, Constanta, Constantina.
Foreign variations: Constanza (Italian, Spanish), Konstanze (German).

CONSUELA—Spanish: Consuelo. "Consolation." A wonderful friend when needed. Consuelo Vanderbilt, American heiress.
Foreign variations: Consuelo (Italian, Spanish).

CORA—Greek: Kore. "The maiden." In Greek mythology Kore was the daughter of the goddess Demeter. Corinne Calvet, actress.
English nickname: Corrie.
English variations: Kora, Corella, Corette, Corrina, Correne.
Foreign variation: Corina (Spanish).

CORABELLE—Greek-French: Kore-Belle. "Beautiful maiden."

CORAL—Latin: Corallum. "Coral from the sea," or Old French: Coral. "Cordial, sincere." Coral Brown, English actress.
English variation: Coraline.
Foreign variation: Coralie (French).

CORDELIA—Middle Welsh: Creiddylad. "Jewel of the sea." In Welsh legends Cordelia was the daughter of King Lear, ruler of the sea. In Shakespeare's *King Lear* she was the only one of his three daughters who loved him.
English nicknames: Cordie, Delia, Della.
Foreign variations: Cordelie (French), Kordula (German).

CORINNE—See Cora.

CORISSA—Latin-Greek: Corissa. "Most maidenly." A feminine and modest lady.
English variation: Corisa.

CORLISS—Old English: Carleas. "Cheerful, good-hearted."

CORNELIA—Latin: Cornelia. "Yellowish or horn-colored," or Latin: Cornel. "Cornel tree." The feminine of Cornelius. Cornelia was a famous Roman mother of twelve children. The cornel tree was sacred to Apollo in Greek myths. St. Cornelia, an early North African Christian martyr; Cornelia Otis Skinner, noted actress and writer.
English nicknames: Cornie, Nela, Nelia, Nelli, Nellie.
English variations: Cornela, Cornelle, Cornela.
Foreign variation: Cornelie (French).

CORONA—Spanish: Corona. "Crown, crowned one."

COSETTE—French: Cosette. "Victorious army." A French feminine nickname from Nicholas.
Foreign variation. Cosetta (Italian).

COSIMA—Greek: Kosmos. "Order, harmony; the world." Feminine form of Cosmo. Heavenly rhapsody, harmony and order was incarnated in the girl. Cosima Wagner, wife of composer Richard Wagner.

CRESCENT—Old French: Creissant. "To increase or create." Foreign variation: Crescentia (Italian).

CRISPINA—Latin: Crispina. "Curly haired." The feminine form of Crispin.

CRYSTAL—Latin: Crystallum. "Clear as crystal." Without deception. Chrystal Herne, noted American actress.
English variation: Chrystal.

CYNARA—Greek: Kinara. "Thistle or artichoke." Beauty protected by thorns. Famed from the writings of Horace, ancient Roman poet, and from Ernest Dowson's poem.

CYNTHIA—Greek: Kynthia. "The moon." Cynthia was an epithet for Artemis or Diana, the moon goddess, who was born on Mount Cynthos on the island of Delos.
English nicknames: Cynth, Cynthie.

CYPRIS—Greek: Kipris. "From the island of Cyprus."

CYRENA—Greek: Kyrene. "From Cyrene." Cyrene was a goddess of Cyrenaica, an ancient north African country. In Greek myths Cyrene was a water nymph loved by Apollo.

CYRILLA—Latin: Cyrilla. "Lordly one." The feminine form of Cyril. A lady of dignity.
Foreign variation: Cirila (Spanish).

CYTHEREA—Greek: Kythereia. "From the island of Cythera." Cytherea was an epithet for Aphrodite or Venus.

D

DACIA—Greek: Dakoi. "From Dacia." Dacia was an ancient eastern European country.

DAFFODIL—Old French: Afrodille. "The daffodil flower." Touched by Pluto and turned to gold from white, according to the Greek myth.

DAGMAR—Old German: Dagomar. "Day glorious" or Old German: Dank-mar. "Famous thinker; glory of the Danes."

DAHLIA—Old Norse: Dal-r. "From the valley." Latin form of the surname of A. Dahl, Swedish botanist, for whom the flower was named.

DAISY—Old English: Daeges-eage. "Eye-of-the-day." A miniature symbol of the sun. In France this flower is called Marguerite. Popularized by the Gay Nineties song "Daisy Bell."

DALE—Old English: Dael. "From the valley." Where nature was liberal with her beauty. Alternate origin, Greek: Damaris. "Heifer, gentle one." Dale Evans Rogers noted actress, entertainer.
English variations: Daile, Dayle.

DAMITA—Spanish: Damita. "Little noble lady." Lili Damita, European actress.

DANICA—Old Slavic: Danika. "Star, morning star." The morning star that awakens the cock to crow.

DANIELA—Hebrew: Dani'el. "God is my judge." Feminine form of Daniel. Danielle Darrieux, French actress.
English variations: **Danella, Danelle.**
Foreign variations: **Danielle** (French), **Daniela** (Spanish).

DAPHNE—Greek: Daphne. "Laurel or bay tree." The fragrant laurel tree branches were used as a crown for victors. Daphne was the daughter of the river god, and was changed into a laurel tree in Greek mythology. Daphne du Maurier, English novelist; Daphne Anderson, English actress.

DARA—Hebrew: Dara. "House of compassion or wisdom." "Charity or compassion is the scope of all God's commands."— Old Proverb. Dara Howard, American actress.

DARCIE—Old French: D'Arcy. "From the fortress." Feminine version of D'Arcy; also Irish Gaelic: Dorchaidhe. "Dark man."

DARIA—Greek: Dareios. "Wealthy, queenly." Feminine form of Darius, from the famous Persian ruler.

DARLENE—Old Anglo-French: Darel-ene. "Little dear one."

DARRELLE—Old Anglo-French: Darel. "Little dear one."
English variations: **Darryl, Daryl.**

DAVIDA—Hebrew: David. "Beloved one." Feminine form of David. Without someone to love, life would be like a day without the sun.
English variation. **Davina.**

DAWN—Old English: Dagian. "The dawn of day." As the sun disperses darkness, so does a beautiful daughter dispel loneliness. Dawn Addams, actress.

DEANNA—See Diana.

DEBORAH—Hebrew: Deborah. "The bee." One who seeks only the sweet in life. Deborah was a famous Biblical prophetess who helped free Israel from the Canaanites. Debbie Reynolds, Deborah Kerr, Debra Paget, Deborah Walley, actresses.
English nicknames: **Deb, Debbie, Debby.**
English variations: **Debora, Debra.**

DECIMA—Latin: Decima. "The tenth Daughter."

DEE—Welsh: Du. "Black; dark one." A brunette beauty. See Diana.

DEIRDRE—Irish Gaelic: Deardriu. "Complete wanderer," or Irish Gaelic: Deirdre. "Sorrow." Deirdre was the tragic heroine of an old Irish legend, the ward of King Conchobor, ancestor of Clan O'Connor. She fell in love and fled to England with Naoise; later when they returned, her lover was killed and she died on his grave.

DELCINE—See Dulcine.

DELFINE—Greek: Delphinion. "The larkspur or delphinium flower." Named for its flower-center which resembles a dolphin-fish or delphinos.
English variations: **Delfina, Delphina, Delphine.**

DELIA—Greek: Delos; Delia. "Visible." Delia was a name for Artemis, the Greek moon goddess who was born on the Isle of Delos.

DELICIA—Latin: Deliciae. "Delightful one." "Rarely, rarely, comest thou, spirit of delight."— Shelley

DELIGHT—Old French: Delit. "Delight or pleasure." A daughter who brought happiness to her parents Delight Evans, American editor, critic.

DELILAH—Hebrew: Delilah. "Languishing or gentle." Delilah was the betrayer of Samson in the Bible.
English variations: Delila, Dalila.

DELLA—See Adelle, Adeline, Adelaide.

DELMA—Spanish: Delmar; French Delmare. "Of the sea." A daughter named for her love of the ocean.

DELORA—See Dolores.

DELORES—See Dolores.

DELPHINE—See Delfine.

DELTA—Greek: Delta. "Fourth letter of the Greek alphabet." A name for a fourth daughter.

DEMETRIA—Greek: Demetrios. "Belonging to Demeter, Greek fertility goddess." St. Demetria, early Christian martyr, died A.D. 363.

DENA—Old English: Denu. "From the valley." Feminine form of Dean.
English variations: Deana, Deane.

DENISE—French: Denise. "Adherent of Dionysus, Greek god of wine." The feminine form of Dennis. Denise Darcel, actress.
English variations: Denice, Denyse.

DESIREE—French: Desirée. "Desired longed-for." A wish for a daughter fulfilled.

DESMA—Greek: Desmos. "A bond or pledge."

DESMONA—Greek: Dys-daimonia. "Ill-starred one." A shortening of Desdemona, famous character in Shakespeare's *Othello*.

DEVA—Sanskrit: Deva. "Divine." A name for the moon goddess.

DEVONA—Old English: Defena. "From Devonshire." Devonshire was named for the ancient Celtic tribe called Defena, believed to mean "Deep valley people."

DEXTRA—Latin: Dexter. "Skillful, dexterous." A genius with her hands.

DIAMANTA—French: Diamant. "Diamondlike." Precious as a rare jewel.

DIANA—Latin: Diana. "Goddess; divine one." Diana was the Roman moon goddess and deity of the hunt. Notable namesakes include actresses Diana Wynyard, Diana Lynn, Diana Dors, Deanna Durbin, Diane Varsi.
English nicknames: Di, Dian, Dee.
English variations: Deana, Deanna, Dianna, Dyana, Dyane.
Foreign variations: Diane (French).

DIANTHA—Greek: Dios-anthus. "Flower of Zeus, divine flower."
English variations: Dianthe, Dianthia.

DIDO—Greek: Dido. Obscure meaning, possibly: "Teacher; enlightener." "Teaching others teaches yourself."—Proverb. Dido, an ancient princess of Tyre, was the reputed founder of the famous North African city of Carthage.

DINAH—Hebrew: Dinah. "Judged." Dinah was a daughter of Jacob and Leah in the Bible. Dinah Maria Craik, 19th-century

English novelist; actresses Dinah
Shore, Dina Merrill.
English variation: **Dina.**

DISA—Old Norse: Diss. "Active sprite," or Greek: Dis.
"Twice or double." Dis was an
ancient Nordic fairy guardian.

DIXIE—French: Dix. "Ten or
tenth." Dixie Land, the Southern
states, was so named without sub-
stantiation, from ten-dollar bills
called "Dixies."

DOANNA—American com-
pound of Dorothy and Anna.

DOCILA—Latin: Docilis. "Gentle, teachable." A woman with
the ability to absorb knowledge.

DOLL—See Dorothy.

DOLORES—Spanish: Dolores.
"Sorrows." Usage from Santa
Maria de los Dolores, referring
to the seven sorrowful occasions
in the life of St. Mary. Dolores
Hart, Dolores del Rio, actresses.
English and Spanish nicknames:
Lola, Lolita.
English variations: **Delores, Del-**
oris, Delora, Dolorita.

DOMINA—Latin: Domina.
"Lady." A beautiful lady, cultured and refined.

DOMINICA—Latin: Dominica.
"Belonging to the Lord." Femi-
nine of Dominic.
Foreign variations: **Dominique**
(French), **Domenica** (Italian),
Dominga (Spanish).

DONALDA—Scotch Gaelic:
Domhnull. "World ruler." The
feminine of Donald.
English variation: **Donia.**

DONATA—Latin: Donatio.
"Donation; gift."

DONIA—See Donalda.

DONNA—Italian: Donna.
"Lady." A cultured and refined
one. Donna Reed, Donna Corcoran, actresses.

Foreign variations: **Doña**
(Spanish).

DORA—Greek: Doron. "Gift."
See Dorothy, Theodora. Dora
D'Istria, Rumanian 19th-century
writer; Dora Keen, American
writer.
English nicknames: **Dori, Dor-**
rie.
English variations: **Doralin,**
Doralynne, Dorelia, Dorena,
Dorette, Doreen.

DORCAS—Greek: Dorkas. "A
gazelle." A graceful woman with
lustrous eyes. In the Bible, Dorcas was raised from the dead by
St. Peter.

DORÉ—French: Doré. "Golden
one." A fair maiden, topaz-
crowned, with azure eyes.

DOREEN—Irish Gaelic: Doire-
ann. "The sullen one." A daughter concerned with the seriousness
of life. See Dora. Doreen Montgomery, American writer.
English variations: **Dorene,**
Dorine.

DORINDA—Greek-Spanish:
Doron linda. "Beautiful gift."

DORIS—Greek: Doris. "From
the ocean." In Greek myths Doris
was the daughter of Oceanus, god
of the sea. Doris Day, actress.
English variations: **Doria, Dor-**
ice, Dorise, Dorris.

DOROTHY—Greek: Dorothea.
"Gift of God." See Theodora.
St. Dorothea, early Christian
martyr; writers Dorothy Thomp-
son, Dorothy Parker, Dorothy
Kilgallen; Dorothy Kirsten, sing-
er; actresses Dorothy Collins,
Dorothy McGuire, Dorothy Pro-
vine.
English nicknames: **Dot, Dottie,**
Dotty, Dol, Dollie, Dolly
English variations: **Dorothea,**
Dorotea, Dorthea, Dorthy.
Foreign variations: **Dorothea**
(German), **Dorothée** (French),
Dorotea (Italian, Spanish).

DRUELLA—Old German: Drugi-self. "Elfin vision."

DRUSILLA—Latin: Drusilla. "Descendant of Drusus, the strong one."
English nicknames: Dru, Drusa, Drucie, Drusie.

DUANA—Irish Gaelic: Dubhain. "Little dark one," or Irish Gaelic: Duan. "Song."
English variations: Duna, Dwana.

DUENA—Spanish: Dueña. "Chaperon." A matron who accompanies unmarried couples to places of entertainment.

DULCIANA—See Dulcie.

DULCIBELLE—See Dulcie.

DULCIE—Latin: Dulcis. "Sweet one." Love is much sweeter than honey.
English variations: Delcine, Dulce, Dulcea, Dulcine, Dulcinea, Dulcibelle, Dulciana.

DURENE—Latin: Durus. "Enduring one."

DYANE—See Diana.

E

EARLENE—Old English: Eorl. "Noble woman." The feminine form of Earl. Alternate, Irish Gaelic: Airleas. "A pledge."
English nicknames: Earlie, Earley.
English variations: Earline, Erlene, Erline.

EARTHA—Old English: Ertha. "The earth." Eartha Kitt, vocalist, actress.
English variations: Erda, Ertha, Herta, Hertha.

EASTER—Old English: Eastre. "Born at Easter time." Eostre was the ancient Anglo-Saxon goddess of spring.

EBBA—Old English: Ebba. "Flowing back of the tide." See Eve.

ECHO—Greek: Echo. "Reflected sound." In Greek myths Echo, a nymph, pined away for the love of Narcissus, until nothing was left but her voice.

EDA—Old English: Eada. "Prosperity, blessedness," or Old Norse: Edda: "Poetry." A dewey-eyed daughter who was given every feminine attribute. Eda Heinemann, American actress. See Edith.

EDANA—Irish Gaelic: Aiden, Eideann. "Little fiery one." A loving child who caught a spark of God's celestial warmth. St. Edana of Ireland, 6th century.

EDE—See Eda. Also Greek: Ede. "Generation." A loving mother blessed by children. Alternate, Old English: Eadda. "Prosperous."

EDELINE—See Adeline.

EDEN—Hebrew: 'eden. "Delight, pleasure." One who typifies the ultimate in femininity.

EDINA—Scotch: Edina. "From the city of Edinburgh," or Old English: Ead-wine. "Prosperous friend." See Edwina. Poetical name for the capital city of Scotland.

EDITH—Old English: Eadgyth. "Rich gift." Edith Wharton, American novelist; Edith Evans, English actress; Edith Hamilton, American mythology writer; Edith Piaf, French chanteuse; Edie Adams, singer, actress; Eydie Gorme, singer.
English nicknames: Eda, Ede, Edie, Eyde, Eydie.
English variations: Editha, Edithe, Ediva, Edyth, Edythe.

Foreign variation: Edita (Italian).

EDIVA—See Edith.

EDLYN—Old English: Eathelin. "Noble little one," or Old Anglo-French: Ead-elin. "Prosperous little one."

EDMONDA—Old English: Eadmund. "Prosperous protector." The feminine of Edmund.
English variation: Edmunda.

EDNA—Hebrew: 'ednah. "Rejuvenation." One who knew the secret of renewal or transformation. Edna, wife of Enoch in the Biblical Apocrypha; Edna St. Vincent Millay, American poet; Edna Ferber, American novelist; Edna May Oliver, American actress.
English nicknames: Ed, Eddie.

EDREA—Old English: Ear-ric. "Prosperous, powerful." Feminine of Edric.
English variation: Edra.

EDWARDINE—Old English: Ead-weard. "Prosperous guardian." Feminine of Edward.

EDWINA—Old English: Eadwine. "Prosperous friend." The feminine of Edward.
English variation: Edina.

EGBERTA—Old English: Ecgbeorht. "Bright, shining sword." Feminine of Egbert.
English variation: Egbertina, Egbertine.

EGLANTINE—Old French: Aiglentine. "Sweetbrier rose; woodbine." A maiden compared to a wild rose. Eglentyne was a prioress in Chaucer's 14th-century writings.

EILEEN—Irish Gaelic: Eibhlin. "Light." The Irish form of Helen. Eileen Farrell, operatic singer; Eileen Heckart, American actress.

EIR—Old Norse: Eir. "Peace, clemency." All hearts are healed by inward peace. Eir was the Norse goddess of healing.

EKATERINA—See Catherine.

ELA—See Elaine, Ella.

ELAINE—See Helen. The old French form of Helen, popularized by Tennyson's "Elaine, the Lily Maid of Astolat."
English variations: Elane, Elayne.

ELATA—Latin: Elatus. "Lofty, elevated." A woman exalted for her beauty and for her womanly accomplishments.

ELBERTA—See Alberta. Clara Elberta Rumph, after whom the Elberta peach was named.

ELDORA—Spanish: El dorado. "Gilded one." A woman adorned with fine clothes and beautiful jewelry.

ELDRIDA—Old English: Eald-raed. "Old, wise counselor." The feminine form of Eldred.

ELEANORE—Old French: Elienor. "Light." An old form of Helen. A woman who disbursed knowledge. Eleanore of Aquitaine, English queen, died 1204; Nell Gwyn, famous 17th-century English actress; Eleonora Duse, Italian actress; Eleanor Roosevelt, wife of President Franklin D. Roosevelt; Eleanor Powell, actress.
English nicknames: El, Ella, Ellie, Nelda, Nell, Nellie, Nelly, Nora.
English variations: Eleanor, Elinor, Elinore, Eleonore, Eleonora, Elnore, Elaine, Leonore, Lenore.
Foreign variations: Eleonora (Italian), Éléonore (French), Leanor (Spanish), Eleonore (German, Danish).

ELECTRA—Greek: Elektra. "Brilliant one." A clever one with thoughts, words and deeds. Electra was the daughter of the hero Agamemnon in Greek history.

ELENA—See Helen. Elena Mercouri, Italian actress.

ELFRIDA—Old English: Aelfraed. "Enfin or good counselor." See Alfreda. Elfreda, second wife of England's 10th-century King Edgar.
English variations: Elfreda, Elfrieda.

ELGA—Gothic: Alhs; Slavic: Olga. "Holy, consecrated." Dedicated to a life of holiness.

ELINOR—See Eleanore.

ELISE—See Elizabeth.

ELISSA—See Elizabeth.

ELIZABETH—Hebrew: Elisheba. "Consecrated to God; oath of God." St. Elizabeth, mother of John the Baptist; Elizabeth I and II, English queens; Elizabeth Barrett Browning, English poet; Elizabeth Rudel Smith, Treasurer of the U.S.; actresses Elizabeth Taylor, Bette Davis, Betta St. John, Betty Grable, Betty Hutton.
English nicknames: Bess, Bessie, Bessy, Beth, Betsey, Betsy, Bett, Betta, Bette, Bettina, Betty, Elsa, Else, Elsie, Libby, Lisa, Lise, Liza, Lizzie, Lizzy.
English variations: Elisabeth, Elisa, Elise, Elissa, Eliza, Elyse, Lisbeth, Lizabeth.
Foreign variations: Elisabeth, Elise, Lisette, Babette (French), Elisabetta, Elisa (Italian), Elisabeth Elsa, Else (German, Dutch, Danish), Isabel, Belita, Elisa, Ysabel (Spanish), Elisabet (Swedish), Eilis (Irish), Ealasaid, Elspeth (Scotch).

ELLA—Old English: Aelf. "Elf; beautiful fairy maiden." A girl with a supernatural beauty. See Eleanore, Ellen. Ella Wheeler Wilcox, American poet.
English nicknames: Ellie, Elly.

ELLAMAY—Compound of Ella and May.

ELLEN—See Helen. Ellen Terry, famous English actress (1848-1928); Ellen Glasgow, author.

ELLICE—Greek: Elias. "Jehovah is God." A feminine form of Ellis and Elias.

ELMA—Greek: Elmo. "Amiable." A woman who had sympathy and affection for her friends. The feminine of Elmo.

ELMIRA—Old English: Aethel-Maere. "Noble, famous one." The feminine of Elmer. See Almira.

ELNA—See Helen.

ELNORA—See Eleanore.

ELOISE—See Louise.

ELRICA—Old German: Alh-ric. "Ruler of all."

ELSA—Old German: Elsa. "Noble one." See Elizabeth. Elsa, bride of Lohengrin in German legends; Elsa Maxwell, writer, lecturer; Elsa Lanchester, actress.

ELSIE—Old German: Elsa. "Noble one." See Elizabeth.

ELVA—Old English: Aelf-a. "Elfin, good." Her parents named their daughter their good fairy.
English variations: Elvia, Elvie, Elfie.
Foreign variations: Ailbhe (Irish).

ELVINA—Old English: Aelfwine. "Elfin friend." A child who had an imaginary playmate, an elf. The feminine form of Elvin.

ELVIRA—Latin: Albinia. "White, blonde." A blonde among dark-haired people. Donna El-

vira, in Mozart's famous opera *Don Giovanni*.
English variation: Elvera.
Foreign variations: Elvire (French), Elvira (Italian).

ELYSE—See Elizabeth.

ELYSIA—Latin: Elysia. "Sweetly blissful." Elysium in Roman myths was the dwelling place of happy souls.

EMERALD—Old French: Esmeraude. "The bright green emerald gem."
English nicknames: Em, Emmie.
English variation: Emerant.
Foreign variations: Emeraude (French), Esmeralda (Spanish).

EMILY—Gothic: Amala. "Industrious one," or Latin: Aemilia. "Flattering, winning one." See Amelia. Emily Brontë, English novelist; Princess Emily, daughter of England's King George II; Emily Dickinson, American poet; Emily Post, etiquette arbiter; Emilie Dionne, of the famous quintuplets.
English nicknames: Em, Emmie, Emmy.
English variations: Emelda, Emilie, Emlyn, Emlynne, Emera.
Foreign variations: Émilie (French), Emilie (German), Emilia (Italian, Spanish, Dutch), Eimile (Irish), Aimil (Scotch).

EMINA—Latin: Eminens. "Lofty, prominent one."

EMMA—Old German: Imma. "Universal one," or German: Amme. "Nurse." Emma Willard, 19th-century American educator; Emma Calvé, opera singer; Lady Emma Hamilton, 18th-century English beauty.
English nicknames: Em, Emmie, Emmi, Emmy.
English variations: Emelina, Emeline, Emelyne, Emmaline.
Foreign variations: Emma (Italian, German), Ema (Spanish).

EMMALINE—See Emma.

EMOGENE—See Imogene.

ENA—Irish Gaelic: Aine. "Little ardent or fiery one." A red-haired, loving Colleen. Princess Victoria Ena, born 1887, later Queen of Spain.

ENGELBERTA—Old German: Engel-berhta. "Bright angel." A little one haloed by golden hair.

ENID—Old Welsh: Enit. "Woodlark, purity." In the old English Arthurian legends Enid was the wife of Geraint. Enid Bennett, silent film actress; Enid Bagnold, English writer.

ENNEA—Greek: Ennea. "Nine; ninth child."

ENRICA—Italian: Enrica. "Ruler of an estate or home." Queen of her domicile. The Italian feminine form of Henry.

EOLANDE—See Yolande.

ERANTHE—Greek: Ear-anthemos. "Spring flower."

ERDA—See Eartha, Herta, Hertha.

ERICA—Old Norse: Eyrekr. "Ever powerful; ever-ruler." Foreign variation: Erika (Swedish).

ERIN—Irish Gaelic: Erinn. "From Ireland." The Emerald Isle, a fair jewel set in a tranquil sea. Erin O'Brien-Moore, actress.

ERLINE—See Earlene.

ERMA—Old German: Heri-man. "Army maid," or Latin: Herminia. "Noble one." Erminie Smith, American ethnologist.
English variations: Erma, Erminia, Erminie, Hermia, Hermine, Herminie, Hermione.

ERNA—Old English: Earn. "Eagle." See Ernestine.
English variation: Ernaline.

ERNESTINE—Old English: Earnest. "Earnest one." The feminine of Ernest. Ernestine Schumann-Heink, famous opera and concert singer.
English nickname: Erna.

ERTHA—See Eartha.

ERWINA—Old English: Earwine. "Sea friend." The feminine of Erwin.

ESME—See Esmeralda.

ESMERALDA—Spanish: Esmeralda. A name for the rarest of all gems. A character in Victor Hugo's *The Hunchback of Notre Dame.*
English nickname: Esme.

ESTA—Italian: Est. "From the East."

ESTELLE—French: Estoile. "A star." A mademoiselle who was the star of her family. Estella Lewis, 19th-century dramatist; Estelle Winwood, actress.
English nicknames: Essie, Stella, Stelle.
English variation: Estella.
Foreign variations: Estelle (French), Estrella, Estrellita (Spanish).

ESTHER—Hebrew: Ester; Persian: Esthur. "A star." The Biblical Esther was queen of Persia; Esther Forbes, American Pulitzer Prize winner, history, 1943; Esther Dale, actress.
English nicknames: Essa, Essie, Ettie, Etty, Hetty.
English variations: Ester, Hester, Hesther.
Foreign variations: Ester (Italian, Spanish), Hester, (Dutch), Eister (Irish).

ETHEL—Old English: Aethel. "Noble one." Ethel Barrymore,

noted American actress; Ethel Merman, American actress.
English variations: Ethelda, Ethelinda, Etheline, Ethelyn, Ethyl.

ETHELINDA—Old German: Athal-lindi. "Noble serpent." The serpent was a symbol of wisdom and life without end. See Ethel.

ETHELJEAN—Modern compound of Ethel and Jean.

ETTA—Old German: Etta. "Little One." See Henrietta.

EUCLEA—Greek: Eukleia. "Glory."

EUDOCIA—Greek: Eudoxos. "Of good respute."
English nicknames: Docie, Doxie, Doxy.
English variations: Eudosia, Eudoxia.

EUDORA—Greek: Eudora. "Generous."
English nickname: Dora.
Foreign variation: Eudore (French).

EUGENIA—Greek: Eugenios. "Well-born; noble." The feminine form of Eugene. Eugenie, Empress of France, 1826-1920; St. Eugenia, 3rd-century Roman martyr; Eugenie Leontovich, actress.
English nicknames: Genie, Gene.
Foreign variations: Eugénie (French), Eugenia (Italian, German, Spanish).

EULALIA—Greek: Eulalos. "Fair speech; well-spoken one." St. Eulalia, 4th-century martyr, patron of Barcelona.
English nicknames: Eula, Lallie.
Foreign variations: Eulalie (French), Eulalia (Italian, Spanish).

EUNICE—Greek: Eunike. "Happy, victorious one." Eunice was the mother of Timothy in the Bible.

EUPHEMIA—Greek: Euphemia. "Auspicious speech; good repute." St. Euphemia, 4th-century virgin martyr, is greatly venerated.
English nicknames: Effie, Effy.
Foreign variations: Euphémie (French), Euphemia (German), Eufemia (Italian, Spanish), Eadaoine (Irish).

EUSTACIA—Latin: Eustathius. "Stable, tranquil," or Latin: Eustachus. "Fruitful." The feminine form of Eustace.
English nicknames: Stacie, Stacey.

EVALEEN—See Eve.

EVANGELINE—Greek: Euangelos. "Bringer of good news." Famous from Longfellow's poem, *Evangeline*, and from Evangeline Booth of the Salvation Army;
Evangeline Adams, noted astrologer.
English nicknames: Eve, Eva, Vangie, Vangy.

EVE—Hebrew: Chavva. "Life-giving." The Biblical mother of mankind wife of the first man, Adam; divine symbol of the blessedness of motherhood. Actresses Eva Le Gallienne, Eve Arden, Eva Bartok, Eva Marie Saint.
English variations: Eva, Eba, Ebba, Evelina, Eveline, Evelyn, Evlyn.
Foreign variations: Eve (French), Eva (German, Italian, Spanish, Danish, Portuguese), Aoiffe, Evaleen (Irish).

EVELYN—See Eve. Also Irish Gaelic: Eibhlin. "Light." A form of Helen.

F

FABIA—Latin: Fabiana. "Bean grower." The feminine of Fabian.

FAITH—Middle English: Fayth. "Belief in God loyalty, fidelity." Faith Domergue, actress.
English nickname: Fay.

FANCHON—French: Françoise. "Free." An old French derivative of Frances. "To free men, threats are impotent."—Cicero.

FANNY—See Frances.

FARICA—See Frederica.

FAUSTINE—Latin: Fausta. "Lucky, auspicious." The feminine form of Faust.
English variations: Faustina, Fausta.
Foreign variations: Faustina (Italian), Faustine (French).

FAVOR—Old French: Favor. "Help, approval; good will conferred."

FAWN—Old French: Faon. "Young deer; reddish-brown colored." A tawny-haired girl, fleet as a deer.

FAY—Old French: Fae. "A fairy or elf," or Irish Gaelic: Feich. "Raven." A tiny child compared to the beneficient fairies. See Faith. Fay Bainter, Fay Compton, Faye Emerson, actresses.

FAYANNE—Compound of Fay and Anne.

FAYETTE—Old French: Fayette. "Little fairy." "O, thou art fairer than the evening air, clad in the beauty of a thousand stars." —Marlowe.

FAYME—Old French: Fame. "Lofty reputation; renown." Authorities eulogized this exalted woman.

FEALTY—Old French: Feelté. "Fidelity, allegiance." "To God, thy country and thy friend be true."—Vaughan.

FEDORA—See Theodora.

FELDA—Old German: Felde. "From the field." From the meadows filled with flowers and grain, this wholesome maiden came.

FELICE—Latin: Felicia. "Happy one." Continuous joy and exuberance encompassed this girl. The feminine form of Felix. Felice is a character in *Piers Plowman*, 14th-century English allegorical poem. Felicia De. Hemans, English poet (1793-1835); Felicia Farr, actress.
English variations: Felicia, Felicity, Felis.
Foreign variations: Félicie, Félise (French), Felicia (Italian), Felicidad (Spanish).

FENELLA—Gaelic Irish: Fionnghuala. "White-shouldered one." A reminder of snowcapped mountains above green fields. Fenella was an elflike character in Scott's *Peveril of the Peak.*
English variation: Finella.

FEODORA—See Theodora.

FERN—Old English: Fearn. "A fern; fernlike." Femininity in green, filigree fern lace.

FERNANDA—Gothic: Fairhonanth. "World-daring; life-adventuring." A feminine form of Ferdinand.
English variations: Ferdinanda, Fernandina.

FIDELIA—Latin: Fidelis. "Faithful one." One whose belief transcends unbelievers. Beethoven opera, *Fidelio;* Imogene called herself "Fidele" in Shakespeare's *Cymbeline.*

FIFI—See Josephine.

FILIPA—See Philippa.

FILMA—Old English: Filmen. "A veil or mist." A maid of ethereal beauty.

FIONA—Irish Gaelic: Fionn. "Fair one." Fiona MacLeod was a character in Sharp's writings.

FLANNA—Irish Gaelic: Flann. "Red-haired." The vivid red of the robin was in this temptress's hair.

FLAVIA—Latin: Flavia. "Yellow-haired one." A blue-eyed daughter crowned with gold.

FLETA—Old English: Fleotig. "Swift, fleet one."

FLEUR—French: Fleur. "A flower." A lovely girl like a lovely flower, is from God's garden.
English variation: Fleurette.

FLEURETTE—See Fleur.

FLORA—Latin: Flora. "Flower." Flora was the Roman goddess of flowers. Flora MacDonald, Scotch 18th-century heroine; Flora Steel, 19th-century English novelist; Flora Robson, English actress.
English nicknames: **Florrie, Florry.**
English variations: **Flore, Floria.**
Foreign variations: **Flore** (French), **Fiora** (Italian), **Flor** (Spanish).

FLORENCE—Latin: Florentia. "Blooming, flourishing, prosperous." Florence Nightingale, founder of nursing system (1820-1910); Florence Reed, actress.
English nicknames: **Flo, Florrie, Flossie.**
English variations: **Florance, Florinda, Floris, Florine.**
Foreign variations: **Fiorenza** (Italian), **Florencia** (Spanish), **Florentia** (German).

FLOWER—Old French: Fleur. "A blossom." How can words describe an orchid or a rose?

FONDA—Middle English: Fonned. "Affectionate, tender"; Latin: Fundus. "Foundation."

FORTUNE—Latin: Fortuna. "Fate; destiny."
Foreign variations: Fortuna (Italian, Spanish).

FRANCES—Latin: Franciscus. "Free one," or "From France." Frances Willard, 19th-century educator; Frances Perkins, former U.S. Secretary of Labor; Francesca da Rimini, 13th-century Italian heroine; Fannie Hurst, American novelist, Fanny Brice, actress and comedienne.
English nicknames: Fan, Fannie, Fanny, Fran, Frannie, Franny, Francie, Francy, Frankie.
English variations: Francine, Francyne.
Foreign variations: Françoise (French), Francesca, Cecca (Italian), Franziska (German), Francisca (Spanish).

FRANCINE—See Frances.

FREDA—See Frieda.

FREDELLA—Modern compound of Frieda and Ella.

FREDERICA—Old German: Fridu-ric. "Peaceful ruler." A woman who exemplified harmony and inward serenity. Frederika, Queen of Greece; Frederika Bremer, 19th-century Swedish novelist.
English nicknames: Freddie, Freddy.
English variations: Frederika, Frerika, Farica.
Foreign variations: Frédérique (French), Federica (Italian, Spanish), Friederike (German).

FREYA—Old Norse: Freyja. "Noble lady." Freya was the Norse goddess of love and beauty.

FRIEDA—Old German: Fridu. "Peaceful one." A fräulein so serene one rested in her presence. See Winifred. Frieda Inescort, actress.
English variations: Freda, Frida.

FRITZI—Old German: Friduric. "Peaceful ruler." A German feminine form of Fritz from Frederick. Fritzi Scheff, famous singer and entertainer.

FRONDE—Latin: Frondis. "A leafy branch."

FULVIA—Latin: Fulvia. "Tawny or yellow colored."

G

GABRIELLE—Hebrew: Gabhriel. "Man of God." An acknowledgment of the infinity and power of God by this woman. The feminine form of Gabriel. Gabriela Mistral, Nobel Prize winner, literature.
English nicknames: Gabie, Gaby.
English variations: Gabriela, Gabriella.

GAEA—Greek: Gaia. "The earth." "The earth a stage which God and nature do with actors fill."—Heywood. Gaia was the Greek deity of the earth, the mother of Uranus.
English variation: Gaia.

GAIL—Old English: Gal. "Gay, lively one." See Abigail. Gail Patrick Jackson, actress, producer; Gail Storm, actress.
English variations: Gale, Gayle.

GALATEA—Greek: Galateia. "Milky white." In the Greek legend, Pygmalion fashioned an ivory statue he called Galatea, which Aphrodite caused to come to life.

GALE—Old Norse: Gala: "To sing; singer." All things of nature sing or have a tone. See Gail, Abigail.

GALIENA—Old German: Galiana. "Lofty one."

GARDA—See Gerda.

GARDENIA—New Latin: Gardenia. "The fragrant white gardenia flower." A name for a girl of beauty. The gardenia was named for Alexander Garden, 18th-century American botanist.

GARLAND—Old French: Garlande. "A wreath or crown of flowers."

GARNET—Middle English: Gernet. "The garnet gem." A girl whose hair compared to the dark red garnet.
English variation: **Garnette**.

GAY—Old French: Gai. "Bright and lively."

GAYLE—See **Gail**.

GAZELLA—New Latin: Gazella. "Gazella or antelope." A lady graceful as a deer and as innocent as a lamb.

GELASIA—Greek: Gelastikos. "Inclined to laughter." A woman like a bubbling spring, whose motivating source was unknown.

GEMMA—Italian: Gemma. "A gem or precious stone." Compared to a precious jewel was this lovely lady.

GENE—See Eugenia. Author Gene Stratton Porter; Gene Tierney, actress.

GENEVA—Old French: Genèvre "Juniper tree." Elegance dressed in green.

GENEVIEVE—Old German: Geno-wefa. "White wave." See Guinevere. St. Geneviève, A.D. 420-519, patron of Paris; Genevieve Tobin, actress.

GEORGETTE—See Georgia.

GEORGIA—Latin: Georgia. "Farmer." The feminine of George. Georgia Neese Clarke, Treasurer of the U.S.; Georgia O'Keefe, artist; Georgette de la Plante, French modiste after whom "Georgette crepe" was was named.
English nicknames: **Georgie, Georgy**.
English variations: **Georgene, Georgette, Georgina, Georgine**.
Foreign variations: **Georgine, Georgienne, Georgette** (French), **Giorgia** (Italian), **Georgina** (German, Dutch).

GEORGIANA—See Georgia.

GERALDINE—Old German: Ger-walt. "Spear-mighty." The feminine of Gerald. Geraldine Farrar, operatic singer; Geraldine Page, actress.
English variation: **Geraldina**.
English nicknames: **Gerrie, Gerry, Jeri, Jerri, Jerry**.
Foreign variations: **Géraldine** (French), **Giralda** (Italian), **Gerhardine** (German).

GERANIUM—Greek: Geranion. "Crane." From usage, refers to the geranium flower.

GERDA—Old Norse: Garth-r. "Enclosure; protection." Gerda was the wife of the god Freyr in Norse myths; also a child in Andersen's fairy tale, *The Snow Queen*.
English variation: **Garda**.

GERMAIN—French: Germaine; Latin: Germanus. "A German." A blonde fräulein, a living representative of her country.

GERTRUDE—Old German: Ger-trut. "Spear-loved." Gertrude was one of the German mythical Valkyries. Notables include St. Gertrude the Great, 13th-century German mystic; Gertrude Atherton, novelist; Gertrude Stein, writer; Gertrude Lawrence, actress.
English nicknames: Gert, Gertie, Gerty, Trudie, Trudy.
Foreign variations: Gertrud (German), Gertrude (French), Gertrudis (Spanish), Geltruda (Italian).

GIACINTA—See Hyacinth.

GILBERTA—Old German: Gisil-berhta. "Brilliant pledge or hostage."
English nicknames: Gillie, Gilly.
English variations: Gilberte, Gilbertina, Gilbertine.

GILDA—Old English: Gyldan. "Covered with gold." An enchanting maiden with a crown of golden hair. Gilda was daughter of Rigoletto in the Verdi opera; Gilda Gray, dancer.

GILLIAN—Latin: Juliana. "Youthful, downy-haired one."
English nicknames: Gill, Gillie, Gilly, Jill.

GINA—See Regina. Gina Lollobrigida, Italian actress.

GINEVRA—See Guinevere.

GINGER—Latin: Gingiber. "Ginger spice or ginger flower." Named for the yellow or tawny ginger flower. See Virginia. Ginger Rogers, actress, dancer.

GISELLE—Old German: Gisela. "Pledge or hostage." A girl held as a hostage in war negotiations. Gisela, daughter of a French king,

married in A.D. 880, Rollo or Rolf, 1st Duke of Normandy, ancestor of William the Conqueror; Gisele MacKenzie, actress, singer.
English variations: Gisela, Gisella, Giselle.
Foreign variations: Gisele (French), Gisela (Italian, Spanish).

GITANA—Spanish: Gitana. "A gypsy."

GITHA—See Gytha.

GLADYS—Old Welsh: Gwladys; Latin: Claudia. "Lame one," or Latin: Gladiolus. "Small sword or gladiolus flower." Gladys Cooper, noted actress.
English nickname: Glad.
English variation: Gleda.

GLEDA—Old English: Gled. "Glowing; glad one." See Gladys.

GLENNA—Old Welsh: Glyn; Irish Gaelic: Ghleanna. "Dweller in a valley or glen." The feminine form of Glenn. Glenda Farrell, Glynis Johns, actresses.
English variations: Glenda, Glynis, Glynnie.

GLORIA—Latin: Gloria. "Glory; glorious one." "The shortest way to glory is to be guided by conscience."—Home. Actresses Gloria Swanson, Gloria de Haven, Gloria Grahame.
English variations: Glori, Gloriana, Gloriane, Glory.

GLORIANA—See Gloria.

GLYNIS—See Glenna.

GODIVA—Old English: Godgifu. "Gift of God." Lady Godiva of Coventry, wife of Leofric, Earl of Mercia, was heroine of the legend and poem by Tennyson.

GOLDIE—Old English: Goldie. "Golden one." A lady compared to the purest of all metals.
English variations: Golda, Goldy.

GRACE—Latin: Gratia. "Graceful, attractive one." A girl who walked in beauty and in rhythm. Grace Coolidge, wife of U.S. President Calvin Coolidge; Grace Moore, singer; Grace George, actress; Princess Grace Kelly Grimaldi of Monaco.
Foreign variations: Grazia (Italian), Engracia (Spanish), Giorsal (Scotch).

GREER—See Gregoria.

GREGORIA—Latin: Gregorius. "Watchful one." A mother's eternal vigilance over her children. A feminine form of Gregory. Greer Garson, actress.
English variation: Greer.

GRETA, GRETCHEN, GRETEL—See Margaret.

GRISELDA—Old German: Grisja-hilde. "Gray battle-maiden." Usage was initiated by a character in Boccaccio's *Decameron*.
English nicknames: Selda, Zelda.
English variations: Chriselda, Grishilda, Grizelda.
Foreign variations: Grishilde, Griseldis (German, Dutch), Griselda (French, Italian).

GUDA—Old English: Goda. "The good one."

GUENNA—See Gwendolyn, Guinevere.

GUIDA—Italian: Guida: "A guide." A woman ordained to guide or teach others. Alternate, Old German: Wido. "Warrior maid."

GUILLA—See Wilhelmina.

GUINEVERE—Old Welsh: Gwenhwyvar. "White wave, white phantom." The wife of King Arthur in English legends. See Gwendolyn, Genevieve.

English variations: Gaynor, Guenna, Gwenore, Jennifer, Genevieve, Vanora.
Foreign variation: Ginevra (Italian).

GUNHILDA—Old Norse: Gunn-hildr. "Warrior battle-maid." A daughter of the Norsemen who fought beside the man she loved. Gunhilda, daughter of a Polish duke, was the queen of Danish King Sweyn Forkbeard and mother of King Canute of Denmark and England, 11th century.

GUSTAVA—Swedish: Gustaf. "Staff of the Goths." A Gothic maid who was the support of the warriors' morale.
English nicknames: Gussie, Gussy.

GWENDA—See Gwendolyn.

GWENDOLYN—Old Welsh: Gwendolyn. "White-browed one." Gwendolyn was the wife of Merlin the magician in old Welsh legends. See Guinevere.
English nicknames: Gwen, Gwennie, Gwenda, Guenna.

GWYNETH—Old Welsh: Gwynedd. "White, blessed one."

GWYNNE—Old Welsh: Gwyn. "White or fair one."

GYPSY—Old English: Gipcyan. "A gypsy, a wanderer." A romantic wanderer from another country. Gypsy Rose Lee, actress.

GYTHA—Old English: Gytha. "A gift," or Old Norse: Guthr. "Warlike." She was a moody girl with a temper unrestrained. The Danish Countess Gytha was the wife of 11th-century Godwin, Earl of Wessex, England.
English variation: Githa.

H

HADRIA—See Adria.

HAGAR—Hebrew: Haghar. "Forsaken." Hagar in the Bible was an Egyptian slave of Sarah, the wife of Abraham. "Abraham sent Hagar with her son into the wilderness."—Gen. 21:14.

HAIDEE—Greek: Aidoios. "Modest; honored." "Modesty is the color of virtue."—Diogenes. Haidee was a Greek girl in Byron's *Don Juan.*

HALCYONE—Greek: Halkyon. "Sea-conceived; kingfisher bird." In Greek myths Halcyone, daughter of Aeolus, in grief for her drowned husband, threw herself into the sea and was changed into a kingfisher.

HALDANA—Old Norse: Half-Dan. "Half Danish." Feminine of Halden.

HALFRIDA—Old German: Hali-frid. "Peaceful heroine," or Old English: Heall-frith. "Peaceful hall or home."

HALIMEDA—Greek: Halimedes. "Thinking of the sea." A lass fascinated by the sea.
English nicknames: **Hallie, Meda.**

HANNAH—Hebrew: Khannah. "Graceful one." See Anne. Hannah in the Bible was the mother of the prophet Samuel.
English nicknames: **Hannie, Hanny, Annie, Nan, Nanny.**
English variations: **Anna, Anne, Hana.**

HARALDA—Old Norse: Haruald. "Army ruler." The feminine of Harold.
English nicknames: **Hallie, Hally.**

HARMONY—Latin: Harmonia. "Concord, harmony." One who knew the harmony and order of nature and the universe.
English variations: **Harmonia, Harmonie.**

HARRIET—Old French: Hanriette. "Estate or home ruler." The highest position attained by women. See Henrietta. Harriet Beecher Stowe, American writer (1812-1896); Harriet Hosmer, American sculptor.

HATTIE—See Henrietta.

HAZEL—Old English: Haesel. "Hazelnut tree." Among the ancient people of Europe the hazel branch was an insignia of rulership.
Foreign variations: **Aveline (French).**

HEATHER—Middle English: Hadder. "The heather flower or shrub." Heather Angel, actress.

HEBE—Greek: Hebe. "Youth." Hebe, daughter of Zeus in Greek myths, was the goddess of youth.

HEDDA—Old German: Hadu. "Strife." Famed from the Ibsen play *Hedda Gabler* and from Hedda Hopper, noted columnist, actress. See Hedwig.
English variations: **Heddi, Heddy, Hedy.**

HEDWIG—Old German: Haduwig. "Strife, fight."
English variations: **Heda, Hedwiga.**
Foreign variations: **Hedwig, Hedda (German), Hedvige (French), Hedy (Slavic).**

HEDY—Greek: Hedy. "Sweet; pleasant." See Hedda, Hedwig. Hedy Lamarr, actress.

HELEN—Greek: Helene. "Light; a torch." A woman whose wisdom and understanding were like a light in the dark. St. Helena, mother of the Emperor Constantine; Helen Keller, deaf, dumb, blind lecturer and writer; Helen Hunt Jackson, author; Helen Hayes, Helen Menken, noted American actresses.
English nicknames: Nell, Nellie, Nelly, Lena, Lina.
English variations: Helena, Helene, Eleanore, Elenore, Elinore, Elaine, Elane, Ella, Ellie, Elna, Ellen, Ellene, Ellyn, Elyn, Ellette, Nellette, Nelliana, Ileana, Elene, Leonora, Leonore, Lenore, Leora, Lora, Lana, Nora, Norah.
Foreign variations: Helena, Helene (German), Hélène (French), Elena (Italian, Spanish).

HELGA—Old German: Halag. "Pious, religious, holy." See Olga.

HELICE—Greek: Helike. "Spiral." Helike was a Greek nymph in mythology.

HELMA—Old German: Helm. "Helmer or protection."
English variation: Hilma.

HELOISE—See Louise. Heloise was a 12th-century French abbess and scholar, renowned for her romance with Abelard.

HENRIETTA—French: Henriette. "Estate or home ruler." A feminine form of Henry. Henrietta Maria, wife of England's King Charles I; Henrietta (Hetty) Green, American financier; Henrietta Crosman, American actress.
English nicknames: Hettie, Hetty, Hattie, Hatty, Ettie, Etta, Netta, Nettie, Netty, Yetta.
English variations: Harriet, Harriette, Harriott, Henriette.

Foreign variations: Henriette (French, German), Hendrika (Dutch), Henrika (Swedish), Enrichetta (Italian), Enriqueta (Spanish), Eiric (Scotch).

HENRIKA—See Henrietta.

HERA—Latin: Hera. "Ruling lady; queen." Hera was the Greek queen of heaven, the wife of Zeus.

HERMIA—See Hermione, Erma.

HERMINA—See Hermione, Erma.

HERMINE—See Hermione, Erma.

HERMIONE—Greek: Hermione. "Of the world or earth." See Erma. In Greek myths Hermione was the daughter of Menelaus and Helen of Troy. She was a queen in Shakespeare's *A Winter's Tale*. Namesakes include Hermione Baddeley, Hermione Gingold, English actresses.
English variations: Hermia, Hermine, Herminia.

HERMOSA—Spanish: Hermosa. "Beautiful." "I loved her for that she was beautiful."—P. J. Bailey.

HERTHA—Old English: Ertha. "Earth." A woman who mothered everyone and everything. Hertha was the old Teutonic goddess of peace and fertility.
English variations: Herta, Eartha, Ertha, Erda.

HESPER—Greek: Hesperos. "Evening or evening star." "The evening star, love's harbinger."—Milton. Hesperia was the Greek name for Italy. See Esther.
English variations: Hespera, Hesperia.

HESTER—Greek: Aster. "Star." See Esther. Hester Prynne, hero-

ine of Hawthorne's *The Scarlet Letter*.
English variation: Hesther.

HIBERNIA—Latin: Hibernia. "Ireland." Green is the island and beautiful, whether it is called Erin, Ireland, or the ancient Hibernia.

HIBISCUS—Latin: Hibiscus. "The marsh-mallow plant and flower."

HILARIA—Latin: Hilaria. "Cheerful one." The feminine form of Hilary. The name Hilaria is in the English "Hundred Roll's" dated 1273.

HILDA—Old German: Hilde. "Battle maid." Hilda was one of the Valkyrs in Norse myths, a beautiful maiden who escorted souls to Valhalla. St. Hild, an abbess, A.D. 614-680.
English variations: Hild, Hilde, Hilda, Hildie, Hildy.

HILDEGARDE—Old German: Hildi-gard. "Battle wand, battle maiden, battle stronghold." Hildegard, chanteuse and actress; Hildegarde Neff, actress; St. Hildegarde, German 11th-century abbess.

HILDEMAR—Old German: Hildi-mar. "Battle-celebrated or glorious." Renowned as a heroine of war.

HILDRETH—Old German: Hildi-reth. "Battle counselor." A feminine adviser on battle strategy.

HILMA—See Helma.

HOLDA—Old German: Holda. "Concealed" or "Beloved." Frau Holda in German myths led the spirits in a swift, celestial flight.
Foreign variations: Holde, Holle, Hulda (German).

HOLLY—Old English: Holen. "Holly tree," or Old English: Halig. "Holy." Named for the decorative Christmas holly; or for a child born at Christmas.

HONEY—Old English: Hunig. "Sweet one." An international term for one beloved. See Honoria.

HONORIA—Latin: Honoria. "Honor; honorable one."
English nicknames: Honey, Nora, Norah, Norry.

HOPE—Old English: Hopa. "Hope, expectation, desire." A name first popularized by the Puritans. Notables: Hope Emerson and Hope Lange, actresses.

HORATIA—Latin: Horatius. "Keeper of the hours." The feminine form of Horace.
English variation: Horacia.

HORTENSE—Latin: Hortensia. "Of the garden, a gardener." Hortense Eugenie Beauharnais, wife of France's ruler Louis Bonaparte; Hortense Alden, actress.
English variation: Hortensia.
Foreign variations: Hortensia (German, Dutch, Danish), Ortensia (Italian).

HUBERTA—Old German: Hugi-beraht. "Brilliant mind." A woman so clever she was honored with this name. The feminine of Hubert.

HUETTE—Old English: Hugi-et. Another name for feminine brilliance. The feminine of Hugh.
English variations: Hughette, Hugette, Huetta.

HULDA—Old German: Hulda. "Gracious or beloved." Hebrew: Huldah. "Weasel." Huldah was an ancient Biblical prophetess.
English nicknames: Huldie, Huldy.

HYACINTH—Greek: Hyakinthos. "Hyacinth flower or purple hyacinth color." A girl who left a memory of color and perfume. English nicknames: Cinthie, Cynthie, Jackie, Jacky.
English variations: Hyacintha, Hyacinthia, Jacintha, Jacinthe.

Foreign variations: Hyacinthe (French), Hyacinthie (German), Giacinta (Italian), Jacinta (Spanish).

HYPATIA—Greek: Hypate. "Highest." Hypatia was a beautiful, wise 5th-century martyred philosopher and mathematician.

I

IANTHA—Greek: Ianthinos. "Violet-colored flower."
English variations: Ianthina, Janthina.

IDA—Old German: Ida. "Industrious," or Old English: Eada. "Prosperous, happy." Mount Ida in Crete was famous in Greek myths, the place where Jupiter was concealed as a baby. Namesakes include Ida Tarbell, writer; Ida Lupino, actress.
English variations: Idalia, Idalina, Idaline.

IDUNA—Old Norse: Iduna. "Lover," or Old German: Ida. "Industrious." In Norse myths Iduna was the keeper of the golden apples of youth.
English variation: Idonia.

IERNE—Late Latin: Ierne. "Ireland."

IGNATIA—Latin: Ignatia. "Fiery, ardent one." A girl whose temper flared between her mirth and tears. The feminine form of Ignatius.

ILA—Old French: Isle. "From the island," or Old English: Ilde. "Battle."

ILEANA—Greek: Iliona. "From the city of Ilion or Troy." Ileana is a name used by Greek royalty.

ILKA—Slavic: Milka. "Flattering or industrious." A woman

honored for her vivacity and perseverance. Ilka Chase, actress-writer.

ILONA—Hungarian: Ilona. "Beautiful one." See Helen. Ilona Massey, actress.

IMOGENE—Latin: Imaginis. "An image or likeness." A small image of her mother. Imogene Coca, comedienne.

IMPERIA—Latin: Imperialis. "Imperial one."

INA—Latin: Ina. A Latin feminine name-suffix added to masculine names. See Catherine. Namesakes: Ina Coolbrith, writer; Ina Claire, Ina Balin, actresses.

INEZ—See Agnes.

INGRID—Old Norse: Ing-rida. "Hero's daughter." Ing was an ancient Norse name for a deity, hero, or son. Ingrid Bergman, actress.
Scandinavian variations: Inga, Inger, Ingunna, Ingaberg.

INIGA—Latin: Ignatia. "Fiery, ardent one." A transposed spelling of Ignatia, from the Spanish "Inigo."

IOLA—Greek: Iole. "Dawn cloud; violet color." In Greek myths Iole was a princess captured by Hercules.
English variation: Iole.

IOLANTHE—Greek: Iolanthe. "Violet flower." Popularized by a light opera by Gilbert and Sullivan. See Yolanda.

IONE—Greek. Iolaos. "Violet colored stone."
English variation: Iona.

IRENE—Greek: Eirene. "Peace." Irene was the Greek goddess of peace. Ierne Joliot-Curie, chemist; Irene Dunne, Irene Franklin, Irina Demich, actresses.
English nicknames: Rene, Rena.
English variations: Irena, Irina, Eirena, Erena.

IRETA—Latin: Iratus. "Angry, enraged one."
English variations: Iretta, Irette.

IRIS—Greek: Iris. "The rainbow, the iris flower." Iris was the messenger of the Greek gods, also representing the rainbow.

IRMA—Latin: Herminia. "High-ranking person," or Old German: Era-man. "Honorable, noble person. See Erma.

IRVETTE—Old English: Earwine. "Sea friend." The feminine form of Irving.

ISA—Old German: Isan. "Iron-willed one." A determined lady with a resolute will. See Isabel. Isa Miranda, Italian actress.

ISABEL—Old Spanish: Ysabel. "Consecrated to God." The Spanish form of Elizabeth. Isabel (Isabella) Queen of Spain, patroness of Columbus; three English queens named Isabel; Isabel Jewell, actress.
English nicknames: Issie, Issy, Bella, Belle, Ib, Isa.
English variations: Isabella, Isabelle.
Foreign variations: Isabeau (French), Isabella (Italian), Isabel (Spanish), Isabelle (German), Iseabal (Scotch).

ISADORA—Greek: Isidora. "Gift of Isis." The feminine form of Isidore. Isadora Duncan, dancer and teacher.

ISIS—Egyptian: Ast. "Supreme goddess or spirit." Isis was the ancient Egyptian goddess of motherhood, fertility, and the moon.

ISLEEN—See Aislinn.

ISOLDE—Old Welsh: Eysllt. "The fair one." In the old English King Arthur legends Isolde or Iseult was the wife of Tristan; Isolde is also in German myths and celebrated from Wagner's opera *Tristan and Isolde*.

ITA—Old Irish Gaelic: Itu. "Thirst." One with a desire for greater truth and knowledge. St. Ita or Ytha of Ireland, 6th century.

IVA—Old French: Ive. "Yewtree." See Jane.
English variation: Ivanna.

IVY—Old English: Ifig. "Ivy vine." The ivy was sacred to Dionysus and Bacchus in Greek and Roman myths. Ivy Baker Priest, former Treasurer of the U.S.

J

JACINTH—See Hyacinth.

JACOBA—Late Latin: Jacoba. "The supplanter." A substitute who attained honor and renown. A feminine form of Jacob, James.
English variations: Jacobina, Jacobine.

JACQUELINE—Old French: Jacqueline. "The supplanter." A feminine form of Jacob, James, Jacques. Jacqueline Kennedy, wife of U.S. President Kennedy; Jacqueline Cochran, aviatrix.
English nicknames: Jackie, Jacky.
English variations: Jacquelyn, Jacquetta, Jackelyn.

JADE—Spanish: Ijada. "Jade stone." No jewel could compare with that priceless gem called "daughter."

JAN—See Jane.

JANE—Hebrew: Y-hohhanan. "God is gracious." A feminine form of John. Jane Austen, English novelist; Jane Addams, social worker; actresses Jane Russell, Jane Powell, Jane Wyman, Jane Fonda, Jan Sterling, Jayne Mansfield.
English nicknames: Janie, Janey, Jeanie, Jeaney, Jennie, Jenny, Netta, Zaneta.
English variations: Jan, Janet, Janette, Janice, Janina, Janna, Jayne, Jean, Jeanne, Jennette, Joan, Joanne.
Foreign variations: Jeanne, Jeannette (French), Johanna (German), Gianina, Giovanna (Italian), Juana, Juanita (Spanish), Sinead, Shena, Sheena (Irish), Sine, Seonaid (Scotch).

JANET—See Jane.

JANICE—See Jane.

JANINA—See Jane.

JANTHINA—See Ianthe.

JARVIA—Old German: Gerhwas. "Spear-keen." Intelligence compared to the keenness of a spear.

JASMINE—Persian: Yasaman. "The jasmine flower."
English variations: Jasmina, Jasmin, Jessamine, Jessamyn.

JAYNE—Sanskrit: Jina. "Victorious one." "The smile of God is victory."—Whittier. See Jane.

JEAN—French: Jeanne. "God is gracious." See Jane. St. Jeanne D'Arc (Joan of Arc), 15th-century French heroine; Jean Simmons, actress.

JEANNETTE—See Jane.

JEMIMA—Hebrew: Yemimah. "A dove." The dove is an ancient symbol of purity and peace. In the Bible Jemima was a daughter of Job.
English nicknames: Jemie, Jemmie, Mimi.

JENNIFER—See Guinevere. Jennifer Jones, actress.

JENNY—See Jane.

JEREMIA—Hebrew: Yirmeyah. "Exalted of the Lord." The feminine form of Jeremiah.
English nicknames: Jeri, Jerrie, Jerry.

JERI—See Geraldine, Jeremia.

JERRI, JERRY—See Geraldine, Jeremia.

JERUSHA—Hebrew: Yerushah. "Possessed or married."

JESSAMINE—See Jasmine.

JESSICA—Hebrew: Yishay. "Wealthy one." Jessica was Shylock's daughter in Shakespeare's *Merchant of Venice*. Jessica Tandy, actress; Jessica Dragonette, singer.
English variations: Jessie, Jessalynn.

JESSIE—See Jessica.

JEWEL—Old French: Juel. "A precious thing or gem."

JILL—See Julia, Gillian. Jill St. John, actress.

JINX—Latin: Inyx. "A charm or spell." One with elegance of grace and beauty that was enchanting. Jinx Falkenburg, actress.
English variation: Jynx.

JOAKIMA—Hebrew: Jehoaiakim. "The Lord will set up or judge." One whom God has lifted up spiritually. The feminine of Joachim.

JOAN—See Jane. Joan Sutherland, opera singer; actresses Joan Crawford, Joan Fontaine.

JOANNA—See Jane.

JOBINA—Hebrew: Iyyobh. "Afflicted, persecuted." "The gem cannot be polished without friction, nor man perfected without trials."—Chinese Proverb.
English variation: Jobyna.

JOCELYN—Old English: Goscelin. "The just one." A feminine variation of Justin.
English variations: Jocelyne, Joceline, Joscelyne, Josceline, Justine.

JOCOSA—Latin: Jocosus. "Humorous, joking." One who had a sense of humor that brought laughter to her home.

JODY—See Judith.

JOHANNA—See Jane.

JOLETTA—See Julia.

JORDANA—Hebrew: Yarden. "The descending." The feminine form of Jordan.

JOSEPHA—See Josephine.

JOSEPHINE—Hebrew: Yoseph. "He shall add; increaser." The feminine of Joseph. Josephine, Empress of France, 1763-1814; Josephine Hull, American actress.
English nicknames: Jo, Josie.
English variations: Josepha, Josephina, Joette, Josette.

Foreign variations: Josephe, Josephine, Fifi, Fifine (French), Josepha (German), Giuseppina (Italian), Josefa, Josefina, Pepita (Spanish), Seosaimhthin (Irish).

JOVITA—Latin: Jovialis. "Joyful."

JOY—Latin: Joia. "Joyful one." She was like a girl enchanted, enraptured by all life.
English variations: Joice, Joyce, Joyous.

JOYCE—French: Joyeuse. "Joyful." See Joy.

JUANITA—See Jane.

JUDITH—Hebrew: Yehudith. "Praised." A woman commended for her patience and womanliness. In the Bible Judith's story is in the Apocrypha; Judith Anderson, Judy Canova, actresses.
English nicknames: Judie, Judy, Jody.
Foreign variations: Giuditta (Italian), Siobhan (Irish), Siubhan (Scotch).

JUDY—See Judith.

JULI—See Julia.

JULIA—Latin: Julia. "Youthful one." The feminine form of Julius. Julia Ward Howe, poet, social worker (1819-1910); Juliana, Queen of the Netherlands; Julia Peterkin, writer; actresses Julia Marlowe, Julie Harris, Julie London.
English nicknames: Julie, Jill, Juli, Gillie.
English variations: Juliet, Julietta, Juliette, Juliana, Julina, Juline, Joletta.
Foreign variations: Giulia, Giulietta (Italian), Julie, Juliette (French), Julia, Julieta (Spanish), Julie (German), Sile (Irish), Sileas (Scotch).

JULIET—See Julia.

JUNE—Latin: Junius. "Born in June." Actresses June Walker, June Havoc, June Haver, June Allyson.
English variations: Junia, Juniata, Junette, Junine.

JUNELLA—Compound of June and Ella.

JUNO—Latin: Juno. "Heavenly one." Juno was the queen of the goddesses in Roman myths.

JUSTINE—Latin: Justus. "The just one." A feminine form of Justus.
English variations: Justina, Justa, Joscelyn.
Foreign variations: Giustina (Italian), Justina (Spanish).

K

KAMA—Sanskrit: Kama. "Love." The Hindu love god Kama, a handsome youth, rode a parrot, carried a bow of sugar cane with a bowstring of bees, each arrow tipped with a flower. Cupid's dart is tipped with honey for the heart.

KARA—See Cara.

KAREN—See Catherine. Karen Horney, noted psychologist, writer.

KARLA—See Charlotte.

KASMIRA—Old Slavic: Kazatimiru. "Commands peace." This woman's presence demanded peace and serenity.

KATHERINE—See Catherine.

KATHLEEN—See Catherine.

KAYE—See Catherine.

KEELY—Irish Gaelic: Cadhla. "Beautiful one." Keely Smith, singer.

KELDA—Old Norse: Kelda. "A spring." A young girl compared to a bubbling stream, pure and undefiled.
English nickname: Kelly.

KELLY—Irish Gaelic: Ceallach. "Warrior maid." Used for both girls and boys. See Kelda.

KERRY—Irish Gaelic: Ciarda. "Dark one."

KETTI—See Catherine. Ketti Frings, writer, dramatist.

KETURA—Hebrew: Qeturah. "Incense." Named for the incense that perfumed the air during religious services.

KEVIN—Irish Gaelic: Caoimhin. "Gentle, lovable."

KIM—Old English: Cyne. "Chief, ruler." Actresses Kim Stanley, Kim Novak, Kim Hunter.

KIMBERLY—Old English: Cyne-burh-leah. "From the royal-fortress meadow."

KINETA—Greek: Kinetikos. "Active one." A flash of light and beauty, then only my lady's perfume.

KIRSTIN—See Christina.

KORA—See Cora.

KOREN—Greek: Kore. "The maiden." The lotus flower cannot compare to a lovely woman.

KYNA—Irish Gaelic: Conn. "Intelligence, wisdom," or Irish Gaelic: Con. "High, exalted." The feminine of Conan.

L

LALA—Slavic: Lala. "The tulip flower." Named for the beautiful tulip that blooms in the early spring.

LALITA—Sanskrit: Lalita. "Pleasing; artless." A woman free from deceit and pretense.

LANA—See Helen, Alanna. Lana Turner, actress.

LANETTE—Old Anglo-French: Lane-et. "From the little lane."

LANI—Hawaiian: Lani. "Sky."

LANNA—See Helen, Alanna.

LARA—Latin: Lara. "Shining, famous one," or Etruscan: Lar. "Lordly." In Roman myths Lara was a daughter of the river god Almo.

LARAINE—Latin: Larus. "Seabird; gull." A maid free as the birds that skim over the sea. See Lorraine. Laraine Day, actress.
English variations: Larine, Larina.

LA REINA—Spanish: La reina. "The queen."
English variations: Lareina, Larena.
Foreign variation: La reine (French)

LARISSA—Greek: Larissa. "Cheerful one."

LARK—Middle English: Larke. "Singing lark or skylark." The lark soars high in the sky as it sings.

LA ROUX—French: Roux. "Red-head."

LASCA—Latin: Lassus: "Weary; weariness."

LASSIE—Middle English: Lasse. "Little girl." A Scotch derivation.

LATONIA—Latin: Latona. "Sacred to Latona." Latona was the mother of Apollo and Diana in Roman myths.

LAURA—Latin: Laurea. "A crown of laurel-leaves." A wreath of laurel-leaves was the ancient emblem of victory. Feminine of Lawrence. Loretta Young, Laura Hope Crews, Laurette Taylor, Lauren Bacall, actresses; Lorna Doone, fictional heroine.
English nicknames: Laurie, Lori, Lorrie.
English variations: Laurel, Lauren, Laureen, Laurena, Laurene, Lauretta, Laurette, Lora, Loren, Lorena, Lorene, Loretta, Lorette, Lorita, Lorna.
Foreign variations: Lorenza (Italian) Laure, Laurette (French), Laura (Spanish, German).

LAUREN—See Laura.

LAVEDA—Latin: Lavare. "Purified one."
English variations: Lavetta, Lavette.

LA VERNE—Old French: La vergne. "From the alder-tree grove," or Latin: Vernis. "Spring-like."

LAVINIA—Latin: Lavare. "Purified," or Latin: Lavinia. "Lady from Latium."
English variation: Lavina.

LEA—See Lee, Leah.

LEAH—Hebrew: Leah. "Weary one." Leah was Jacob's wife in the Bible.
English variations: Lea, Lee.

LEALA—Old French: Leial. "Faithful, loyal one."
English variations: Lealia, Lealie.

LEANA—See Liana.

LEATRICE—Compound of Leah and Beatrice. Leatrice Joy, actress.

LEDA—See Letitia. In Greek myths Leda was the mother of Helen of Troy.

LEE—Old English: Leah. "From the pasture meadow," or Irish Gaelic: Laoidheach. "Poetic." Lee Patrick, actress.

LEILA—Arabic: Layla. "Dark as night." The magic of the night was in this maiden's eyes and in her fragrant hair. Leila was the heroine of an ancient Persian legend, "Leila and Majnun."
English variations: Leilia, Lela, Lila.

LEILANI—Hawaiian: Lei-Lani. "Heavenly flower." Was it the wild ginger blossom or the bird-of-paradise flower for which this girl was named?

LELA—See Leila.

LEMUELA—Hebrew: Lemu'el. "Consecrated to God." The feminine of Lemuel.

LENA—Latin: Lena. "She who allures." See Madeline, Helen. Lena Horne, singer, actress.
English variation: Lina.

LENIS—Latin: Lenis. "Smooth, soft, mild." A white lily that walked and talked, was this fair woman.
English variations: Lena, Lene, Leneta, Lenita, Lenos.

LENORE—See Eleanore, Helen.

LEODA—Old German: Leute. "Woman of the people." Hope and beauty, strength and faith, a woman who personified her nation.
English variation: Leota.

LEOLA—Latin: Leo. "Lion." A feminine form of Leo.

LEOMA—Old English: Leoma. "Light, brightness." A radiant girl whose very presence seemed clothed in splendor.

LEONA—French: Léonie. "Lion." A woman with the strength, courage, and fortitude of a lioness.
English variations: Leonie, Leoine, Leonelle.

LEONARDA—Old Frankish: Leon-hard. "Lion-brave."
Foreign variations: Leonarde (Italian), Leonarda (German, Spanish).

LEONORE—See Eleanore, Helen. Leonora, heroine of Beethoven's opera *Fidelio;* Leonora Speyer, American poet.

LEONTINE—Latin: Leo. "Lion-like." Leontyne Price, opera singer.
English variation: Leontyne.

LEOPOLDINE—Old German: Leut-pald. "Bold for the people."
English variations: Leopolda, Leopoldina.

LEOTA—See Leoda.

LESLIE—Scotch Gaelic: Liosliath. "Dweller at the gray fortress." An old castle clothed in vines, flowers and memories.
English variation: Lesley.

LETA—See Letitia.

LETHA—Greek: Lethe. "Forgetfulness." In Greek myths, the river of oblivion whose waters caused forgetfulness.
English variations: Lethia, Leitha, Leithia, Leda, Leta.

LETITIA—Latin: Laetitia. "Gladness." The joyousness of spring was in this maiden's heart. English nicknames: Leta, Leda, Letty, Tish. English variations: Leticia, Lettice. Foreign variations: Letizia (Italian), Léetice (French), Leticia (Spanish).

LETTY—See Letitia.

LEVANA—Late Latin: Levana. "The rising sun." A sister of the dawn. The Roman goddess Levana was the patron of childbirth, lifting newborn children from the earth.

LEVINA—Middle English: Levene. "A flash, lightning." A beautiful girl whose presence could light up the darkest day.

LEWANNA—Hebrew: Lebhanah. "The beaming, white one; the moon." A girl so pure and fair they named her for the moon.

LEXINE—See Alexandra.

LEYA—Spanish: Ley. "Loyalty or law."

LIANA—French: Liane. "A climbing vine." English variations: Liane, Lianna, Lianne, Leana.

LIBBY—See Elizabeth. Libby Holman, actress, chanteuse.

LILA—See Leila, Lillian. Lila Lee, actress.

LILAC—Persian: Nilak. "Bluish color; a lilac flower." A girl of Persia distinguished for her blue-black hair.

LILIAN—See Lillian.

LILITH—East Semitic: Lilitu. "Belonging to the night." Lilith, the first wife of Adam in ancient eastern mythology.

LILLIAN—Latin: Lilium. "A lily flower." A girl named for the beautiful lily-of-the-valley. Lillian Russell, actress, singer (1861-1922); Lily Pons, opera singer; Lillian Gish, Lillian Roth, actresses. English nicknames: Lil, Lili, Lilli, Lilly, Lily. English variations: Lilian, Liliana, Liliane, Lilyan, Lilias. Foreign variations: Lili (German), Lis (French), Lilias (Scotch).

LILY—See Lillian.

LINA—See Lena, Caroline, Adeline.

LINDA—Spanish: Linda. "Pretty one." "Truth exists for the wise, beauty for the feeling heart."—Schiller. Actresses Linda Darnell, Linda Christian, Linda Watkins. English variations: Lynda, Lindy.

LINETTE—Old French: Linette. "The linnet bird," based on Latin: Linum. "Flax." The linnet feeds on flax seeds. In the King Arthur legends Lynette was the beloved of Gareth. English variations: Linnet, Linetta, Lynette.

LINNEA—Old Norse: Lind. "Lime-tree." Named after the beautiful tree dressed up in spring blossoms.

LISA—See Elizabeth. Lisa Del Giocondo, subject of Da Vinci's "Mona Lisa."

LISBETH—See Elizabeth.

LITA—See Carmel.

LIVIA—See Olivia.

LIZABETH—See Elizabeth. Lizabeth Scott, actress.

LODEMA—Old English: Ladmann. "Pilot or guide." A lady with a magnetic personality, who was a leader of others.

LOIS—See Louise.

LOLA—See Dolores, Charlotte. Lola Montez, renowned 19th-century actress.

LOLITA—See Dolores.

LONA—Middle English: Al-one. "Solitary, lone one." A lady waiting for her knight in armor.

LORA—See Laura, Helen.

LORELEI—German: Lurlei. "Siren of the River Rhine."

LORENA—See Laura.

LORETTA—See Laura.

LORI—See Laura.

LORNA—See Laura.

LORRAINE—Old German: Lothar-ingen. "Place of Lothar." Lothar, an ancient warrior name, meant "Famous army." Lotharingen was known by the French as the Duchy of Lorraine.
English variation: Loraine.

LOTTA—See Charlotte.

LOTUS—Greek: Lotos. "The lotus flower." The sacred Nile River lily of ancient Egypt.

LOUELLA—See Luella.

LOUISE—Old German: Hlutwig. "Famous warrior-maid." Louisa M. Alcott, author; Louise de la Valliere, 17th-century French beauty; Luisa Tetrazzini, opera singer.
English nicknames: Lu, Lou, Lulie, Lulu.
English variations: Louisa, Eloisa, Eloise, Aloisa, Aloisia, Aloysia, Alison, Allison, Ludwiga, Lois, Loise, Louisette, Loyce.
Foreign variations: Louise, Héloise, Lisette (French), Luise, Ludovika (German), Luisa (Italian, Spanish), Liusadh (Scotch), Labhaoise (Irish).

LOVE—Old English: Lufu. "Tender affection."

LOYCE—See Louise. Loyce Whiteman, singer.

LUANA—Old German-Hebrew: Lud-khannah. "Graceful battle maid." Popularized by the heroine of the stage play, *Bird of Paradise.* Luana Patten, actress.
English nicknames: Lou, Lu.
English variations: Luane, Louanna, Luwana.

LUCIANNA—Italian compound from Lucy and Anne. Lucianna Paluzzi, Italian actress.

LUCILLE—See Lucy. Lucille Ball, film and television actress; St. Lucilla, 3rd-century Roman martyr.

LUCINDA—See Lucy. A 17th-century poetic spelling of Lucy. English nickname: Cindy.

LUCRETIA—Latin: Lucretia. "Riches; reward." Good deeds bring lasting compensation. Lucretia, a virtuous Roman wife, was immortalized in Shakespeare's poem, *The Rape of Lucrece.* Lucrezia Borgia, Italian Duchess of Ferrara (1480-1519); Lucretia Mott, 19th-century American reformer; Lucrezia Bori, opera singer.
Foreign variations: Lucrèce (French), Lucrezia (Italian), Lucrecia (Spanish).

LUCY—Latin. Lucia. "Light; bringer of light." One who brings knowledge to humanity. St. Lucy of Syracuse, famous 3rd-century virgin martyr; Lucy Stone, 19th-century pioneer in advancement of women.
English nicknames: Lou, Lu, Luce.
English variations: Luciana, Lucida, Lucinda, Lucile, Lucille, Lucette.

Foreign variations: Lucie, Lucienne (French), Lucie (German), Lucia (Italian), Lucia, Luz (Spanish), Liusadh (Scotch), Luighseach (Irish).

LUDELLA—Old English: Hludaelf. "Famous elf." A pixy maid named for the legendary spirits of the land.

LUDMILLA—Old Slavic: Ljudumilu. "Beloved by the people." A girl whose charm was modesty. Ludmilla Tcherina, noted ballerina.
Foreign variation: Ludmila (German).

LUELLA—Old English: Hludaelf. "Famous elf." Louella O. Parsons, noted columnist; Luella Gear, actress.
English variations: Louella, Loella, Luelle.

LUNETTA—Italian: Lunetta. "Little moon." Derived from Luna, the name of the Roman moon goddess.

LUPE—Spanish-Mexican: Santa Maria de Guadalupe. A shortening through usage of the last syllables of the saint's name. Alternate, Latin: Lupus. "Wolf." Lupe Velez, actress.

LURLINE—German: Lurlei. "Siren." Circe, the temptress of Ulysses, was another siren. See Lorelei. Lurline Matson, wife of the founder of the shipping lines, after whom several liners were named.
English variations: Lura, Lurleen, Lurlene, Lurette.

LUVENA—Middle-English-Latin: Luve-ena. "Little beloved one."

LYDIA—Greek: Lydia. "A woman of Lydia." Lydia, an ancient country of Asia Minor, was famed for its kings, Midas and Croesus, who became symbols of wealth.
Foreign variations: Lydie (French), Lidia (Italian, Spanish).

LYNN—Old English: Hlynn. "A waterfall or pool below a fall." Lynn Fontanne, famous actress; Lynn Bari, film actress.

LYRIS—Greek: Lyristes. "Player on a lyre or harp." One whose music brought a glimpse of paradise.
English variation: Lyra.

LYSANDRA—Greek: Lysander. "Liberator of men." The feminine of Lysander, an ancient Greek hero-name. One who freed the souls of men from the mundane things of earth.

M

MAB—Irish Gaelic: Meadhbh. "Mirth, joy." Mab, Queen of the Fairies in Irish myths, was used in that role by Shakespeare in *Romeo and Juliet*.
English variations: Mave, Meave, Mavis.
Foreign variations: Mab, Meave (Irish), Mavis (French).

MABEL—Latin: Amabilis. "Lovable one." "All true love is grounded on esteem."—Buckingham. Mabel Walker Willebrandt, U.S. attorney.
English variations: Mabelle, Mable, Maybelle.
Foreign variations: Mabelle (French), Maible (Irish), Moibeal (Scotch).

MADELINE—Greek: Magdalene. "From Magdala." Magdala, meaning "Elevated, magnificent," on the Sea of Galilee in Palestine, was the birthplace of St. Mary Magdalene, whose sins were forgiven by Jesus Christ. Namesakes include Madeline, daughter of King Francis I of France, who became queen of James V of Scotland; Madeline Bridges, poet; Madeleine Carroll, actress.
English nicknames: Mada, Maddie, Maddy, Mala, Lena, Lina, Maud.
English variations: Madeleine, Madalena, Madelon, Madlen, Madlin, Madel, Madella, Madelle, Magdala, Magdalen, Magdalene, Malena, Malina, Marleen, Marlene, Marline.
Foreign variations: Madelaine, Madeleine, Madelon (French), Magdalena, Madalena (Spanish), Magdalene, Marlene, Madlen, Magda, Mady (German), Maddalena (Italian), Maighdlin (Irish).

MADELLE—See Madeline.

MADGE—See Margaret.

MADORA—See Media.

MADRA—Spanish: Madre. "Mother." A woman blessed by motherhood.

MAE—See May.

MAGDA—See Madeline, Maida.

MAGDALENE—See Madeline.

MAGGI—See Margaret.

MAGNILDA—Old German: Magan-hildi. "Powerful battle maiden," or Latin-German: Magn-hildi. "Great battle maiden." A heroine name.

MAGNOLIA—New Latin: Magnolia. "Magnolia flower and tree." A flower from heaven, resting in its mother's arms. The magnolia was named for Pierre Magnol, 17th-century French botanist.
English nicknames: Mag, Maggie, Nola, Nolie.

MAHALA—Hebrew: Mahalah. "Tenderness." Mahalia Jackson, noted singer.
English variations: Mahalah, Mahalia.

MAIA—See Mary.

MAIDA—Old English: Maegth. "A maiden." A girl enchanting as the song of Circe.
English nicknames: Maidie, Mady.
English variations: Maidel, Mayda, Mayde, Maydena.
Foreign variations: Magd, Mady, Magda (German).

MAISIE—See Margaret.

MAJESTA—Latin: Majesta. "Majestic one." As magnificent as a mountain dressed in sunlit clouds. Majesta or Maia, consort of Vulcan, was the Roman goddess of the month of May.

MALA—See Madeline. Mala Powers, actress.

MALINA—See Madeline, Malinda.

MALINDA—Greek: Meilichos. "Mild, gentle one." Soft and sweet as a day in spring.
English nicknames: Mallie, Mally, Lindy.
English variations: Malinde, Melinda, Malena, Malina, Melina.

MALVA—Greek: Malako. "Soft, slender," or Latin: Malva. "Mallow flower."
English variation: Melva, Melba.

MALVINA—Irish Gaelic: Maolmin. "Polished chief." The feminine of Malvin and Melvin. In ancient Irish myths that were called the Fenian Cycle, Malvina was a heroine.
English nicknames: Malva, Malvie, Melva, Melvie, Mal, Mel.
English variations: Malvina, Melvina, Melvine.

MANETTE—See Mary.

MANON—See Mary.

MANUELA—Spanish: Manuela. "God with us." A Spanish feminine form of Emmanuel.

MARA—Hebrew: Marah. "Bitter." A form of Mary, a name claimed by Naomi in the Biblical Book of Ruth. Namesakes include Mara English, Mara Corday, actresses.
English variations: Maralina, Maraline.

MARALINE—See Mara.

MARCELLA—Latin: Marcella. "Belonging to Mars; martial one." A feminine form of Marcus. Marcella, a Roman widow, was a 4th-century disciple of St. Jerome; Marcella Sembrich, operatic soprano.
English nicknames: Marcie, Marcy.
English variations: Marcelle, Marcellina, Marcelline, Marcile, Marcille.
Foreign variations: Marcelle (French), Marcela (Spanish).

MARCIA—Latin: Marcia. "Belonging to Mars; martial one." A feminine form of Marcius and Marcus. St. Marcia was an early Christian martyr.
English nicknames: Marcie, Marcy.
English variations: Marcelia, Marcile, Marcille, Marchita, Marquita, Marsha.

Foreign variations: Marcie (French), Marcia (Italian).

MARCILE—See Marcella, Marcia.

MARELDA—Old German: Marhildi. "Famous battle maiden." English variation: Marilda.

MARELLA—See Mary.

MARETTA—See Mary.

MARGARET—Latin: Margarita. "A pearl." Honoring Margaret, patron saint of Scotland. Notables: Princess Margaret of England; Margaret Mitchell, author of *Gone with the Wind;* Margaret Mead. sociologist; Margaret Leech, historian; actresses Margaret Sullavan, Margaret O'Brien.
English nicknames: Marga, Marge, Margie, Margo, Madge, Mag, Maggie, Maggi, Maisie, Meg, Meta, Greta, Peg, Peggie, Peggy, Rita.
English variations: Margareta, Margarita, Margery, Margory, Marget, Margette, Margalo, Marguerite, Marjorie, Marjory, Miriam.
Foreign variations: Margherita (Italian), Margarita, Rita (Spanish), Marguerite, Margot (French), Margarethe, Margarete, Grete, Gretal, Grethel, Gretchen (German), Margarete (Danish), Margaretha (Dutch), Mairghread (Irish, Scotch).

MARGOT—See Margaret.

MARI—See Mary. Mari Aldon, actress.

MARIA-MARIE—See Mary.
Namesakes: Maria Theresa, Empress of Austria (1717-1780); Marie Curie, co-discoverer of radium; Maria Tallchief, ballerina; actresses include Marie Dressler, Marie Wilson, Marie McDonald.

MARIAN—Hebrew-English: Mary-Anne. "Bitter-graceful," or Old French: Mari-on. "Little Mary." See Mary, Anne. St. Mariana, Spanish, "Lily of Madrid," 1565-1624; Marian Anderson, singer.
English variations: Marion, Mariana, Marianna, Marianne, Maryanne.
Foreign variations: Marianna (Italian), Marianne (French), Mariana (Spanish), Marianne (German).

MARIETTA—See Mary.

MARIGOLD—English: Marygold. "The golden marigold flower." A girl with hair like yellow gold.

MARILYN—See Mary. Marilyn Miller, Marilyn Monroe, Marilyn Maxwell, actresses.
English variations: Marilin, Marylin.

MARINA—Latin: Marina. "Of the sea." St. Marina of Alexandria, early Christian martyr; Princess Marina of Greece was married to Prince George of England, 1934.

MARJORIE—Old French: Margerie. "A pearl." An early form of Marguerite, the French spelling of Margaret. Marjorie Kinnan Rawlings, writer; actresses Marjorie Lawrence, Marjorie Main, Marjorie Rambeau.
English nicknames: Marge, Margie, Margy, Margo, Marje, Marjie, Marjy.
English variations: Marjory, Margery, Margory.
Foreign variations: Meadhbh (Irish), Marcail (Scotch).

MARLA—See Mary. Marla English, actress.

MARLENE—See Madeline. Marlene Dietrich, actress.
English variations: Marleen, Marleene, Marlena, Marline.

MARMARA—Greek: Marmareous. "Flashing, glittering, radiating." A name expressing great personal charm and magnetism.

MARSHA—See Marcia.

MARTHA—Aramaic: Martha. "Lady or mistress." A woman of discretion, the queen of her home. Martha was the sister of Mary and Lazarus in the Bible. The most famous American with this name was Martha Washington; others include Martha Raye and Martha Hyer, actresses.
English nicknames: Mart, Marta, Marth, Martie, Marty, Mattie, Matty, Pat, Patty.
English variations: Marthena, Martita, Martella.
Foreign variations: Marthe (French, German), Marta (Italian, Spanish, Swedish), Moireach (Scotch).

MARTINA—Latin: Martina. "Martial, warlike one." A name from planet Mars, which the ancients called the god of war.
English nicknames: Marta, Martie, Marty, Tina.
Foreign variation: Martine (French).

MARVEL—Old French: Merveille. "A miracle; a wonderful thing." A baby is a miracle of God.
English variations: Marva, Marvela, Marvella, Marvelle.

MARY—Hebrew: Marah; Miryam. "Bitter or bitterness." Call me not Naomi (the pleasant), call me Mara (the bitter) for the Almighty hath dealt very bitterly with me."—Ruth, 1:20. Marah was the Hebrew word for the bitter resin myrrh, used in Biblical times as incense and perfume. Mary honors the Blessed Virgin. Namesakes include Mary, Queen of Scots; Mamie Eisenhower; writers Mary Roberts Rinehart,

Mary Austin, Mary Chase; actresses Mary Pickford, Mary Martin, Mary Nash, Maria Schell, Mamie Van Doren.
English nicknames: Mame, Mamie, Mayme, May, Mari, Moll, Mollie, Molly, Polly.
English variations: Mara, Maria, Marie, Maretta, Marette, Marella, Marietta, Marilla, Marilyn, Marla, Marya, Miriam, Muriel.
Foreign variations: Marie, Manette, Manon, Maryse (French), Maria. Marita, Mariquita (Spanish), Maire, Maura, Maureen, Mearr, Moira, Moire, Moya, Muire (Irish), Marya (Slavic), Mairi, Moire, Muire (Scotch).

MARYANN—A compound of Mary and Ann. See Marian.

MARYLOU—A compound of Mary and Louise.

MARYRUTH—A compound of Mary and Ruth.

MARYSE—See Mary.

MATHILDA—Old German: Mat-hilde. "Mighty battle-maiden." Matilda was the queen of William the Conqueror, Norman-French ruler who subjugated England in 1066; Matilda Heron, 19th-century actress; Maude Adams, actress.
English nicknames: Mat, Mattie, Matty, Tilda, Tillie, Tilly.
English variations: Matilda, Maud, Maude.
Foreign variations: Mathilde (German, French), Matelda (Italian), Matilde (Spanish), Maitilde (Irish).

MATTEA—Hebrew: Mattithyah. "Gift of God." A feminine form of Matthew.
English variations: Matthea, Matthia, Mathea, Mathia.

MAUDE—See Mathilda.

MAUREEN—Irish Gaelic: Mairin. "Little Mary." See Mary. Alternate, Old French: Maurin. "Of dark complexion." A feminine form of Maurice. Maurine Neuberger, U.S. Senator; Maureen O'Hara, actress.
English variations: Mora, Moira, Moreen, Moria, Maurine.
Foreign variations: Morena (Spanish), Maurizia (Italian).

MAUVE—Latin: Malva. "Violet or lilac colored." A name for a violet-eyed little girl.
English variation: Malva.

MAVIS—French: Mauvis. "Song thrush." See Mab.

MAXINE—Latin: Maxima. "Greatest." In legend and in history, greatness of character is recorded. Maxine Elliott, Maxene Andrews, actresses.
English nicknames: Maxie, Maxy.

MAY—Latin: Maia. "Great one." Used for daughters born in May. Maia was the Roman goddess of spring, wife of Vulcan. See Mary. Dame May Whitty, May Robson, actresses.
English variations: Mae, Maia, Maya, Maye.

MAYBELLE—Latin-French: Maia-belle. "Great and beautiful one." See Mabel.

MAYDA—See Maida.

MAYME—See Mary.

MEARA—Irish Gaelic: Meara. "Mirth."

MEDIA—Greek: Medeon. "Ruling," or Latin: Media. "Middle child." Medea was an ancient Greek enchantress.
English variations: Medea, Madora, Medora.

MEDORA—See Media.

MEGAN—Greek: Megas. "Great, mighty one," or Irish Gaelic: Meghan. "Margaret."

MEHITABEL—Hebrew: Meheytabel. "Benefited by God." Popularized by the *Archie and Mehitabel* stories by Don Marquis.
English variations: Mehetabel, Mehitabelle.
English nicknames: Hetty, Hitty.

MELANIE—Greek: Melanos. "Black or dark." An epithet for Demeter in Greek myths; she wore dark clothing as the earth goddess of winter.
English nicknames: Mel, Mellie.
English variations: Melanie, Melany.

MELANTHA—Greek: Melanthos. "Dark flower."

MELBA—See Malva.

MELICENT—See Millicent.

MELINA—Latin: Melinus. "Canary-yellow colored." See Madeline, Malinda, Carmel. A girl named for the domesticated yellow song bird.

MELINDA—See Malinda.

MELISSA—Greek: Melissa. "Honey; a bee."
English nicknames: Mellie, Melly, Millie, Milly, Lissa.
English variations: Melicent, Melisent, Melitta, Melessa, Melisse, Millicent, Millisent, Melita.

MELVA—See Malva, Malvina.

MELVINA—See Malvina.

MERCEDES—See Mercy.

MERCIA—Old English: Mercia. "From the kingdom of Mercia." From the 6th to 9th centuries Mercia comprised central England.

MERCY—Middle English: Merci. "Compassion, pity." Primary usage is from the Spanish "Santa Maria de las Mercedes," "Our Lady of Mercy." Mercy Warren, American writer and patriot (1728-1814).
Foreign variation: Mercedes (Spanish).

MEREDITH—Old Welsh: Maredud. "Mortal day," or Old Welsh: Meredydd. "Guardian from the sea." Also a masculine name.
English nickname: Merry.
English variation: Meridith.

MERLE—Latin: Merula. "Thrush; blackbird." A brunette beauty of ancient Rome. Also used as a masculine name. Merle Oberon, actress.
English variations: Merl, Merlina, Merline, Meryl, Myrlene, Merola.

MERNA—See Myrna.

MEROLA—See Merle.

MERRY—Middle English: Merie. "Mirthful; pleasant." See Meredith. Merry Anders, actress.

MERTICE—Old English: Maertisa. "Famous and pleasant." English variation: Merdyce.

MERYL—See MERLE.

MESSINA—Latin: Messena. "That which is in the middle; a middle child."

META—Latin: Meta. "The measurer; a goal." A young lady who planned her life and worked to fulfill her visions. See Margaret.

METIS—Greek: Metis. "Wisdom; skill." Metis was the first wife of Zeus, the Greek king of the gods.

MICHAELA—Hebrew: Mikhael. "Who is like God?" A feminine form of Michael.

English nicknames: Mickie, Micky.
English variations: Michaelina, Michaeline, Michelina, Micheline, Micaela, Mikaela.
Foreign variations: Michel, Michelle (French), Michaella (Italian), Miguela, Miguelita (Spanish).

MIGNON—French: Mignon. "Dainty, graceful, darling." A lovely maiden who seemed to fly on winged mercurial feet. Heroine of the Ambroise Thomas opera and of Goethe's *Wilhelm Meister*.
French variation: Mignonette.

MILDRED—Old English: Mildraed. "Mild counselor," or Old English: Mild-thryth. "Mild power." Mildred Natwick, actress; Mildred MacAfee, Navy WAVE head, World War II.
English nicknames: Mil, Millie, Milly.
English variation: Mildrid.

MILLICENT—Old German: Amala-sand. "Industrious and true." See Melissa.
English nicknames: Mil, Millie, Milly, Lissa.
English variations: Melicent, Mellicent, Milicent, Milissent, Millisent.
Foreign variations: Melisande (French), Melisenda (Spanish).

MIMI—See Miriam. Mimi is the heroine of the Puccini opera *La Boheme*. Mimi Benzell, actress.

MINA—See Minna, Wilhelmina. Mina Ellis, Canadian author and explorer.

MINDY—See Minna. Mindy Carson, singer.

MINERVA—Greek: Menos. "Force, purpose," or Latin: Minerva. "The thinking one." A woman whose clever reason exceeded that of the women of her day.

Minerva was the highest goddess of Rome, coupled with Jupiter and Juno.
English nicknames: Min, Minnie, Minny.
Foreign variation: Minette (French).

MINNA—Old German: Minne. "Love." Medieval German Minnesingers were ballad singers of noble birth. See Wilhelmina.
English nicknames: Min, Mina, Minnie, Minda, Mindy.
English variations: Minetta, Minette.

MINNIE—See Minna, Minerva, Wilhelmina. Minnie Maddern Fiske, noted actress.

MINTA—Greek: Mintha. "The mint plant." So sweet, this child was a reminder of a garden of pungent mint.
English variation: Mintha.

MIRA—Latin: Mira. "Wonderful one."
English variations: Mirilla, Mirella, Mirelle, Myra, Myrilla.

MIRABELLE—Spanish: Mirabella. "Beautiful looking one."
English variations: Mirabel, Mirabella.

MIRANDA—Latin: Miranda. "Admirable; extraordinary."

MIRIAM—Hebrew: Miryam. "Bitter." See Mary. The Biblical Miriam was the sister of Moses and Aaron. Miriam Hopkins, Mitzi Green, actresses.
English nicknames: Mimi, Minnie, Mitzi.

MIRNA—See Myrna.

MITZI—See Miriam.

MODESTY—Latin: Modesta. "Modest one." A humble girl free from vanity and ostentation.
Foreign variations: Modesta (Italian), Modestia (Spanish), Modestine (French).

MOIRA—Greek: Moirai. "Merit," or Irish Gaelic: Moire. "Great one." Also an Irish form of Mary, Martha, and Agnes. Moira Shearer, actress. See Mary.

MOLLY—See Mary. Molly Picon, actress.

MONA—Greek: Monos. "One; single one," or Italian: Mona. "My lady," or Irish Gaelic: Muadhnait. "Noble one." Famous from Da Vinci's painting, *Mona Lisa*. Mona Freeman, actress. See Monica.

MONICA—Late Latin: Monica. "Admonition; advice." A woman who counseled others in behaviorism. Honoring St. Monica, 4th century, mother of St. Augustine. Monica Lewis, actress, singer.
English nickname: Mona.
Foreign variation: Monca (Irish).

MOREEN—See Maureen.

MORGANA—Old Welsh: Morgant. "Shore of the sea." In ancient English legends Morgan Le Fay was the sister of King Arthur.

MORIA—See Maureen.

MORNA—See Myrna.

MOSELLE—Hebrew: Mosheh. "Taken out of the water." A French feminine form of Moses.
English variation: Mozelle.

MURIEL—Greek: Myrrha. "Myrrh; bitter." See Mary. Muriel Kirkland, actress.
English variations: Murial, Meriel.
Foreign variations: Muireall (Scotch), Muirgheal (Irish).

MUSETTA—Old French: Musette. "A quiet, pastoral aria or song." Musetta is a character in Puccini's *La Boheme*.

MUSIDORA—Greek: Mousadoros. 'Gift of the Muses." The Greek Muses were nine goddesses who presided over songs, art, poetry and the sciences.

MYRA—Greek: Mirias. "Abundance." See Mira. Myra Hess, noted pianist.

MYRLENE—See Merle.

MYRNA—Irish Gaelic: Muirne. "Polite, gentle." Called a lady for her manners and her looks. Myrna Loy, actress.
English variations: Merna, Mirna, Moina, Morna, Moyna.

MYRTLE—Greek: Myrtos. "The myrtle." A tribute to obstacles overcome. Myrtle was the ancient Greek symbol of triumph and victory.
English variations: Myrta, Myrtia, Myrtis, Mirtle, Mertle, Mertice, Myrtice.

N

NADA—Slavic: Nada. "Hope." English variation: Nadine.

NADINE—See Nada.

NAIDA—Latin: Naiadis. "A water or river nymph."

NAIRNE—Scotch Gaelic: Amhuinn. "From the alder-tree river." Used also as a masculine name.

NANCY—An enlargement of Nan. See Anne. Namesakes include Nancy Hanks, mother of Abraham Lincoln; Nancy Kelly, Nancy Kwan, actresses.

NANETTE—See Anne. A variation of Nan. Nanette Fabray, actress.

NAOMI—Hebrew: Naomi. "The pleasant one." "And the name of the man was Elimelech, and the name of his wife Naomi."—Ruth 1:2.
English variations: Naoma, Noami.

NAPEA—Latin: Napaea. "She of the valleys." Illusive girl of mythical fame, seen by dreamers and poets. In Greek myths Napaea was a nymph of the valleys and glens.

NARA—Old English: Nearra. "Nearer or nearest one."

NARDA—Latin: Nardus. "Fragrant ointment." When this dream of loveliness passed by, she left a fragrance in one's memory.

NATA—Hindustani: Nat. "A rope-dancer." The girl moved rhythmically as if she were enchanted by sweet music.

NATALIE—Latin: Natalis. "Birthday or natal day." Natalie Talmadge, Natalie Wood, actresses.
English nicknames: Nat, Nattie, Natty, Nettie, Netty.
English variations: Natala, Natalia, Nataline, Nathalia, Nathalie, Noel, Noelle, Novella.
Foreign variations: Natalie, Noelle (French), Natalia (Spanish), Natasha (Slavic).

NATHANIA—Hebrew: Nathan. "A gift," or "Given of God." A feminine form of Nathan.
English variation: Nathene.

NATIVIDAD—Spanish: Natividad. "Christmas, born at Christmas."

NEALA—Irish Gaelic: Niall. "Champion." A feminine form of Neal and Neil.

NEBULA—Latin: Nebula. "Mist, vapor, a cloud." She was beauty, sunlit clouds, blue sky, stars of the night.

NEDA—Slavic: Nedjelja. "Born on Sunday," or Old English: Eadweard. "Prosperous guardian," a feminine form of Ned from Edward. Nedda is the heroine of the Leoncavallo opera *Pagliacci*.
English variation: Nedda.

NELDA—Old English: At-theneldre. "From a home at the eldertree," or a development of Nell and Nellie from Eleanore.

NELLIE—See Helen, Cornelia, Eleanore. Nellie Melba, opera singer; Nellie Tayloe Ross, former Wyoming governor.
English variations: Nelly, Nellis, Nelle, Nell, Nela, Nelda, Nelia, Nella, Nelita, Nelina.

NELLWYN—Greek-Old English: Helene-wine. "Light or bright friend."

NEOLA—Greek: Neos. "Youthful one."

NEOMA—Greek: Neomenia. "The new moon." "What is there in thee, moon! That thou shoulds't move my heart so potently."—Keats.

NERINE—Greek: Nereos. "A swimmer; one from the sea." A form of Nereis, an ancient seanymph.
English variations: Nerice, Nerissa.

NERISSA—See Nerine.

NESSA—A development of Nessie. See Agnes.

NETTA—A development of Antonia, Henrietta, Jeannette.

NEVA—Spanish: Nieve. "Snow or extreme whiteness." Fair and bright as a snowcapped, sunlit mountain in winter. See Nevada.

NEVADA—Spanish: Nevada. "White as snow." English nickname: Neva.

NEYSA—A development of Agnes. Neysa McMein, artist.

NICOLE—Greek: Nikolaos. "Victorious army, victorious people." A girl who successfully represented her people. A feminine form of Nicholas. Nicole Maurey, actress. English nicknames: Nickie, Nicky, Nikki. English variations: Nicola, Nichola, Nicolina, Nicoline.

NIKE—Greek: Nike. "Victory."

NIKKI—See Nicole.

NILA—Latin: Nilus. "The River Nile of Egypt." Nile blue were the eyes of their daughter. Also a development of Nela from Cornelia.

NINA—Spanish: Niña. "Girl." A daughter surrounded by a bright nimbus of parental love. Nina Cecilia Bowes-Lyon, mother of Queen Elizabeth, wife of George VI of England; Nina Foch, actress. English variations: Ninetta, Ninette.

NINON—See Anne.

NISSA—Scandinavian: Nisse. "A friendly elf or brownie." A wee little miniature of a woman, snuggled safe in her mother's arms.

NITA—See Anne, Jane. Also Choctaw Indian: Nita. "A bear."

NIXIE—Old German: Nichus. "A little water-sprite." Lovers saw this fairy when the moon was full.

NOAMI—See Naomi.

NOELLE—See Natalie.

NOKOMIS—Chippewa Indian: Nokomis. "Grandmother."

NOLA—Late Latin: Nola. "A small bell," or Irish Gaelic: Nuallan. "Famous." English variation: Nolana. See Olivia.

NOLANA—See Nola.

NOLETA—Latin: Nolentis. "Unwilling." English variation: Nolita.

NONA—Latin: Nona. "Ninth child." English nickname: Nonie.

NORA—See Eleanore, Honoria. Nora Perry, poet, journalist (1841-1896).

NORBERTA—Old German: Nor-beraht. "Brilliant heroine," or Old Norse: Njorth-r-biart-r. "Brilliance of Njord." Njord was the ancient Norse deity of the winds and of seafarers. A feminine form of Norbert.

NORDICA—German: Nordisch. "From the north." An adventuress from the land of the midnight sun.

NORMA—Latin: Norma. "A rule, pattern or precept." A lady of perfection. Popularized by Bellini's opera Norma. Norma Shearer, Norma Talmadge, actresses.

NORNA—Old Norse: Norn. "A Norn or Viking goddess of fate."

NOVIA—Latin: Nova. "Young person," or Latin: Novicius. "Newcomer." English variation: Nova.

NUALA—Irish Gaelic: Nuala from Fionnghuala. "Fair-shouldered one."

NUMIDIA—Latin: Numidia. "A nomad, or one from Numidia." A girl who liked to travel.

NYDIA—Latin: Nida. "From the nest." A sweet seedling cradled in her parents' house.

NYSSA—Greek: Nyssa. "Starting point," or Latin: Nisus. "Striver toward a goal." The journey's end is personified in this girl's name.

NYX—Greek: Nyx. "Night," or Latin: Nix. "Snowy or white haired." A Greek goddess who personified the night.

O

OBELIA—Greek: Obelos. "A pointed pillar."

OCTAVIA—Latin: Octavia. "Eighth child." The feminine of Octavius.
English nicknames: Tavie, Tavy.
Foreign variations: Ottavia (Italian), Octavie (French).

ODELETTE—French: Odelette. "A little ode or lyric song." A mademoiselle whose voice was a melodious rondeau.
English variation: Odelet.

ODELIA—Old Anglo-French: Odel. "Little wealthy one." A feminine form of Odell. Odette Myrtil, actress.
English variations: Odella, Odelinda, Odilia, Otha, Othilia, Odette, Ottilie.

ODESSA—Greek: Odysseia. "The Odyssey, a long journey." A form from the ancient Greek epic poem of the travels of Odysseus. The Russian city of Odessa, founded by Catherine the Great in 1794, was a namesake.

ODETTE—See Odelia.

OLA—See Olga.

OLGA—Old Norse: Halag. "Holy one." A saintly woman who dedicated her services to God. Olga was a favorite name in the imperial Russian family. St. Olga, 10th-century duchess of Kiev.
English variations: Olva, Olivia, Olive, Elga.

OLINDA—Latin: Olida. "Fragrant." This child was compared to a sweet-smelling herb.

OLIVE—Latin: Olivia. "Olive tree or olive branch." The olive branch was symbolic of peace. St. Olivia was a virgin Christian martyr of Carthage. Olive Schreiner, English writer (1862-1920); Olivia de Havilland, actress.
English nicknames: Ollie, Olly, Livia, Nollie, Nola, Livvie.
English variations: Olivia, Olivette, Olva, Olga.

OLYMPIA—Greek: Olympia. "Of Olympus; heavenly one." Named for the beautiful canopy of stars that light the earth at night.
Foreign variations: Olympe (French), Olympie (German), Olimpia (Italian).

OMA—Arabic: Amir. "Commander." The feminine of Omar.

ONA—Latin and Irish Gaelic: Una. "Unity." See Una. Ona Munson, actress; Oona Chaplin, wife of comedian Charlie Chaplin, Oona White, choreographer.
Foreign variations: Oonagh, Oona (Irish).

ONAWA—American Indian: Onawa. "Wide-awake one." A vigilant Indian maiden, keen and observant of life's dangers and joys.

OPAL—Sanskrit: Upala. "A precious stone." The magical gem of the ancients, that had captured the colors of heaven.
English variations: Opalina, Opaline.

OPHELIA—Greek: Ophis. "Serpent," or Greek: Ophelos. "Help," or Greek: Ophelimos. "Useful." The serpent was an ancient insignia for wisdom. A serpent with its tail in its mouth symbolized eternity, that is, no beginning or end. Ophelia is a famous character in Shakespeare's *Hamlet.*
English variations: Ofelia, Ofilia. Foreign variation: Ophélie (French).

ORA—Latin and Old English: Ora. "Shore or seacoast," or Latin: Aurum. "Gold."
English variations: Orabel, Orabelle.

ORALIA—Latin: Aurelia. "Golden." A precious girl with shining yellow hair and sun-kissed skin to match.
English variations: Oriel, Orielda, Oriole, Oriola, Orielle, Orlena, Orlene, Oralie.

ORDELLA—Old German: Ordalf. "Elfin spike or spear."

OREA—Greek: Orea. "Of the mountain."

ORELA—Latin: Oracula. "A divine announcement." As this woman listened, she learned.

ORENDA—Iroquois Indian: Orenda. "Magic power."

ORIANA—Latin: Oriens. "The dawning," or Latin: Aurea. "Golden one." In the medieval story *Amadis of Gaul,* Oriana was the beloved of Amadis.

ORIEL—See Oralia.

ORLENA—See Oralia.

ORNA—Irish Gaelic: Odharnait. "Pale or olive color."

ORPAH—Hebrew: Orpah. "A fawn." "My beloved is like a roe or a young hart."—The Song of Solomon, 2:9.

ORSA—See Ursula.

ORVA—Old English: Ord-wine. "Spear friend." The feminine of Orvin.

OTTILIE—See Odelia.

OZORA—Hebrew: Uzziye. "Strength of the Lord."

P

PALLAS—Greek: Pallas. "Wisdom; knowledge." Names of old pagan gods still last, though they belong to ages past. Pallas was a name for the Greek Athena who represented wisdom.

PALMA—Latin: Palma. "A palm." Used for a child born on Palm Sunday.
English variations: Palmira, Palmyra.

PALOMA—Spanish: Paloma. "A dove." Who has not heard a baby coo as softly as a mourning dove, English variations: Palometa, Palomita.

PAMELA—Greek: Pam-meli. "All-honey." Pamela was invented by Sir Philip Sidney in 1590 for a character in *Arcadia.* Namesakes: Pamela Tiffin, Pamela Mason, actresses.

English nicknames: Pam, Pammy.
English variations: Pamella, Pamelina.

PANDORA—Greek: Pan-doron. "The all-gifted one." A maiden imbued with many talents. Pandora in the Greek myth was given a sealed box that contained all human ills, which escaped when she opened it.

PANPHILA—Greek: Panphilos. "The all-loving one." "Love can neither be bought nor sold; its only price being love."—Proverb.

PANSY—French: Pensée. "A thought." "There's rosemary, that's for remembrance; . . . and there is pansies, that's for thoughts."—Shakespeare, *Hamlet*.

PANTHEA—Greek: Pantheios. "Of all the gods." The Roman Pantheon was built to honor all the ancient gods.

PARNELLA—Old French: Pernel. "Little rock." A feminine form of Parnell from Peter.
English variation: Pernella.

PARTHENIA—Greek: Parthenos. "Maidenly."

PATIENCE—French: Patience. "Endurance with fortitude." This name was eulogized by our perseverant Pilgrim fathers.

PATRICIA—Latin: Patricius. "Noble one." The feminine form of Patrick. St. Patricia, 7th century, is one of the patrons of Naples, Italy. Patrice Munsel, opera singer; Patricia McCormick, champion diver; Patty Berg, champion golfer; actresses Patrice Wymore, Patti Page.
English nicknames: Pat, Patti, Pattie, Patsy, Patty.
Foreign variations: Patrice (French), Patrizia (Italian).

PAULA—Latin: Paulus. "Little." Small in stature but big in love and constancy. Used in honor of St. Paul the Apostle, and St. Paula, a 3rd-century Nicomedian martyr. Pauline Lord, Paula Prentiss, Paula Raymond, Paulette Goddard, actresses.
English nicknames: Pauly, Polly.
English variations: Paulette, Pauline, Paulita.
Foreign variations: Paule, Paulette, Pauline (French), Paola, Paolina (Italian), Paula, Paulina (Spanish).

PAULINE—See Paula.

PEACE—Latin: Pacis. "Tranquillity." "Let us therefore follow after the things that make for peace." Philippians.

PEARL—Late Latin: Perla. "A pearl." Oh pearl of flawless beauty, your enchantment is your purity. Pearl Buck, writer; Pearl White, silent screen star.
English variations: Pearla, Pearle, Pearline.

PEGGY—See Margaret. Peggy Ashcroft, Peggy Wood, actresses.

PELAGIA—Greek: Pelagos. "From the sea." Man's longing and imagination have made him see beautiful mermaids enticing ships at sea.

PENELOPE—Greek: Penelope. "Worker of the web; weaver." Patiently our ancestors in days gone by, wove soft skeins into cloth to glorify and cover man. In Greek myths Penelope wove each day and unraveled the cloth at night. Namesakes: Penny Singleton, actress.
English nicknames: Pen, Penny.

PENTHEA—Greek: Pentheus. "Mourner," or Greek: Penta. "Fifth child."

PEONY—Latin: Paeonia. "The god of healing." Sacred to Pan, the Greek god, and also to Apollo. A flower name.

PEPITA—See Josephine.

PERDITA—Latin: Perdita. "The lost." The king's daughter in Shakespeare's *The Winter's Tale*.

PERFECTA—Spanish: Perfecta. "Perfect, accomplished one."

PERNELLA—See Parnella.

PERSEPHONE—Greek: Persephonia. "Sacred to the goddess Persephone." Persephone was the Greek deity of the underworld.

PERSIS—Latin: Persis. "A woman from Persia." St. Paul honored Persis in the Bible.

PETRA—Latin: Petra. "Rock." One strong and everlasting like the Great Pyramid of Gizeh.
English variations: Petronia, Petronella, Petronilla.
Foreign variations: Pierette, Perrine (French), Petronille (German).

PETUNIA—Tupi Indian: Petum. "Reddish-purple flowered petunia." The talismanic flower name of an Indian maid.

PHEBE—See Phoebe.

PHEDRA—Greek: Phaidra. "Bright one." Phaidra was a daughter of King Minos and the wife of Theseus in ancient Crete.

PHILANA—Greek: Philein. "Loving." A lover of all God's creations, this girl was beloved by all.
English variations: Philene, Philina, Philida.

PHILANTHA—Greek: Philanthos. "Flower lover." "Floral apostles that in dewy splendor weep without woe, and blush without a crime."—Horace Smith.

PHILBERTA—Old English: Fela-beorht. "Very brilliant one."

PHILIPPA—Greek: Philippos. "Lover of horses." Famed in history from Philippa of Hainault, queen of England's 13th-century King Edward III.
English nicknames: Phil, Phillie.
Foreign variations: Filippa (Italian), Felipa (Spanish), Philippine (German).

PHILOMELA—Greek: Philomelos. "Lover of song." A woman who heard the melodies of all nature. A name for the nightingale.

PHILOMENA—Greek: Philomene. "Lover of the moon." A Grecian who never slumbered; when the moon was full she walked in silver sheen.

PHOEBE—Greek: Phoibe. "Bright one." The feminine of Phoebus, a name for the sun god Apollo. St. Phoebe of Corinth, 1st century; Phoebe Cary, poet.
English variation: Phebe.

PHOENIX—Greek: Phoinix; Egyptian: Bennu. "The heron or eagle," or "The rejuvenated and reincarnated one." The legendary bird that lived 500 years, was consumed by fire and rose in youthful freshness from its ashes.

PHYLLIS—Greek: Phyllis. "A green branch." A mythological princess changed into an almond tree. Actresses Phyllis Haver, Phyllis Calvert.
English variations: Phillis, Phyllys.
Foreign variation: Filide (Italian).

PIERETTE—See Petra.

PILAR—Spanish: Pilar. "A fountain-basin or pillar." What is woman, but the foundation of her family. A Spanish designation for the Virgin Mary. Pilar Wayne, wife of John Wayne, actor.

PIPER—Old English: Pipere. "A pipe player." Piper Laurie, actress.

PLACIDA—Latin: Placidus. "Gentle, peaceful one."

PLATONA—Greek: Platos. "Broad-shouldered." A feminine form of Plato, the great Greek philosopher.

POLLY—See Mary, Paula. Polly Bergen, singer, actress.

POLLYANNA—Compound of Polly and Anne.

POMONA—Latin: Pomona. "Fruitful." Pomona was the Roman goddess of fruit.

POPPY—Latin: Papaver. "A poppy flower." A beautiful flower that intoxicates.

PORTIA—Latin: Portio. "An offering." A gift to God of frankincense and bitter myrrh. Also the title of an ancient Roman clan, Porcius. Leading character in Shakespeare's *Merchant of Venice*.

PRIMA—Latin: Primus. "First child."

PRIMAVERA—Spanish: Primavera. "Springtime." Soft hair and docile eyes bathed in the springtime air.

PRIMROSE—Latin: Primula. "Little first one." A little spring rose bowing low in the rain, giving thanks.

PRISCILLA—Latin: Priscilla. "From past or primitive times." St. Priscilla was a 1st century hostess to St. Peter at Rome. Priscilla Mullins, wife of John Alden, famous in New England history. English nicknames: Pris, Prissie.

PROSPERA—Latin: Prosperus. "Favorable, auspicious.

PRUDENCE—Latin: Prudentia. "Foresight; intelligence." A prescience of things to come was a gift of this girl. Prudence Penny, home economics columnist. English nicknames: Pru, Prue.

PRUNELLA—French: Prunelle. "Prune colored; the color of sloe plums." Prunella dressed in purple.

PSYCHE—Greek: Psyche. "Soul or mind."

PYRENA—Greek: Pyrene. "Fiery one," or "Fruit kernel." Pyrene was loved by Hercules; her grave is in the Pyrenees. Fire means "of the light." The kernel could signify the heart or hearth of the home.

PYTHIA—Greek: Python. "A prophet or diviner." Pythia was the name of the priestesses of the old Greek oracle of Apollo at Delphi.

Q

QUEENA—Old English: Cwen. "A queen." "Grace was in her steps, heaven in her eye, in every gesture dignity and love."—Milton.
English nickname: Queenie.

QUERIDA—Spanish: Querida. "Beloved."

QUINTINA—Latin: Quinctus. "Fifth child." A feminine form of Quintin and Quentin.

R

RABI—Arabic: Rabi. "Spring or harvest."

RACHEL—Hebrew: Rachel. "A ewe." The personification of gentleness and patience while suffering. Rachel was the Biblical wife of Jacob, the mother of Joseph and Benjamin.
English nicknames: Rae, Ray.
Foreign variations: Rachele (Italian), Raquel (Spanish), Rachelle (French), Rahel (German), Raoghnailt (Scotch).

RADELLA—Old English: Raedaelf. "Elfin counselor."

RADINKA—Slavic: Radinka. "Active one." Life is a joyful pageant for the active and alert.

RADMILLA—Slavic: Rad-milu. "Worker for the people."

RAE—Old English: Ra. "A doe deer." "Make haste, my beloved, and be thou like to a roe or to a young hart upon the mountains of spices."—The Song of Solomon. See Rachel.

RAINA—See Regina.

RAISSA—Old French: Raison. "Thinker, believer." How wonderful to think of earth and trees, of stars and mankind.

RAMONA—Spanish: Ramona. "Mighty or wise protector." A feminine form of Raymond, celebrated from the Helen Hunt Jackson novel *Ramona*.
English variation: Ramonda.

RANI—Hindu: Rani. "A queen."
English variations: Ranee, Rania.

RAPHAELA—Hebrew: R'phael. "Healed by God."

Foreign variation: Rafaela (Spanish).

RASIA—See Rose.

RAY—See Rachel.

REBA—See Rebecca.

REBECCA—Hebrew: Ribqah. "Bound." In the Old Testament, Rebecca was the wife of Isaac.
English nicknames: Reba, Beckie, Becky, Bekki.
English variations: Rebekah, Rebeka.
Foreign variations: Rébecca (French), Rebekka (German, Swedish), Rebeca (Spanish).

REGINA—Latin: Regina. "A queen."
English nicknames: Reggie, Rina, Gina.
English variations: Regan, Raina, Reyna.
Foreign variations: Reine (French), Reina (Spanish), Rioghnach (Irish).

RENATA—Latin: Renata. "Born again." Renewal of faith or reincarnation. Renata Tebaldi, opera singer.
English nicknames: Rene, Renee, Rennie.
Foreign variations: Renée (French), Renate (German)

RENE—See Irene, Renata.

RENEE—See Renata.

RENITA—Latin: Reniti. "Resister." A rebellious rebel.

RESEDA—Latin: Reseda. "The mignonette flower."

REVA—Latin: Revalesco. "To regain strength."

REXANA—Latin-English: Rex-Anne. "Regally graceful."

RHEA—Greek: Rhea. "A stream," or Latin: Rhaea. "A poppy." Rhea was the mother of the gods in the old Greek religion. English variation: Rea.

RHETA—Greek: Rhetor. "An orator."

RHODA—See Rose.

RHODANTHE—Greek: Rhodanthe. "Rose flower." "Sweetest little fellow everybody knows, don't know what to call him, but he's mighty like a rose." F. L. Stanton.

RHODIA—See Rose.

RIA—Spanish: Ria. "A river mouth."

RICADONNA—English-Italian: Rica-donna. "Ruling lady." "Oh thou are fairer than the evening air, clad in the beauty of a thousand stars."—Dr. Faustus.

RICARDA—Old English: Richard. "Powerful ruler." The feminine of Richard.
English nicknames: Rickie, Ricky, Dickie.

RILLA—Low German: Rille. "A stream or brook."
English variation: Rillette.

RINA—See Regina.

RISA—Latin: Risa. "Laughter." "The man that loves and laughs must sure do well."—Pope. Risë Stevens, opera singer.

RITA—See Margaret. Rita Hayworth, Rita Moreno, Rita Gam, actresses.

RIVA—French: Rive. "Riverbank, shore."

ROANNA—Compound of Rose and Anne.

ROBERTA—Old English: Hroth-beorht. "Shining with fame." Roberta La Rue, noted hydrologist; Roberta Peters, operatic singer.
English nicknames: Bobbie, Bobby, Bertie.
English variations: Robina, Robinia, Robinette, Bobbette.
Foreign variations: Robine (French), Ruperta (German).

ROCHELLE—French: Rochelle. "From the little rock." An old French directional landmark.
English variations: Rochella, Rochette.

RODERICA—Old German: Ruod-rik. "Famous ruler." A feminine form of Roderick.
English nicknames: Roddie, Roddy, Rickie.

ROHANA—Hindu: Rohan. "Sandalwood." A reminder of sweet incense.

ROLANDA—Old German: Ruod-lant. "From the famous land." A feminine form of Roland.
Foreign variations: Rolande (French), Orlanda (Italian).

ROMILDA—Old German: Ruom-hildi. "Glorious battle maid."

ROMOLA—Latin: Romula. "Lady of Rome." The title and heroine of a George Eliot novel.
English variations: Romella, Romelle.

RONALDA—Old Norse: Rognuald. "Mighty power." The feminine form of Ronald.

ROSABEL—Compound of Rose and Belle.
English variation: Rosabelle.

ROSALIE—See Rose.

ROSALINDA—Spanish: Rosalinda. "Beautiful rose." Rosalind Russell, actress.
English variations: Rosalind, Rosalynd, Rosaline, Roseline.

ROSAMOND—Old German: Rozo-mund. "Famous protectress."
English variation: Rosamund.
Foreign variations: Rosmunda (Italian), Rosemonde (French), Rosamunda (Spanish), Rozamond (Dutch).

ROSANNA—English: Roseanne. "Graceful rose."

ROSE—Greek: Rhodos. "A rose." St. Rose of Lima, died 1617; Rosa Ponselle, opera singer; Rose Hawthorne Lathrop, poet, philanthropist.
English nicknames: Rosie, Rosy, Zita.
English variations: Rosalie, Rosalia, Rosella, Roselle, Rosetta, Rosette, Rosina, Rasia, Rozella, Rhoda, Rhodia.
Foreign variations: Rosa (Italian, Spanish, Danish, Dutch, Swedish), Rois (Irish), Rosette (French), Rosita (Spanish).

ROSELLEN—Compound of Rose and Helen.

ROSEMARY—English: Rosemary. "The rose of St. Mary," or Latin: Rosmarinus. "Dew of the sea," for the rosemary herb. Rosemary Clooney, singer, entertainer.
English variation: Rose Marie.

ROSETTA—See Rose.

ROUX—See La Roux.

ROWENA—Old English: Hroth-wine. "Famous friend."

Rowena was a heroine of ancient British legends.

ROXANNE—Persian: Raokhshna. "Brilliant one." Roxana is famous as the wife of Alexander the Great, ancient world-conqueror; Roxanne is heroine of Rostand's classic, *Cyrano de Bergerac.*
English nicknames: Roxie, Roxy.
English variations: Roxana, Roxanna, Roxine.

ROYALE—Old French: Roial. "Regal one." A feminine form of Roy.

RUBY—Old French: Rubi. "The ruby gem." A girl whose lips were compared to this beautiful gem. Ruby Keeler, actress.
English variations: Rubie, Rubia, Rubina.

RUDELLE—Old German: Ruod. "Famous one." This person's importance was incorporated into her name.

RUELLA—Compound of Ruth and Ella.

RUFINA—Latin: Rufus. "Red-haired." A feminine form of Rufus.

RULA—Latin: Regula. "A ruler." A sovereign of her country.

RUPERTA—See Roberta.

RUTH—Hebrew: Ruth. "Compassionate, beautiful." "And Ruth said, entreat me not to leave thee or to return from following after thee: for whither thou goest, I will go." Ruth I:16. Ruth M. Stuart, writer (1856-1919); Ruth Gordon, Ruth Roman, actresses.

S

SABA—Greek: Saba. "Woman of Saba or Sheba." A name glamorized by the vibrant Queen of Sheba who visited the fabulously rich King Solomon.

SABINA—Latin: Sabina. "A Sabine lady." The ancient Sabine country was near Rome. St. Sabina was a 1st-century Roman martyr.
English variation: Savina.
Foreign variations: Sabine (French, German, Dutch), Saidhbhin (Irish).

SABRA—Hebrew: "To rest."

SABRINA—Latin: Sabrina. "From the boundary line." Famous from the play *Sabrina Fair* by Samuel Taylor, and the film *Sabrina*.

SADIE—See Sarah.

SADIRA—Persian: Sadar. "The lotus tree." Dreamy one, like the legendary lotus eaters.

SALINA—Latin: Salina. "From the salty place."

SALLY—See Sarah.

SALOME—Hebrew: Shalom. "Peace." The personification of tranquillity. Salome was the daughter of Herodias in the New Testament.
English variations: Saloma, Salomi.
Foreign variation: Salomé (French).

SALVIA—Latin: Salvia. "Sage." A fragrant herb used for cooking.
English variation: Salvina.

SAMANTHA—Aramaic: Samantha. "A listener." An attentive, teachable one.

SAMARA—Hebrew: Shemariah. "Guarded by God."

SAMUELA—Hebrew: Shemuel. "His name is God." An affirmation of faith. A feminine form of Samuel.
English variations: Samella, Samelle, Samuelle.

SANCIA—Latin: Sancia. "Sacred; inviolable."
Foreign variations: Sancha, Sanchia (Spanish).

SANDI—See Alexandra.

SANDRA—See Alexandra.

SAPPHIRA—Greek: Sappheiros. "Sapphire gem or sapphire-blue color." Eyes analogous to the sapphire. Modern usage from the Willa Cather novel *Sapphira and the Slave Girl*.
English variations: Saphira, Sapphire.

SARAH—Hebrew: Sarah. "Princess." Sarah was the wife of Abraham and the mother of Isaac in the Bible. She was first named Sarai meaning "Quarrelsome," but when Sarai was changed to Sarah it became "Princess" and "One who laughed." Namesakes: Sarah Doremus, American philanthropist; Sara Teasdale, poet; famous actresses Sarah Siddons and Sarah Bernhardt.
English nicknames: Sal, Sallie, Sally, Sadie, Sadye.
English variations: Sara, Sari, Sarene, Sarine, Sarette, Sadella, Zara, Zarah, Zaria.
Foreign variations: Sara (French, German, Italian, Spanish), Sorcha (Irish), Salaidh, Morag (Scotch).

SAVANNA—Old Spanish: Sabana. "An open plain." A señorita from the mesa.

SAVINA—See Sabina.

SAXONA—Old English: Saxan. "A Saxon; one of the sword-people." The Roman conquerors of Germany applied this name to the natives because they battled with short swords; now applied to persons of English descent.

SCARLETT—Middle English: Scarlett. "Scarlet colored." Famous from Scarlett O'Hara, heroine of *Gone with the Wind*.

SEBASTIANE—Latin: Sebastianus. "August, reverenced one." A feminine form of Sebastian. English variation: Sebastiana.

SECUNDA—Laitn: Secunda. "Second child."

SELENA—Greek: Selene. "The moon," or Latin: Coelina. "Heavenly." Selena Royle, actress.
English nicknames: Sela, Selie, Celie, Sena, Selia.
English variations: Selene, Selina, Selinda, Celene, Celina, Celinda.

SELIA—See Selena.

SELINDA—See Selena.

SELMA—See Anselma. Selma Lagerlöf, Swedish novelist.

SEMELE—Latin: Semele. "Once; a single time." Semele was the Greek earth goddess, daughter of Cadmus and mother of Dionysus.

SEMIRA—Hebrew: Shemiramoth. "The height of the heavens." Semiramis, the older form of Semira, was famous from an ancient Assyrian queen.

SENA—See Selena.

SEPTIMA—Latin: Septima. "Seventh child."

SERAPHINA—Hebrew: Seraphim. "Burning or ardent one." The Biblical Seraphim were fiery, purifying ministers of Jehovah. St. Seraphina was a 15th-century Italian abbess.
English variations: Serafina, Serafine, Seraphine.

SERENA—Latin: Serena. "Fair, bright, serene one."

SERILDA—Old German: Sarohildi. "Armored battle maid."

SHARLEEN—See Caroline.

SHARON—Hebrew: Sharai. "A princess," or from place-name usage, Hebrew: Sharon. "A plain." A princess compared to the Rose of Sharon for her exotic beauty.
English nicknames: Sherry, Shari, Sharry.

SHEBA—See Saba.

SHEENA—Irish Gaelic: Sine. "God is gracious." A form of Jane.

SHEILA—Irish Gaelic: Sile. An Irish spelling of Cecilia, Sabina.
English variations: Sheela, Sheelah, Sheilah, Seila.

SHELLEY—Old English: Scelfleah. "From the meadow on the ledge." Shelley Winters, actress.

SHEREE—See Charlotte.

SHERRILL—See Charlotte.

SHERRY—See Charlotte, Sharon.

SHERYL—See Charlotte, Shirley.

SHIRLEY—Old English: Scirleah. "From the bright meadow." Shirley MacLaine, Shirley Jones, Shirley Knight, actresses.
English nicknames: Shir, Shirl.
English variations: Shirlee, Shirlie, Shirleen, Shirlene, Sheryl.

SIBYL—Greek: Sibylla. "A prophetess." There were ten Sibyls in the classic myths, prophetesses located in various Mediterranean countries. Sybil Thorndike, noted English actress.
English nicknames: Sib, Sibbie, Sibby.
English variations: Sybil, Sybilla, Sybille, Sibilla, Sibille, Sibyll, Sibelle.
Foreign variations: Sibylle (French, German), Sibylla (Dutch), Sibeal (Irish).

SIDNEY—See Sydney.

SIDONIA—See Sydney.

SIDRA—Latin: Sidera. "Belonging to the stars; glittering." Divine lady, can it be that you are from a greater solar system?

SIGFREDA—Old German: Sigifrith. "Victorious and peaceful." An obtainer of inward serenity. A feminine form of Siegfried.

SIGNA—Latin: Signa. "A signer." Your signature was left on my heart.

SIGRID—Old Norse: Sigrath. "Victorious counselor." Sigrid Undset, Norwegian writer; Sigrid Gurie, actress.

SILVIA—See Sylvia.

SIMONA—Hebrew: Shim'on. "Hearer; one who hears." My love hears the whisper of the flowers and fairy bells, and the celestial lights of angels. A feminine form of Simeon and Simon. Simone Signoret, French actress.
Foreign variations: Simone, Simonette (French).

SIRENA—Greek: Seiren. "A sweetly singing mermaid siren." Refers to the mythical Greek sirens whose fatal beauty and songs lured men to their death.

SOLITA—Latin: Solitaria. "Alone; solitary." "I love tranquil solitude and such society as is quiet, wise and good."—Shelley.

SOLVIG—Old German: Sigilwig. "Victorious battle maid."

SONYA—See Sophie.

SOPHIE—Greek: Sophia. "Wisdom." "'Tis wise to learn; 'tis godlike to create."—J. G. Saxe. St. Sophia, a 1st century Christian martyr; Sophia Smith, founder of Smith College; Sonja Henie, Norwegian actress, ice skater; Sophia Loren, actress.
English variations: Sophia, Sophy.
Foreign variations: Sofie (French, Danish, Dutch), Sofia (Italian, Spanish), Sonja, Sonya (Slavic, Scandinavian), Sadhbh, Sadhbha (Irish), Beathag (Scotch).

SOPHRONIA—Greek: Sophronia. "Sensible one." A woman with the innate gift of discerning facts from fiction.
Foreign variations: Sonja, Sonya (Scandinavian, Slavic).

SORCHA—Irish Gaelic: Sorcha. "Bright one."

SPRING—Old English: Springan. "The springtime of the year." Spring Byington, actress.

STACEY—See Anastasia.

STACIA—See Anastasia.

STAR—Old English: Steorra. "A star." See Esther.

STELLA—See Estelle. Stella Stevens, actress.

STEPHANIE—Greek: Stephanos. "Crowned one." Honoring St. Stephana of Italy, 1457-1530. A feminine form of Stephen.
English nicknames: Stefa, Steffie, Stepha.
English variations: Stephania, Stephana, Stevana, Stevena.
Foreign variations: Stéphanie (French), Stephanie (German).

STORM—Old English: Storm. "A tempest or storm." Sudden storms are short; then shines the sun. Storm Jameson, English author.

SUNNY—English: Sunny. "Bright, cheerful, genial."

SUSAN—Hebrew: Shoshannah. "Lily or graceful lily." Ivory skin enhanced by jet-black hair. St. Susanna was a 3rd-century Roman martyr. Susan B. Anthony, American reformer; Susan Glaspell, writer; Susan Hayward, Susan Strasberg, Zsa Zsa Gabor, actresses.
English nicknames: Sue, Susie, Susy, Suzie, Suzy, Suki, Sukey.
English variations: Susanna, Susannah, Suzanna, Susanne, Susette, Suzette.
Foreign variations: Susanne (French, German), Susanna (Italian), Susana (Spanish), Zsa Zsa (Hungarian nickname), Sosanna (Irish), Siusan (Scotch).

SYBIL—See Sibyl.

SYDNEY—Old French: Saint-Denis. "From St. Denis, France," or Phoenician: Sidon. "From the city of Sidon." A feminine form of Sidney.

SYLVIA—Latin: Silva. "From the forest." A romantic name from Italy. Sylvia Porter, columnist; Sylvia Sidney, actress. English variations: Silva, Sylva, Silvana, Sylvana, Zilvia. Foreign variations: Silvie (French), Silvia (Italian, Spanish).

SYNA—Greek: Syn. "Together." Companionship for two like minds and hearts.

T

TABITHA—Greek: Tabitha. "Gazelle." A child of grace with lustrous eyes like the gentle gazelle.

TACITA—Latin: Tacito. "Silent." One who knew the virtue of silence when others talked.

TALITHA—Aramaic: Talitha. "Maiden."

TALLULAH—Choctaw Indian: Talula. "Leaping water." The joyous song of water playing leapfrog over rocks can exalt the saddest heart. Tallulah Bankhead, actress.
English nicknames: Tallie, Tally.

TAMARA—Hebrew: Tamar. "Palm tree." Painters, poets, and lovers of beauty eulogize the palm.
English nicknames: Tammie, Tammy.

TAMMY—Hebrew: Tema. "Perfection." See Tamara, Thomasa. Tammy Grimes, Tammy Marihugh, actresses.

TANGERINE—English: Tangierine. "Girl from the city of Tangier, Morocco."

TANSY—Middle Latin: Tanacetum. "Tenacious one." A woman so persistent that she was characterized by her name.

TARA—Irish Gaelic: Torra. "Rocky pinnacle or crag." Tara was the ancient capital of the Irish kings.

TEMPEST—Old French: Tempeste. "Stormy one."

TERENTIA—Greek: Tereos. "Guardian," or Irish Gaelic: Toirdealbach. "Shaped like the god Thor." A feminine form of Ter-

ence. Characterized as like the Norse thunder god Thor.
English nicknames: **Teri, Terri, Terrie, Terry.**

TERESA—See Theresa.

TERI—See Terentia, Theresa.

TERRY—See Terentia, Theresa. Terry Moore, actress.

TERTIA—Latin: Tertia. "Third child."

TESSA—Greek: Tessares. "Fourth child." See Theresa.
English nicknames: **Tess, Tessie.**

THADDEA—Greek: Thaddaios. "Courageous one." A feminine form of Thaddeus.
English variations: **Thada, Thadda.**

THALASSA—Greek: Thalassa. "From the sea."

THALIA—Greek: Thaleia. "Blooming; luxuriant." "A lovely being, scarce formed or moulded, a rose with all its sweetest leaves yet unfolded."—Byron, *Don Juan.* In Greek myths Thalia was one of the three Graces and the Muse of Comedy.

THEA—Greek: Thea. "Goddess." An extraordinary beauty.

THEANO—Greek: Theanoma. "Divine name." Theano was the wife of Pythagoras.

THECLA—Greek: Thekla. "Divisely famous." St. Thecla was a follower of St. Paul.
English variations: **Tecla, Thekla.**

THEDA—See Theodora, Theodosia. Theda Bara, actress, 1890-1955.

THELMA—Greek: Thele. "A nursling." A little person still dependent on her mother. Thelma Ritter, actress.

THEODORA—Greek: Theodoros. "Gift of God." A feminine form of Theodore. See Dorothy. Famous from Theodora, 6th-century Roman Empress of the East.
English nicknames: **Theda, Dora.**
Foreign variations: **Teodora (Italian, Spanish), Fedora, Feodora, (Slavic).**

THEODOSIA—Greek: Theodosia. "God-given."
English nicknames: **Theda, Dosia, Dosie.**
Foreign variations: **Teodosia (Italian), Feodosia (Slavic).**

THEOLA—Greek: Theologos. "Speaker with God."

THEONE—Greek: Theonoma. "God's name."

THEOPHANIA—Greek: Theophaneia. "Appearance of God."

THEOPHILA—Greek: Theophilos. "Beloved of God."

THEORA—Greek: Theoro. "Watcher, contemplater." The power behind man's evolutionary progression is thought.

THERA—Greek: Thera. "Wild, untamed."

THERESA—Greek: Theriso. "Reaper." One who personified man at harvest time, reaping the results of his labor. St. Theresa of Avila in Castile, 1515-1582, Spanish nun, mystic, and writer, was one of the most widely appreciated women in religious history. Teresa Wright, actress.
English nicknames: **Teri, Terri, Terrie, Terry, Tessa, Tessie, Tessy, Tracie, Tracy, Zita.**
English variations: **Teresa, Terese, Teressa, Teresita.**
Foreign variations: **Thérèse (French), Therese (German), Teresa (Italian, Spanish), Toireasa (Irish).**

THETIS—Greek: Thetis. "Positive, determined one." In Greek myths she was the mother of Achilles.

THIRZA—Hebrew: Tirzah. "Pleasantness."

THOMASA—Greek: Thomas. "A twin." One was a counterpart of the other. A feminine form of Thomas.
English nicknames: Tommie, Tommy, Tammy.
English variations: Thomasina, Thomasine, Tomasina, Tomasine.

THORA—Old Norse: Thori-r. "Thunder." A same for the old Norse god Thor.

THORBERTA—Old Norse: Thor-biartr. "Brilliance of Thor." A feminine form of Thorbert.

THORDIS—Old Norse: Thori-dyss. "Thor-spirit." The spirit of the storm made its voice heard.
English variation: Thordia.

THYRA—Greek: Thyreos. "Shield-bearer." Could it be that she wore protective armor around her heart?

TIBELDA—Old German: Theudo-bald. "Boldest of the people." A lady unafraid.

TIBERIA—Latin: Tiberia. "Of the river Tiber."
English nicknames: Tibbie, Tibby.

TILDA—See Mathilda.

TIMOTHEA—Greek: Timotheos. "Honoring God." A feminine form of Timothy.
English nicknames: Timmie, Timmy.

TINA—See Christine. Also used independently.

TITA—Latin: Titulus. "A title of honor."

TITANIA—Greek: Titan. "Giant." The Titans were primordial Greek deities of gigantic size. Titania was the Queen of the Fairies in Shakespeare's *Midsummer Night's Dream.*

TOBY—Hebrew: Tobhiyah. "The Lord is good." A feminine form of Tobias. Toby Wing, actress.

TONIA—See Antonia.

TOPAZ—Latin: Topazos. "A topaz gem."

TOURMALINE—Singhalese: Toramalli. "A carnelian or tourmaline gem." The pink carnelian could not compare with this blonde beauty.

TRACY—Latin: Thrasius. "Bold or courageous," or Irish Gaelic: Treasach. "Battler." See Theresa.

TRAVIATA—Italian: Traviata. "One who goes astray." Made famous by the Verdi opera *La Traviata.*

TRILBY—Italian: Trillare. "To sing with trills." A name coined by George du Maurier for the heroine of the novel *Trilby,* who became a beautiful singer.

TRISTA—Latin: Triste. "Melancholy." One who seemed to have a secret sorrow, all her own, until she smiled.

TRIXIE—See Beatrice. Trixie Friganza, entertainer (1870-1955).

TRUDA—Old German: Truda. "Loved one."
English nickname: Trudie.

TRYPHENA—Latin: Tryphaena. "Delicate one."

TUESDAY—Old English: Tiwesdaeg. "Born on Tuesday." Tuesday Weld, actress.

TULLIA—Irish Gaelic: Taith-leach. "Peaceful, quiet one." A feminine form of the Irish "Tully."

TZIGANE—Hungarian: Czigany. "A gypsy." A Romany maid whose heart was filled with music and adventure.

U

UDA—Old German: Udo. "Prosperous one."
English variation: Udelle.

ULA—Old German: Ula. "Owner of an inherited estate."

ULIMA—Arabic: Alim. "Wise, learned one."

ULRICA—Old German: Alh-ric. "All-ruler."

ULTIMA—Latin: Ultima. "The most distant, aloof one."

ULVA—Gothic: Wulfila. "Wolf." The wolf was a medieval symbol of courage.

UNA—Latin: Una. "One, together." A devoted pair often become one. Una Merkel, Una O'Connor, actresses.

UNDINE—Latin: Unda. "A wave." Undine was a water sprite in classic myths.

URANIA—Greek: Ourania. "Heavenly." Urania was the Greek Muse of Astronomy.

URSULA—Latin: Ursa. "A she-bear." A fearless brown-haired signorina compared to the courageous bear. Ursula Theiss, actress.
English nicknames: Ursa, Ursie, Ursy, Orsa.
English variations: Ursuline, Ursola, Orsola.
Foreign variations: Ursule (French), Orsola (Italian), Ursola (Spanish).

V

VALA—Gothic: Waljan. "Chosen one." How wonderful it is to be selected and preferred to all the children.

VALBORGA—Old German: Waldburga. "Protecting ruler."

VALDA—Old Norse: Uald. "Governor; ruler."
English variation: Velda.

VALENTINA—Latin: Valentis. "Strong, healthy one." A girl flushed with the beauty of good health. St. Valentina was a 4th-century virgin martyr.

English nicknames: Val, Vallie.
English variations: Valentine, Valentia, Valeda, Valida.

VALERIE—Old French: Valeriane. "Strong." A woman whose strength and success were in her persistence. St. Valerie was a 3rd-century martyr. Valerie Taylor, English actress.
English nicknames: Val, Vallie.
English variations: Valeria, Valery, Valoree.
Foreign variations: Valérie (French), Valeria (Italian).

VALESKA—Old Slavic: Valdislava. "Glorious ruler." A feminine form of Vladislav.

VALONIA—Latin: Valles. "From the vale or hollow."

VANESSA—New Latin: Vanessa. "A genus of butterflies." A handsome woman compared to the butterfly that symbolized rejuvenation or renewal. Vanessa Brown, actress.
English nicknames: Van, Vannie, Vanny, Vanna, Vania.

VANNA—See Vanessa.

VANORA—Old Welsh: Gwenhwyvar. "White wave." A development of Guinevere.

VARINA—Slavic: Varvara. "Stranger." A Slavic development of Barbara.

VASHTI—Persian: Vashti. "Beautiful one," or "Thread of life." Vashti was the queen of King Ahasuerus in the Biblical Book of Esther.

VEDA—Sanskrit: Veda. "Knowledge." What is knowledge but wisdom married to intuition? Veda Ann Borg, actress.
English variation: Vedis.

VEDETTE—Italian: Vedetta. "Guardian or sentinel."

VEGA—Arabic: Waqi. "The falling one." Referring to the bright star Vega when it sinks below the horizon.

VELDA—See Valda.

VELIKA—Old Slavic: Velika. "Great one."

VELMA—See Wilhelmina.

VELVET—Middle English: Velouette. "Velvety." A beauty with velvet skin and hair as black as smoke.

VENTURA—Spanish: Ventura. "Happiness and good luck."

VENUS—Latin: Venus. "Loveliness, beauty." Venus, the name for the goddess of beauty and love, personified feminine perfection.
English variations: Venita, Vinita, Vinny, Vinnie.

VERA—Latin: Verus: "True." A woman of constancy and truth. Vera Miles, actress.
English variations: Vere, Verena, Verene, Verina, Verine, Verla.

VERBENA—Latin: Verbenae. "Sacred boughs."

VERDA—See Verna.

VERENA—Old German: Varin. "Defender; protector." See Verna.

VERNA—Latin: Verna. "Springlike." A spring nymph, sunkissed, dressed in green and crowned with bright blossoms. Verna Felton, actress.
English variations: Verne, Verneta, Vernita, Verda, Verena, Vernis, Virna, Virina.

VERONICA—See Bernice. St. Veronica wiped the face of Jesus Christ as he was on his way to Calvary. Namesakes: Veronica Lake, Veronica Cartwright, actresses.
English nicknames: Vonnie, Vonny.

VESPERA—Latin: Vesper. "The evening star."

VESTA—Latin: Vesta. "She who dwells or lingers." Vesta was the Roman goddess of the household and of flocks and herds.

VEVAY—See Vivian.

VEVILA—Irish Gaelic: Bebhinn. "Melodious, harmonious lady." Oh, sweet lady, lover of life and all its splendor, never can you be at war with people, nature or yourself.

VICKI—See Victoria.

VICTORIA—Latin: Victoria. "Victory." Famous from Queen Victoria of England (1819-1901); Queen Victoria of Spain, wife of Alphonso XIII; Vicki Baum, author.
English nicknames: Vic, Vickie, Vicki, Vicky.
English variation: Victorine.
Foreign variations: Vitoria (Spanish), Vittoria (Italian), Victoire (French).

VIDA—Hebrew: Dawid. "Beloved one." A feminine form of David.

VIDONIA—Portuguese: Vidonho. "A vine branch." A delicate tendril from the parental stock.

VIGILIA—Latin: Vigilis. "Awake and alert."

VIGNETTE—French: Vignette. "Little vine." Tiny, tender, clinging vine, held so gently in mother's arms.

VILLETTE—French: Ville. "From the country estate."

VIÑA—Spanish: Viña. "From the vineyard." Vina Delmar, author.

VINCENTIA—Latin: Vincentius. "Conquering one." A feminine form of Vincent.

VINITA—See Venus.

VIOLET—Old French: Violete. "A violet flower." Violet Kemble Cooper, Violet Heming, actresses.
English variations: Viola, Violetta, Violette, Iolanthe, Yolanda, Yolande, Yolanthe.

Foreign variations: Viola, Viole, Violette (French), Violetta (Italian), Violante (Spanish, Portuguese.)

VIRGILIA—Latin: Virgilius. "Rod or staff bearer."

VIRGINIA—Latin: Virginia. "Maidenly." Virginia Dare, born at Roanoke, Virginia, in 1587, was the first white child born in America of English parents. Virginia Mayo, Virginia Gray, actresses.
English nicknames: Virgie, Virgy, Ginger, Ginnie, Ginny.
Foreign variations: Virginie (French, Dutch), Virginia (Italian, German).

VIRIDIS—Latin: Viridis. "Fresh blooming, green."

VITA—Latin: Vita. "Life." Spirit or energy that imbues and motivates all living things.
English variations: Veta, Vitia.

VIVIAN—Latin: Viva. "Alive." Saint Vivian or Vibiana was an early martyr. Vivienne Della Chiesa, singer; actresses Vivien Leigh, Vivian Vance, Vivian Blaine, Vivienne Segal.
English nicknames: Viv, Vivie.
English variations: Viviana, Vivien, Vivienne, Vivyan.
Foreign variations: Vivienne (French), Viviana (Italian)

VOLANTE—Italian: Volante. "Flying one." One who seemed to float on wings of energy, love and hope.

VOLETA—Old French: Volet. "A flowing veil."

VONNY—See Veronica.

W

WALDA—Old German: Waldo. "Ruler."
English variation: Welda.

WALLIS—Old English: Waleis. "One from Wales, Welshman." This beauty came from the wet, mossy, fern-filled glens of Wales. Feminine form of Wallace. Wallis Warfield, Duchess of Windsor.
English nicknames: Wallie, Wally.

WANDA—Old German: Wando, Wendi. "Wanderer." A dream-led daughter, roaming over glen and dell seeking violets in the snow. Wanda Hendrix, actress.
English nicknames: Wandie, Wendy.
English variations: Wandis, Wenda, Wendeline.

WANETTA—Old English: Wann. "Pale one."

WARDA—Old German: Warto. "Guardian." A feminine form of Ward.

WELDA—See Walda.

WENDY—See Wanda. Wendy Hiller, Wendy Barrie, actresses.

WILHELMINA—Old German: Willi-helm. "Resolute Protector." A feminine form of William. Famous from Wilhelmina, Queen of Holland. Notables: Willa Cather, novelist; Wilma Rudolph, track champion.
English nicknames: Willie, Willy, Minnie, Minny, Billie, Billy, Helma.

English variations: Wilhelma, Wilhelmine, Willamina, Willa, Willette, Wilmette, Wilma, Wylma, Vilma, Willabelle.
Foreign variations: Guillelmine, Guillemette (French), Wilhelmine (German, Danish), Guglielma (Italian), Guillelmina (Spanish), Vilhelmina (Swedish).

WILLA—See Wilhelmina.

WILLABELLE—See Wilhelmina.

WILMA—See Wilhelmina.

WINEMA—Modoc Indian: Winema. "Woman chief." The Indian chieftainess of her tribe, wise with innate wisdom.

WINIFRED—Old German: Wini-frid. "Peaceful friend." Winifred Holt, American sculptor, philanthropist.
English nicknames: Winnie, Winny.

WINOLA—Old German: Wini-holdo. "Gracious friend."

WINONA—Sioux Indian: Winona. "First-born daughter." All nature hushed; the birds and lisping stream began to sing a greeting song to their first-born daughter.
English variations: Winonah, Wenona.

WYNNE—Old Welsh: Wyn. "Fair, white."

X

XANTHE—Greek: Xanthos. "Yellow." A sweet nestling with hair of soft, cobweb gold.

XAVIERA—Spanish Basque: Javerri; Xaver. "Owner of the new house." A feminine form of Xavier. She watched the building of her house and waited to transform it into heaven, like women of the world have done since Eve.

XENIA—Greek: Xenia. "Hospitable one."
English variations: Xena, Xene, Zenia.

XYLONA—Greek: Xylon. "From the forest."

Y

YEDDA—Old English: Giddian. "To sing; singer."
English variation: Yetta.

YETTA—Old English: Geatan. "To give; giver." See Henrietta, Yedda.

YNEZ—See Agnes.

YOLANDA—Greek: Iolanthe. "Violet flower." See Violet, Iolanthe. Yolande, queen of Scotland's King Alexander III, 1249-1286; Yolanda Veloz, dancer.

English variations: Eolande, Iolande.
Foreign variations: Yolande (French), Yolanda (Italian).

YVETTE—See Yvonne. Yvette Guilbert, Yvette Mimieux, actresses.

YVONNE—Old French: Yves. "Yew-bow." Yvonne Printemps, Yvonne de Carlo, actresses.
English variations: Yvette, Yevette.

Z

ZADA—Arabic: S'ad. "Lucky one."

ZANDRA—See Alexandra.

ZANETA—See Jane.

ZARA—Hebrew: Zarah. "East; dawn brightness."

ZEA—Latin: Zea. "A kind of grain." A girl compared to a field of ripened grain.

ZELDA—See Griselda.

ZELIA—Greek: Zelos. "Zeal." A devoted or ardent one." Zelia Nuttall, American archaeologist.
English variations: Zele, Zelie, Zelina.

ZELMA—See Anselma.

ZENA—See Xenia, Zenobia.

ZENAIDA—See Zenobia.

ZENDA—See Zenobia.

ZENIA—See Xenia, Zenobia.

ZENINA—See Zenobia.

ZENNA—See Zenobia.

ZENOBIA—Greek: Zenbios. "Given life by Jupiter or Zeus." Jupiter or Zeus was the head of the gods of antiquity. Zenobia was the 3rd-century A.D. ruler of the Syrian city-state of Palmyra. English variations: Zena, Zenaida, Zenda, Zenna, Zenia. Foreign variation: Zénobie (French).

ZERA—Hebrew: Zera'im. "Seeds." Progeny that will mature and have seedlings of their own.

ZERLINDA—Hebrew-Spanish: Zarah-linda. "Dawn-beautiful." English variation: Zerlinda.

ZETA—Greek: Zeta. "The letter 'Z,' 6th letter of the Greek alphabet."

ZEVA—Greek: Siphos. "Sword."

ZILLA—Hebrew: Zillah. "Shadow." A little, inseparable image of her mother.

ZINNIA—New Latin: Zinnia. "The zinnia flower." Named for German Prof. J. G. Zinn, 18th century. English variation: Zinia.

ZIPPORA—Hebrew: Zipporah. "Beauty; trumpet; or sparrow." Zipporah was the Biblical wife of Moses.

ZITA—See Rosita, Theresa.

ZOE—Greek: Zoe. "Life." A sweet, animated existence with eternal potentials. Zoe Akins, dramatist.

ZONA—Latin: Zona. "A girdle." Zona was applied as a name for the belt of Orion in the great constellation. Zona Gale, author.

ZORA—Slavic: Zora. "Aurora or dawn." English variations: Zorina, Zorine.

ZSA ZSA—See Susan.

A

AARON—Hebrew: Aharon. "Lofty or exalted." Aaron, brother of Moses, qualified and enlightened, was exalted as the first high priest of the Hebrews. Aaron Burr, 3rd Vice-President of the United States.
English variation: Aron.
Foreign variation: Haroun (Arabic).

ABBOTT—Old English: Abod from Arabic: Abba. "Abbey father." A man named "The Father" for his magnitude of soul. Abbott Thayer, American painter (1849-1921).
Foreign variations: Abboid (Gaelic), Abott, Abbe (French), Abad (Spanish).

ABEL—Hebrew: Heb-hel. "Breath, evanescence." The breath of life is transitory in duration. Abel was the second son of Adam and Eve.

ABELARD—Old German: Adelhard. "Nobly resolute." Pierre Abelard, 12th-century French philosopher, renowned for his romance with Heloise.

ABNER—Hebrew: Abhner. "Father of Light." What is light but wisdom; what is light but love. Abner Doubleday, American Civil War military leader.

ABRAHAM—Hebrew: Abraham. "Father of the multitude." The most exalted founder of the Hebrew people. Abraham Lincoln, 16th United States President.
English nicknames: Abe, Abie, Bram.
Foreign variations: Abramo, Abrahamo (Italian), Abrahán (Spanish), Ibrahim (Arabic).

ABRAM—Hebrew: Abram. "The lofty one is father." One who had a realization of the incomprehensible infinity of God. Abram Newkirk, American Episcopal bishop, 1824-1901.
English nicknames: Abe, Abie.
Foreign variations: Abramo (Italian), Bram (Dutch).

ACE—Latin: As. "Unity." A kindly man with a feeling of unity with all mankind.
English nickname: Acey.

ACKERLEY—Old English: Aecer-leah. "Dweller at the acre meadow."
English nickname: Ack.

ACKLEY—Old English: Ac-leah. "Dweller at the oak-tree meadow."
English nickname: Ack.

ADAIR—Scotch Gaelic: Athdara. "From the oak-tree ford." James Adair (1710-1780), American writer.

ADALARD—Old German: Adal-hard. "Noble and brave." St. Adalard, c. 751-827, abbey founder in Saxony.

ADAM—Hebrew: Adham. "Man of the red earth." "And God created Adam of the red dust of the earth, and breathed into his nostrils life."
English nicknames: Ad, Ade.
Foreign variations: Adán (Spanish), Adamo (Italian) Adao (Portuguese), Adhamh (Irish and Scotch).

ADDISON—Old English: Addison. "Son of Adam." Addison Verrill, American zoologist.

ADELBERT—See Albert.

ADLAI—Hebrew: Adlai. "My witness, my ornament." A man living the word of God. Adlai E. Stevenson, statesman.

ADLER—Old German: Adlar. "Eagle." Keen of mind and vision. Alfred Adler (1870-1937), Austrian psychiatrist and psychologist.

ADNEY—Old English: Addaneye. "Dweller on the noble-one's island."

ADOLPH—Old German: Adalwolf. "Noble wolf" or "Noble hero." A brave warrior. Adolph Zukor, noted motion picture pioneer; Adolphe Menjou, noted actor; Adolpho Lopez Mateos, President of Mexico.
English nicknames: Ad., Dolf, Dolph
Foreign variations: Adolf (German, Swedish, Dutch, Danish), Adolphus (Swedish), Adolfo (Spanish, Italian), Adolphe (French).

ADON—Phoenician: Adon. "Lord." Adon was a sacred Hebrew name for God.
Foreign variation: Adonis (Greek).

ADRIAN—Latin: Ater. "Dark one." A brunette, nicknamed by a fair-haired people. Adrian Stokes, British painter (1854-1935); Adrian, motion picture costume designer.
English variation: Hadrian.
Foreign variations: Adriano (Italian), Adrien (French), Adrián (Spanish).

ADRIEL—Hebrew: Adriyel. "From God's congregation." An exalted one.

AENEAS—Greek: Aineías. "The praised one." The legendary defender of Troy, memorialized in Greek song and story.
English variation: Eneas.
Foreign variations: Enne (French), Eneas (Spanish).

AHERN—Gaelic Irish: Eachthighearn. "Horse-lord" or "Owner of many horses." Brian Aherne, noted actor.
English and Irish variations: Ahearn, Aherin, Aherne, Hearne, Hearn.

AHREN—Old Low German: Ahren: "Eagle."

AIDAN—Gaelic Irish: Aodhan. "Little fiery one." A man of fire whose temper flared between his mirth and tears. St. Aidan, famous Irish monk, died A.D. 651.
English variation: Eden.

AIKEN—Old North English: Ad-ken. "Little Adam." A small reflection of his father. Conrad Aiken, American poet.
English variations: Aikin, Aickin.

AINSLEY—Old English: Ainesleah. "The awe-inspiring one's meadow."

ALAN—Irish Gaelic: Alain. "Handsome, cheerful, harmonious one." Alan Ladd, American actor; Alan Jay Lerner, lyricist and librettist; H. Allen Smith, American writer.
English variations: Allan, Allen, Allyn, Aland.
Foreign variations: Alain (French), Alano (Italian, Spanish), Ailean (Scotch), Ailin (Irish).

ALARIC—Old German: Alhric: "Ruler of all" or Old German: Adal-ric: "Noble ruler." Famous as a 4th-century king of the Visigoths. Alaric Watts, English poet and journalist, 1797-1864.
Foreign variations: Alarico (Spanish), Alrik (Swedish).

ALASTAIR—Scotch Gaelic: Alasdair, a form of Alexander. "Defender of men."

English variations: Allister, Alister, Alaster.

ALBEN—Latin: Albinus. "Fair complexioned one." Alben Barkley, Vice President of the United States. St. Alban, English martyr, died A.D. 303.
English variations: Albin, Alban.
Foreign variations: Aubin (French), Alban (Irish), Alva (Spanish).

ALBERN—Old English: Aethelbeorn. "Noble warrior."

ALBERT—Old English: Aethelberht. "Noble and brilliant or illustrious." Albert Einstein, scientist (1879-1955); King Albert of Belgium, ruled 1909-1934.
English nicknames: Al, Albie, Bert.
English variations: Elbert, Adelbert.
Foreign variations: Albrecht, Adalbert (German), Aubert (French), Alberto (Italian; Spanish), Ailbert (Scotch).

ALBIN—See Alben.

ALCOTT—Old English: Aldcott. "Dweller at the old cottage."

ALDEN—Old English: Aldwine. "Old, wise protector or friend." John Alden, Pilgrim settler in 1620 at Plymouth, Massachusetts.
English variations: Aldin, Aldwin, Aldwyn, Elden, Eldin.

ALDER—Old English: Aler. "At the alder-tree."

ALDIS—Old English: Ald-hus. "From the old house." An ancient home filled with memories. Aldous Huxley, writer.
English variations: Aldous, Aldus.

ALDO—Old German: Ald. "Old and wise." Aldo Ray, American actor. Aldo Manutius, Italian printer (1449-1515).

ALDRICH—Old English: Aldric. "Old, wise ruler." Thomas Bailey Aldrich (1836-1907), American writer, poet, novelist.
English variations: Aldric, Eldric.
Foreign variation: Audric (French).

ALDWIN—Old English: Aldwine. "Old friend or protector."
English variation: Eldwin.

ALERON—Middle Latin: Alerio. "Eagle."

ALEXANDER—Greek: Alexandros. "Helper and defender of mankind." Alexander the Great, Macedonian world conqueror, died 323 B.C.; Alexander Hamilton, American statesman.
English nicknames: Alex, Alexis, Alec, Sandy, Sander, Saunders.
Foreign variations: Alister, Alasdair (Scotch), Alsandair (Irish), Alessandro (Italian), Alejandro (Spanish), Alexio (Portuguese), Alexandre (French, Portuguese), Aleksandr (Russian).

ALEXIS—See Alexander. Alexis Carrell (1873-1944), French surgeon and writer.
Foreign variation: Alejo (Spanish).

ALFONSO—See Alphonso.

ALFORD—Old English: Aldford. "The old ford or river-crossing." A shallow place in the river.

ALFRED—Old English: Aelfraed. "Good or elfin counselor." King Alfred the Great of England, benevolent ruler from A.D. 871 to 901 was the most famous person in history by this name; Alfred Hitchcock, film and television director, producer.
English nicknames: Al, Alf, Alfie.
Foreign variations: Alfredo (Italian, Spanish), Ailfrid (Irish).

ALGER—Old German: Adal-gar. "Noble spearman." Horatio Alger, American writer of juvenile stories (1834-1899).
English variation: **Algar**.

ALGERNON—Old French: Algrenon. "Man with a mustache or beard." Algernon Swinburne, famous 19th-century English poet.
English nicknames: **Algie, Algy**.

ALISON—Old English: Adalson: "Noble one's son." Also English: Alice-son; Old German-French: Alh-som. "Holy or sacred fame." A sweet presence born of love. Sir Archibald Alison, British historian (1792-1867).
English nickname: **Al**.
English variation: **Allison**.

ALLAN—See Alan.

ALLARD—Old English: Alh-hard. "Sacred and brave," or Old English: Aethel-hard. "Noble, brave." Good deeds made this man a hero to his people.
Foreign variation: **Alard** (French).

ALLEN—See Alan.

ALLISON—See Alison.

ALLISTER—See Alastair.

ALMO—Old English: Aethelmaer. "Noble and famous."

ALONZO—See Alphonso.

ALOYSIUS—Late Latin: Aloisius. "Famous warrior." See Lewis. St. Aloysius, 1568-1591, a Jesuit of Lombardy.
English variations: **Aloys, Lewis, Louis**.
Foreign variations: **Louis** (French), **Ludwig** (German), **Alabhaois** (Irish).

ALPHONSO—Old German: Adal-funs. "Noble and ready." Alphonso Taft, U.S. Secretary of War, 1876; Alphonso XIII, King of Spain, 1886-1931; Alphonse Daudet, famous 19th-century French writer.
English variation: **Alfonso**.
Foreign variations: **Alfonso** (Spanish, Italian, Swedish), **Alonso** (Spanish), **Alphonse** (French), **Alfons** (German, Swedish), **Alphonsus** (Irish), **Affonso** (Portuguese).

ALPIN—Pictish-Scotch: Alpin from Latin: Albinus. "Blond one." Clan MacAlpin, descendants of Kenneth MacAlpin, claim to be the oldest Scotch clan.

ALROY—Irish Gaelic: Giolla-ruaidh. "Red-haired youth."

ALSTON—Old English: Aethelstun. "Noble one's estate."

ALTMAN—Old German: Altmann. "Old, wise man." St. Altman, founder of Benedictine Abbey, Austria (1020-1091).

ALTON—Old English: Ald-tun. "Dweller at the old town or estate."

ALVA—Latin: Albinus. "Blond one. Thomas Alva Edison, American inventor (1847-1931).
Foreign variation: **Alba** (Spanish).

ALVAH—Hebrew: Alvah. "Exalted one."

ALVIN—Old German: Alh-win. "Friend of all" or Adal-win, "Noble friend."
English variations: **Alwin, Alwyn, Alvan**.
Foreign variations: **Aloin, Aluin** (French), **Aluino** (Spanish), **Alwin** (German).

ALVIS—Old Norse: Alviss. "All-wise." The dwarf Alviss in Nordic mythology demanded the daughter of the god Thor in marriage.

AMASA—Hebrew: Amasa. "Burden bearer." A patriarch who shared the troubles and misfortunes of others. Amasa Walker, American political economist. (1799-1875).

AMBROSE—Greek: Ambrotos. "Divine, immortal one." One animated with a spirit both mortal and divine. St. Ambrose, 4th-century Bishop of Milan, Italy; Ambrose Bierce, noted American writer.
Foreign variations: Ambrogio, Ambrosi (Italian), Ambroise (French), Ambrosio (Spanish), Ambrosius (German, Swedish, Dutch), Ambros (Irish).

AMERIGO—See Emery. Amerigo Vespucci, Italian explorer after whom America was named.

AMERY—See Amory.

AMMON—Egyptian: Amen. "The hidden." "No man shall see the face of God." St. Ammon the Great, one of the earliest and greatest hermit-monks, died A.D. 350.

AMORY—Old German: Alhmar-ric. "Divine, famous ruler." An ancestor who seemed endowed with wisdom from on high.
English variation: Amery.

AMOS—Hebrew: Amos. "A burden." Life's burdens are often heavy until we face our problems. Amos was an 8th-century Biblical prophet. Amos Bronson Alcott (1799-1888), American teacher, philosopher.

ANATOLE—Greek: Anatolios. "Man from the East." A stranger to the West. Anatole France, French writer (1844-1924); Anatole Litvak, motion picture director.
Foreign variation: Anatol (Slavic), Anatolio (Spanish).

ANDERS—See Andrew.

ANDREW—Greek: Andreas. "Strong, manly." St. Andrew the Apostle is the patron saint of Scotland. St. Andrew's "X"—shaped cross appears on the British flag and on innumerable coats-of-arms of Scotch and English families. Andrew Jackson, 7th President of United States; Andrew Carnegie (1837-1919), Scotch-American steel magnate and philanthropist. André Maurois, French writer.
English nicknames: Andie, Andy.
Foreign variations; Andreas (German, Dutch, Swedish), André (French), Andrés (Spanish), Andrea (Italian), Andrej (Slavic), Aindreas (Scotch and Irish), Anders (Swedish).

ANGELO—Italian: Angelo. "Angel or Messenger." Pope John XXIII (Angelo Roncalli); Angelo Angelucci, 19th-century Italian author.
English nickname: Angie.

ANGUS—Scotch Gaelic: Aonghus. "Unique strength, one-choice." Famous as a strong man in his country. Angus or Aonghus, grandson of Niall of the Nine Hostages, 10th-century Irish ruler, was ancestor of many Irish and Scotch clans.

ANNAN—Celtic: Anant. "From the stream."

ANSCOM—Old English: Aenescumb. "Dweller in the valley of the awe-inspiring one." A strange, unusual man dwelling alone with his family.
English variation: Anscomb.

ANSEL—Old French: Ancel. "Adherent of a nobleman." See Anselm.
English variation: Ansell.

ANSELM—Old German: Ans-helm. "Divine helmet." A man with a helmet that arrows touched but could not penetrate. St. Anselm, the Father of Scholasticism, died A.D. 1109.
English nicknames: Anse, Ansel.
Foreign variations: Anselme (French), Anselmi (Italian), Anselmo (Spanish, Portuguese), Anshelm (German).

ANSLEY—Old English: Aene's-leah. "From the awe-inspiring one's pasture meadow."

ANSON—Old English: Aene's son. "Awe-inspiring one's son." Anson Burlingame, American diplomat (1820-1870).

ANSTICE—Greek: Anastasios. "Resurrected one."
English variation: Anstiss.

ANTHONY—Latin: Antonius. "Inestimable, priceless one." St. Anthony the Great, died A.D. 356, early Christian hermit; St. Anthony of Padua, died A.D. 1231, patron saint of the poor; Anthony Wayne, American Revolutionary War general; Anthony Eden, British Prime Minister; actors include Anthony Quinn, Anthony Quayle, Tony Martin, Tony Randall, Tony Curtis.
English nicknames: Tony.
Foreign variations: Antonio (Spanish, Italian, Portuguese), Antoine (French), Anton, Antonius (German, Swedish), Anntoin (Irish).

ANWELL—Welsh-Celtic: Anwyl. "Beloved or dear one."
English variations: Anwyl, Anwyll.

ANYON—Welsh-Celtic: Einion. "Anvil." Anvils were used to fashion armor for brave knights in the Middle Ages.

ARCHARD—Anglo-French-German: Erchan-hardt. "Sacred, powerful."
English variation: Archerd.

ARCHER—Old English: Archere. "Bowman, archer."

ARCHIBALD—Anglo-French-German: Erchan-bold. "Sacred, noble and bold." Archibald Mac-Leish, American poet and dramatist.
English nicknames: Arch, Archie.
Foreign variations: Archaimbaud, Archambault (French), Archibaldo (Spanish), Gilleasbuig (Scotch), Archimbald (German).

ARDEN—Latin: Ardens. "Ardent, fiery."
English variation: Ardin.

ARDLEY—Old English: Arda-leah. "From the home-lover's meadow."

ARDOLPH—Old English: Ardwolf. "Home-loving wolf." A fierce warrior changed by love into a gentle man.

ARGUS—Greek: Argos. "Watchful guardian." A vigilant whose keen eyes saw everything. Argus in Greek mythology was the giant with a hundred eyes. Legend says that these eyes later ornamented the peacock's tail feathers.

ARGYLE—Scotch Gaelic: Arregaithel. "From the Land of the Gaels, an Irishman."

ARIC—Old English: Alh-ric. "Sacred ruler."
English nicknames: Ric, Rick, Ricky.

ARIES—Latin: Aries. "A ram." Born in April, the first sign of the Zodiac; his parents called him Aries for "The Ram."

ARLEDGE—Old English: Hare-lache. "Dweller at the hare or rabbit lake." A lake where rabbits played and danced to mystic music made by frogs.

ARLEN—Irish Gaelic: Airleas. "Pledge." A man of truth and common sense who kept his vow to God. Michael Arlen, English writer; Richard Arlen, American actor.

ARLEY—Old English: Hara-leah. "From the rabbit meadow." English variation: Harley.

ARMAND—Old German: Hariman. "Army-man." Armand was patron saint of the Netherlands. English variation: Armin.

ARMSTRONG—Old English: Arm-strang. "Strong of arm (in battle)."

ARNALL—Old German: Arnhold. "Eagle-gracious." A sharp-sighted man with the courtesy of a gentleman. English variation: Arnell.

ARNETT—Old Franco-English: Arnet. "Little eagle." English variations: Arnatt, Arnott.

ARNEY—Old German: Arni. "Eagle." Arne Garborg, Norwegian author (1851-1924). English variation: Arnie. Foreign variation: Arne (Norwegian).

ARNO—Old German: Arn-wulf. "Eagle-wolf." A fighter with the vision of an eagle and the courage of a wolf. Peter Arno, American cartoonist. Foreign variations: Arnou, Arnoux (French).

ARNOLD—Old German: Arnwald. "Eagle-ruler" or "Strong as an eagle." Arnold Bennett, famous English novelist (1867-1931). Foreign variations: Arnaldo (Spanish), Arnoldo (Italian), Arnaud (French).

ARNOT—Old Franco-German: Arn-ot. "Little eagle." English variation: Arnott.

ARTEMAS—Greek: Artemas. "Gift of Artemis." St. Artemas, 1st century, was one of St. Paul's disciples. Artemas Ward, American Revolutionary War general (1727-1800).

ARTHUR—Cymric-Welsh: Arth-wr. "Noble one" or "Bearman." King Arthur, semi-legendary 6th-century English ruler was the subject of many romantic tales. Arthur Balfour, British statesman (1848-1930); Art Linkletter, television personality. English nicknames: Art, Artie. Foreign variations· Arturo (Spanish, Italian), Artair (Scotch), Artur (Irish), Artus (French).

ARUNDEL—Old English: Arndell. "Dweller at the eagle dell."

ARVAD—Hebrew: Arvad. "Wanderer." Arpad, who died in A.D. 907, was the national hero of Hungary. Foreign variation: Arpad (Hungarian).

ARVAL—Latin: Arvalis. "Cultivated land." Welsh: Arvel. "Wept-over." English variation: Arvel.

ARVIN—Old German: Hariwin. "Army or people's friend." A friend who loved all men and thought them equal.

ASA—Hebrew: Asa. "Physician." A true physician who healed both mind and body. The Biblical Asa was a Judean king. Asa Gray, American botanist (1810-1888).

ASCOT—Old English: Est-cot. "Dweller at the east cottage." English variation: Ascott.

ASHBURN—Old English: Aescburne. "Ash-tree brook." Where ash-trees were held earthbound by the brook's soft joyous song.

ASHBY—Old English: Aesc-by. "Ash-tree farm."

ASHER—Hebrew: Asher. "Happy one." A boy quick to laugh. Asher Durand, American painter and engraver (1796-1886).

ASHFORD—Old English: Aescford. "Dweller at the ash-tree ford."

ASHLEY—Old English: Aescleah. "Dweller at the ash-tree meadow."

ASHLIN—Old English: Aesclin. "Dweller at the ash-tree pool."

ASHTON—Old English: Aesctun. "Dweller at the ash-tree farm."

ASHUR—East Semitic: Ashur. "Warlike one." Ashur-banipal and Ashur-nasirpal were ancient Assyrian kings.

ASWIN—Old English: Aescwine. "Spear-friend or protector."

ATHERTON—Old English: Aethre-tun. "Dweller at the spring-farm."

ATLEY—Old English: Atteleah. "Dweller at the meadow." A meadow where birds sing love songs to its beauty.

ATWATER—Old English: Attewater. "Dweller at the water." This family lived where water flowed in great profusion. Wilbur Atwater, American chemist (1844-1907).

ATWELL—Old English: Attewelle. "Dweller at the spring."

ATWOOD—Old English: Attewode. "At the forest." George Atwood, English mathematician (1746-1807).

ATWORTH—Old English: Atte-worthe. "At the farmstead."

AUBERT—See Albert.

AUBIN—Old French: Aubin. "Fair, blond one." A youth whose hair caught the sun's bright rays that turned it gold.

AUBREY—Old French: Albaric. "Blond ruler, elf ruler, spirit ruler." A king whose blond hair formed a crown of gold upon his noble head. Aubrey Beardsley, 19th-century English painter. Foreign variation: **Alberik** (Swedish).

AUDRIC—Old German: Adalric. "Noble ruler." An old one, rich in knowledge and experience.

AUDWIN—Old German: Adalwine. "Noble friend."

AUGUST—Latin: Augustus. "Majestic dignity; exalted." Augustus Caesar, 63 B.C.–14 A.D., first Roman emperor; Augustus John, famous Welsh painter (1878-1961); Auguste Renoir, noted French painter (1841-1919).
English nickname: **Gus**.
English variation: **Augustus**.
Foreign variations: **Agosto** (Italian), **Auguste**, (French), **Augusto** (Spanish), **Aguistin** (Irish).

AUGUSTINE—Latin: Augustinus. "Belonging to Augustus." St. Augustine, Oracle of the Western Church, A.D. 354-430.
English variations: **Austin, Austen**.

AUSTIN—See Augustine. Austin Chamberlain, English politician (1863-1937).

AVENALL—Old French: Avenelle. "Dweller at the oat field." Oat fields ripening in the sun bring thoughts of cakes and honey.
English variations: **Avenel, Avenell**.

AVERELL—Middle English: Averil. "Born in the month of April," or Old English: Efer-hild. "Boar-warrior." Averell Harriman, American statesman.
English variations: Averil, Averill.

AVERY—Old English: Aelf-ric. "Elf-ruler." Legendary, mischievous elfin ruler of primeval Britain. Avery Hopwood, American playwright.

AXEL—Old German: Apsel. "Father of peace." Scandinavian form of the Hebrew Absalom. Axel Wennergren, Swedish industrialist; Axel Munthe, Swedish writer (1857-1949).

AXTON—Old English: Aecce's-stane. "Sword-wielder's stone."

AYLMER—Old English: Aethelmaere. "Noble-famous one," or Old English: Aegel-maere. "Awe-inspiring, famous." John Aylmer, bishop of London (1521-1594); Felix Aylmer, English actor.

AYLWARD—Old English: Aegel-weard. "Awe-inspiring guardian," or Old English: Aethelweard. "Noble guardian."

AYLWORTH—Old English: Aegel-weorth. "Awe-inspiring one's farmstead."

B

BAILEY—Old French: Bailli. "Bailiff or steward." Men trusted him.
English variations: Baillie, Baily, Bayley.

BAINBRIDGE—Old English: Ban-brigge. "Bridge over white water." Commodore William Bainbridge (1774-1833), American naval officer.

BAIRD—Irish Gaelic: Bhaird. "Ballad singer." A singer who put sweet words to music. Baird, a 13th-century chieftain, founded the Scotch clan Baird.
English variation: Bard.

BALBO—Latin: Balbus. "The indistinct speaker." General Italo Balbo, prominent in World War II.
Foreign variations: Bailby (French), Balbi (Italian).

BALDEMAR—Old German: Balde-mar. "Bold or princely and famous."
Foreign variation: Baumer (French).

BALDER—Old English: Baldhere. "Bold army." An extremely brave army leader; or Old Norse: Baldr. "Prince." Balder was the god of peace in old Norse mythology.
Foreign variations: Baldur (Norse), Baudier (French).

BALDRIC—Old German: Baldric. "Bold or princely ruler." St. Baldric was a 7th-century French religious leader. Baldric, a landowner, is listed in the 11th-century English Domesday Book.
Foreign variation: Baudric (French).

BALDWIN—Old German: Baldwin. "Bold friend or protector." Forceful man, courageous and strong. Baldwin of Flanders was a famous 11th-century King of Jerusalem; Baudouin is the present King of Belgium, born 1930.
Foreign variations: Balduin (German, Swedish, Danish), Baudoin (French), Baldovino (Italian).

BALFOUR—Gaelic-Pictish: Baile-four. "From the pasture place." Balfour, a noted Scotch name, is from a town in Fifeshire.

BALLARD—Old German: Baldhardt. "Bold, strong." A hero strong of character as well as physique.

BALTHASAR—Greek: Baltasaros. "May the Lord protect the king." Balthasar was one of the Three Wise Men or Magi who brought gifts to the Christ Child. Foreign variations: Belshazzar (Hebrew), Baltasar (German, Swedish), Balthasar (French), Baldassare (Italian).

BANCROFT—Old English: Benecroft. "From the bean field." A bean grower in medieval days.

BANNING—Irish Gaelic: Banain. "Little blond one." Old English: Bana-ing. "Son of the slayer."

BARCLAY—Old English: Berc-leah. "Dweller at the birchtree meadow." Barclay is a famous Scotch clan name. Barclay V. Head, English numismatist, (1844-1914).
English variation: Berkeley.

BARD—Irish Gaelic: Bard. "Poet and singer."
Foreign variations: Baird (Scotch), Barde (French).

BARDOLF—Old English: Barda-wulf. "Axe-wolf." A fearless man who wielded an axe in battle. Bardolfus is listed in the English Curia Regis Rolls, A.D. 1205.
English variations: Bardolph, Bardulf, Bardulph.
Foreign variations: Bardoul, Bardou (French).

BARDRICK—Old English: Barda-ric. "Axe-ruler."

BARLOW—Old English: Baerhloew. "Dweller at the bare hill." Alternate origin, Old English: Bar-hloew. "Boar-hill."

BARNABAS—Greek: Barnabas. "Son of exhortation or consolation." An heir of his father who taught spiritual truths. St. Barnabas was a companion of St. Paul; Barnaby Rudge, a character in Dickens' writings.
English nicknames: Barnaby, Barney, Barny.
Foreign variations: Barnabé (French), Barnaba, Barna (Italian), Bernabé, Barnebás (Spanish).

BARNABY—See Barnabas.

BARNARD—See Bernard. St. Barnard, 9th-century French archbishop.

BARNETT—Old English: Boern-et. "Nobleman; leader."

BARNUM—Old English: Beorn's-ham. "Nobleman's home." Phineas T. Barnum, famous American circus owner and showman (1810-1891).

BARON—Old English: Baron. "Nobleman, warrior." James Baron, American Navy Commodore (1769-1851).
English variation: Barron.

BARR—Old English: Barre. "A gateway." Medieval villages were protected by walls and gates. Alternate origin, Old German: Ber. "Bear." Robert Barr, Scotch novelist, journalist (1850-1912).

BARRET—Old German: Berowalt. "Bear-mighty." A man with great strength. Baret was a landowner in the English Domesday Book, 11th century; Barrett Wendell, American author-educator.
English variation: Barrett.

BARRIE—See Barry.

BARRIS—Old Welsh: Ab-Harry. "Son of Harry."

BARRY—Irish Gaelic: Bearach. "Spearlike or pointed." A man seen as a spear. Alternate origin, Old French: Bari. "Barrier or arm." American actors include Barry Sullivan and Barry Nelson.

BARTHOLOMEW—Hebrew: Bar-Talmai. "Son of the furrows; farmer." St. Bartholomew was one of the twelve Apostles; Bartel Fonkman, American Congressman. English nicknames: Bart, Bartel, Barth, Bat. Foreign variations: Barthélemy, Bartholomé (French), Bartholonaus, Barthel (German), Barolomeo (Italian), Bartolome (Spanish), Parlan (Scotch), Bartholomeus (Swedish, Dutch).

BARTLEY—Old English: Barteah. "Bart's meadow." Bartley Crum, author. Foreign variation: Beartlaidh (Irish).

BARTON—Old English: Bereun. "Barley-estate or farmstead." A place where barley grew and viewers dreamed of amber ale and beer. Barton MacLane, American actor. English nickname: Bart.

BARTRAM—Old English: Beorht-hramm. "Glorious raven." A hero who was a descendant of Viking kings. The raven was the Viking armorial symbol. John Bartram, American botanist (1699-1777). English variation: Barthram.

BASIL—Latin: Basileolus. "Kingly, magnificent." St. Basil the Great, A.D. 329-379, was founder of the Greek Orthodox Church; Basil Rathbone, actor. Foreign variations: Basile (French), Basilio (Italian, Spanish, Portuguese), Basilius (German, Swedish, Dutch), Vassily (Russian).

BAXTER—Old English: Back-stere. "Bread-baker." The town's folk loved the baker's loaves and cakes. Baxter Ward, American television commentator. English nickname: Bax.

BAYARD—Old English: Bayhard. "Reddish-brown haired and powerful." The Chevalier Bayard, medieval French knight, was renowned for courage and honor; Bayard Taylor, 19th-century American essayist. English nickname: Bay. Foreign variations: Biaiardo, Baiardo (Italian).

BEACHER—Old English: Becere. "Dweller by the beech tree." An old locality name. English nicknames: Beach, Beachy, Beech, Beechy. English variation: Beecher.

BEAGAN—Irish Gaelic: Beagan. "Little one." An endearing nickname. English variation: Beagen.

BEAL—Old French: Bel. "Handsome one." A Beau Brummel, admired by women and envied by men. William J. Beal (1838-1924), American botanist. English variations: Beale, Beall.

BEAMAN—Old English: Beomann. "Beekeeper."

BEAMER—Old English: Bemeere. "Trumpeter." A trumpeter who blasted the silence that preceded war.

BEATTIE—Irish Gaelic: Biadhtaiche. "Public victualer." A distributor of provisions for the people of a town. Sir David Beatty, English Admiral (1871-1936). English variations: Beatie, Beaty, Beatty.

BEAU—Old French: Beau. "Handsome one." Beau Brummell, admired by women and envied by men, a 19th-century English dandy.

BEAUFORT—Old French: Beau-fort. "From the beautiful stronghold." Where old stones clothed in moss and vine were a memorial to brave men. Henry Beaufort, English 15th-century cardinal.

BEAUMONT—Old French: Beau-mont. "From the beautiful mountain." A mountain, star and cloud crowned, jeweled and perfumed by multicolored flowers. Francis Beaumont, famous English dramatist (1584-1616).

BECK—Middle English: Bek. "A brook." A lonesome brook looking for a river. Walter Bec listed in the 11th-century English Domesday Book.

BEECHER—See Beacher. Henry Ward Beecher, 19th-century American clergyman.

BELDEN—Old English: Beldene. "Dweller in the beautiful glen." A valley lost in beauty and in dreams.
English variation: Beldon.

BELLAMY—Old French: Bellamy. "Handsome friend." Faithful friend, as glorious as Apollo. Ralph Bellamy, American actor.

BEN—Hebrew: Ben. "Son." Also a nickname for Benjamin. Ben Jonson, 17th-century English dramatist; Ben-Hur, fictional character.
English variation: Benn.

BENDIX—See Benedict.

BENEDICT—Latin: Benedictus. "Blessed one." St. Benedict, A.D. 490-542, founder of Benedictine Order of monks; Benito Juarez, 19th-century President of Mexico; Benedict Arnold, American Revolutionary War general.
English nicknames: Ben, Benedick, Bennet, Bendix, Dick.
Foreign variations: Benedikt (German, Swedish), Benoit (French), Benedetto (Italian), Benedicto, Benito (Spanish), Bengt (Swedish).

BENITO—See Benedict.

BENJAMIN—Hebrew: Binyamin. "Son of the right hand." The Biblical Benjamin was Jacob's youngest son who carried out his father's wishes; Benjamin Franklin, American statesman (1706-1790); Benjamin Fairless, American industrialist; Benny Goodman, orchestra leader; Beniamino Gigli, famous opera tenor.
English nicknames: Ben, Bennie, Benjy, Benny.
Foreign variations: Beniamino (Italian), Benjamin (French, Spanish), Beathan (Scotch).

BENNETT—French-Latin: Benet. "Little blessed one." A man blessed with a happy disposition and good health. Bennett Cerf, American publisher.

BENONI—Hebrew: Benoni. "Son of my sorrow." Jacob's youngest son in the Bible was named Benoni by Rachel, who died at his birth. He was renamed Benjamin by his father.

BENSON—Hebrew-English: Ben-son. "Son of Benjamin." Also shortened from Benedict-son. Benson Lossing, American historian (1813-1891); Benson Fong, actor.

BENTLEY—Old English: Beonet-leah. "From the bent-grass meadow." The grassy lea where birds and crickets, owls and toads rehearsed their varied songs. Richard Bentley, 18th-century English critic.

BENTON—Old English: Beonettun "From the bent-grass farm." Grass like green brush strokes on the canvas of the earth. Thomas Hart Benton, American statesman (1782-1858).

BERESFORD—Old English: Beres-ford. "From the barley-ford." Where a river ran through a waving field of gold. Charles Beresford, English admiral.

BERG—German: Berg. "From the mountain."

BERGER—French: Berger. "Shepherd." Berger is listed in the 11th-century English Domesday Book.

BERK—See Burke.

BERKELEY—See Barclay.

BERN—Old German: Berin. "Bear." A proud protector of his people. Bern is listed in the 11th-century English Domesday Book. English variations: Berne, Bernie, Berny.

BERNARD—Old German: Berin-hard. "Brave as a bear." Bold as a bear, a courageous soldier. St. Bernard of Clairvaux, 12th century, and St. Bernard of Menthon, died 1008; Bernard Baruch, American financier, economist, statesman.
English nicknames: Barney, Barny, Bernie, Berny.
English variation: Burnard.
Foreign variations: Bernhard (German, Swedish), Bernardo (Italian, Spanish), Barnard (French), Bearnard (Scotch, Irish).

BERT—Old English: Beorht. "Shining, glorious one." See also Albert, Herbert. Bert Parks, entertainer; Bert Lahr, comedian; Burt Lancaster, actor.

BERTHOLD—Old German: Bercht-wald. "Brilliant ruler." St. Berthold of France founded the Carmelite Order, 12th century. Berthold Auerbach, 19th-century German novelist.
English nicknames: Bert, Bertie.
English variation: Bertold.
Foreign variations: Berthoud (French), Bertoldi (Italian).

BERTON—Old English: Beorht-tun. "Brilliant one's estate," or Old English: Burh-tun. "Fortified town."
English nicknames: Bert, Bertie.

BERTRAM—Old English: Beorht-hram. "Brilliant raven." The raven was symbolic of wisdom. St. Bertrand, 7th-century evangelizer of France and Flanders; Bertram Goodhue, noted American architect (1860-1929); Bertrand Russell, English writer and philosopher.
Foreign variations: Bertrand (French), Beltrán (Spanish), Bertrando (Italian).

BEVAN—Welsh: Ab-Evan. "Son of the well-born or youthful one." A noble man without a title.
English variations: Beaven, Beavan, Beven.

BEVIS—Old French: Beaveis. "Fair view."
Foreign variation: Beauvais (French).

BICKFORD—Old English: Bic-ca-ford. "Hewer's ford." Charles Bickford, American actor.
English nickname: Bick.

BING—Old German: Binge. "From the kettle-shaped hollow." Bing Crosby, noted actor and singer.

BINK—North English: Bink. "Dweller at the bank or slope."

BIRCH—Old English: Beorc. "At the birch tree." Samuel Birch, 19th-century English Egyptologist.
English variation: Birk.

BIRKETT—Middle English: Birk-hed. "Dweller at the birch headland." A tree-covered promontory that extended into the sea. Birket Foster, English painter (1825-1899).

BIRKEY—North English: Birkey. "From the birch-tree island."

BIRLEY—Old English: Byre-leah. "Cattle shed on the meadow."

BIRNEY—Old English: Burne-ig. "Dweller on the brook-island." James Birney, 19th-century American politician.
English variation: Burney.

BIRTLE—Old English: Bird-hil. "From the bird hill."

BISHOP—Old English: Biscop. "The bishop." Sir Henry Bishop, English composer (1786-1855).

BLACK—Old English: Blaec. "Dark complected." James Black, American lawyer and prohibition leader (1823-1893).

BLADE—Old English: Blaed. "Prosperity, glory."

BLAGDEN—Old English: Blaec-dene. "From the dark valley." A shadowed valley whose precipitous walls obscured the sun.

BLAINE—Irish Gaelic: Blian. "Thin, lean one." St. Blane, 6th century Scotch bishop; James G. Blaine, 19th-century American statesman.
English variation: Blayne.

BLAIR—Irish Gaelic: Blar. "From the plain or field." Francis Blair, American politician, Civil War general (1821-1875).

BLAISE—See Blaze.

BLAKE—Old English: Blac. "Fair haired and fair complexioned," or Old English: Blaec. "Dark one." Robert Blake, 17th-century English admiral.

BLAKELEY—Old English: Blaec-leah. "From the black meadow."

BLAKEY—Old English: Blac-ey. "Little fair-haired one."

BLANCO—Spanish: Blanco. "Blond, white." A strange mutation, beloved by his race.

BLAND—Latin: Blandus. "Mild, gentle one."

BLANE—See Blaine.

BLANFORD—Old English: Bland-ford. "Gray-haired one's river crossing."

BLASE—See Blaze.

BLAYNE—See Blaine.

BLAZE—Latin: Blasius. "Stammerer." Some philologists say, "Torch or firebrand" from Old German: Blas. St. Blaze, world renowned 4th-century Armenian bishop, patron of physicians.
English variations: Blaise, Blase, Blayze.
Foreign variations: Blaise (French), Blasien (German), Biagio (Italian), Blas (Spanish), Blasius (Swedish).

BLISS—Old English: Bliss. "Joyful one." A joyful person even in adversity. Bliss Perry, American author, editor.

BLYTHE—Old English: Blythe. "Merry one."

BOAZ—Hebrew: Boaz. "In the Lord is strength." In the Bible Boaz was a pillar of wisdom in the Temple of the Lord. Boaz was the husband of Ruth.
English variations: Boas, Boase.

BODEN—Old French: Bodin. "Herald, messenger." Town crier of news before they had newspapers.

BOGART—Old German: Bogo-hardt. "Bow-strong." Humphrey Bogart, actor.

BONAR—Old French: Bonaire. "Kind, gentle, good." Bonar Law, British statesman (1858-1923).
English variation: Bonner.

BONIFACE—Latin: Bonifacius. "Doer of good." A lucky, fortunate one. St. Boniface, the Apostle of Germany, born in England, A.D. 675. Boniface Amerbach, 16th-century German scholar.
Foreign variations: Bonifacius (German, Swedish, Dutch), Bonifacio (Italian, Spanish).

BOONE—Old French: Bone. "Good one." Daniel Boone, American explorer (1735-1820).

BOOTH—Old Norse: Bothi. "Herald," or Middle English: Bothe. "Dweller in a hut." Booth Tarkington, American novelist (1869-1946).
English variations: Both, Boothe, Boot, Boote.

BORDEN—Old English: Bardene. "From the boar-valley."

BORG—Norse: Borg. "Castle dweller."

BORIS—Slavis: Boris. "Battler." A warrior, able bodied and strong, a threat to tyrants. St. Boris, King of Bulgaria, died A.D. 907; Boris Godunov, 17th-century Russian czar; Boris Karloff, noted actor.

BOSWELL—Old French: Bosvile. "Forest-town." A town built in the woods where violets bloom in spring. St. Boswell, 7th-century abbot of Melrose, Scotland; James Boswell, 18th-century Scotch biographer.

BOSWORTH—Old English: Bos-worth. "At the cattle-enclosure." A hedged enclosure that kept marauders out and cattle in. Joseph Bosworth, 19th-century English clergyman; Hobart Bosworth, American actor.

BOTOLF—Old English: Botewolf. "Herald-wolf." A professional herald who went from door to door shouting town news in person. St. Botolph, famous 7th-century English abbot, for whom Boston, England, and Boston, Massachusetts, were named.

BOURKE—See Burke.

BOURNE—Old English: Bourne. "From the brook." A small brook whose song was a whisper and a sigh. See also Burne.

BOWEN—Old Welsh: Ab-Owen. "Son of the well-born or youthful one," or Gaelic: Buadhachan. "Little victorious one." Francis Bowen, 19th-century American author.

BOWIE—Irish Gaelic: Buidhe. "Yellow-haired." Col. James Bowie, American scout, died 1836.

BOYCE—Old French: Bois. "From the forest." A woodland dweller whose contact with the town was rare. William Boyce, English composer (1710-1799).

BOYD—Irish Gaelic: Buidhe. "Blond one." E. Boyd Smith, American artist, illustrator; William Boyd, actor.

BOYNE—Irish Gaelic: Bo-find. "White cow." Named for a rare white cow that grazed in the fields of lush grass. Famous Battle of the Boyne, Ireland, 1690.

BRAD—Old English: Brad. "Broad, wide place." See also Bradley, Bradford.

BRADBURN—Old English: Brad-bourne. "Broad brook." A peaceful place where speckled trout teased dragonflies.

BRADEN—Old English: Braddene. "From the wide valley."

BRADFORD—Old English: Bradford. "From the broad river crossing." William Bradford, famous 17th-century New England governor; Bradford Dillman, actor.

BRADLEY—Old English: Brad-leah. "From the broad meadow." Henry Bradley, 19th-century English philologist.
English nicknames: Brad, Lee.

BRADY—Irish Gaelic: Bradach. "Spirited one," or Old English: Brad-ig. "From the broad-island." "Diamond Jim" Brady; William A. Brady, theatrical producer; Scott Brady, actor.
English nickname: Brad.

BRAINARD—Old English: Bran-hard. "Bold raven." A man who feared no one. The raven was symbolic of bravery. David Brainerd, American missionary to the Indians (1718-1747).
English variation: Brainerd.

BRAM—See Bran, Abraham. Bram Stoker, English writer of *Dracula* (1847-1912).

BRAMWELL—Old English: Braem-wiella. "From the bramble-bush spring." Bramwell Fletcher, actor.

BRAN—Old Celtic: Brann. "Raven." The dove, the raven and the phoenix bird are symbols of continued life or rebirth. Prince Bran, Gaelic Irish legends say, sailed to a sunny land in the southern seas, returning after a hundred years, still a young man.
English variation: Bram.

BRAND—Old English: Brand. "Firebrand." Great energy and self-confidence made this man eloquent. In Norse myths Brand was the grandson of Woden, king of the gods.

BRANDER—Old Norse: Brandr. "Sword; firebrand." Brander Matthews, American educator, writer.

BRANDON—Old English: Brand-dun. "From the beacon hill." A mount with a beacon light shining bright. Brandon Peters, Brandon de Wilde, actors.

BRANT—Old English: Brant. "Proud one," or Old English: Brand. "Firebrand." Joseph Brant, 1742-1807, Mohawk Indian war chief.

BRAWLEY—Old English: Bra-leah. "From the hillslope meadow."

BRENDAN—Irish Gaelic: Breandan. "Little raven." A brave, bold man, even in his youth. St. Brendan, famous 6th-century Irish leader, patron of sailors; Brendan Behan, Irish playwright.

BRENT—Old English: Brent. "Steep hill. George Brent, actor.

BRETT—Celtic: Bret. "Briton." A native of the isle the Romans called Brittania. Bret Harte, famed 19th-century American writer.
English variation: Bret.

BREWSTER—Old English: Brewstere. "Brewer." William Brewster, American Pilgrim leader.

BRIAN—Celtic: Bri-an. "Strength, virtue, honor." All three attributes make a leader. Brian Boru, most famous of all Irish kings, A.D. 926-1014; actors include Brian Aherne, Brian Keith, Brian Donlevy.
English variations: Briant; Brien, Brion, Bryan, Bryant, Bryon.
Foreign variation: Briano (Italian).

BRICE—Celtic-Welsh: Brys. "Quick one." Indisputable swiftness helped this man to excell, as did the Greek Olympian.
English variation: Bryce.

BRIDGER—Old English: Brigge-ere. "Dweller at the bridge; bridge-builder." Jim Bridger, American explorer, frontier scout, 19th century.

BRIGHAM—Middle English: Brigge-ham. "Dweller at the

bridge enclosure." A bridge fringed by heliotrope and heather. Brigham Young, American religious leader (1801-1877).

BROCK—Old English: Brok. "Badger." A badger inn-sign gave this man his name. Brock Pemberton, theatrical producer. English nicknames: **Broc, Brockie, Brok.**

BROCKLEY—Old English: Broc-leah. "From the badger meadow." Where badgers built great burrows below the pasture grass.

BRODERICK—Middle English: Brod-rig. "From the broad ridge," or Welsh: Ab-Roderick. "Son of famous ruler." Broderick Crawford, actor.

BRODIE—Irish Gaelic: Broth. "A ditch." An individual who built a canal to irrigate his land. Brodie is a famous Scotch clan name. Sir Benjamin Brodie was surgeon to the British royal family in the mid-1800s.
English variation: **Brody.**

BROMLEY—Old English: Brom-leah. "Dweller at the broom-meadow." A place where yellow broom grows.

BRONSON—Old English: Brunson. "Son of the brown one." Bronson Howard, American dramatist, journalist (1842-1908).

BROOK—Middle English: Brok. "Dweller at the brook." Where a romanticist heard a small brook whispering to the flowers.
English variation: **Brooke.**

BROOKS—Middle English: Broks. "Dweller at the brooks." Where brooks met and merged to become a tumbling river. Brooks Atkinson, American drama critic.

BROUGHER—Old English: Burghere. "Fortress resident."

BROUGHTON—Old English: Burg-tun. "From the fortress town." A large town below the fortress walls.

BROWN—Middle English: Brun. "Dark, reddish complexion." John Brown, 19th-century American abolitionist.

BRUCE—Old French: Bruis. "Dweller at the thicket." Robert the Bruce, Scotland's famous king, liberated his land from England in the 1300s.

BRUNO—Italian: Bruno. "Brown haired one." St. Bruno, founder of the Carthusian Order of monks, died A.D. 1101. Bruno Walter, orchestra conductor.

BRYAN—See Brian. William Jennings Bryan, American lawyer and politician.

BRYANT—See Brian. Bryant Washburn, silent screen actor.

BRYCE—See Brice.

BUCK—Old English: Boc. "Buck deer." Nature gave this man the grace and swiftness of a deer. Buck Jones, silent screen Western actor.

BUCKLEY—Old English: Boc-leah." "Dweller at the buck-deer meadow." James Buckley, American religious leader (1836-1920).

BUDD—Old English: Boda. "Herald or messenger." The messenger of kings, the herald of the town. Also a nickname from Richard. Budd Schulberg, American novelist; Buddy Baer, actor. English variations: **Bud, Budde, Buddie, Buddy.**

BUNDY—Old English: Bondig. "Free man." A man who earned his freedom from his overlord.

BURBANK—Old English: Burh-bank. "Dweller on the castle hill-slope." Luther Burbank, famous American horticulturist.

BURCH—Middle English: Birche. "Birch tree." A birch tree haunted by wild birds marked this ancestor's home site.

BURCHARD—Old English: Burgh-hard. "Strong as a castle." A youth whose strength was compared to a castle that had withstood war and troubled times. Burchard was a famous 12th-century French abbot.
Foreign variations: Burckhardt, Burkhart (German), Burgard, Burgaud (French).

BURDETT—Old French: Bordet. "Little shield." A soldier who was firm against all evil.

BURDON—Old English: Burh-don. "Dweller at the castle hill."

BURFORD—Old English: Burh-ford. "Dweller at the castle-ford." An ancient castle-ford where cattle, sheep, and brave men crossed.

BURGESS—Middle English: Burgeis. "Citizen of a fortified town." An impregnable place of protection. Burgess Meredith, actor.

BURKE—Old French: Burc. "Dweller at the fortress." Sir John Burke, famous English genealogist and heraldic expert, 19th century; Bourke Hickenlooper, U.S. Senator.
English variations: Berk, Berke, Bourke, Burk.

BURKETT—Old French: Burcet. "From the little stronghold."

BURL—Old English: Byrle. "Cup-bearer." A server of wine to the lord of a medieval castle. Burl Ives, folk singer and actor.

BURLEY—Old English: Burh-leah. "Dweller at the castle meadow."
English variation: Burleigh.

BURNABY—Old Norse: Biorn-byr. "Warrior's estate." Frederick Burnaby, 19th-century English traveler.

BURNARD—See Bernard.

BURNE—Old English: Bourne. "Brook." A lonesome brook looking for a river.
English variations: Bourn, Bourne, Burn, Byrne.

BURNELL—Old French: Brunel. "Little brown-haired one." Arthur Burnell, English orientialist (1840-1882).

BURNETT—Middle English: Burnet. "Little brown-complected one." Burnet Maybank, U.S. Senator.

BURNEY—Old English: Bureig. "Dweller at the brook island."

BURR—Old Norse: Burr. "Youth." Burr Tillstrom, actor.

BURRELL—Old French: Burel. "Reddish-brown complexion."

BURT—See Bert.

BURTON—Old English: Burh-tun. "Dweller at the fortified town." Burton Holmes, noted American traveler, lecturer.

BUSBY—Scotch-Norse: Bus-byr. "Dweller at the village in the thicket." Busby Berkeley, choreographer.

BYFORD—Old English: Bi-ford. "Dweller by the river crossing."

BYRAM—Old English: Byre-ham. "Dweller at the cattle-shed place." A cattle shelter on a family estate.

BYRD—Old Ɛnglish: Byrd. "Birdlike." Nicknamed a "bird" because of his quick actions. Admiral Richard E. Byrd, American Antarctic explorer.

BYRLE—See Burl.

BYRNE—See Bourne.

BYRON—Old French: Buiron. "From the cottage or country estate." Where nature was magnanimous in its magnificence. George, Lord Byron, famous English poet (1788-1824).

C

CADBY—Old Norse-English: Cada's-byr. "Warrior's settlement. A soldier who founded the town called Cadby.

CADDOCK—Old Welsh: Cadawg. "Battle keenness." Strategy in battle results in victory.

CADELL—Old Welsh: Cad-el "Battle spirit." An aptitude for war made this man a hero. St. Cadell of Wales, 7th century.

CADMAN—Old Anglo-Welsh: Cad-man. "Battle man." Charles Wakefield Cadman, American composer.

CADMUS—Greek: Kadmos. "Man from the East." Legendary hero, founder of Grecian Thebes, who brought the alphabet to his people.

CAESAR—Latin: Caesar. "Long-haired or hairy"; through usage, "Emperor." Cesar Romero, actor. Foreign variations: Cäsar (German), Cesare (Italian), César (French, Spanish, Portuguese), Caesar (Swedish, Danish).

CAIN—Hebrew: Cain. "Possession or possessed." The first son of Adam and Eve, who murdered his brother Abel.

CALDER—Old English: Call-dwr. "The brook."

CALDWELL—Old English: Cald-wiella. "Cold spring." A cold, sweet spring where wild birds sing and cattle pause to drink.

CALEB—Hebrew: Kaleb. "Bold one" or "Dog." Fearless and courageous in danger. Caleb Young Rick, American poet (1872-1943). English nickname: Cale.

CALEY—Irish Gaelic: Caol-aidhe. "Thin, slender." His spirit seemed enclosed in steel, he was so strong and lithe.

CALHOUN—Irish Gaelic: Coill-cumhann. "From the narrow forest." Narrow woods between two green meadows. John C. Calhoun, American statesman (1782-1850).

CALVERT—Old English: Calf-hierde. "Calf-herder." A man who loved cattle, green pastures and the pungent smell of pines. Sir George Calvert, founder of Maryland (1580-1632).

CALVIN—Late Latin: Calvinus. "Bald one." Calvin Coolidge, 30th U.S. President. English nickname: Cal. Foreign variations: Calvino (Italian, Spanish).

CAMDEN—Anglo-Gaelic: Camdene. "From the crooked or winding valley." The glade was enhanced by wild rose bushes. William Camden, English scholar (1551-1623).

CAMERON—Scotch Gaelic: Cam-shron. "Wry or crooked nose." A man whose crooked nose gave him individuality; founder of clan Cameron. Cameron Mitchell, actor.
English nickname: Cam.

CAMPBELL—Scotch Gaelic: Cam-beul. "Wry or crooked mouth." When Campbell spoke men listened; founder of clan Campbell.
English nicknames: Cam, Camp.

CANUTE—Old Norse: Knut-r. "Knot." Immovable and steadfast in his resolutions. Canute or Knut was King of England and Denmark, A.D. 1017-1035; Knute Rockne, famous American football coach (1888-1931).
Foreign variation: Knut (Scandinavian).

CAREY—Old Welsh: Caerau. "Dweller at the castles." Medieval castles were well-fortified homes. Cary Grant, actor; Cary Middlecoff, golfer.
English variation: Cary.

CARL—See Charles. Also, Old German: Karl. "Farmer." A tiller of the soil who transformed it into a garden fit for kings. Carl Sandburg, noted American poet, author; Carl Hayden, U.S. Senator; Carl Reiner, actor.

CARLETON—Old English: Carla-tun. "Farmer's settlement." Where neighbors exchanged new seeds and gossip. Carleton Carpenter, actor; Carlton Chapman American painter (1860-1925).
English variation: Carlton.

CARLIN—Old Gaelic Irish: Cearbhallan. "Little champion."
English variation: Carling.

CARLISLE—Old English: Caerluel. "Castle tower." The tower was a fortress of defense. John G. Carlisle, American statesman (1835-1910).

CARMICHAEL—Scotch Gaelic: Cara-michil. "Friend of St. Michael," or Scotch Gaelic: Kermichil. "From Michael's stronghold."

CARNEY—Irish Gaelic: Cearnach. "Victorious." A soldier of the king, a man well trained and trusted.
English variation: Carny.

CAROL—See Carroll.

CAROLLAN—Irish Gaelic: Cearbhallain. "Little champion." A small warrior but immensely brave.

CARR—Old Norse: Kiarr. "Dweller at a marsh." A family progenitor who built his home beside a swamp.
English variations: Karr, Kerr.

CARRICK—Irish Gaelic: Carraig. "Rocky headland." A dweller whose home was surrounded by the sea.

CARROLL—Irish Gaelic: Cearbhall. "Champion." Lewis Carroll, famous author (1832-1898); J. Carroll Naish, actor.

CARSON—Middle English: Carson. "Son of the dweller at a marsh." Jack Carson, actor; Johnny Carson, comedian.

CARSWELL—Old English: Caerse-wiella. "Dweller at the watercress spring." Where small fish played hide-and-seek.

CARTER—Old English: Cartere. "Cart driver." Carter Glass, U.S. Senator; Carter Dickson, English author.

CARTLAND—Scotch-English: Caraid-land. "Land between the streams."

CARVELL—Old French: Caraville. "Spearman's estate, marshy estate."
English variation: Carvel.

CARVEY—Gaelic Irish: Cearrbhach. "Athlete, game-player." Physical agility and strength were held in high esteem in old Erin.

CARY—See Carey.

CASEY—Irish Gaelic: Cathasach. "Valorous, brave, watchful." A maintainer of order by constant vigilance. Casey Stengel, baseball manager.

CASH—Latin: Cassius. "Vain one."
English variation: Cass.

CASIMIR—Old Slavic: Kazatimiru. "Commands-peace." A leader at peace with himself and the world. Casimir the Pacific was Poland's great 11th-century king.
Foreign variations: Casimiro (Spanish), Kasimir (German, Slavic).

CASPAR—Persian: Kansbar. "Treasure-master." See Gaspar.
English nickname: Cass.
English variations: Casper, Gaspar, Gasper.

CASS—See Cash, Caspar.

CASSIDY—Irish Gaelic: Casidhe. "Ingenious, clever one; curly-haired one."

CASTOR—Greek: Kastor. "Beaver." A nicksame first applied to a man of diligence and determination. Castor was one of the Greco-Roman "Heavenly Twins" known as "The Gemini."

CATHMOR—Irish Gaelic: Cathaoir-mor. "Great warrior."

CATO—Latin: Catus. "Sagacious, wise one." Cato the Elder and Younger were famous ancient Roman patriots.

CAVAN—Irish Gaelic: Caomhan. "Handsome one."
English and Irish variation: Kavan.

CAVELL—Old French: Cavel. "Little active one."

CAWLEY—Scotch-Norse: MacAmhlaidh. "Ancestral relic." A sacred talisman from his predecessors suggested this man's name.

CECIL—Latin: Caecilius. "Dim-sighted or blind." The blind often have a super sense that is their compensation. Notables include Cecil Rhodes, English South African administrator (1853-1902); Cecil B. De Mille, famous film director, producer; Cecil S. Forester, English novelist.
English nickname: Cece.
Foreign variations: Cécile (French), Cecilius (Dutch).

CEDRIC—Old English: Caddaric. "Battle chieftain." A character in Scott's *Ivanhoe*. Sir Cedric Hardwicke, noted English actor.

CHAD—Old English: Cadda. "Warlike." St. Chad, English bishop, 7th century.

CHADWICK—Old English: Cadda-wic. "Warrior's estate or town." Sir Edwin Chadwick, English social reformer (1800-1890).

CHALMERS—Old Scotch: Chalmer "Son of the overseer or chamberlain."

CHANCE—Middle English: Chance. "Good fortune." So-named because fortune seemed to smile on this man's endeavors. See Chauncey.

CHANCELLOR—Middle English: Chaunceler. "King's secretary." A learned man invested with authority and secrecy.
English nicknames: Chance, Chaunce.

CHANDLER—Middle English: Chaundler; Old French: Chandelier. "Candle maker." Howard Chandler Christy, noted illustrator (1873-1952).

CHANNING—Old French: Chanoine. "Canon; church dignitary." Channing Pollock, American dramatist.
English nickname: Chan.

CHAPMAN—Old English: Ceapmann. "Merchant." Chapman Revercomb, U.S. Senator; Roy Chapman Andrews, noted explorer.

CHARLES—Old German: Karl; Latin: Carolus. "Strong, manly." Charles I, King of England, 1600-1649; Charles Darwin, English naturalist, 1809-1882; Charles de Gaulle, President of France; actors Charles Boyer, Charles Laughton, Charles Ruggles.
English nicknames: Charley, Charlie, Chick, Chuck.
Foreign variations: Karl, Carl (German, Swedish), Carlo (Italian), Carlos (Spanish), Karel (Dutch), Teàrlach (Scotch).

CHARLTON—Old English: Carla-tun. "Peasant's farmstead or town." Charlton Heston, actor.

CHASE—Old French: Chacier. "Hunter." W. M. Chase, American painter (1849-1916); Salmon P. Chase, former U.S. Secretary of the Treasury.

CHATHAM—Old English: Cadda-hamm. "Soldier's land." Named for a royal land grant.

CHAUNCEY—Middle English: Chanceler. "Chancellor church official." A diligent man who earned his good fortune. Chauncey Depew, American lawyer; Chauncey Olcott, entertainer (1860-1932).
English nicknames: Chance, Chancey, Chaunce.

CHENEY—Old French: Chesne. "Dweller at the oak forest." John Vance Cheney, American author (1848-1922).
English variation: Cheyney.

CHESTER—Old English: Ceaster. "Dweller at the fortified army camp." Chester A. Arthur, 21st President of the U.S.; Chester Bowles, American diplomat.
English nicknames: Ches, Chet.

CHETWIN—Old English: Cetewind. "From the cottage on the winding path."

CHEYNEY—See Cheney.

CHILTON—Old English: Celdtun. "From the spring farm."

CHRISTIAN—Greek: Christos. "Believer in Christ, anointed one." A follower of Christ's teachings. St. Christian, 12th-century bishop of Clogher; a long line of Danish kings named Christian, beginning in 1448; Christian Hahnemann, founder of homeopathy; Christian Herter, American statesman.
English nicknames: Chris, Chrissy, Christie, Christy.
Foreign variations: Kristian (Swedish), Chrétien (French), Christiano (Italian, Spanish).

CHRISTOPHER—Greek: Christoforos. "Christ-bearer." Used in honor of St. Christopher, 3rd century martyr, protector of travelers; Christopher Columbus, discoverer of America, known as Cristoforo Colombo in Italy and Cristóbal Colon in Spain; Christopher Fry, English dramatist.
English nicknames: Chris, Chrissy, Kit.
Foreign variations: Cristóbal (Spanish), Christophe (French), Cristoforo (Italian), Christoph, Christophorus (German), Kristofor (Swedish), Christoffer (Danish), Gillecriosd (Scotch).

CHURCHILL—Old English: Circe-hyll. "Dweller at the church-hill." Sir Winston Churchill, English statesman, writer.

CIAN—Irish Gaelic: Céin. "Ancient." He lived so long that people called this patriarch "ancient." The most famous Cian was the son-in-law of Ireland's celebrated 11th-century king, Brian Boru.

CICERO—Latin: Cicero. "Vetch or chick-pea." Named for his field of bright chick-peas. Cicero, died 43 B.C., was a noted Roman orator and statesman.

CLARE—Latin: Clarius. "Famous, illustrious one." Clair Engle, U.S. Senator.
English variation: **Clair**.

CLARENCE—Latin: Clarensis. "Famous one." Noted from Clarence Darrow, famous attorney; Clarence Mackay, American industrialist.

CLARK—Old French: Clerc. "Scholar." A learned man whose wisdom illuminated other eager minds. Clark Gable, noted actor (1901-1961).

CLAUDE—Latin: Claudius. "The lame one." A handicap may become a stimulus for great achievements. Famous from two Roman emperors in the 1st and 3rd centuries A.D.; Claudian, 5th-century Roman poet; Shakespearean characters named Claudio; Claude Debussy, French composer; Claude Pepper, U.S. Senator; Claude Rains, actor.
Foreign variations: **Claude** (French), **Claudio** (Italian, Spanish), **Claudius** (German, Dutch).

CLAUS—See Nicholas.

CLAY—Old English: Claeg. "From the place of clay." Sun-baked clay can be made productive by water, patience, and a plow. Henry Clay, American statesman (1777-1852).

CLAYBORNE—Old English: Claeg-borne. "From the clay-brook." Where blue water bubbled from white clay.
English nickname: **Clay**.
English variations: **Claiborn**, **Claybourne**.

CLAYTON—Old English: Claeg-tun. "From the clay estate or town."

CLEARY—Irish Gaelic: Cleirach. "Scholar." One who has gained knowledge from old books and parchments.

CLEMENT—Latin: Clementis. "Gentle, kind one." St. Clement of the 1st century; six medieval Popes; Clément Delibes, French operatic composer (1836-1891); Clemens Brentano, German dramatist (1778-1842); Clement Attlee, British statesman, Clement Moore, American author of *The Night Before Christmas*.
English nicknames: **Clem**, **Clemmy**, **Clim**.
Foreign variations: **Clemente** (Italian, Spanish), **Klemens** (German), **Clément** (French), **Clemens** (Danish), **Clementius** (Dutch).

CLEVE—See Clive, Cleveland.

CLEVELAND—Old English: Clif-land. "From the clif-land." Cleveland Amory, American author; Cleveland Abbe, American scientist (1883-1916).
English nicknames: **Cleve**, **Clevie**.

CLIFF—Old English: Clif. "From the steep rock or cliff." See Clifford. Cliff Robertson, actor; Cliff Arquette (Charley Weaver) American comedian.

CLIFFORD—Old English: Cliff-ord. "From the cliff-ford." A rock landmark at a river crossing. Clifford Case, U.S. Senator.
English nicknames: **Clif**, **Cliff**.

CLIFTON—Old English: Cliftun. "From the cliff-estate or town." Clifton Webb, actor; Clifton Fadiman, literary critic.

CLINTON—Old English: Clinttun. "From the headland-estate or town." Clinton Anderson, U.S. Senator; Clint Walker, American actor.
English nickname: **Clint.**

CLIVE—Old English: Clif. "From the cliff." An ancestor who took his name from his home on a precipice. Clive Brook, English actor.
English variations: **Cleve, Clyve.**

CLOVIS—Old German: Chlodwig. "Famous warrior." An early spelling of Ludwig or Lewis. Clovis, A.D. 481-511 founded the Frankish dynasty of French kings.
Foreign variation: **Clodoveo** (Spanish).

CLUNY—Irish Gaelic: Cluainach. "From the meadow." An old man who reminisced on meadows damp with morning dew.

CLYDE—Welsh: Clywd. "Warm," or Scotch Gaelic: Cleit. "Rocky eminence; heard from afar." From the famous River Clyde in Scotland. Clyde Cessna, American aircraft pioneer; Clyde Reed, U.S. Senator.

COBB—See Jacob.

COLAN—See Colin.

COLBERT—Old English: Ceolbeorht. "Brilliant seafarer," or Old German: Kuhl-berht. "Cool, calm, brilliant."
English variations: **Colvert, Culbert.**

COLBY—Old Anglo-Norse: Kolbyr. "From the black or dark settlement." Bainbridge Colby, U.S. Secretary of State.

COLE—See Nicholas. Cole Porter, American composer.

COLEMAN—Old English: Colemann. "Adherent of Nicholas," or Irish Gaelic: Column-an. "Little dove." St. Colman, patron of Austria, died 1012; Ronald Colman, actor.
English variation: **Colman.**

COLIN—Irish Gaelic: Coilin. "Child; cub," or French-Greek: Nicolin. "Victorious army." Colin Clive, Colin Keith-Johnston, English actors.
English variation: **Colan.**
Foreign variation: **Cailean** (Scotch).

COLLIER—Old English: Colier. "Charcoal merchant; miner." Collier Young, American film and television executive.
English variations: **Colier, Colis, Collyer, Colyer.**

COLTER—Old English: Coltere. "Colt-herder." There was no drudgery in the herder's work, for he loved horses.

COLTON—Old English: Coletun. "From the dark estate or town." Walter Colton, American editor, writer (1797-1851).

COLVER—See Culver.

CONAN—Celtic: Kunagnos. "Intelligence, wisdom," or Irish Gaelic: Conan. "High, exalted." St. Conan, Irish bishop on the Isle of Man, died 648; Sir Arthur Conan Doyle, English writer, creator of Sherlock Holmes.

CONLAN—Irish Gaelic: Connlan. "Hero."
English variations: **Conlin, Conlon.**

CONRAD—Old German: Kuonraet. "Bold counselor." A man unprejudiced, not afraid to tell the truth. St. Conrad of Hildesheim, 12th-century follower of St. Francis; Konrad Adenauer, German Chancelor; Konrad Bercovici, author; Conrad Hilton, American hotel executive.

English nicknames: Con, Connie, Cort, Curt.
Foreign variations: Konrad, Kort, Kurt (German), Konrad (Swedish), Conrade (French), Conrado (Italian, Spanish), Koenraad (Dutch).

CONROY—Irish Gaelic: Conaire. "Wise one."

CONSTANTINE—Latin: Constantinus. "Firm, constant one." Constantine the Great, 4th-century Roman emperor; Constantine, King of Greece (1868-1923).
Foreign variations: Costantino (Italian), Constantin (French, German, Danish), Constantino (Spanish), Konstantin (Swedish).

CONWAY—Irish Gaelic: Conmhaighe. "Hound of the plain." Conway Tearle, actor.

COOPER—Old English: Cupere. "Barrel maker." A skilled artisan who fashioned barrels for commerce.
English nickname: Coop.

CORBETT—Old French: Corbet. "Raven." A man with the courage of Vikings. The raven emblem symbolized wisdom and was used on flags and shields of the Norse Viking conquerors of Normandy and northwest France. Harvey W. Corbett, noted American architect.
English variations: Corbet, Corbin, Corby.

CORBIN—See Corbett.

CORCORAN—Irish Gaelic: Corcurachan. "Of reddish complexion." W. W. Corcoran, American financier, art collector (1798-1888).

CORDELL—Old French: Cordel. "Little rope-maker," or "Little rope." Cordell Hull, U.S. Secretary of State.

COREY—Irish and Scotch Gaelic: Coire. "Dweller by a hollow or by a seething pool." Corey Ford, American author.
English variation: Cory.

CORMICK—Irish Gaelic: Corbmac. "Charioteer." A man who had great skill in handling horses.
English and Irish variations: Cormac, Cormack.

CORNELIUS—Latin: Cornelius. "Horn colored; hornlike," or Late Latin: Cornolium. "Cornel-cherry tree." St. Cornelius, 1st century A.D.; Cornelius Vanderbilt, 19th-century American capitalist; Cornelius Ryan, author.
Foreign variations: Cornelio (Italian, Spanish, Portuguese), Cornélius (French).

CORNELL—Old French: Corneille. "Horn colored hair." A man whose hair was the color of rich cream. Cornel Wilde, actor.
English variations: Cornall, Cornel.

CORT—Old Norse: Kort-r. "Short," or Old German: Kort. "Bold." See Conrad.

CORWIN—Old Franco-English: Cor-wine. "Heart friend." "Greater love hath no man than this, that a man lay down his life for his friends." John 15:13.

CORYDON—Greek: Korudon. "Helmeted or crested one."

COSMO—Greek: Kosmos. "Order, harmony; the universe." Studies of the order, regularity and harmony of the universe make a student a philosopher. St. Cosmos, 3rd-century Christian martyr, patron of physicians; Cosmo the Elder and Cosmo the Great, medieval de' Medici rulers of Florence, Italy.
Foreign variations: Cosme (French), Cosimo (Italian, Spanish).

COURTLAND—Old English: Court-land. "Dweller at the farmstead or court land."
English nickname: Court.

COURTNEY—Old French: Courtenay. "Dweller at the farmstead or court." Courtney Riley Cooper, American writer.

COVELL—Old English: Cofahealh. "Dweller at the cave slope." A descriptive landmark.

COWAN—Irish Gaelic: Cobhan. "Hillside hollow." A valley filled with grass and flowers and sweet perfume. Alternate source Irish Gaelic: Comhghan. "A twin."

COYLE—Irish Gaelic: Cathmaol. "Battle follower." A soldier who liked the game of war and hidden danger.

CRADDOCK—Old Welsh: Caradoc. "Abounding in love; beloved." A gentleman who expressed love and affection. Renowned from Caradoc, heroic 1st-century King of Wales.

CRAIG—Scotch Gaelic: Creag. "Dweller at the crag." Craig Stevens, American actor.

CRANDELL—Old English: Cran-dell. "Dweller at the crane valley."
English variation: Crandall.

CRANLEY—Old English: Cranleah. "From the crane meadow." Where long-shanked birds assembled.

CRANSTON—Old English: Crans-tun. "From the crane estate or town." The cranes owned the large estate and the people were their tenants.

CRAWFORD—Old English: Crawe-ford. "From the crow-ford." Crawford Long, American scientist (1815-1878).

CREIGHTON—Middle English: Creke-tun. "Dweller at the creek estate or town." Creighton Hale, actor.

CRISPIN—Latin: Crispus. "Curly haired." St. Crispin, 3rd century, the patron of shoemakers. Foreign variations: Crispino (Italian), Crépin (French), Crispus (German), Crispo (Spanish), Krispijn (Dutch).

CROMWELL—Old English: Cromb-wiella. "Dweller at the crooked or winding spring." The crooked spring was sweet for all its meandering. Oliver Cromwell, English ruler 1653-1658.

CROSBY—Old Norse: Krossby-r. "Dweller at the shrine of the Cross." Made famous by the Crosby family of entertainers.
English variations: Crosbey, Crosbie.

CROSLEY—Old English: Crosleah. "From the cross-meadow." An old cross was a directional landmark on the meadow.

CULBERT—See Colbert.

CULLEN—Irish Gaelic: Cuilthinn. "Handsome one." An attractive man, gracious and dexterous. William Cullen Bryant, American poet (1794-1878).
English variations: Cullan, Cullin.

CULLEY—Irish Gaelic: Coille. "At the woodland." Great logs dispersed the winter's chill.
English variation: Cully.

CULVER—Old English: Colfre. "The dove." A symbol of peace to all nations.
English variation: Colver.

CURRAN—Irish Gaelic: Curadhan. "Champion or hero." A man who excelled in all he did.
English nicknames: Currey, Currie, Curry.

CURTIS—Old French: Curteis. "Courteous one." A gentleman in manners and in words. General Curtis LeMay, U.S. Air Force Chief of Staff; Curtis Wilbur, U.S. Secretary of the Navy. English nickname: Curt.

CUTHBERT—Old English: Cuth-beorht. "Famous, brilliant." St. Cuthbert of England died A.D. 687.

CYNRIC—Old English: Cyne-ric. "Powerful and royal." The blood of kings flowed in this proud princes' veins.

CYPRIAN—Greek: Kupris. "Man from the island of Cyprus." Regarded as an immigrant until he became a citizen of a new land. Cyprus was the mythical birthplace of Venus; its name means "Place of Venus." St. Cyprian, 3rd century.
Foreign variation: Cipriano (Spanish).

CYRANO—Greek: Kurene. "From Cyrene." Cyrene was the capital city of Cyrenaica in ancient north Africa. Famous from *Cyrano de Bergerac*, hero of classic drama by Rostand, modeled on a 17th-century soldier-poet.

CYRIL—Greek: Kyrillos. "Lordly one." A good man without a scepter or crown. St. Cyril of Alexandria, A.D. 376-444; Cyril N. Parkinson, English author; Cyril Ritchard, actor.
Foreign variations: Cyrille (French), Cirillo (Italian), Cyrill (German), Cirilo (Spanish), Cyrillus (Danish, Swedish, Dutch).

CYRUS—Old Persian: Kurush. "The sun." Named for the old pagan sun god, portrayed in medieval plays. Cyrus the Great was the 5th-century B.C. founder of the Persian Empire; Cyrus McCormick, American inventor (1809-1884).
English nickname: Cy.
Foreign variation: Ciro (Spanish).

D

DACEY—Irish Gaelic: Deasach. "Southerner."
English variation: Dacy.

DAG—Old Norse: Dag-r. "Day or brightness." The Norse god Dag was born of light and love, while night (Nott) was born of chaos. Dag Hammarskjold (1903-1961), UN Secretary General.

DAGAN—East Semitic: Dagan. "The earth," or "Little fish." Dagan, the Babylonian god of earth was once called the god of water and fish, and later the god of the earth and agriculture.
West Semitic variation: Dagon.

DAGWOOD—Old English: Daegga's wode. "Bright one's forest." Made famous from the comic strip character Dagwood.

DALBERT—Old English: Deal-beorht. "Proud, brilliant one," or Old English: Dael-beorht. "Shining valley." A valley dressed in green and perfumed by flowers. Delbert Mann, stage and motion picture director.
English variation: Delbert.

DALE—Old English: Dael. "Dweller in the valley." Dale Carnegie, writer and lecturer; Dale Robertson, actor.

DALLAS—Scotch Gaelic: Daileass. "From the waterfall-field or ravine-field." George Dallas (1792-1804), American statesman after whom Dallas, Texas, was named.

DALTON—Old English: Daeltun. "From the valley estate or town." John Dalton, English scientist (1766-1844).

DALY—Irish Gaelic: Dalach. "Counselor." Arnold Daly, actor; John Daly, radio and TV personality.

DALZIEL—Scotch Gaelic: Dalyell. "From the little field."

DAMON—Greek: Damon. "Constant one, "or Greek: Damas. "Tamer." Damon and Pythias, ancient Pythagorean scholars, valued friendship more than life. Damon was truly the "Constant one." Damon Runyon, American writer.
Foreign variations: **Damien** (French), **Damiano** (Italian), **Damian** (German).

DAN—Hebrew: Dan. "Judge." See Daniel.

DANA—Old English: Dane. "Man from Denmark." Dane Clark, Dana Andrews, actors; Richard Henry Dana, novelist.

DANBY—Old Norse: Dan-rby-r. "From the Dane's settlement." Francis Danby, English painter (1793-1861).

DANIEL—Hebrew: Daniyel. "God is my judge." God is the judge of man's conduct. Daniel, the Biblical Hebrew prophet; Daniel Boone, American explorer; Daniel Defoe, 18th-century English author of *Robinson Crusoe;* Daniel Taradash, film writer; actors Dan Dailey, Danny Thomas, Danny Kaye, Dan Duryea.
English nicknames: **Dan, Dannie, Danny.**

Foreign variations: **Danielle** (Italian), **Dane** (Dutch), **Daniel** (German, French, Spanish, Swedish), **Dàniel** (Scotch).

DARBY—Irish Gaelic: Diarmaid. "Free man," or Old Norse: Dyr-by-r. "From the deer estate." A place where deer and fawns could play unharmed by hunters. John Nelson Darby, founder of Plymouth Brethren; George Derby, American humorist.
English variation: **Derby.**

DARCY—Old French: D'Arcy. "From the fortress," or Irish Gaelic: Dorchaidhe. "Dark man." A mighty stronghold against attackers. Baron Thomas Darcy, English statesman, religious rebel (1467-1537).
English variations: **Darsey, Darsy.**

DARIUS—Greek: Dareious. "Wealthy one." Original usage in honor of Darius the Great, ancient Persian king; St. Darius, early Christian martyr; Darius Milhaud, music composer.

DARNELL—Old English: Derne-healh. "From the hidden nook." A secret place where dreamers came to dream.

DARRELL—Old French: Darel. "Little dear or beloved one." Darryl Zanuck, noted film producer.
English variations: **Daryl, Darryl.**

DARREN—Irish Gaelic: Dearan. "Little great one." Darren McGavin, actor.

DARRICK—See Derrick.

DARSEY—See Darcy.

DARTON—Old English: Deortun. "Deer park or estate." A little paradise where deer had found a haven.

DAVID—Hebrew: David. "Beloved one." Famous from the Biblical David, King of Israel and St. David, 6th century, patron saint of Wales; David Livingstone, British explorer; David Ben-Gurion, Premier of Israel; David Brinkley, commentator; actors David Warfield, David Niven, David Wayne.
English nicknames: **Dave, Davie, Davy.**
Foreign variations: **Davide** (French), **Davidde** (Italian), **Daibidh** (Scotch).

DAVIN—Old Scandinavian: Dagfinn-r. "Brightness of the Finns." The Finns like glowing candles in the dark, gave forth their knowledge to other men.

DAVIS—Old English: Davidsone. "Son of the beloved one." Old English and Scotch contraction of "David's son."

DEAN—Old English: Dene. "Dweller in the valley." Dean Acheson, American statesman; Dean Rusk, U.S. Secretary of State; Dean Martin, actor.

DEARBORN—Old English: Dere-bourne. "From the deerbrook." The deer came there to drink at dusk. Walter F. Dearborn, American educator.

DEDRICK—Old German: Dietrich. "Ruler of the people." See **Theodoric.**

DEEMS—Old English: Demasone. "Son of the judge." Deems Taylor, American composer, writer.

DELANO—Old French: De la Noye. "From the place of the nut trees." Where squirrels and small boys picnic. Franklin Delano Roosevelt, 32nd U.S. President.

DELBERT—Old English: Daegel-beorht. "Day-bright." See **Dalbert.**
English nicknames: **Del, Bert.**

DELLING—Old Norse: Delling-r. "Very shining one." A cheerful face makes a sad heart rejoice.

DELMER—Old French: De la Mare. "From the sea." Delmer Daves, film director, writer.

DELWYN—Old English: Dealwine. "Proud friend," or Old English: Daegel-wine. "Bright friend," or Old English Daelwine. "Valley-friend." A man who was friend to everyone.
English variation: **Delwin.**

DEMAS—Greek: Demas. "Popular one." Demas was a Greek, dignified, but approved by everyone.

DEMETRIUS—Greek: Demetrios. "Belonging to Demeter, Greek fertility goddess." One can never fashion jewels as beautiful as dewdrops on a rose. Demetrius, a silversmith of Ephesus, fomented disturbances against St. Paul.
Foreign variations: **Demetre** (French), **Demetrio** (Italian), **Dmitri** (Russian).

DEMOS—Greek: Demos. "The people." A spokesman for the populace.

DEMPSEY—Irish Gaelic: Diomasach. "Proud one." Jack Dempsey, American boxing champion.

DEMPSTER—Old English: Dema-stere. "The judge." A seeker after truth and when he found the truth, he judged. Arthur J. Dempster, American physicist (1885-1950).

DENBY—Old Norse: Dan-r by-r. "From the Dane's settlement."

DENIS—See Dennis.

DENLEY—Old English: Dene. "Dweller in the valley meadow."

DENMAN—Old English: Deneman. "Valley resident." Denman Thompson, American actor.

DENNIS—Greek: Dionys-os. "God of wine." Handsome man, happy as Dionysus who drank the elixir of Bacchus. Dennis Day, singer; actors Dennis King, Dennis O'Keefe, Dennis Morgan, Dennis Weaver.
English nicknames: Den, Denney, Denny.
English variations: Denis, Denys, Dion.
Foreign variations: Dionisio (Italian, Spanish), Dionysus (German), Denis Irish).

DENNISON—Old English: Dennis-sone. "Son of Dennis." Denison Clift, author, director.

DENTON—Old English: Denetun. "From the valley estate or town."

DENVER—Old English: Deneofer. "Dweller at the valley edge." James W. Denver, U.S. Congressman and Territorial Governor (1812-1892).

DERBY—See Darby.

DEREK—See Derrick.

DERMOT—Irish Gaelic: Diarmaid. "Free man."
English variation: Dermott.

DERRICK—Old German: Dietrich. "Ruler of the people." Derek Bond, Dirk Bogarde, actors; Dirk Bouts, 15th-century Dutch painter.
English variations: Derek, Dirk.

DERRY—Irish Gaelic: Dearg. "The red one."

DERWARD—Old English: Deor-ward. "Deer warden or guardian."

DERWIN—Old English: Deorawine. "Beloved friend."

DESMOND—Irish Gaelic: Deasmumhan. "Man from south Munster." Munster, now a south Irish province, was an ancient kingdom.

DEVERELL—Old Welsh-English: Dufr-healh. "From the riverbank." A home among white dogwood and yellow broom.

DEVIN—Irish Gaelic: Daimhin. "Poet, savant." A poet who put his higher thoughts into words.

DEVLIN—Irish Gaelic: Dobhailen. "Fierce valor." A fierce man, brave against opposition.

DEWEY—Old Welsh: Dewi. "Beloved one." A Welsh form of the Biblical David. Admiral George Dewey, hero of Spanish-American War; Thomas E. Dewey, American lawyer, politician; Dewey Martin, actor.

DE WITT—Old Flemish: De Witt. "Blond one." De Witt Clinton, American statesman (1769-1828).

DEXTER—Latin: Dexter. "Dexterous one." Timothy Dexter, 18th-century American merchant; Anthony Dexter, actor.
English nicknames: Deck, Dex.

DIAMOND—Old English: Daeg-mund. "Bright protector," or Old French: Diamant. "A diamond."

DIEGO—See James.

DIGBY—Old Norse: Diki-by-r. "From the dike settlement." A man from the land where dikes kept the sea at bay. K. H. Digby, 19th-century English author.

DILLON—Irish Gaelic: Diolmhain. "Faithful one." A faithful friend is hard to find.

DION—See Dennis.

DIRK—See Derrick.

DIXON—Old English: Dikkesone. "Son of Richard." See Richard. Joseph Dixon, American inventor (1799-1869); Maynard Dixon, American Western painter.

DOANE—Old English: Doune. "From the down or hill." G. W. Doane, 19th-century U.S. clergyman.

DOLAN—Irish Gaelic: Dubhlachlan. "Black haired." Robert E. Dolan, composer, conductor.

DOMINIC—Latin: Dominicus. "Born on Sunday, the Lord's Day," or "Belonging to the Lord." A boy born on Sunday, dimpled and fresh as a flower. St. Dominic (1170-1221), Spanish founder of Dominican Order.
English nicknames: Dom, Dommie, Nick.
English variations: Dominick.
Foreign variations: Domenico, Dominico (Italian), Domingo (Spanish), Dominique (French), Dominik (Slavic).

DONAHUE—Irish Gaelic: Donn-chadh. "Brown warrior."
English nicknames: Don, Donn.

DONALD—Scotch Gaelic: Domhnall. "World-mighty, world-ruler." Donald of the Isles, famous chief of clan MacDonald, died 1289; actors Donald Crisp, Don Ameche, Donald O'Connor.
English nicknames: Don, Donnie, Donny.

DONATO—Latin: Donatio. "A gift." "God has given some gifts to the whole human race, from which no one is excluded."— Seneca. St. Donatian, 4th-century bishop of Rheims.

DOOLEY—Irish Gaelic: Dubhlaoch. "Dark hero." Dr. Tom Dooley, famous medical pioneer.

DORIAN—Greek: Dorios. "From the sea, from Doria." The Dorians were ancient Hellenic settlers of Greece. Usage from the fictional hero of Oscar Wilde's *Picture of Dorian Gray*.

DORY—French: Doré. "Golden haired."

DOUGLAS—Scotch Gaelic: Dubh-glas. "From the black or dark water." A famous Scotch clan name. Notables: General Douglas MacArthur; Douglas Dillon, U.S. Secretary of the Treasury; Douglas Fairbanks, Jr., actor.
English nickname: Doug.
English variations: Douglass, Dugald.

DOW—Irish Gaelic: Dubh. "Black haired." Boy with black hair blended with the night, but eyes that were blue as the dawn. Neal Dow, 19th-century American reformer.
English variation: Dowie.

DOYLE—Irish Gaelic: Dubhghall. "Dark stranger." A sable-haired newcomer, most enchanting.

DRAKE—Middle English: Draca. "Owner of the 'Sign of the Dragon' Inn." The picture of a Draca or Dragon was a familiar English medieval trademark on shops and hostelries. Sir Francis Drake, 16th-century English navigator.

DREW—Old Welsh: Dryw. "Wise one," or Old German: Drugi. "Vision, phantom," or Old German: Drud. "Strength." Drew Pearson, noted columnist.

DRUCE—Old Anglo-Welsh: Dryw-sone. "Son of the wise man."

DRURY—Old French: Druerie. "Sweetheart; darling."

DRYDEN—Old English: Dryge-dene. "From the dry valley." John Dryden, 17th-century English poet.

DUANE—See Dwayne.

DUDLEY—Old English: Dudda-leah. "From the people's meadow." Dudley Field Malone, noted American attorney; Dudley Digges, actor; Dudley Beck, American cyclotron inventor. English nicknames: Dud, Dudd.

DUFF—Irish Gaelic: Dubh-thach. "Dark complexioned one." A fair haired boy with sun tanned skin. Dubh-thach was the Arch-Poet of King Laeghaire of Ireland, whom St. Patrick converted A.D. 433. English variation: Duffy.

DUGALD—See Douglas.

DUGAN—Irish Gaelic: Dubh-gan. "Dark complexioned."

DUKE—Old French: Duc. "Leader."

DUNCAN—Scotch Gaelic: Donn-chadh. "Brown warrior." Duncan, King of Scotland, 1034-1040, was murdered by Macbeth; Duncan Phyfe, furniture designer; Duncan Hines, international gourmet. English nickname: Dunc.

DUNLEY—Old English: Dun-leah. "From the hill meadow."

DUNMORE—Scotch Gaelic: Dun-mor. "Great hill fortress." A fortified hill that enemies could not take.

DUNN—Old English: Dunn. "Dark complexioned one." A dark stranger to the fair haired men of Britain. James Dunn, actor.

DUNSTAN—Old English: Dun-stan. "Brown stone, brown fortress." A locational landmark. St. Dunstan was a 10th-century Archbishop of Canterbury.

DUNTON—Old English: Dun-tun. "From the hill estate or town."

DURANT—Latin: Durantis. "The enduring one." Will Durant, American writer, educator.

DURWARD—Old English: Duru-weard. "Gate keeper." A man who admitted or rejected visitors to the town. Durward G. Hall, U.S. Congressman.

DURWIN—Old English: Deor-wine. "Beloved friend." A friend who loved all men.

DUTCH—German: Deutsch. "The German."

DWAYNE—Irish Gaelic: Dubhain. "Little dark one." Dwayne Hickman, actor. English variation: Duane.

DWIGHT—Old Dutch: Wit. "White or blond one." Dwight D. Eisenhower, 34th U.S. President; Dwight Deere Wiman, theatrical producer.

DYLAN—Old Welsh: Dylan. "From the sea." People wondered if this man was washed ashore from the sea. Dylan was the ancient Welsh deity of the ocean. Dylan Thomas, poet (1914-1953).

E

EACHAN—Irish Gaelic: Eachan. "Little horse." A boy, playful as a colt on a frosty morn.

EARL—Old English: Eorl. "Nobleman; chief." A princely man exalted by his friends. Alternate: Irish Gaelic: Airless. "A pledge." Earl Van Dorn, Confederate Civil War leader; Erle Stanley Gardner, author; Errol Flynn, actor; Earl Warren, Chief Justice of the United States.
English variations: Earle, Erl, Erle, Errol.

EATON—Old English: Ea-tun. "From the riverside estate." Eaton Hodgkinson, English physicist (1789-1861).

EBENEZER—Hebrew: Eben-haezer. "Stone or rock of the help." The stone erected by Samuel in the Bible to commemorate defeat of the Philistines Ebenezer Horsford, American chemist (1818-1893).
English nicknames: Eb, Eben.

EBERHARD—Old German: Ebur-hardt. "Wild-boar brave." A person compared to a brave boar protecting its young. Eberhard Schrader, German archaeologist (1836-1908).

EBNER—See Abner.

EDBERT—Old English: Eadbeorht. "Prosperous, brilliant." A seeker after knowledge.

EDEL—Old German: Adal. "Noble one." In heritage, in words, in deeds, truly magnanimous.

EDELMAR—Old English: Aethel-maere. "Noble, famous."

EDEN—Hebrew: 'eden. "Place of delight and pleasure." Each man builds an Eden of his own and calls it paradise. Eden Phillpotts, Anglo-Indian novelist; Sir Anthony Eden, English statesman.

EDGAR—Old English: Ead-gar. "Prosperous spearman." Edgar, 10th-century king of England; Edgar Allan Poe, American writer; Edgar Guest, American poet; Edgar Bergen, entertainer.
English nicknames: Ed, Eddie, Eddy, Ned.
Foreign variations: Edgar (German), Edgardo (Italian), Edgard (French).

EDISON—Old English: Eadward-sone. "Son of Edward." Thomas A. Edison, American inventor.
English variation: Edson.

EDMUND—Old English: Eadmund. "Prosperous protector." A gentleman who prospered by helping others. Edmund Halley, English scientist (1656-1742); St. Edmund, 9th-century English ruler; Edmund Spenser, 16th-century English poet; Eamon de Valera, Irish president; Edmond O'Brien, Edmund Gwenn, actors.
English nicknames: Ed, Eddie, Eddy, Ned.
Foreign variations: Eamon (Irish), Edmundo (Spanish), Edmond (French, Dutch).

EDOLF—Old English: Ead-wulf. "Prosperous wolf."

EDRIC—Old English: Ead-ric. "Prosperous ruler."
English nicknames: Ed, Ric.

EDSEL—Old English: Ead-sele. "A prosperous man's manor house or hall." A rich benefactor of his people. Edsel Ford, American manufacturer.

EDWALD—Old English: Ead-weald. "Prosperous ruler."

EDWARD—Old English: Ead-ward. "Prosperous guardian." A trusted warden of other people's property. Edward I, II, III, IV, V, VI, VII, VIII, kings of England; Edward Teach, 18th-century English pirate; Eddie Cantor, comedian.
English nicknames: Ed, Eddie, Eddy, Ned, Ted, Teddy.
Foreign variations: Eduardo (Italian, Spanish, Portuguese), Edouard (French), Eduard (German, Dutch), Edvard (Swedish, Danish).

EDWIN—Old English: Ead-wine. "Prosperous friend." Sir Edwin Arnold, 19th-century English poet; Edwin Stanton, U.S. Secretary of War; Edwin Booth, famous American actor; Edwin Arlington Robinson, American poet.
English nicknames: Ed, Eddie, Eddy.
Foreign variation: Eduino (Italian, Spanish).

EGAN—Irish Gaelic: Aodhagan. "Ardent, fiery one."

EGBERT—Old English: Ecg-beorht. "Bright, shining sword." Egbert the Great, King of the West Saxons and first king of England.

EHREN—Old German: Ehren. "Honorable one."

EINAR—Old Norse: Ein-her. "Warrior leader." A famous leader in battle. The Einherjar were kings and heroes of the Norse Valhalla or heaven. Einar Ingvald, noted linguist, professor.

ELBERT—See Albert. Elbert Hubbard, American author, editor (1856-1915); Elbert Thomas, U.S. Senator.

ELDEN—Old English: Aelf-dene. "Elf valley." A legendary place where elves were said to dwell.

ELDER—Old English: Aeldra. "Dweller at the elder tree." A home sheltered from sun and storm by a large elder tree.

ELDON—Old English: Ealh-dun. "From the holy hill." A descriptive name for a shrine built in veneration of God on a high hill. Sir Eldon Gorst, English administrator (1861-1911).

ELDWIN—See Aldwin.

ELEAZAR—Hebrew: El'azar. "To whom God is a help." St. Eleazar, follower of St. Francis.
Foreign variations: Eléazar (French), Eleazaro (Spanish).

ELI—Hebrew: Eli. "Jehovah" or "The Highest." A sacred name for the Lord. Eli Whitney, American inventor (1765-1825); Ely Culbertson, bridge expert.
English variation: Ely.

ELIAS—See Elijah.

ELIHU—Hebrew: Eli-hu. "God, the Lord." Elihu Root, American statesman, Nobel prize winner.

ELIJAH—Hebrew: Eli-yah. "Jehovah is my God." Elias Ashmole, 17th-century English antiquarian; Elias Howe, American inventor (1819-1867); Elie Faure, French writer; Elia Kazan, noted director.
English variations: Elias, Ellis.
Foreign variations: Elia (Italian), Elie (French), Elias (German, Dutch), Elías (Spanish).

ELISHA—Hebrew: Eli-sha. "God, my salvation." Elisha Grau, American inventor (1835-1901); Elisha Cook, Jr., actor.
Foreign variations: Eliseo (Italian, Spanish), Elisée (French.

ELLARD—Old English: Ealh-hard. "Sacred, brave," or Old English: Aethel-hard. "Noble, brave."

ELLERY—Middle English: Eller-ey. "From the elder-tree island." William Ellerey, American Revolutionary patriot; Ellery Queen, fictional detective.
English variation: Ellerey.

ELLIOT—Hebrew-French: Eli-yah-ot. "Jehovah is my God." Elliott Coues, American naturalist (1842-1899); Elliott Nugent, actor.
English variation: Elliott.

ELLIS—See Elijah.

ELLISON—Old English: Elle-sone. "Son of Ellis."

ELMER—Old English: Aethel-maere. "Noble-famous." Elmer Davis, commentator (1890-1958); Elmer Rice, dramatist.
English variation: Aylmer.

ELMO—Italian: Elmo. "Helmet; protector." St. Elmo or Erasmus, patron of seamen; Elmo Lincoln, silent film actor.

ELMORE—Old English: Elm-mor. "Dweller at the elm-tree moor."

ELROY—Old French: Le roy. "The king." Elroy is a transposition of Le Roy. Elroy Hirsch, athlete, actor.

ELSDON—Old English: Aethelis-dun. "Noble one's hill," or "Ellis-hill."

ELSON—See Ellison.

ELSTON—Old English: Aethelis-tun. "Noble one's estate or town," or Old English: Aethelstan. "Noble-stone."

ELSWORTH—Old English: Aethelis-worth. "Noble one's estate."

ELTON—Old English: Eald-tun. "From the old estate or town."

ELVIN—See Elwin.

ELVIS—Old Norse: Alviss. "All wise." Elvis Presley, singer, actor.

ELVY—Old English: Aelf-wig. "Elfin warrior."

ELWELL—Old English: Eald-wiella. "From the old spring." Gone are the ancient Druids who drank the sweet water from this spring.

ELWIN—Old English: Aelf-wise. "Elfin friend."
English variation: Elvin.

ELWOOD—Old English: Eald-wode. "From the old forest." Trees twisted and bent by the storms of time. Thomas Ellwood, English writer (1639-1713); Elwood Bowles, noted California attorney.
English variation: Ellwood.

ELY—See Eli.

EMANUEL—See Emmanuel.

EMERSON—See Emery.

EMERY—Old German: Amalric. "Industrious ruler," or Old German: Ermin-ric. "Joint- or co-ruler." Emmerich Kalman, German composer; Emory Upton, U.S. Civil War leader; Emory Parnell, actor.
English variations: Emmery, Emory, Emerson.
Foreign variations: Emmerich (German), Amerigo (Italian), Emeri (French).

EMIL—Gothic: Amal. "Industrious one," or Latin: Aemilius. "Flattering, winning one." Emile Zola, 19th-century French writer; Emil Jannings, noted actor.
Foreign variations: Emile (French), Emilio (Spanish).

EMMANUEL—Hebrew: Immanu-el. "God with us." God is within the hearts of good men. Emanuel the Great, Portuguese king (1469-1521).
English variation: Immanuel.
English nicknames: Mannie, Manny.
Foreign variations: Emanuele (Italian), Manuel (Spanish), Emanuel (German).

EMMETT—Old German: Amalhardt. "Industrious-strong," or Old English: Aemete. "An ant." Emmett Kelly, famed American circus clown.
English variations: Emmet, Emmit, Emmott.

EMORY—See Emery.

ENEAS—See Aeneas.

ENNIS—Irish Gaelic: Aonghus. "One-choice," or "Only choice," or Greek: Ennea. "Ninth child."

ENOCH—Hebrew: Khanok. "Consecrated, dedicated." Enoch, the Biblical patriarch, was father of Methuselah. Enoch Arden, hero of tale by Tennyson; Enoch Pond, American theologian.

ERASMUS—Greek: Erasmios. "Lovable; worthy of love." Worthy of the respect of man and of the love of God. St. Erasmus or St. Elmo, patron of sailors; Erasmus D. Preston, American astronomer (1851-1906).
English nicknames: Ras, Rasmus.
Foreign variations: Erasmo (Italian, Spanish), Erasme (French).

ERASTUS—Greek: Erastos. "Beloved." A giver of love, beloved in return.
English nicknames: Ras, Rastus.
Foreign variation: Eraste (French).

ERIC—Old Norse: Ei-rik-r. "Ever powerful; ever-ruler." Erich Ludendorff, German general; Eric the Red, Norwegian Viking hero; Eric Johnston, motion picture industry leader; Eric Ambler, English author.
English nicknames: Ric, Rick, Ricky.
Foreign variations: Erik (Scandinavian), Erich (German).

ERLAND—Old English: Eorlland. "Nobleman's land."

ERLING—Old English: Eorlsone. "Nobleman's son."

ERMIN—See Herman.

ERNEST—Old English: Earnest. "Earnest one." Ernest Hemingway, American author; Ernest C. Watson, physicist; Ernest Dowson, English poet; actors Ernie Kovacs, Ernest Borgnine.
English nicknames: Ernie, Erny.
Foreign variations: Ernst (German), Ernesto (Italian, Spanish), Ernestus (Dutch).

ERROL—See Earl.

ERSKINE—Scotch Gaelic: Airdsgainne. "From the height of the cleft." Erskine Nical, Scotch painter; Erskine Caldwell, novelist.

ERWIN—Old English: Ear-wine. "Sea friend." See Irving. Erwin Schroedinger, German physicist.

ESMOND—Old English: Estmund. "Gracious protector." A courteous, well-mannered guardian.

ESTE—Italian: Est. "From the East." A man from the east who came to the west. Estes Kefauver, U.S. Senator.
English variation: Estes.

ETHAN—Hebrew: Eythan. "Firmness, strength." Ethan Allen, Revolutionary War leader; *Ethan Frome,* novel by Edith Wharton.

EUGENE—Greek: Eugenios. "Well-born, noble." There were four Popes named Eugene; Prince Eugen of Austria, medieval leader in the Crusades; Eugene O'Neill, American dramatist.
English nickname: Gene.
Foreign variations: Eugenio (Italian, Spanish, Portuguese), Eugen (German), Eugène (French), Eugenius (Dutch).

EUSTACE—Latin: Eustathius. "Stable, tranquil," or Latin: Eustachus. "Fruitful." A man honored for his productive land. St. Eustace, Roman soldier, was martyred in A.D. 118 and is the patron of hunters.
Foreign variations: Eustache (French), Eustazio (Italian), Eustasius (German), Eustquio (Spanish), Eustatius (Dutch).

EVAN—Irish Gaelic: Eoghan; Old Welsh: Owein. "Well-born one; young warrior." An image of his noble ancestors.
English variations: Ewan, Ewen, Owen.

EVERARD—Old English: Eferhard. "Strong or brave as a boar." Sir Everard Home, Scotch surgeon (1756-1832); Everett Dirksen, U.S. Senator.
English nickname: Ev.
English variations: Evered, Everett.
Foreign variations: Eberhard (German), Evraud (French), Everardo (Italian), Everhart (Dutch).

EVERETT—See Everard.

EVERLEY—Old English: Eferleah. A meadow where wild boars fought and dug up tubers.

EWALD—Old English: Aewweald. "Law-powerful." A barrister or interpreter of English laws.
English variation: Evald.

EWERT—Old English: Eweheorde. "Ewe-herder." A herder of white ewes that grazed on an emerald green field.

EWING—Old English: Aewwine. "Law-friend." A lawyer who used the law to protect his fellow men.

EZEKIEL—Hebrew: Yekhezqel. "Strength of God." Ezekiel, great Hebrew Biblical prophet.
English nickname: Zeke.
Foreign variations: Ezechiel (French), Ezechiele (Italian), Ezechiel (German, Dutch), Ezequiel (Spanish).

EZRA—Hebrew: Ezra. "Help, helper." Famous Hebrew prophet of the Bible. Ezra Pound, American poet; Ezra Stone, actor.
Foreign variations: Esdras (French, Spanish), Esra (German).

F

FABIAN—Latin: Fabianus. "Bean-grower." A medieval agriculturist who knew his husbandry. Fabius, Roman general, 200 B.C., defeated the invader Hannibal; Pope Fabian, 3rd century; Fabian Forte, actor, singer.
Foreign variations: Fabio, Fabiano (Italian), Fabien (French).

FABRON—South French: Fabron. "Little blacksmith." An apprentice who desired to learn a trade.
Foreign variations: Fabre (French), Fabroni (Italian).

FAGAN—Irish Gaelic: Faodhagan. "Little fiery one." A tempestuous boy, explosive in everything he did.
English variation: Fagin.

FAIRLEY—See Farley.

FANE—Old English: Faegen. "Glad; joyful." A person whose laughter was as contagious as the wild birds' happy song.

FARLEY—Old English: Faerleah. "From the bull or sheep meadow." Farley Granger, actor. English variations: **Fairlie, Fairleigh, Farly.**

FARNELL—Old English: Fearnhealh. "From the fern slope." English variations: **Farnall, Fernald.**

FARNHAM—Old English: Fearn-hamm. "From the fern field."

FARNLEY—Old English: Fearn-leah. "From the fern meadow."

FAROLD—Old English: Faerwald. "Mighty traveler." A man who gained wisdom and strength from his travels.

FARR—Old English: Faer. "Traveler."

FARRAND—See Ferrand.

FARRELL—Irish Gaelic: Fearghal. "Most valorous one," or "Champion, warrior." English variations: **Farrel, Ferrell.**

FARRIS—See Ferris.

FAUST—Latin: Faustis. "Lucky, auspicious." A man favored by God with good omens. Dr. Faustus, legendary 15th-century necromancer was used as hero of Gounod's opera *Faust*, and Goethe's drama. Faustus Socinus 16th-century Italian reformer. Foreign variation: Fausto (Italian).

FAY—Irish Gaelic: Feich. "Raven." The raven symbolized wisdom in medieval Europe. Richard D. Fay, American educator. English variation: **Fayette.**

FELIX—Latin: Felix. "Fortunate, lucky one." Felix Adler, 19th-century ethical reformer; Felix Morley, writer on economics; Felix Bracht, 19th-century German painter. There are over 70 saints named Felix. Foreign variations: Felix (French), Felice (Italian), Félix (Spanish).

FELTON—Old English: Feldtun. "From the field estate or town."

FENTON—Old English: Penntun. "Marsh farm or estate." Land that was drained for cultivation.

FEODOR—See Theodore.

FERDINAND—Gothic: Fairhonanth. "World-daring; life-adventuring." A lover of life and travel. Historically famous were Ferdinand the Great, 11th-century Spanish king; Ferdinand Magellan, Portuguese navigator, Hernando Cortez, conqueror of Mexico. Modern namesakes include Fernando Lamas, actor. English nicknames: Ferd, Ferdie. Foreign variations: **Ferdinando** (Italian), **Fernando, Hernando** (Spanish).

FERGUS—Irish Gaelic: Fearghus. "Very choice one." Ten saints Fergus are listed in the Martyrology of Donegal. Feargus O'Connor, Irish chartist (1794-1855). English nickname: Fergie.

FERNALD—See Farnall.

FERRAND—Old French: Ferrant. "Iron-gray hair." Hair that hid a great man's thoughts. English variations: **Farrand, Farrant, Ferrant.**

FERRIS—Irish Gaelic: Feoras. "Peter, 'The Rock'" or "Very choice one." A man stable and firm as a mighty stone. English variation: **Farris.**

FIDEL—Latin: Fidelis. "Faithful, sincere." St. Fidelis of Sigmaringen, "Advocate of the Poor"; Fidel Castro, notorious Cuban leader.
Foreign variations: Fidele (French), Fidelio (Italian).

FIELDING—Old English: Felding. "Dweller at the field." All nature was a garden for this man.

FILBERT—Old English: Felabeorht. "Very brilliant one." English variation: Philbert. Foreign variations: Filberto (Italian, Spanish), Filberte (French).

FILMER—Old English: Felamaere. "Very famous one." Millard Fillmore, 13th U.S. President.
English nickname: Fil.
English variations: Filmore, Fillmore.

FILMORE—See Filmer.

FINDLAY—See Finley.

FINLEY—Irish Gaelic: Fionnghalac. "Little fair-haired valorous one," or Irish Gaelic: Fionnlaoch. "Fair soldier." Finlay Currie, actor.
English nicknames: Fin, Lee.
English variations: Findlay, Findley, Finlay.

FINN—Irish Gaelic: Fionn. "Fair-haired and complexioned," or Old German: Fin. "From Finland." A tow-headed boy with sky-blue eyes. Finn Ronne, Antarctic explorer.

FIRMIN—Old French: Firmin. "Firm, strong one."

FISKE—Middle English: Fiske. "Fish." Used by an ancestor from his medieval shop-sign. Fiske Kimball, American architect (1888-1955).

FITCH—Middle English: Fitche. "European marten or ermine." A man whose hair was as yellow as summer ermine. John Fitch, American steamboat inventor (1743-1798).

FITZ—Old French: Filz. "Son." Introduced to Britain by the Normans and altered from "Filz" to "Fitz."

FITZGERALD—Old English: Fitz-Gerald. "Son of spear-mighty." See Gerald. Fitzgerald Molloy, historian.

FITZHUGH—Old English: Fitz-Hugh. "Son of the intelligent one." Fitzhugh Lee, Virginia governor (1835-1905).

FLANN—Irish Gaelic: Flann. "Red-haired one." A bonnie lad with hair as russet as the frost-kissed leaves in fall.

FLAVIUS—Latin: Flavius. "Golden-yellow hair." Flavius Valens, eastern Roman Emperor, 4th century; Flavius Josephus, famous Jewish historian, 1st century.

FLETCHER—Middle English: Fleccher. "Arrow-featherer." A man named for his dexterity in putting feathers on arrows.

FLINN—See Flynn.

FLINT—Old English: Flynt. "A stream." In America we call obsidian "flint," but in Britain it was an ancient word for a brook.

FLOYD—See Lloyd.

FLYNN—Irish Gaelic: Floinn. "Son of the red-haired man." English variation: Flinn.

FORBES—Irish Gaelic: Fearbhirigh. "Man of prosperity," or Irish Gaelic: Forba. "Owner of fields."

FORD—Old English: Ford. "River crossing." Henry Ford, American manufacturer.

FORREST—Old French: Forest. "Dweller at a forest." Forrest Tucker, actor.
English variation: Forest.

FORRESTER—Middle English: Forester. "Forest guardian." A warden who watched for fire and illegal hunters.
English nicknames: Forrie, Foss.
English variations: Forester, Forster, Foster.

FORSTER—See Forrester.

FORTUNE—Old French: Fortune. "Lucky one." Fortune seemed to smile on this happy man. St. Fortunatus, 6th-century Bishop of Poitiers, France.
Foreign variations: Fortunio (Italian), Fortuné (French).

FOSS—See Forrester.

FOSTER—See Forrester.

FRANCHOT—See Francis.

FRANCIS—Latin: Franciscus. "Free man," or "Frenchman." A man subservient only to his government. St. Francis of Assisi, 1181-1226; Lord Francis Bacon, English philosopher (1561-1626); Francisco Pizarro, 15th-century Spanish conquistador; Franz Josef Hayden, composer; Franchot Tone, actor.
English nicknames: Fran, Frank.
Foreign variations: Francois, Franchot (French), Franciskus, Franz (German), Francesco (Italian), Francisco (Spanish, Portuguese), Frans (Swedish), Frants (Danish).

FRANK—Old French: Franc. "Free man." See Franklin, Francis. Frank Sinatra, actor, singer; Frank Conroy, Frank Lovejoy, actors.

FRANKLIN—Middle English: Frankeleyn. "Free holder of land." A man who earned his freedom from his overlord. Franklin D. Roosevelt, 32nd U.S. President.
English nicknames: Frank, Frankie.
English variations: Franklyn, Francklin, Francklyn.

FRASER—See Frazer.

FRAYNE—Middle English: Fren. "Stranger; foreigner," or Old French: Frayne. "Dweller at the ash-tree." Stephen Le Fren recorded in England, 1273.
English variations: Fraine, Frean, Freen, Freyne.

FRAZER—Old French: Frasier. "Strawberry," or Old English: Frisa. "Curly-haired one; Frisian Dutchman."
English variations: Fraser, Frasier, Frazier.

FREDERICK—Old German: Fridu-rik. "Peaceful ruler." A man not greedy or aggressive. Frederick the Great, Prussian King, 1740-1786; Fritz Kreisler, violinist; Fredric March, actor.
English nicknames: Fred, Freddie, Freddy.
English variations: Frederic, Fredric, Fredrick.
Foreign variations: Friedrich, Fritz (German), Fréderic (French), Federigo (Italian), Federico (Spanish), Fredrik (Swedish), Frederik (Danish, Dutch).

FREEMAN—Old English: Freoman. "Free man." A man free from an overlord, ranked with the landed gentry.

FREMONT—Old German: Frimunt. "Free or noble protector." General John C. Frémont (1813-1890); Fremont Older, American writer, publisher (1856-1935).

FREWIN—Old English: Freo-wine. "Free, noble friend." Freo-wine, descendant of Woden, was ancestor of the early English kings of Wessex.
English variation: Frewen.

FREY—Old English: Fre. "Lord." Frey was the ancient Norse god of prosperity, peace and fertility.

FRICK—Old English: Freca. "Bold man."

FRIDOLF—Old English: Fridu-wulf. "Peaceful wolf." A peaceful man with wolf-like courage.

FRITZ—See Frederick.

FULLER—Middle English: Ful-lere. "Cloth-thickener." A man who moistened and pressed cloth.

FULTON—Old English: Fugel-tun. "Dweller at the fowl-enclo-sure." A fenced-in place for poul-try or game-birds. Alternate, Old English: Fula-tun. "People's es-tate." Rev. Fulton J. Sheen, Amer-ican clergyman, author; Fulton Lewis, commentator.

FYFE—Pictish-Scotch: Fibh. "From Fifeshire, Scotland."

G

GABLE—Old French: Gabel. "Little Gabriel."

GABRIEL—Hebrew: Gabriel. "Man of God." The Archangel of the Annunciation. Gabriel An-dral, French physician, writer (1797-1853); Gabriel Heatter, commentator.
English nicknames: Gabe, Gabie, Gabby.
Foreign variations: Gabriele, Gabriello (Italian), Gabriel (German, French, Spanish).

GAGE—Old French: Gage. "Pledge." A man who dedicated his life to God.

GAIL—See Gale.

GAIR—Irish Gaelic: Gearr. "Short one."

GALE—Old English: Gal. "Gay, lively one." A boy with energy and happiness to spare. Alternate, Irish Gaelic: Gall. "Foreigner." Gale Gordon, actor.
English variations: Gail, Gaile, Gayle.

GALEN—Irish Gaelic: Gaelan. "Little bright one." A small lad,

wise beyond his years. Galen Drake, radio personality.

GALLAGHER—Irish Gaelic: Galchobhar. "Foreign helper or eager helper." A man from another land.

GALLOWAY—Old Gaelic: Gallgaidheal. "Man from the land of the stranger Gaels." A Scottish Celt of the Highlands.
English variations: Galway, Gallway.

GALTON—Old English: Gafol-tun. "Owner of a rented estate." It was considered unusual to lease land in the Middle Ages.

GALVIN—Irish Gaelic: Gael-bhan. "Bright, shining white," or Irish Gaelic: Gealbhan. "Spar-row."
English variations: Galvan, Gal-ven.

GAMALIEL—Hebrew: Gamal-yel. "Recompense of God." Re-warded for his devotion and serv-ice to God. Gamaliel the Elder, 1st-century teacher of the Apostle Paul; Gamaliel Bradford, Amer-ican biographer (1863-1932).

GANNON—Irish Gaelic: Gionnan. "Little fair complexioned one."

GARDNER—Middle English: Gardiner. "A gardener." A man named for his fine vegetables, fruits, and flowers. Gardiner Spring, American clergyman, author (1785-1873); Gardner McKay, actor.
English variations: Gardener, Gardiner.

GAREY—See Gary.

GARFIELD—Old English: Garafeld. "Triangular field," or Old English: Gari-feld. "War or battle-spear field. James Garfield, 20th U.S. President.

GARLAND—Old English: Gariland. "From the spear-land," or Old French: Garlande. "Wreath of flowers or leaves."

GARMAN—Old English: Garmann. "Spearman." An expert with the spear.

GARMOND—Old English: Garmund. "Spear protector."
English variations: Garmon, Garmund.

GARNER—Old French: Garnier. "Guardian army; army guard."

GARNETT—Old English: Garnyd. "Spear-compulsion," or Late Latin: Granatus. "A seed; pomegranate seed."
English variation: Garnet.

GARNOCK—Old Welsh: Gwernach. "Dweller by the alderriver."

GARRETT—Old English: Garhard. "Spear-brave; firm-spear." Garrett Hobart, 24th Vice President of the U.S.
English variations: Garrard, Garrett, Garret, Garritt, Gerard.
Foreign variation: Gearoid (Irish).

GARRICK—Old English: Garric. "Spear-ruler." A ruler proficient with his lance.

GARROWAY—Old English: Gar-wig. "Spear-warrior." Dave Garroway, television personality.
English variation: Garraway.

GARTH—Old Norse: Garth-r. "From the garden."

GARTON—Old English: Garatun. "Dweller at the triangular farmstead."

GARVEY—Irish Gaelic: Gairbhith. "Rough peace," or Irish Gaelic: Garbhach. "Rough one." An intricate paradox meaning probably, "Peace after much controversy."

GARVIN—Old English: Garwine. "Spear-friend."
English variation: Garwin.

GARWOOD—Old English: Gyr-wode. "From the fir forest."

GARY—Old English: Gari. "Spear; spearman." Gari Melchers, American painter; Gary Cooper, Gary Merrill, Gary Crosby, actors.
English variations: Gari, Garey, Garry.

GASPAR—Persian: Kansbar. "Treasure-master." Gaspar was one of the three Wise Men or Magi in the Bible; Gaspar Cortereal, Portuguese navigator, 1450-1501.
English variations: Caspar, Casper, Gasper, Kaspar, Kasper, Jasper.
Foreign variations: Gaspard (French), Gasparo (Italian), Kaspar (German).

GASTON—French: Gascon. "Man from Gascony, the Land of the Basques." Gaston Plante, French physicist, 19th century.

GAVIN—Old Welsh: Gwalchmai. "From the hawk field." Sir

Gawain, nephew of King Arthur in the medieval Round Table romances; Gavin Douglas, Scotch 16th-century poet.
English variations: Gavan, Gaven, Gawen, Gawain.

GAYLE—See Gale.

GAYLORD—Old French: Gaillard. "Lively one."
English variations: Gayler, Gaylor, Gallard.

GAYNOR—Irish Gaelic: Mac-Fionnbharr. "Son of the fairhead."
English variations: Gainer, Gainor, Gayner.

GEARY—Middle English: Gery. "Changeable one." One who vacillates.
English variations: Gearey, Gery.

GEOFFREY—See Jeffrey, Godfrey.

GEORGE—Latin: Georgius. "Land-worker; farmer." St. George, patron of England, 4th century; English kings George I to VI; George Washington, 1st U.S. President; George Gershwin, composer; actors George Burns, George Nader, George Montgomery, George Raft.
English nicknames: Georgie, Georgy, Geordie.
Foreign variations: Georg (German, Danish, Swedish), Giorgio (Italian), Jorge (Spanish), Georges (French), Geòras (Scotch).

GERALD—Old German: Gerwalt. "Spear-mighty," or Old German: Ger-wald. "Spear-ruler." Gerald Massey, English poet (1828-1907); Sir Gerald du Maurier, famous English actor.
English nicknames: Gerry, Jerry.
Foreign variations: Géralde, Geraud, Giraud (French), Giraldo (Italian), Gerold (German), Gearalt (Irish).

GERARD—Old English: Garhard. "Spear-brave; spear-strong." Gerhard Mercator, 16th-century Flemish geographer; Gerhart Hauptmann, German dramatist, Gerard Hopkins, English poet.
English nicknames: Gerry, Jerry.
English variations: Gerrard, Gerhard.
Foreign variations: Gerhardt, Gerhard (German), Geraud (French), Gerardo, Gherardo (Italian), Gerardo (Spanish), Gerhard (Danish, Swedish), Gearard (Irish).

GERONIMO—See Jerome.

GIBSON—Old English: Gibbesone. "Son of Gilbert." See Gilbert.

GIDEON—Hebrew: Gid-on. "Hewer or feller; destroyer." A man who cut down trees. Gideon in the Bible ruled Israel for forty years; Gideon Granger, U.S. Postmaster General (1767-1822).

GIFFORD—Old English: Gifuhard. "Gift-brave." Gifford Pinchot, Pennsylvania governor.
English nicknames: Giff, Giffy.
English variations: Giffard, Gifferd.

GILBERT—Old English: Giselbeorht. "Brilliant pledge or hostage." A brilliant man held as security for the performance of certain actions. Gilbert Chesterton, English writer; Gilbert Roland, actor.
English nicknames: Gil, Gill, Gib, Gibb, Bert.
Foreign variations: Giselbert, Gilbert (German), Guilbert (French), Gilberto (Italian, Spanish), Gilibeirt (Irish), Gilleabart (Scotch).

GILBY—Old Norse: Gisl-by-r. "Pledge or hostage's estate," or Irish Gaelic: Giolla-buidhe. "Yellow-haired lad."
English variation: Gilbey.

GILCHRIST—Irish Gaelic: Gi-olla-Chriost. "Servant of Christ." Foreign variation: Gillecriosd (Scotch).

GILES—Old French: Gilles. "Youthful; downy-bearded one," or Latin: Egidius. "Shield bearer." Gilles Menage, French scholar (1613-1692); Giles Fletcher, English dramatist (1588-1623). Foreign variations: Gilles, Egide (French), Egidio (Italian), Egidius (German, Dutch), Gil (Spanish).

GILLETT—Old French: Gille-et. "Little Gilbert." See Gilbert. Gelett Burgess, American writer, illustrator; William Gillette, actor. English variations: Gelett, Gelette, Gillette.

GILMER—Old English: Gisel-maere. "Famous hostage." A noted man held captive from another land.

GILMORE—Irish Gaelic: Giol-la-Mhuire. "Adherent of St. Mary." English variations: Gillmore, Gilmour.

GILROY—Irish Gaelic: Giolla-ruaidh. "Servant of the red-haired youth."

GIRVIN—Irish Gaelic: Garbh-han. "Little rough one." A riotous boy, stormy and tempestuous. English variations: Girvan, Girven.

GLADWIN—Old English: Glaed-wine. "Kind, cheerful friend."

GLANVILLE—Old French: Glande-ville. "From the oak-tree estate."

GLENDON—Scotch Gaelic: Glen-dun. "From the glen-for-tress."

GLENN—Old Welsh: Glyn; Irish Gaelic: Ghleanna. "Dweller in a glen or valley." Glyn Phil-pot, English painter; Glenn Ford, Glenn Hunter, actors. English nicknames: Glennie, Glenny. English variations: Glen, Glyn, Glynn.

GLYNN—See Glenn.

GODDARD—Old German: Gode-hard. "Divinely firm" or "God-firm." As unchanging as the laws of the universe. English variations: Godard, Godart, Goddart. Foreign variations: Godard (French), Gotthart (German), Gotthard (Dutch).

GODFREY—Old German: Gott-fried. "Divinely peaceful." Gottfried Leibnitz, German 17th-century mathematician; Godfrey Weitzel, Civil War leader; Godfrey Tearle, actor. English variations: Goeffrey, Jeffrey. Foreign variations: Gottfried (German, Dutch), Goffredo (Italian), Godofredo (Spanish), Godefroi (French), Gottfrid (Swedish), Goraidh (Scotch), Gothfraidh (Irish).

GODWIN—Old English. God-wine. "Divine friend," or "Friend of God." Godwin, 11th-century Earl of Wessex. English variation: Goodwin. Foreign variation: Godewyn (Dutch).

GOLDING—Old English: Gold-ing. "Son of the golden one." Golding Bird, English physicist.

GOLDWIN—Old English: Gold-wine. "Golden friend." Goldwin Smith, Canadian author (1823-1910).

GORDON—Old English: Gara-dun. "From the triangular or gore-shaped hill." A pie-shaped hill between two plains. Cele-

brated from the Scotch Clan Gordon. Gordon Alexander, American biologist, writer; Gordon MacRae, singer, actor.
English nicknames: Gordie, Gordy.
English variations: Gordan, Gorden.

GORMAN—Irish Gaelic: Gorman. "Little blue-eyed one."

GOUVERNEUR—French: Gouverneur. "Chief ruler; governor." Gouverneur Morris, American statesman (1752-1816).

GOWER—Old Welsh: Gwyr. "Pure one." Sordidness cannot besmirch the pristine soul. Gower Champion, actor, dancer, director.

GRADY—Irish Gaelic: Grada. "Noble, illustrious."

GRAHAM—Old English: Graeg-hamm. "From the gray land or gray home." Graham MacNamee, commentator.

GRANGER—Old English: Grangere. "Farmer." A man who knew the joy of new, productive fields.

GRANT—Middle English: Grand. "Great one." Grant Wood, American painter (1892-1942).

GRANTLAND—Old English: Grand-land. "From the great grassy plain." Grantland Rice, sportsman, film producer.

GRANVILLE—Old French: Grande-ville. "From the great estate or town." Land, majestic in its immensity. Granville Hall, American psychologist.

GRAYSON—Middle English: Grayve-sone. "Son of the reeve or bailiff. Grayson Kirk, educator.

GREELEY—Old English: Graegleah. "From the gray meadow." Horace Greeley, 19th-century journalist, founder of Republican Party.

GREGORY—Latin: Gregorious. "Watchman; watchful one." A man vested with authority and alertness. St. Gregory the Great, 540-604; 16 Popes were named Gregory; Gregory Peck, actor; Gregory (Pappy) Boyington, Marine ace.
English nicknames: Greg, Gregg.
Foreign variations: Gregor, Gregorius (German), Gregoire (French), Gregoor (Dutch), Gregorio (Italian, Spanish, Portuguese), Griogair (Scotch), Greagoir, Grioghar (Irish).

GRIFFITH—Old Welsh: Gruffudd. "Fierce chief," or Old Welsh: Gruffin. "Ruddy one." A ferocious leader against his country's enemies.

GRISWOLD—Old German: Gris-wald. "From the gray forest."

GROVER—Old English: Grafere. "From the grove of trees." Grover Cleveland, 22nd and 24th U.S. President.

GUNTHER—Old Norse: Gunnr-har. "Battle-army." A name from the military forces of his country.
English and Scandinavian variations: Gunnar, Gunner, Gunter.

GUSTAVE—Swedish: Gustaf. "Staff of the Goths." Gustavus Adolphus, 16th-century Swedish king; Gustave Doré, 19th-century French illustrator; Gustave Flaubert, 19th-century French writer.
English nicknames: Gus, Gussie.
Foreign variations: Gustav (German), Gustaf (Swedish), Gustavo (Italian, Spanish), Gustave (French) Gustaff (Dutch).

GUTHRIE—Gaelic: Gaothaire. "From the windy place," or Old German: Gund-heri. "Army warrior." Guthrie McClintic, noted theatrical producer.

GUY—Old German: Wido. "Warrior," or Latin: Vitus. "Life." Guy de Maupassant, French writer (1850-1893); actors Guy Bates Post, Guy Madison.

Foreign variations: **Guido** (German, Swedish, Italian, Spanish), **Guy** (French).

GWYNN—Old Welsh: Gwyn. "Fair, blond one." Gwyn was the deity of the underworld in Welsh myths.
English variation: **Gwyn**.
Foreign variation: **Guin** (Gaelic).

GYLES—See Giles.

H

HACKETT—Old Franco-German: Hack-et. "Little hacker." A boy who learned his woodsman-father's trade.

HADDEN—Old English: Haeth-dene or Haeth-dun. "From the heath- valley or hill."
English variations: **Haddan Haddon**.

HADLEY—Old English: Haeth-leah. "From the heath meadow." Uncultivated land waiting for the plows of men.
English variation: **Hadleigh**.

HADWIN—Old English: Haetho-wine. "War-friend." A soldier of his king and country.

HAGEN—Irish Gaelic: Hagan. "Little, young one."
English variations: **Hagan, Haggan**.

HAGLEY—Old English: Haga-leah. "From the hedged pasture." A natural enclosure formed by a thicket.

HAIG—Old English: Haga. "Dweller at the hedged enclosure."

HAKON—Old Norse: Hakon. "Of the high or exalted race." Hakon has been the name of many Norwegian kings.
Norse variations: **Haakon, Hako**.

HALBERT—Old English: Hale-beorht. "Brilliant hero." An intelligent, celebrated, fearless man.

HALDEN—Old Norse: Half-Dan. "Half-Dane." A man half Danish and half English. Halfdan was the name of many Norwegian rulers.
English variations: **Halfdan, Haldan**.

HALE—Old English: Haele. "Hero," or Old English: Heall. "From the Hall." Hale Hamilton, actor.

HALEY—Irish Gaelic: Ealadhach. "Ingenious, scientific."

HALFORD—Old English: Healh-ford. "From the hillslope-ford," or Old English: Heall-ford. "From the manor house ford."

HALL—Old English: Heall. "Dweller at the hall or manor house." Hall Caine, English novelist (1853-1931).

HALLAM—Old English: Heal-um. "Dweller at the slopes." Where hills slope downward to the sea.

HALLEY—Old English: Heall-leah. "From the Manor House meadow," or Old English: Halig. "Holy." Edmund Halley, English astronomer (1656-1742).

HALLIWELL—Old English: Halig-wiella. "Dweller by a holy spring." That spring which can quench the thirst for truth. Halliwell Hobbes, actor.

HALLWARD—Old English: Heall-weard. "Hall warden or guardian." A guard in the armor of noble loyalty, allowing no harm to enter.

HALSEY—Old English: Hals-ig. "From Hal's island." An individual who dreamed of returning without knowing why, except for the memory of a still lagoon.

HALSTEAD—Old English: Heall-stede. "From the manor house place." A place where each chore was a delight and each leisure moment a melody.
English variation: Halsted.

HALTON—Old English: Healh-tun. "From the hillslope estate." Unrestricted vision of limitless boundaries.

HAMAL—Arabic: Hamal. "Lamb."

HAMAR—Old Norse: Hammar. "A symbol of the ingenuity of man."

HAMILTON—Old English: Hamela-tun. "Home-lover's estate" or "Wether-sheep enclosure." Hamilton Fish, U.S. Secretary of State (1869-1877).

HAMLET—Old Franco-German: Hamo-elet. "Little home." Hamlet, Prince of Denmark, famous Shakespearean character.

HAMLIN—Old Franco-German: Hamo-elin. "Little home-lover." Hamlin Garland, American writer.

HANFORD—Old English: Hean-ford. "From the high-ford."

HANLEY—Old English: Hean-leah. "From the high pasture."

HANS—See John. Hans Christian Andersen, 19th-century Danish writer.

HARBERT—See Herbert.

HARBIN—Old Franco-German: Hari-beorht-in. "Little, glorious warrior." A small person efficient in handling an army. See Herbert.

HARCOURT—Old Franco-German: Hari-court. "From the fortified farm." A farm that became a training place for soldiers.

HARDEN—Old English: Haradene. "From the hare-valley." J. Harden Peterson, U.S. Congressman.
English variation: Hardin.

HARDING—Old English: Heard-ing. "Brave one's son."

HARDWIN—Old English: Heard-wine. "Brave friend." Not ostentatious, but a friend of honor.

HARDY—Old German: Harti. "Bold and daring." Distinctive in his courage, this person was noble in character. Hardy Kruger, actor.
English variations: Hardey, Hardie.

HARFORD—Old English: Hara-ford. "From the hare-ford," or Old English: Here-ford. "Army-ford."

HARGROVE—Old English: Hara-graf. "From the hare-grove."
English variation: Hargrave.

HARLAN—Old English: Hari-land. "From the army-land," or Old English: Hara-land. "Hare-land." Where hares were so plentiful people were intruders. Harlan Bushfield, U.S. Senator.

HARLEY—Old English: Hara-leah. "From the hare-pasture." Harley Kilgore, U.S. Senator.
English variation: Arley.

HARLOW—Old English: Harihloew. "Army-hill; fortified hill." An army encampment. Harlow Shapley, astronomer; Harlow Curtice, industrialist.

HARMAN—See Herman.

HARMON—See Herman.

HAROLD—Old Norse: Haruald. "Army-ruler." Notables include Harold II, last Saxon king of England (1022-1061): Harold Arlen, composer; Harold Lloyd, actor; Harold Macmillan, British Prime Minister.
English nicknames: Hal, Harry.
English variations: Harald, Herold.
Foreign variations: Harald (Swedish, Danish), Araldo (Italian), Herold (Dutch), Aralt (Irish), Harailt (Scotch).

HARPER—Old English: Hearpere. "Harp player." A musician whose melodies brought his listeners delight.

HARRIS—Old English: Hanrysone. "Son of Harry." Harrison Smith Morris, American editor, poet; Harrison Cady, illustrator.
English variation: Harrison.

HARRISON—See Harris.

HARRY—Old English: Hari. "Army man." See Henry, Harold. Harry S Truman, 33rd U.S. President.

HART—Old English: Heort. "Hart-deer." From an old shop-sign that pictured a red stag deer. Hart Crane, American poet (1899-1932).

HARTFORD—Old English: Heort-ford. "Stag-ford." A clear, shallow spot where deer could cross the stream.

HARTLEY—Old English: Heort-leah. "Hart-deer pasture." A meadow green and fertile, where deer grazed. Hartley Coleridge, English writer, poet (1796-1846); J. Hartley Manners, dramatist.

HARTMAN—Old German: Hart-mann. "Strong, austere man," or Old English: Heortman. "Stag-deer keeper."

HARTWELL—Old English: Heort-wiella. "Hart-deer spring." Where wild deer came to drink.

HARTWOOD—Old English: Heort-wode. "Hart-deer forest."

HARVEY—Old German: Herwig. "Army-warrior." One who protects his country. Alternate, Old Breton French: Hueru. "Bitter, severe." Harvey W. Wiley, American chemist; Harvey Firestone, American industrialist; Harvey Kuenn, baseball star.
English nickname: Harv.
English variation: Hervey.

HASLETT—Old English: Haesel-heafod. "Hazel-tree headland." Hazel-trees at the top of the path. William Hazlett Upson, writer.
English variation: Hazlett.

HASTINGS—Old English: Haestingas. "Son of the severe, violent one." Stern and strict, the father reared his son to be a man. Hastings was a 9th-century Scandinavian Viking leader; Hastings Keith, U.S. Congressman.

HAVELOCK—Old Norse: Hafleik-r. "Sea-contest." Triumph was his in a fierce battle with the sea. Havelock the Dane was an ancient legendary character; Havelock Ellis, English psychological writer.

HAVEN—Old English: Haefen. "Place of safety."

HAWLEY—Old English: Hagaleah. "From the hedged meadow." Twisted and thorny hedges were a deterrent against intruders.

HAYDEN—Old English: Haga-dene. "From the hedged valley." A mile of lane, hedged, bright with fragrant wild roses.
English variation: Haydon.

HAYWARD—Old English: Haga-ward. "Hedged enclosure keeper."

HAYWOOD—Old English: Haga-wode. "From the hedged forest." A tangled labyrinth shielded forest and animals from man. Heywood Broun, literary critic (1888-1937).
English variation: Heywood.

HEATH—Middle English: Hethe. "Heath or wasteland."

HEATHCLIFF—Middle English: Hethe-clif. "From the heath-cliff."

HECTOR—Greek: Hektor. "Holds fast; steadfast." A hero who held his enemies at bay. In Greek history Hector was the bravest Trojan warrior.
Foreign variations: Ettore (Italian), Eachunn (Scotch).

HENDRICK—See Henry.

HENRY—Old German: Heim-rik. "Ruler of an estate, a home, or private property." Henry VIII, English king; Henry Hudson, English and Dutch navigator; Henry Ward Beecher, American 19th-century clergyman; Henry Fonda, Henry Hull, actors; Henri Bernstein, French dramatist.
English nicknames: Harry, Hank, Hal.
English variations: Hendrick, Henri.
Foreign variations: Heinrich (German), Enrico (Italian), Henri (French), Enrique (Spanish), Hendrik (Dutch, Danish), Henrik (Swedish), Eanruig (Scotch), Hanraoi (Irish).

HERBERT—Old German: Heri-beraht. "Army-brilliant; glorious warrior." Herbert Hoover, 31st U.S. President; Herbert George Wells, English author; Herbert Lom, actor.
English nicknames: Herb, Herbie, Bert.
English variations: Harbert, Hebert.
Foreign variations: Erberto (Italian), Heriberto (Spanish), Hoireabard (Irish).

HERMAN—Old German: Heri-mann. "Army-man; warrior," or Latin: Herminius. "High ranking person." Herman Melville, Herman Wouk, American writers.
English nicknames: Herm, Hermie.
English variations: Ermin, Harman, Harmon.
Foreign variations: Hermann (German, Danish), Armand (French), Armando (Spanish), Ermanno (Italian).

HERNANDO—See Ferdinand.

HERRICK—Old German: Heri-rik. "Army ruler."

HERVEY—See Harvey. Hervey Allen, American author.

HEWE—See Hugh.

HEWETT—Old Franco-German: Hugi-et. "Little Hugh." See Hugh.
English variation: Hewitt.

HEYWOOD—See Haywood.

HIATT—See Hyatt.

HILARY—Latin: Hilarius. "Cheerful, gay one." A man who never saw a cloud on a rainy day. St. Hilary or Hilarius, Latin writer, Bishop of Poitiers; Hilaire Belloc, famous French and English writer.
English variations: Hillary, Hillery.
Foreign variations: Hilarius (German, Danish, Dutch, Swedish), Hilaire (French), Ilario (Italian), Hilario (Spanish, Portuguese).

HILDEBRAND—Old German: Hild-brand. "War-sword." Named for his sword used in war. Hildebrand was an ancient legendary German hero.

HILLIARD—Old German: Hild-hard. "Battle-brave."
English variations: Hillier, Hillyer.

HILTON—Old English: Hylltun. "From the hill estate." Conrad Hilton, hotel magnate; Jack Hylton, English impresario.
English variation: Hylton.

HIRAM—Hebrew: Hiram. "Most noble one." One endowed with high mental, moral and spiritual values. Hiram, King of Tyre, aided King Solomon in building his famous temple; Hiram Johnson, U.S. Senator.
English nicknames: Hi, Hy.

HOBART—Old German: Hohberht. "High-brilliant." A person high in intelligence and leadership. Alternate, Old German: Hugi-beraht. "Brilliant mind." Hobart Bosworth, silent screen actor.

HOGAN—Irish Gaelic: Ogan. "Youth."

HOLBROOK—Old English: Hol-broc. "Dweller at the brook in the hollow." Holbrook Blinn, actor.

HOLCOMB—Old English: Holcumb. "Deep valley." Between two perpendicular cliffs there was a green meadow.

HOLDEN—Old English: Holdene. "From the hollow in the valley.

HOLLIS—Old English: Hollies. "From the holly-tree grove."

HOLMES—Middle English: Holmes. "From the river islands." Holmes Herbert, English actor.

HOLT—Old English: Holt. "From the forest."

HOMER—Greek: Homeros. "Pledge; security." A devout man who made a solemn promise to carry out an action. Homer, renowned Greek poet, 9th-century B.C.; Homer Ferguson, Homer Capehart, U.S. Senators.
Foreign variations: Homerus (German, Dutch), Homère (French), Omero (Italian).

HORACE—Latin: Horatius. "Keeper of the hours; light of the sun." A sage who taught the regularity of the seasons and the hours. Horace was an ancient Roman poet. Notables: Horatio Nelson, British admiral; Horatio Alger, American author; Horace Mann, American educator; Horace Greeley, American journalist.
English variation: Horatio.
Foreign variations: Horatius (German), Horacio (Spanish, Portuguese), Orazio (Italian), Horats (Dutch).

HORTON—Old English: Hartun. "From the gray estate."

HOUGHTON—Old English: Hoh-tun. "From the estate on the bluff."

HOWARD—Old English: Heahweard. "Chief guardian." Entrusted by law with the care of the people. Howard Hanson, composer; Howard Keel, actor.
English nickname: Howie.

HOWE—Old German: Hoh. "High; eminent one," or Middle English: How. "Hill."

HOWELL—Old Welsh: Howel. "Little alert one." Howell Cobb, U.S. Secretary of the Treasury (1815-1868).

HOWLAND—Middle English: How-land. "Dweller at the hilly land."

HUBERT—Old German: Hugi-beraht. "Brilliant mind or spirit." A genius who could create, reason, and make decisions. St. Hubert, 7th-century French bishop; Hubert Walker, 12th-century English statesman.
English nicknames: Hugh, Hube, Bert.
Foreign variations: Uberto (Italian), Huberto (Spanish), Hubert, Hugibert (German), Hoibeard (Irish).

HUDSON—Old English: Hod-sone. "Son of the hooded one." A father who wore a hooded woolen cloak.

HUEY—See Hugh.

HUGH—Old English: Hugi. "Intelligence; spirit." Rare complimentary name for a clever, brilliant man. The English St. Hugh of Lincoln erected Lincoln Cathedral, 13th century; Hugh Black, Scotch theologian, author; Hugh O'Brian, actor.
English nicknames: Huey, Hughie, Hughy.
Foreign variations: Hugo (German, Spanish, Swedish, Dutch, Danish), Hugues (French), Ugo (Italian), Aodh (Irish), Aoidh (Scotch).

HULBERT—Old German: Huldi-beraht. "Graceful-brilliant." A boy who walked as if he walked to music.
English variations: Hulbard, Hulburd, Hulburt.

HUMBERT—Old German: Hun-beraht. "Brilliant Hun," or Old German: Haim-beraht. "Brilliant supporter." Humbert or Umberto I, King of Italy, died 1900.
Foreign variations: Umberto (Italian).

HUMPHREY—Old German: Hun-frid. "Peaceful Hun," or Old German: Haim-frid. "Peace-support." Sir Humphrey Gilbert,

English explorer (1539-1583); Humphrey Bogart, actor.
English nicknames: Hump, Humph.
English variations: Humfrey, Humfry.
Foreign variations: Humfried (German, Dutch), Onfroi (French), Onofredo (Italian), Onofré, Hunfredo (Spanish), Humfrid (Swedish).

HUNTER—Old English: Hun-tere. "A hunter." A hunter of wild game for food and sport. Hunter Gardner, actor.
English variation: Hunt.

HUNTINGDON—Old English: Huntan-dun. "Hunter's hill." A hill abounding in game.

HUNTINGTON—Old English: Huntan-tun. "Hunting-estate." Huntington Hartford, theatrical producer.

HUNTLEY—Old English: Hunta-leah. "From the hunter's meadow." Huntley Gordon, actor.

HURLBERT—Old English: Herle-beorht. "Army-brilliant." A clever leader in war.

HURLEY—Irish Gaelic: Murt-huile. "Sea-tide." A man who loved the tide and sea.

HURST—Middle English: Hurst. "Dweller at the forest.
English variation: Hearst.

HUTTON—Old English: Hoh-tun. "From the estate on the projecting ridge."

HUXFORD—Old English: Huc's-ford. "Hugh's-ford."

HUXLEY—Old English: Huc's-leah. "Hugh's meadow."

HYATT—Old English: Heah-yate. "From the high gate." A family who lived by a city gate. A. Hyatt Verrill, American explorer.

HYDE—Old English: Hid.
"From the hide, an acreage that supported one family." Hyde Clark, English philologist, engineer (1815-1895).

HYMAN—Hebrew: Hhayim.
"Life." The divine energy that animates all life and brings it into existence. Hyman Rickover, Admiral, U.S. Navy.

I

IAN—Scotch Gaelic: Iaian.
"God is gracious." See John. Ian Hunter, Ian Keith, actors; Ian Fleming, author.

IGNATIUS—Latin: Ignatius.
"Fiery or ardent one." Ignace Jan Paderewski, Polish pianist (1860-1941); Ignazio Silone, Italian author.
English variations: Ignace, Ignatz.
Foreign variations: Ignaz (German), Ignace (French), Ignazio (Italian), Ignacio (Spanish), Ignatius (Dutch).

IMMANUEL—See Emanuel.

INGEMAR—Old Norse: Ingamar. "Famous-son." Notables: Ingemar Johansson, Swedish boxer; Ingmar Bergman, Swedish film executive.

INGER—Old Norse: Ing-harr.
"A son's army."
Foreign variations: Ingar, Ingvar (Scandinavian).

INGLEBERT—Old German: Engel-berht. "Angel-brilliant." Unusually intelligent.
English variations: Englebert, Engelbert.

INGRAM—Old Norse: Inghram. "Ing's raven; the son's raven." The ancient Norse hero name "Ing" meant "Son." The raven depicted wisdom.

INNIS—Irish Gaelic: Inis.
"From the river-island."
English variations: Innes, Inness, Iniss.

IRA—Hebrew: Ira. "Watchful one." Ira Allen, a founder of Vermont (1751-1814); Ira Gershwin, lyricist.

IRVIN, IRVINE—See Irving.

IRVING—Old English: Earwine. "Sea friend," or Old Welsh: Erwyn. "White river." Irvin S. Cobb, humorist (1876-1944); Irving Stone, writer; Irving Berlin, composer; Sir Henry Irving, famous English actor.
English variations: Irvin, Irvine, Irwin, Erwin.

IRWIN—See Irving.

ISAAC—Hebrew: Yitshhaq. "He laugheth." It was said this child laughed when he was born. Notables: Sir Isaac Newton, English scientist; Isaac Stern, violinist.
English nicknames: Ike, Ikey, Ikie.
Foreign variations: Isaak (German), Isacco (Italian), Izaak (Dutch).

ISHAM—Old English: Isen-ham. "From the iron-one's estate." A man so firm and stern his friends called him Iron. Isham Jones, orchestra leader.

ISIDORE—Greek: Isidoros.
"Gift of Isis." Isis, the Egyptian goddess, was wife of Osiris. Isidore Rabi, physicist.
English nicknames: Issy, Izzy.
Foreign variations: Isidor (German), Isidro (Spanish), Isidoro (Italian).

IVAN—See John.

IVAR—Old Norse: Iv-har. "Yew-bow army." Ivor, son of Alan, king of Brittany, A.D. 683; Ivar Aasen, Norwegian author; Ivor Novello, English actor-playwright.
English variations: Iver, Ivor.

IVEN—Old French: Iven. "Little yew-bow." This name was applied to a boy who had a bow made of yew-wood.

IVES—Old English: Ives. "Son of yew-bow." Figurative meaning, "Little archer."
English variation: Yves.

J

JACK—French: Jacques. "The supplanter." See John, Jacob.

JACKSON—Old English: Jaksone. "Son of Jack."

JACOB—Hebrew: Ya'aqob. "The supplanter." A man who replaced another. Used in honor of the Biblical patriarch Jacob, son of Abraham. Jacob Epstein, Polish sculptor. See James.
English nicknames: Jake, Jakie, Jack, Cob, Cobb.
Foreign variations: Jayme (Old Spanish), Jacobo (Spanish), Jacques (French), Jakob (German), Giacobo, Giacopo, Giacomo, Iacovo (Italian).

JACQUES—See Jacob.

JAGGER—North English: Jager. "Carter, teamster." A transporter of things by wagon.

JAMES—Old Spanish: Jayme. "The supplanter." See Jacob. St. James, one of the twelve apostles; Diego (James) Velasquez, 17th-century Spanish painter; James Boswell, Scotch biographer (1740-1795); James Joyce, Irish author; James Donald, James Cagney, James Stewart, actors.
English nicknames: Jim, Jimmie, Jimmy, Jamie.
Foreign variations: Jaime, Diego (Spanish), Giacomo (Italian), Seamus (Irish).

JARMAN—Old German: Hariman. "The German." This man earned his sobriquet because he came from Germany.
English variation: Jerman.

JARVIS—Old German: Gerhwas. "Spear-keen." Widely known as an expert with the spear.
English variation: Jervis.

JASON—Greek: Iason. "Healer." A Greek who had a knowledge of healing. Jason was among the ancient Greek heroes. Jason Robards, Jr., actor.

JASPER—Old French: Jaspre. "Jasper stone." A beautiful gem of various colors. See Gaspar. Jasper Cropsey, American painter.

JAY—Old French: Jaie. "Blue jay." Named for the saucy blue jay. Jay (Dizzy) Dean, baseball star.

JEAN—See John.

JED—Hebrew: Yedidiyah. "Beloved of the Lord." A modern shortening of Jedediah. Jed Harris, theatrical producer.

JEFFERSON—Old English: Geffrey-sone. "Son of Jeffrey." Jefferson Davis, President, Confederate States of America, 1861-1865.

JEFFREY—Old French: Geof-
froi. "Divinely peaceful." See
Godfrey. Actors Jeffrey Hunter,
Jeff Chandler, Geoffrey Horne.
English nicknames: Jeff, Jeffy.
English variations: Jefferey,
Geoffrey, Godfrey.

JEREMY—Hebrew: Yirm'yah.
"Appointed of Jehovah." A mod-
ern form of Jeremiah. Jeremy
Taylor, 17th-century English
bishop, author.
English nickname: Jerry.
Foreign variations: Jeremias
(German, Dutch), Jéréme
(French), Geremia (Italian),
Jeremias (Spanish).

JEROME—Latin: Hieronymus.
"Sacred or Holy Name." Jerome
Salinger, writer; Jerome Kern,
composer; Jerome Courtland, ac-
tor.
English nicknames: Gerry, Jerry.
English variations: Jerrome,
Gerome.

JESSE—Hebrew: Yishay.
"Wealth." A man rich in valu-
able resources. Jesse Crawford,
organist; Jesse Owens, track star;
Jess Willard, boxer.
English nicknames: Jess, Jessie.

JOEL—Hebrew: Yoel. "The
Lord is God." Joel McCrea, actor.

JOHN—Hebrew: Yehokhanan.
"God is gracious." Honoring St.
John the Apostle and St. John
the Baptist. Notables: John F.
Kennedy, U.S. President; Johann
Sebastian Bach, composer; Johan-
nes Brahms, composer; John Ed-
gar Hoover, FBI chief; Colonel
John Glenn, Jr., U.S. astronaut;
actors John Gielgud, John Barry-
more, John Wayne, John Beal.
English nicknames: Johnnie,
Johnny, Jack, Jackie.
English variations: Jon, Jonn
Zane.
Foreign variations: Johann, Jo-
hannes (German), Jean
(French), Juan (Spanish), Gio-
vanni (Italian), Ivan (Slavic),
John (Swedish), Eoin, Seain,
Seann, Shane (Irish), Iaian
(Scotch).

JONAS—Hebrew: Yonah.
"Dove." A man so-called because
he was peace-loving and serene.
Jonas Salk, noted physician.

JONATHAN—Hebrew:
Y-honathan. "Jehovah's gift."
Jonthan was the son of Saul and
the friend of David in the Bible.
Jonathan Edwards, 18th-century
American theologian; Jonathan
Swift, English author; Jonathan
Winters, comedian.

JORDAN—Hebrew: Yarden.
"Descender." The descending
river of Palestine.
Foreign variations: Jourdain
(French), Giordano (Italian).

JOSEPH—Hebrew: Yoseph.
"He shall add." This man will
add to his learning by experience.
Honoring St. Joseph of the Bible.
Namesakes: Franz Joseph Haydn,
Austrian composer; Giuseppe
Verdi, opera composer; Joe Di-
Maggio, baseball star; Joseph Cot-
ten, actor.
English nicknames: Joe, Joey.
Foreign variations: Giuseppe
(Italian), José (Spanish), Iosep
(Irish), Seosaidh (Scotch).

JOSHUA—Hebrew: Yehoshua.
"God of salvation." Joshua Logan, American dramatist, director, and producer.
English nickname: Josh.

JUDD—Hebrew: Y-hudhah.
"Praised." Eulogized by those
who knew him. A modern form
of Judah.

JULIAN—Latin: Julianus. "Be-
longing to Julius." See Julius.
Julian Eltinge, impersonator;
Julian Hawthorne, author.

JULIUS—Latin: Julius. "Youthful; downy-bearded one." A nick-

name for a very young, unshaven man. Jules Verne, French author; Jules Massenet, French composer; Julius LaRosa singer.
English nickname: Jule.
Foreign variations: Jules (French), Julio (Spanish), Giulio (Italian).

JUSTIN—Old French: Justine. "Upright, just one." A Frenchman who earned this name by his actions. The name of two 5th-century Byzantine emperors.
Foreign variations: Giustino (Italian), Justino (Spanish).

JUSTIS—Old French: Justice. "Justice." A man who upheld justice.
English variation: Justus.
Foreign variations: Giusto (Italian), Justo (Spanish), Juste (French), Justus (German).

K

KANE—Irish Gaelic: Cain. "Tribute," or Irish Gaelic: Cathan. "Little, warlike one." Known as a small, rebellious boy.
English variations: Kain, Kaine, Kayne.

KARL—See Charles.

KARNEY—See Kearney.

KARR—See Carr.

KASPAR—See Gaspar.

KAVAN—See Cavan.

KAY—Old Welsh: Cai. "Rejoicer," or Irish Gaelic: MacKay. "Fiery." Sir Kay was one of the knights of King Arthur's Round Table.

KEANE—Middle English: Kene. "Bold, sharp one." Designated as a smart and unafraid man. Alternate, Irish Gaelic: Caoin. "Handsome one."
English variations: Kean, Keen, Keene.

KEDAR—Arabic: Kadar. "Powerful." An Arab, physically strong and forceful.

KEEFE—Irish Gaelic: Caomh. "Handsome, noble, gentle, lovable." A complimentary name for a favorite son. Keefe Brasselle, actor.

KEEGAN—Irish Gaelic: Aodhagan. "Little fiery one."

KEELAN—Irish Gaelic: Caolan. "Little, slender one." Seven Irish saints were called Caolan.

KEELEY—Irish Gaelic: Cadhla. "Handsome."
English variations: Kealy, Keely.

KEENAN—Irish Gaelic: Cianan. "Little ancient one." A small man, old and wise. Three Irish saints were called Cianan; Keenan Wynn, actor.
English variation: Kienan.

KEITH—Irish Gaelic: Caith. "From the battle place." A man who lived by an old battlefield. Alternate: Old Welsh: Coed. "From the forest." Keith Andes, Keith Baxter, actors.

KELL—Old Norse: Kelda. "From the spring."

KELLER—Irish Gaelic: Ceileachan. "Little companion."

KELLY—Irish Gaelic: Ceallach. "Warrior." A brave soldier of the king.
English variation: Kelley.

KELSEY—Old Norse: Kiolls-ig. "Dweller at ship-island."

KELVIN—Irish Gaelic: Caol-abhuinn. "From the narrow river."
English variations: **Kelvan, Kelven.**

KEMP—Middle English: Kempe. "Warrior, champion."

KENDALL—Old English: Caindale. "From the clear-river valley or bright valley."
English variations: **Kendal, Kendell.**

KENDRICK—Irish Gaelic: MacEanraic. "Son of Henry," or Old English: Cyne-ric. "Royal ruler."

KENLEY—Old English: Cyneleah. "Dweller at the royal meadow."

KENN—Old Welsh: Cain. "Clear, bright water." Water as bright as polished silver.

KENNARD—Old English: Cene-hard. "Bold, strong."

KENNEDY—Irish Gaelic: Cinneididh. "Helmeted head," "Helmeted chief." An old Scotch and Irish clan name.

KENNETH—Irish Gaelic: Coinneach. "Handsome one," Old English: Cyne-ath. "Royal oath." Kenneth MacAlpin Scotch king, A.D. 843-858; Kenneth Keating, U.S. Senator.
English nicknames: **Ken, Kenney, Kenny.**

KENRICK—Old English: Cene-ric. "Bold ruler." A man without fear. Alternate, Old English: Cyne-ric. "Royal ruler."

KENT—Old Welsh: Cant. "White, bright." Kent Taylor, Kent Smith, actors.

KENTON—Old English: Cyne-tun. "From the royal estate."

KENWARD—Old English: Cene-ward. "Bold guardian," or Old English: Cyne-ward. "Royal guardian."

KENWAY—Old English: Cene-wig. "Bold warrior." An aggressive and obstinate fighter. Alternate, Old English: Cyne-wig. "Royal warrior."

KENYON—Irish Gaelic: Ceannfhionn. "White headed." Kenyon Nicholson, American dramatist.

KERMIT—Irish Gaelic: Diarmaid. "Free man." A man who answered only to his God. Kermit Roosevelt, son of U.S. President Theodore Roosevelt.

KERN—Irish Gaelic: Ceirin. "Little dark one."

KERR—Irish Gaelic: Carra. "Spear." See Carr. Alternate, Irish Gaelic: Ciar. "Dark one." John Kerr, actor.

KERRY—Irish Gaelic: Ciarda. "Son of the dark one."

KERWIN—Irish Gaelic: Ciardubhan. "Little, jet-black one." A sun-tanned boy with coal black hair and soft brown eyes. Kerwin Mathews, actor.
English variations: **Kerwen, Kirwin.**

KESTER—Old English: Caster. "From the Roman army camp." A stranger from the Roman conqueror's fort in ancient Britain.

KEVIN—Irish Gaelic: Caoimhin. "Gentle, lovable." Kevin McCarthy, actor.
English variations: **Kevan, Keven.**

KEY—Irish Gaelic: MacAoidh. "Son of the fiery one."

KIERAN—Irish Gaelic: Ciaran. "Little dark-complexioned one."

KILLIAN—Irish Gaelic: Cillin. "Little warlike one."

KIM—Old English: Cyne. "Chief, ruler."

KIMBALL—Old Welsh: Cynbel. "Warrior chief," or Old English: Cyne-bold. "Royal and bold."
English variations: Kimble, Kimbell.

KING—Old English: Cyning. "Ruler." King Vidor, motion picture director.

KINGSLEY—Old English: Cinges-leah. "From the king's meadow."
English variation: Kinsley.

KINGSTON—Old English: Cingestun. "Dweller at the king's estate."

KINGSWELL—Old English: Cinges-wiella. "Dweller at the king's spring."

KINNARD—Irish Gaelic: Cinnard. "From the high hill."

KINNELL—Irish Gaelic: Cinnfhail. "From the head of the cliff."

KINSEY—Old English: Cynesige. "Royal, victorious one."

KIPP—North English: Kip. "Dweller at the pointed hill."

KIRBY—Old Norse: Kirkja-byr. "From the church village." Kirby Grant, actor.
English variation: Kerby.

KIRK—Old Norse: Kirkja. "Dweller at the church." Kirk Douglas, actor.

KIRKLEY—Old North English: Circe-leah. "Church-meadow."

KIRKWOOD—Old North English: Circe-wode. "From the church forest." A church in a forest clearing.

KIRWIN—See Kerwin.

KNIGHT—Middle English: Kniht. "Soldier." David Knight, actor.

KNOX—Old English: Knocks. "From the hills."

KNUT—See Canute.

KONRAD—See Conrad.

KURT—See Conrad.

KYLE—Irish Gaelic: Caol. "From the strait."

KYNE—Old English: Cyne. "Royal one." Peter B. Kyne, author.

L

LACH—Old English: Laec. "Dweller by the water."
English variation: Lache.

LACHLAN—Scotch Gaelic: Laochail-an. "Warlike one," or Scotch Gaelic: Loch-lainn. "From the water."

LACY—Latin: Latiacum. "From Latius' estate." From the Roman's manor house.

LADD—Middle English: Ladde. "Lad or attendant."

LAIBROOK—Old English: Ladbroc. "Path by the brook." A trail perfumed by flowers and pussy willows.

LAIDLEY—Old English: Ladleah. "From the watercourse meadow." A man-made canal that watered a thirsty pasture.

LAIRD—Scotch: Laird. "Landed proprietor." One of the landed gentry.

LAMAR—Old German: Land-mari. "Land famous."

LAMBERT—Old German: Land-bercht. "Land-brilliant." English nicknames: Bert, Bertie. Foreign variations: Landbert (German), Lamberto (Italian).

LAMONT—Old Norse: Log-mann. "Law-man; lawyer." A man of law and letters. English variations: Lamond, Lammond.

LANCE—Old French: L'Ancelot. "Attendant or adherent." A modern short form of the old English "Lancelot." Lance Fuller, actor.

LANDER—Middle English: Launder. "Launderer," or Middle English: Landere. "Owner of a grassy plain." English variations: Landor, Landers.

LANDON—See Langdon.

LANE—Middle English: Lane. "From the narrow road." The old English Hundred Rolls of A.D. 1273 list Cecil "In the Lane." Lane Chandler, actor.

LANG—Old Norse: Lang-r. "Long or tall man." A Scandinavian so-called because of his great height. Andrew Lang, English writer (1844-1912).

LANGDON—Old English: Lang-dun. "Dweller at the long hill." A hill that seemed to cut the plain in two. English variation: Landon.

LANGFORD—Old English: Lang-ford. "Dweller at the long ford." A shallow, wide river where man and beast could cross.

LANGLEY—Old English: Lang-leah. "From the long meadow." Samuel P. Langley, U.S. astronomer (1834-1906).

LANGSTON—Old English: Langs-tun. "Tall man's estate or town." A man remembered for his height and his rich land.

LANGWORTH—Old English: Lang-worth. "From the long enclosure." A place fenced in by thicket and by hedge.

LARS—See Lawrence.

LARSON—Scandinavian: Lars-son. "Son of Lars." See Lawrence.

LATHAM—Old Norse: Hlathum. "From the barns." Multiple shelters for livestock.

LATHROP—Old English: Lath-throp. "From the barn-farmstead." A meadow dominated by a large, bright-colored barn.

LATIMER—Middle English: Latimer. "Interpreter." An esteemed man versed in many languages.

LAURENCE—See Lawrence.

LAWFORD—Old English: Hloew-ford. "From the ford at the hill."

LAWLER—Irish Gaelic: Leath-labhra. "Mumbler; half-speaker." A boy who talked so low, some said he mumbled.

LAWLEY—Old English: Hloew-leah. "From the hill-meadow." A fragrant green pasture tucked between two hills.

LAWRENCE—Latin: Laurens. "Laurel-crowned one." A man crowned by the emblem that personified victory and distinction. St. Laurence, celebrated 3rd-century martyr; Lorenzo de' Medici, 15th-century Florentine ruler; Lauritz Melchior, noted singer; Lawrence Welk, orchestra leader;

Sir Laurence Olivier, Laurence Harvey, English actors.
English nicknames: Larry, Lauren, Laurie, Lawry, Loren, Lorin, Lon, Lonnie.
English variations: Laurence, Larrance, Lawrance.
Foreign variations: Lorenz, Laurenz (German), Laurent (French), Lorenzo (Italian, Spanish), Lorenz, Lauritz (Danish), Lars (Swedish), Laurens (Dutch), Labhras (Irish), Labhruinn (Scotch).

LAWSON—Old English: Lawesone. "Son of Lawrence." Son of the victory-crowned one.

LAWTON—Old English: Hlowe-tun. "From the hill-town or estate."

LAZARUS—Hebrew: El'azar. "God will help." Lazaro Cardenas, Mexican statesman.
Foreign variations: Lazaro (Italian, Spanish), Lazare (French).

LEAL—Middle English: Lele. "Loyal; faithful." A man true to his friends, and trustworthy.

LEANDER—Greek: Leiandros. "Lion-man." Leander was famous in Greek myths.
Foreign variations: Léandre (French), Leandro (Italian, Spanish).

LEE—Old English: Leah. "From the pasture meadow," or Irish Gaelic: Laoidheach. "Poetic." A sweet, green meadow where poets come to dream. Lee De Forest, American inventor; actors Lee Bowman, Lee J. Cobb.
English variation: Leigh.

LEGGETT—Old French: Legat. "Envoy or delegate."
English variations: Leggitt, Liggett.

LEIF—Old Norse: Leif. "Beloved one." A man endeared to many people. Leif Erickson, famous Norse explorer.

LEIGH—See Lee.

LEIGHTON—Old English: Leah-tun. "Dweller at the meadow farm." Leighton Noble, orchestra leader.

LEITH—Scotch Gaelic: Leathan. "Broad, wide river." A great, slow river banked with wild roses, ferns and shrubs.

LELAND—Old English: Leahland. "From the meadow-land." In April the meadow was dressed in white, soft blooms, and green.

LEMUEL—Hebrew: Lemu'el. "Consecrated to God." Parents who pledged their son to serve God.
English nicknames: Lem, Lemmie.

LENARD—See Leonard.

LENNON—Irish Gaelic: Leannan. "Little cloak."

LENNOX—Scotch Gaelic: Leamhnach. "Abounding in elm trees." Where elm trees were filled with happy birds.

LEO—Latin: Leo. "Lion." A designation of honor for a man of bravery. Thirteen popes were named Leo; Leo Tolstoy, Russian novelist; Leo Durocher, baseball manager.

LEON—French: Leon. "Lionlike." Leon Blum, French statesman (1872-1950); Leon Brunin, Belgian painter; Leon Ames, actor.

LEONARD—Old Frankish: Leon-hard. "Lion-brave." Leonardo da Vinci Italian painter, sculptor, architect; Leonard Bernstein, composer-conductor.
English nicknames: Len, Lennie, Lenny.
English variations: Leonerd, Lennard.
Foreign variations: Leonardo (Italian, Spanish), Léonard (French), Leonhard (German).

LEOPOLD—Old German: Leutpald. "Bold for the people." Leopold I, II, III, Kings of Belgium; Leopold Stokowski, noted orchestra conductor.
Foreign variations: Léopold (French), Luitpold, Leupold (German), Leopoldo (Italian, Spanish).

LEROY—Old French: Le Roy. "King." A person who was given the title of king for his royal bearing, or for the part he played in a religious pageant. Le Roy Prinz, motion picture producer, director.
English nicknames: Lee, Roy.

LESLIE—Scotch Gaelic: Liosliath. "Dweller at the gray fortress." A fortress old and tempered by the elements. Leslie Banks, Leslie Howard, noted English actors.

LESTER—Latin: Ligera-castra. "Chosen camp; legion camp." The Roman army pitched camp in an advantageous place. Lester B. Pearson, Canadian statesman.
English nickname: Les.

LEVERETT—Old French: Leveret. "Young rabbit." A nickname for an active, joyous youth. Leverett Saltonstall, U.S. Senator.
English nickname: Lev.

LEVERTON—Old English: Laefer-tun. "From the rush-farm."
English nickname: Lev.

LEVI—Hebrew: Lewi. "Joined; united." A Hebrew who tried to link men closer to their God. Levi in the Bible was a son of Jacob and Leah.

LEWIS—See Louis.

LINCOLN—Old English: Lincolne. "From the colony by the pool." Abraham Lincoln, American President, was the famous prototype of this name; Lincoln Steffens, writer, lecturer.
English nickname: Linc.

LIND—Old English: Lind. "Dweller at the linden or lime tree." A yellow-flowered linden tree spread its branches over this family's residence.
English variation: Linden.

LINDBERG—Old German: Linde-berg. "Linden tree hill." Where birds could watch the people from the trees. Charles A. Lindbergh, famous flier.
English nickname: Lindy.

LINDELL—Old English: Lind-dael. "Dweller at the linden tree valley." Trysting place for lovers who picked the heart-shaped linden leaves.

LINDLEY—Old English: Lind-leah. "At the linden tree meadow." Lindley Bickworth, U.S. Congressman.

LINDON—See Lyndon.

LINDSEY—Old English: Lindes-ig. "Pool-island." Lindsay Crosby, entertainer, singer.
English variations: Lindsay, Linsay, Linsey.

LINFORD—Old English: Lindford. "From the linden tree ford."

LINK—Old English: Hlinc. "From the bank or ridge."

LINLEY—Old English: Linleah. "From the flax field."

LINN—See Lynn.

LINTON—Old English: Lin-tun. "From the flax enclosure." A home enclosed by fields of fragrant flax.

LINUS—Greek: Linos. "Flax-colored hair." A name for a boy with flaxen hair. Linus Pauling, scientist.

LIONEL—Old French: Lionel. "Young lion." A youth, tawny-haired and unafraid. Lionel Barrymore, actor.
Foreign variation: Lionello (Italian).

LITTON—Old English: Hlith-tun. "Hillside town or estate."

LLEWELLYN—Old Welsh: Llyw-eilun. "Like a ruler." Llew-ellyn the Great was a 13th-century Welsh ruler.

LLOYD—Old Welsh: Llwyd. "Gray-haired one." Lloyd George, English statesman; Lloyd Nolan, Lloyd Bridges, actors.
English variation: Floyd.

LOCKE—Old English: Loc. "Dweller by the stronghold or enclosure." W. J. Locke, English novelist.

LOGAN—Scotch Gaelic: Lagan. "Little hollow." Logan is a famed Scotch clan name.

LOMBARD—Latin: Longobard. "Long bearded one." A luxurious beard was an emblem of distinction centuries ago.

LON—Irish Gaelic: Lonn. "Strong, fierce." Enemies thought this man ferocious, but friends knew him as kindly. See Lawrence. Lon Chaney and Lon Chaney, Jr., actors.

LOREN—See Lawrence.

LORIMER—Middle English: Lorimer. "Saddle, spur and bit maker." A skilled artisan in the Middle Ages.

LORIN—See Lawrence.

LORING—Old German: Lothar-ing. "Son of famous-in-war." Son of the leader of a victorious army. Loring "Red" Nichols, orchestra leader.

LOUIS—Old German: Hlut-wig. "Famous warrior." Honoring St. Louis, 13th century king of France; Louis Joliet, 17th century French explorer; Ludwig von Beethoven, German composer; Luigi Pirandello, Italian play-wright; Louis Pasteur, French chemist; Louis Calhern, Louis Jourdan, actors.
English nicknames: Lou, Lew, Louie.
English variation: Lewis.
Foreign variations: Ludwig (German), Luigi, Lodovico (Italian), Luis (Spanish), Lode-wijk (Dutch), Ludvig (Swed-ish), Lugaidh (Irish), Luthais (Scotch).

LOVELL—Old English: Leof-el. "Little beloved one," or Old French: Louvel. "Little wolf." Lowell Thomas, commentator, writer.
English variation: Lowell.

LOWELL—See Lovell.

LOYAL—Old French: Loial. "True, faithful, unswerving."

LUCAS—See Luke.

LUCIAN—Latin: Lucianus. "Descendant of Lucius." See Luke.
Foreign variations: Luciano (Italian), Lucien (French).

LUCK—See Luke.

LUDLOW—Old English: Leodh-loew. "Dweller at the prince's hill."

LUDWIG—See Louis.

LUKE—Latin: Lucius. "Light-bringer of light or knowledge." Spiritual truth can convert the darkness of ignorance into light and intelligence. Primary usage commemorates St. Luke the Evangelist. Lucius Beebe colum-nist, publisher.
English variations: Lucas, Lucian, Lucius, Luck.
Foreign variations: Lucas (Ger-man, Dutch, Danish, Irish), Luc (French), Luca (Italian), Lucio (Spanish), Lukas (Swedish), Lucais (Scotch).

LUNDY—French: Lundi. "Born on Monday," or Scotch: Lundie. "Island grove."

LUNN—Irish Gaelic: Lonn. "Strong, fierce."

LUNT—Old Norse: Lund-r. "From the grove."

LUTHER—Old German: Hlutheri. "Famous warrior." Luther Adler, actor; Luther Burbank, horticulturist.
Foreign variations: **Lothaire** (French), **Lotario** (Italian), **Lutero** (Spanish).

LYLE—Old French: Del isle. "from the isle." An emigrant from an island. Lyle Talbot, actor. English variation: **Lyell.**

LYMAN—Middle English: Leyman. "Meadow-man." A man who walked in purple clover and thought of paradise.

LYNDON—Old English: Linddun. "Dweller at the lime tree or linden tree hill." Lyndon B. Johnson, U.S. Vice-President. English variation: **Lindon.**

LYNN—Old Welsh: Llyn. "From the pool or waterfall." English variation: **Lyn.**

M

MACADAM—Scotch Gaelic: MacAdhamh. "Son of Adam." A descendant of the "man of the red earth." See Adam.

MACDONALD—Scotch Gaelic: MacDomhnall. "Son of worldmighty." Macdonald Carey, actor.

MACDOUGAL—Scotch Gaelic: MacDubhgall. "Son of the dark stranger."

MACKINLEY—Irish Gaelic: MacCinfhaolaidh. "Learned or skillful leader." William McKinley, 25th U.S. President.

MACMURRAY—Irish Gaelic: MacMuireadhaigh. "Son of the mariner." Fred MacMurray, actor.

MACY—Old French: Macey. "From Mathew's estate."

MADDOCK—Old Welsh: Madawc. "Good and beneficient." A champion of mankind's welfare. Madoc was a renowned 12th-century Welsh ruler.
English variations: **Madoc, Madock, Madog.**

MADDOX—Old Anglo-Welsh: Maddock-son. "The benefactor's son." See Maddock.

MADISON—Old English: Mahthild-son. "Son of war-mighty." Heir of the valiant warrior. James Madison, 4th U.S. President.

MAGEE—Irish Gaelic: MacAodha. "Son of the fiery one."

MAGNUS—Latin: Magnus. "Great one." A man excellent in physical and mental proclivities. Magnus was the name of many important Norwegian kings.

MAITLAND—Old English: Maed-land. "Dweller at the meadowland."

MAJOR—Latin: Major. "Greater." A champion without competition.

MALCOLM—Scotch Gaelic: Mael-Coluim. "Disciple of St. Columba." Malcolm Canmore (Malcolm III), 11th-century Scotch king; Sir Malcolm Campbell, racing car specialist.

MALIN—Old English: Maht-hild-in. "Little war-mighty one."

MALLORY—Old German: Madel-hari. "Council-army; army counselor," or Old French: Mail-hair-et. "Unfortunate-strong."

MALONEY—Irish Gaelic: Maoldhomhnaigh. "Devoted to Sunday worship."

MALVIN—Irish Gaelic: Maol-min. "Polished chief," or Old English: Maethel-wine. "Council-friend." See Melvin.
English nickname: Mal.

MANDEL—German: Mandel. "Almond." A man characterized for his long, oval eyes.
English nickname: Manny.

MANFRED—Old English: Mann-frith. "Peaceful man, peaceful hero."

MANLEY—Old English: Mann-leah. "From the man's or hero's meadow."

MANNING—Old English: Mann-ing. "Son of the hero."

MANSFIELD—Old English: Maun-feld. "From the field by the small river." Mike Mansfield, U.S. Senator; Richard Mansfield, American actor.

MANTON—Old English: Mann-tun. "From the hero's estate."

MANUEL—See Emmanuel.

MANVILLE—Old French: Manne-ville. "From the great estate." Miles and miles of fertile land tilled by the hands of man.

MARCEL—Latin: Marcellus. "Little hammer; little warlike one." Marcel Proust, French novelist (1871-1922); Marcel Wittrisch, German singer.
Foreign variations: Marcellus (French), Marcello (Italian), Marcelo (Spanish).

MARCUS—See Mark.

MARDEN—Old English: Mere-dene. "From the pool-valley."

MARIO—Latin: Marius. "Martial one." Mario Pei, author, linguist; Mario Lanza, noted singer.

MARION—Old French: Mari-on. "Little Mary." A French masculine form of Mary.
Foreign variation: Mariano (Spanish).

MARK—Latin: Marcus. "Warlike one." Celebrated from Marco Polo, Italian traveler (1254-1324); Mark Twain, writer (1835-1910). Main usage from St. Mark the Evangelist.
English variation: Marcus.
Foreign variations: Marc (French), Marco (Italian), Markus (German, Swedish, Dutch, Danish), Marco, Marcos (Spanish).

MARLAND—Old English: Mere-land. "From the lake land."

MARLEY—Old English: Mere-leah. "From the lake meadow."

MARLON—Old French: Esmerillon. "Little falcon or hawk." A hunter named for his trained falcon. Marlon Brando, actor.
English variation: Marlin.

MARLOW—Old English: Mere-hloew. "From the hill by the lake." Christopher Marlowe, 16th-century English dramatist.
English variation: Marlowe.

MARMION—Old French: Mermeion. "Very small one." Marmion was the medieval hero of Sir Walter Scott's balladic poem *Marmion*.

MARSDEN—Old English: Mersc-dene. "Dweller at the marshy valley."
English variation: Marsdon.

MARSH—Old English: Mersc. "From the marshy place." Violets, vines, and fronding ferns splendorized the marsh.

MARSHALL—Middle English: Marschal. "Steward; horse-keeper." An attendant to the lord of a manor. Marshall Field III, publisher, philanthropist (1893-1956); Marshall Jewell, U.S. Postmaster General under President Grant; Marshall Thompson, actor.

MARSTON—Old English: Meres-tun. "Dweller at the lake-farm."

MARTIN—Latin: Martinus. "Warlike one." A name taken from Mars, the Roman war god, from whom the planet was named. Martin Luther, German religious reformer (1483-1546); Martin Van Buren, 8th U.S. President; Martin Johnson, famed African explorer.
English nicknames: Martie, Marty, Mart.
English variations: Marten, Marton.
Foreign variations: Martino (Italian, Spanish), Martín (Spanish), Martijn (Dutch), Martainn (Scotch).

MARVIN—Old English: Maerwine. "Famous friend," or Old English: Mere-wine. "Sea friend." Marvin Camrus, research physicist.
English nickname: Marv.

MARWOOD—Old English: Mere-wode. "From the lake-forest."

MASLIN—Old French: Masselin "Little Thomas."
English variation: Maslen.

MASON—Old French: Masson. "Stone-worker." A master-builder who worked with stone. James Mason, actor.

MATHER—Old English: Maethhere. "Powerful-army." Cotton Mather, American theologian, writer (1663-1728).

MATTHEW—Hebrew: Mattithyah. "Gift of Jehovah." St. Matthew was one of the twelve Apostles; Matthew Arnold, 19th-century English writer; Matthew Ridgway, U.S. Army general.
English nicknames: Mat, Matt, Mattie, Matty.
English variations: Mathew, Mathias, Mattias.
Foreign variations: Mathieu (French), Matthäus (German), Matteo (Italian), Mateo (Spanish), Mattheus (Swedish, Dutch), Matthaeus (Danish), Mata (Scotch).

MAURICE—Late Latin: Mauricius. "Dark-complexioned one." A man with jet-black hair and eyes that sparkled like the wine of Bacchus. Maurice Maeterlinck, Belgian writer; Maurice Evans, Maurice Chevalier, actors.
English nicknames: Maurie, Maury, Morrie.
English variations: Morris, Morrell.
Foreign variations: Maurizio (Italian), Moritz (German), Mauricio (Spanish), Maurits (Dutch), Maolmuire (Scotch).

MAXIMILIAN—Latin: Maximilianus. "Greatest in excellence." A Roman considered as the epitome of self-perfection. Maximilian, Holy Roman Emperor (1459-1519); Maximilian, Emperor of Mexico (1864-1867); Maximilian Schell, actor; Maxim Gorki, Russian novelist.
English nicknames: Max, Maxie, Maxy, Maxim.
Foreign variations: Maximilien (French), Maximo, Maximiliano (Spanish), Massimiliano (Italian), Maximilianus (Dutch).

MAXWELL—Old English: Mac-cus-wiella. "Capable-influential one's spring," or "Large spring." Maxwell Anderson, playwright; Max Reinhardt, theatrical producer; Max Beerbohm, English author; Maxwell Perkins, famous editor.
English nicknames: Max, Maxie, Maxy.

MAYER—Latin: Major. "Greater one." Because he was first in competition among all contestants.

MAYFIELD—Old English: Maga-feld. "From the warrior's field."

MAYHEW—Old French: Mahieu. "Gift of Jehovah. God gave to this devoted man the gift of reason without prejudice. A variation of Matthew.

MAYNARD—Old German: Megin-hard. "Powerful, brave." Maynard Dixon, Western painter.
Foreign variation: Menard (French).

MAYO—Irish Gaelic: Magheo. "From the plain of the yew trees." Yews were used for making bows in the Middle Ages.

MEAD—Old English: Maed. "From the meadow." The scent of fresh-mowed hay lingered long in this lad's memories. Meade Minnegerode, author.

MEDWIN—Old English: Maeth-wine. "Powerful friend."

MELBOURNE—Old English: Myln-burne. "From the mill-stream." Mills were built on streams to obtain water power for grinding grain.
English variations: Melburn, Milburn.

MELDON—Old English: Myln-dun. "Dweller at the mill-hill."

MELVILLE—Old French: Amal-ville. "From the industrious-one's estate." Melville Fuller, Chief Justice of the U.S. (1888-1910); Melville Cooper, actor.

MELVIN—Old English: Mael-wine. "Sword friend or speech-friend," or Irish Gaelic: Maol-min. "Polished chief." A long, sharp weapon was the constant companion of brave knights. Melvyn Douglas, actor.
English nickname: Mel.
English variations: Malvin, Melvyn.

MENDEL—East Semitic: Min'da. "Knowledge, wisdom." A man who gained knowledge by experience and study. L. Mendel Rivers, U.S. Congressman.

MERCER—Middle English: Mercer. "Merchant, storekeeper."

MEREDITH—Old Welsh: Meredydd. "Guardian from the sea." Meredith Willson, composer, conductor.

MERLE—French: Merle. "Blackbird." A black-haired youth named for the common blackbird.

MERLIN—Middle English: Merlion. "Falcon or hawk." An individual wise and cunning as a hawk. Merlin was a famous 5th-century adviser and magician. Merlin Hull, U.S. Congressman.

MERRILL—Old French: Mer-el. "Little famous one."

MERRITT—Old English: Maer-et. "Little famous one."

MERTON—Old English: Mere-tun. "From an estate or town by a lake."

MERVIN—Old English: Maere-wine. "Famous friend," or Scotch Gaelic: Muir-finn. "Beautiful sea." Mervyn Le Roy, noted motion picture producer, director.
English variations: Merwin, Merwyn.

MEYER—German: Meier. "Steward; farmer." A personal attendant and confidant of a king. The later interpretation was "farmer."

MICHAEL—Hebrew: Mikhael. "Who is like God," A spiritual and orderly one who practiced absolute truth. Honoring the archangel St. Michael. Michael Arlen, writer; Mickey Mantle, baseball star; Mickey Rooney, actor; Mike Todd, motion picture producer.
English nicknames: Mike, Mickie, Micky.
English variation: Mitchell.
Foreign variations: Michel (French). Michele (Italian), Miguel (Spanish), Mikael (Swedish), Micheil (Scotch), Mischa (Slavic).

MILES—Late Latin: Miles. "Soldier, warrior." Miles Standish, leader in the founding of New England.
English variation: Myles.

MILFORD—Old English: Mylnford. "Dweller at the mill-ford."

MILLARD—Old French: Emille-hard. "Flattering, winning and strong." Millard Fillmore, 13th U.S. President; Millard Tydings, U.S. Senator.

MILLER—Middle English: Millere. "Grain-grinder; flour-miller."

MILO—Latin: Milon. "Miller." Honored as the man who helped to feed the people of his town.

MILTON—Old English: Mylntun. "Dweller at the mill-town." Milton Berle, comedian, actor.

MILWARD—Old English: Myln-weard. "Mill-keeper."

MINER—Old French: Mineor. "A miner," or Latin: Minor. "Young person." Minor Watson, actor.
English variation: Minor.

MISCHA—See Michael. Mischa Elman, famed violinist.

MITCHELL—Middle English: Michell. "Who is like God,," See Michael. Mitch Miller, musician, entertainer.
English nickname: Mitch.

MODRED—Old English: Modraed. "Courageous counsellor." A brave diplomat who advised his people.

MONROE—Irish Gaelic: Moineruadh. "From the red swamp." A marsh that was filled with red and brown reeds. James Monroe, 5th U.S. President.
English variations: Monro, Munro, Munroe.

MONTAGUE—French: Montaigu. "Dweller at the pointed hill. Montague Love, actor.
English nicknames: Monte, Monty.

MONTGOMERY—Old French: Mont-Gomeric. "From the wealthy-one's hill or hill-castle." Montgomery Blair, U.S. Postmaster General under President Lincoln; Montgomery Clift, actor.
English nicknames: Monte, Monty.

MOORE—Old French: More. "Dark-complexioned." A dark and handsome man like Shakespeare's Moor in *Othello*. Alternate, Middle English: More. "From the wasteland."

MORELAND—Old English: Mor-land. "From the moor-land."

MORGAN—Old Welsh: Morcan. "White sea." Dweller by majestic, foamy breakers. Morgan Beatty, commentator.
English variation: Morgen.

MORLEY—Old English: More-leah. "From the moor meadow." A rush and fern filled pasture.

MORRIS—See Maurice. Morris R. Cohen, philosopher, educator (1880-1947).

MORRISON—Old English: More-sone. "Son of Maurice." See Maurice. Morrison Waite, Chief Justice of the United States, 1874-1888.

MORSE—Old English: More-s. "Son of the dark-complexioned one."

MORTIMER—Old French: Morte-mer. "From the still water." Quiet, deep, peaceful water, resting. Alternate, Irish Gaelic: Muircheartaigh. "Sea-director." English nicknames: **Mort, Mortie.**

MORTON—Old English: Mortun. "From the moor estate or town." The village was built near uncultivated wasteland. Morton Gould, composer, conductor; Mort Sahl, comedian. English nicknames: **Mort, Mortie.**

MORVEN—Irish Gaelic: Morfinn. "Great, fair-complexioned one." A blond giant in strength and intelligence. English variation: **Morfin.**

MOSES—Hebrew: Mosheh. "Taken out of the water," or Egyptian: Mesu. "Child." Honoring the great Hebrew prophet, lawgiver and Israelite leader. English nicknames: **Mose, Mosie, Moe, Moss.** Foreign variations: **Moise** (French, Italian), **Moisés** (Spanish), **Mozes** (Dutch).

MUIR—Scotch Gaelic: Muir. "From the moor or wasteland." Undrained, peaty wasteland in Britain is usually covered with heath or shrubs. John Muir, Scotch-American naturalist.

MUNROE—See Monroe.

MURDOCK—Scotch Gaelic: Muireadhach. "Prosperous from the sea."

MURPHY—Irish Gaelic: Murchadh. "Sea warrior." A protector of his country's shoreline.

MURRAY—Scotch Gaelic: Morogh. "Mariner, sea-warrior." A seaman who manned primitive galleys or sailing ships.

MYLES—See Miles.

MYRON—Greek: Myron. "Fragrant ointment, sweet oil." Myron Taylor, American diplomat; Myron McCormick, actor.

N

NAIRN—Scotch Gaelic: Amhuinn. "Dweller at the alder-tree river."

NALDO—See Reginald.

NATHAN—Hebrew: Nathan. "A gift," or "Given of God." Endowed with the gift of prophecy, Nathan saved Solomon's kingdom. Nathan Hale, American Revolutionary War patriot; Nathan Broch, columnist; Nathan Milstein, violinist. English nicknames: **Nat, Nate.**

NATHANIEL—Hebrew: Nethan-el. "Gift of God." A gifted disciple of Christ in the Bible. Nathaniel Hawthorne, 19th-century American writer. English nicknames: **Nat, Nate.** Foreign variations: **Natanael, Nataniel** (Spanish).

NEAL—Irish Gaelic: Niall. "Champion." Niall of the Nine Hostages, who died in A.D. 919, famous Irish ruler, was founder of the celebrated clan O'Neill. Neil Hamilton, actor.
English variations: Nial, Neall, Neale, Neil, Neill, Neel, Niels, Niles.
Foreign variations: Nels, Niels, Nils (Scandinavian), Niall (Scotch).

NELSON—English: Neil-son. "Champion's-son." Nelson Rockefeller, New York governor; Nelson Doubleday, publisher; Nelson Eddy, singer, actor.
English variations: Nealson, Nilson.

NEMO—Greek: Nemos. "From the glen or glade." Famed from Captain Nemo, Jules Verne character in *Twenty Thousand Leagues under the Sea* and *Mysterious Island*.

NESTOR—Greek: Nestor. "Departer or traveler." Figurative meaning "Wisdom." A ruler of ancient Pylos who aided the Greek victory in the Trojan War by giving wise advice.

NEVILLE—Old French: Neuveville. "From the new estate." Land reclaimed from the forest was called "Neuve-ville." Neville Chamberlain, English statesman; Neville Brand, actor.
English variations: Nevil, Nevile.

NEVIN—Irish Gaelic: Giollanaebhin. "Worshipper of the saint." A spiritual relation established with an illuminated saint. Alternate, Old German: Nefen. "Nephew." Ethelbert Nevin, composer.
English variation: Niven.

NEWELL—Old English: Niewheall. "From the new Hall or manor house," or Old French: Nouel. "A kernel."
English variation: Newall.

NEWLAND—Old English: Niew-land. "Dweller on reclaimed land." Francis Newlands (1847-1917), interested in land reclamation, was a credit to this name.

NEWLIN—Old Welsh: Newydd-llyn. "Dweller at the new pool."
English variation: Newlyn.

NEWMAN—Old English: Niew-man. "Newcomer." The townspeople welcomed the stranger to their community. John Henry Cardinal Newman, English prelate (1801-1890).

NEWTON—Old English: Niewtun. "From the new estate or new town." Newton Baker, Secretary of War under President Woodrow Wilson.

NIAL—See Neal.

NICHOLAS—Greek: Nikolaos. "Victorious army; victorious people." St. Nicholas, the wonder worker, was a 4th-century bishop of Myra, the patron of children. Nikolaus Copernicus, 16th-century Polish astronomer; Nicholas Murray Butler, educator; Nicholas Longworth, U.S. statesman.
English nicknames: Nick, Nicky, Nik, Nikki, Nichol, Nicol, Cole, Claus.
Foreign variations: Nicolas (French), Nicolo, Nicola, Niccolo (Italian), Nicolas (Spanish), Nikolaus (German), Neacail (Scotch), Nicolaas (Dutch).

NIGEL—Latin: Nigellus. "Dark one." A brunette man among fair haired people. Nigel Patrick, Nigel Bruce, English actors.

NILES—See Neal. Niles Trammell, television, radio executive.

NIXON—Old English: Nicson. "Son of Nicholas." See Nicholas.

NOAH—Hebrew: Noah. "Rest; comfort." A descendant of Adam;

at God's command Noah built the Ark that saved his family from the flood. Noah Webster, lexicographer (1758-1843); Noah Beery, actor.
Foreign variations: Noé (French, Spanish), Noach (Dutch), Noak (Swedish).

NOBLE—Latin: Nobilis. "Well-known and noble." Noble Johnson, U.S. Congressman.

NOEL—French: Noel. "Born at Christmas." Noel Coward, English playwright, actor, producer.
English variation: Nowell.
Foreign variations: Natale (Italian), Natal (Spanish).

NOLAN—Irish Gaelic: Nuallan. "Famous, noble." A man honored by his countrymen.

NORBERT—Old German: Norberaht. "Brilliant hero," or Old Norse: Njorth-r-biart-r. "Brilliance of Njord." Njord was the ancient Norse deity of the winds and of seafarers.

NORMAN—Old French: Normand. "A Northman." A stranger, strong and blond, from the fjords of the Norsemen. Norman Rockwell, artist; Norman Bel Geddes, stage designer; Norman Vincent Peale, clergyman, author.
English nicknames: Norm, Normie, Normy.

NORRIS—Old French: Noreis. "Northerner." A man from the Land of the Vikings.

NORTHCLIFF—Old English: North-clif. "From the north cliff." Lord Northcliffe was publisher of the *London Times* until his death in 1922.

NORTHROP—Old English: North-thorp. "From the north farm."
English variation: Northrup.

NORTON—Old English: Northtun. "From the north estate or north town."

NORVILLE—Old Anglo-French: North-ville. "From the north estate.
English variations: Norvel, Norvil.

NORVIN—Old English: Northwine. "Friend from the north." English variations: Norwin, Norwyn.

NORWARD—Old English: North-weard. "Northern guardian." A tall Scandinavian became the people's guardian.

NORWELL—Old English: North-wiella. "From the north spring."

NORWOOD—Old English: North-wode. "From the north forest." A primitive wilderness of trees, a haven for wild game.

NOWELL—See Noel.

NYE—Middle English: At-theneye. "Dweller at the island."

O

OAKES—Middle English: Okes. "Dweller at the oak trees."

OAKLEY—Old English: Acleah. "From the oak meadow." A

place where sheep and cattle could escape the summer sun.

OBERT—Old German: Od-bert. "Wealthy, brilliant one."

OCTAVIUS—Latin: Octavius. "Eighth born child." Octavius was a Roman imperial name. Octavius Roy Cohen, American writer.
English variation: **Octavus.**

ODELL—Old Anglo-French: Odel. "Little wealthy one," or Middle English: Wode-hull. "From the forested hill."

ODOLF—Old German: Od-wulf. "Wealthy wolf." The name "wolf" was applied to men of courage in the Middle Ages.

OGDEN—Old English: Okedene. "From the oak valley." Ogden Mills, former U.S. Secretary of the Treasury; Ogden Reid, U.S. Congressman; Ogden Nash, writer.

OGILVIE—Pictish-Scotch: Ogilbinn. "From the high peak."

OGLESBY—Old English: Oegels-by. "Awe-inspiring." A man so literate he held the illiterate spellbound.

OLAF—Old Norse: Oleif-r. "Ancestral relic." A talisman or amulet that was held in high esteem by this Scandinavian. Five Norwegian kings were named Olaf, the first in A.D. 995.
Foreign variations: **Olav** (Norse), **Amhlaoibh** (Irish).

OLIN—A distortion of Olaf. Olin Johnston, U.S. Senator.

OLIVER—Old Norse: Olvaer-r. "Kind, affectionate one," or Old French: Oliver. "Olive tree." Named from the olive tree that was a symbol of peace. Oliver Cromwell, 17th-century English ruler; Oliver Wendell Holmes, U.S. Supreme Court Justice, 1902-1932.
English nicknames: **Ollie, Olley, Olly.**
Foreign variations: **Olivier** (French), **Oliviero** (Italian), **Oliverio** (Spanish).

OLNEY—Old English: Ollan-eg. "Olla's island."

OMAR—Arabic: Omar. "Most high; richness; first son; follower of the Prophet." There are diverse Arabic meanings for Omar. Omar Khayyam, 12th-century Persian poet; Omar Bradley, U.S. Army general.

ONSLOW—Old English: Ondeshloew. "Zealous one's hill." Onslow Stevens, actor.

ORAM—Old English: Orahamm. "From the riverbank enclosure." The river's steep bank was a barrier against unwanted intruders.

ORAN—Irish Gaelic: Odhran. "Pale complexioned one." A boy so fair he was considered pallid. Oren Long, U.S. Senator.
English variations: **Oren, Orin, Orran, Orren, Orrin.**

ORESTES—Greek: Oreias. "Mountaineer." In the myths Orestes was the son of the hero Agamemnon.

ORFORD—Old English: Orfford. "Dweller at the cattle-ford." A place where cattle walked in clear, cool, shallow water.

ORION—Greek: Orion. "Son of fire," or "Son of light." A giant hunter in Greek myths, who was slain by Artemis and became the giant constellation of Orion.

ORLAN—Old English: Ordland. "From the pointed land." Where the land tapered and projected into the sea.
English variation: **Orland.**

ORLANDO—See Roland.

ORMAN—Old English: Ordman. "Spearman." A knight so clever with his spear that he earned this nomenclature. Alternate, Old English: Orme-man. "Ship-man."

ORMOND—Old English: Ord-mund. "Spear-protector," or Old English: Orme-mund. "Ship-protector."

ORO—Spanish: Oro. "Golden one." A blue eyed boy with golden hair that glistened in the morning sun.

ORRICK—Old English: Har-ac. "Dweller at the ancient oak tree." Where the tree in silent dignity guarded the valley.

ORRIN—See Oran.

ORSON—Old English: Ord-sone. "Spearman's son," or Old French: Ourson. "Little bear." Orson Welles, Orson Bean, actors. English variation: Urson.

ORTON—Old English: Ora-tun. "From the shore-farmstead or town." A verdant farm by the lake's moist shore.

ORVAL—Old English: Ord-wald. "Spear-mighty." A youth deemed mighty and quick as Hercules with his spear.

ORVILLE—Old French: Auri-ville. "From the golden estate or town." The meadow was filled with goldenrod and yellow grain. Orville Wright, aviation pioneer (1871-1948).

ORVIN—Old English: Ord-wine. "Spear-friend."

OSBERT—Old English: Os-beorht. "Divinely brilliant." A leader the people said was inspired. Sir Osbert Sitwell, English poet.

OSBORN—Old English: Os-beorn. "Divine warrior." A man blessed by God. Alternate, Old Norse: As-biorn. "Divine bear."

OSCAR—Old Norse: Os-kar. "Divine spear; divine spearman." A soldier's spear that seemed to be blessed by God. Namesakes include the Swedish kings Oscar I and Oscar II; Oscar Dystel, eminent publisher and executive; Oscar Hammerstein, II, librettist, producer.

OSGOOD—Old Norse: Asgaut. "Divine Goth." A benefactor descended from the valiant Goths. Osgood Perkins, actor.

OSMAR—Old English: Os-maer. "Divinely glorious."

OSMOND—Old English: Os-mund. "Divine protector." English variation: Osmund.

OSRED—Old English: Os-raed. "Divine counselor." A man inspired by God.

OSRIC—Old English: Os-ric. "Divine ruler."

OSWALD—Old English: Os-weald. "Divinely powerful." Oswald Spengler, German philosophical writer (1880-1936); Ozzie Nelson, actor, orchestra leader. English variation: Oswell.

OTHMAN—Old German: Otho-mann. "Prosperous man."

OTIS—Greek: Otos. "Acute or keen of hearing," or Old German: Otho. "Wealthy." Otis Skinner, actor (1858-1942); Otis Pike, U.S. Congressman.

OTTO—Old German: Otto, Otho. "Prosperous, wealthy one." A popular imperial German name. Prince Otto Bismarck-Schonhausen, German statesman (1815-1898); Otto Kruger, actor.

OWEN—Old Welsh: Owein. "Well-born one; young warrior." A man of good breeding and manners. Owen Roberts, U.S. Supreme Court Justice; Owen Wister, American author. English variation: Evan.

OXFORD—Old English; Oxnaford. "From the oxen ford." A place where teams of oxen crossed the river.

OXTON—Old English: Oxnatun. "From the ox-enclosure." A pasture fenced in and filled with oxen.

P

PADDY—See Patrick.

PADGETT—French: Paget. "Young attendant." A devoted attaché to his superior.
English variations: Padget, Paget.

PAGE—French: Page. "Attendant, youthful attendant." Page Belcher, U.S. Congressman.

PALMER—Old English: Palmere. "Palm-bearing pilgrim." A pilgrim who returned from the Holy Land with a palm branch.

PARK—Old English: Pearroc. "Dweller at the enclosed land or park." A tract of land where animals were protected. Mungo Park, 18th-century Scotch explorer.
English variation: Parke.

PARKER—Middle English: Parker. "Park keeper or guardian."

PARKIN—Old English: Perekin. "Little Peter." A small replica of his father.

PARLE—Old French: Pierrel. "Little Peter."

PARNELL—Old French: Pernel. "Little Peter."

PARR—Old English: Pearr. "Dweller at the cattle enclosure." Old thornfence thickets kept marauders out and cattle in.

PARRISH—Middle English: Parisch. "From the church area."

PARRY—Old Welsh: Ap-Harry. "Son of Harry." Edward W. Parry, English Arctic explorer (1790-1855).

PASCAL—Italian: Pascale; Pasquale. "Born at Easter." A child born at the Jewish Passover or Christian Easter. St. Paschal was a 9th-century pope.

PATRICK—Latin: Patricius. "Noble one." Honoring St. Patrick, 5th century missionary, patron saint of Ireland. Patrick Henry, American statesman; Patrick McCarran, U.S. Senator; Patrick O'Neal, Pat Boone, actors.
English nicknames: Pat, Paddy.
Foreign variations: Patrizius (German), Patrice (French), Patrizio (Italian), Patricio (Spanish), Padruig (Scotch), Padraic, Padraig (Irish).

PATTON—Old English: Beadutuh. "From the combatant's estate." A man honored for his prowess in battle.
English variations: Patten, Pattin, Paton.

PAUL—Latin: Paulus. "Little." Paul was a missionary of Christianity, a dynamo of energy and faith, who gave his name to men of every land. Paul Cézanne, French painter; Pablo Casals, Spanish cellist; actors Paul Muni, Paul Newman, Paul Henreid.
Foreign variations: Paolo (Italian), Pablo (Spanish).

PAXTON—Old English: Paeccstun. "From the combatant's estate."
English nickname: Pax.

PAYNE—Latin: Paganus. "Villager; one from the country." John H. Payne, composer of "Home Sweet Home."

PAYTON—Old English: Paegastun. "Dweller at the fighter's estate." Peyton Randolph, President of the 1st American Congress (1723-1775).
English variation: Peyton.

PEDRO—See Peter.

PELL—Old English: Paella. "Mantle or scarf." A loose, sleeveless cloak designated the wearer.

PELTON—Old English: Pelltun. "From an estate by a pool."

PENLEY—Old English. Pennleah. "Enclosed pasture-meadow."

PENN—Old German: Bannan. "Commander," or Old English: Penn. "Enclosure." William Penn, English Quaker, founded Pennsylvania.

PENROD—Old German: Bannruod. "Famous commander." Popularized from Booth Tarkington's stories of Penrod.

PEPIN—Old German: Peppi. "Petitioner" or "Perseverant one." Pepin the Short, 8th-century king of the Franks, was the father of the Emperor Charlemagne.
English nicknames: Pepi, Peppi.

PERCIVAL—Old French: Perceval. "Valley-piercer." A knight of King Arthur's court who sought the holy grail. Percy Bysshe Shelley, English poet.
Nicknames: Perce, Percy, Perc.
English variations: Parsefal, Parsifal, Perceval.

PERKIN—Old English: Perekin. "Little Peter." A son of the Fisherman of Galilee. Sir William Perkin, English chemist (1838-1907).

PERRIN—Old French: Perin. "Little Peter." A tiny individual with his father's name.

PERRY—Middle English: Perye. "From the pear tree," or Old

Anglo-French: Pierrey. "Little Peter." Perry Como, singer, entertainer.

PERTH—Pictish-Celtic: Pert. "Thorn-bush thicket." A Scotch county and town and an Australian city are called Perth.

PETER—Latin: Petrus. "Rock or stone." Honors St. Peter, acclaimed as the first Pope of the Catholic Church. Peter the Great, Russian Emperor; Pierre Curie, French chemist; Peter O'Toole, Peter Ustinov, actors.
English nicknames: Pete, Petie, Petey.
Foreign variations: Pietro, Pedro, Pero, Piero (Italian), Pedro (Spanish), Peadair (Scotch), Pierre (French), Petrus (German), Peadar (Irish), Pieter (Dutch).

PEVERELL—Old French: Piperel. "Piper or whistler." Famous from the novel *Peveril of the Peak* by Sir Walter Scott.
English variations: Peverel, Peveril.

PEYTON—See Payton.

PHELAN—Irish Gaelic: Faolan. "Little wolf." "Wolf" was a complimentary name for courage.

PHELPS—West English: Phelips. "Son of Philip." A son of Philip who loved his prancing horses.

PHILIP—Greek: Philippos. "Lover of horses." St. Philip was one of the twelve Apostles. Philip Barry, American dramatist; Prince Philip, husband of England's Queen Elizabeth II; Philip Merivale, noted actor; Phil Harris, orchestra leader.
English nickname: Phil.
Foreign variations: Filippo (Italian), Felipe (Spanish), Philippe (French), Philipp (German), Pilib, Filib (Irish), Filip (Swedish).

PHILLIPS—Old English: Philips. "Son of Philip." Phillips Brooks, clergyman, author of "O Little Town of Bethlehem."

PHILO—Greek: Philo. "Loving; friendly." Judaeus Philo was a 1st-century Jewish philosopher; Philo Vance, fictional detective created by S. S. Van Dine.

PHINEAS—Greek: Phinees. "Mouth of brass." Phineas T. Barnum famous showman.

PICKFORD—Old English: Picford. "From the ford at the peak."

PICKWORTH—Old English: Pica-worth. "From the hewer's estate." A cutter of trees for constructional usage.

PIERCE—Old Anglo-French: Piers. "Rock or stone." A man named from an old stone landmark where he lived. An early variation of Peter. Franklin Pierce, 14th U.S. President; Pierce Butler, U.S. Supreme Court Justice, 1922-1939.

PIERRE—See Peter.

PITNEY—Old English: Bitanig. "Persevering one's island." He matched his wits and strength against the elements of nature.

PITT—Old English: Pyt. "From the hollow or pit," or Old German: Bittan. "Desire; longing."

PLATO—Greek: Platos. "Broad one; broad-shouldered." Plato, world famous Greek philosopher, 427-347 B.C.

PLATT—Old French: Plat. "From the flat land."

POLLOCK—Old English: Pauloc. "Little Paul." A boy called Pollock instead of Junior. Sir Frederick Pollock, English author (1845-1937).

POMEROY—Old French: Pommeraie. "From the apple orchard."

PORTER—French: Portier. "Gatekeeper," or French: Porteur. "Porter."

POWELL—Old Welsh: Ap-Howell. "Son of Howell." See Howell.

PRENTICE—Middle English: Prentice. "A learner or apprentice."

PRESCOTT—Old English: Preost-cot. "From the priest's dwelling." A residence near the parsonage. W. H. Prescott, historian (1796-1859).

PRESLEY—Old English: Preostleah. "Dweller at the priest's meadow." J. B. Priestley, English author and playwright.
English variations: Pressley, Priestley.

PRESTON—Old English: Preost-tun. "Dweller at the priest's place." Preston Foster, actor.

PREWITT—Old French: Preuet. "Little valiant one."
English variation: Pruitt.

PRICE—Old Welsh: Ap-rhys. "Son of the ardent one." The son of a kind and loving man.

PRIMO—Italian: Primo. "First child born to a family." Primo de Rivera, Spanish statesman (1873-1930).

PROCTOR—Latin: Procurator. "Administrator." A man designated to execute the will of his superiors.
English variations: Procter, Prockter.

PRYOR—Old French: Priour. "Head of a priory." A sacred position designated by the church. Arthur Pryor, noted composer and band master.
English variation: Prior.

PUTNAM—Old English: Puttan-ham. "From the commander's estate or pit-dweller's estate."

Q

QUENNEL—Old French: Quesnel. "Dweller at the little oak tree." An isolated tree was a travelers' landmark.

QUENTIN—See Quinton.

QUIGLEY—Irish Gaelic: Coigleach. "Distaff." The part that held the flax on the family spinning wheel.

QUILLAN—Irish Gaelic: Cuilean. "Cub." A proud father's endearing name for his son.

QUIMBY—Old Norse: Kuanby-r. "Dweller at the woman's estate."
English variations: Quinby, Quenby.

QUINCY—Old French: Quincey. "Dweller at the fifth son's estate." Celebrated from John Quincy Adams, 6th U.S. President.

QUINLAN—Irish Gaelic: Caoinlean. "Well-shaped one." An athlete famed for his strength and physical perfection.

QUINN—Irish Gaelic: Cuinn. "Wise; intelligent."

QUINTON—Latin: Quinctus. "Fifth child," or Old English: Cwen-tun. "From the queen's estate or town." An adherent who faithfully served her royal highness. St. Quentin, martyred in A.D. 287 in France; Quentin Burdick, U.S. Senator.

R

RAD—Old English: Raed. "Counselor." Noted as a legal adviser for an embassy.

RADBERT—Old English: Raedbeorht. "Brilliant counselor." Knowledge of the law and of people made this adviser popular.

RADBORNE—Old English: Read-burne. "From the red stream." A stream whose bed was filled with red iron silt washed there by melting snows.

RADCLIFF—Old English: Read-cliff. "Dweller at the red cliff." The cliff was bathed with orange, scarlet and vermillion at sunset.

RADFORD—Old English: Read-ford. "From the red ford."

RADLEY—Old English: Read-leah. "Red pasture-meadow." Emerald green grass on fertile red loam.

RADNOR—Old English: Readan-oran. "At the red shore."

RADOLF—Old English: Raedwulf. "Swift wolf; counsel wolf." An adviser of warriors.

RAFAEL—See Raphael.

RAFFERTY—Irish Gaelic: Rabhartach. "Prosperous and rich."

RALEIGH—Old English: Raleah. "Dweller at the roe-deer meadow." Sir Walter Raleigh, English explorer (1552-1618). English variation: Rawley.

RALPH—Old English: Raed-wulf. "Swift wolf or counsel wolf." A brave adviser. Ralph Waldo Emerson, philosopher, poet (1803-1882); Ralph Bunche, United Nations official; Ralph Bellamy, Ralph Forbes, actors. English variations: Ralf, Raff, Rolf, Rolph.
Foreign variation: Raoul (French).

RALSTON—Old English: Raed-wulf-tun. "Dweller at Ralph's estate or town."

RAMBERT—Old German: Regin-beraht. "Mighty-brilliant." St. Rambert, 7th century.

RAMON—See Raymond.

RAMSDEN—Old English: Ramm-dene. "Ram's valley."

RAMSEY—Old English: Hraem's-eg. "Raven's island," or Old English: Ram-eg. "Ram's island."
English variation: Ramsay.

RANDALL—See Randolph.

RANDOLPH—Old English: Rand-wulf. "Shield-wolf." A war shield that made its owner invincible. Randolph Scott, actor. English nicknames: Rand, Randy.
English variations: Randolf, Randall, Randell.

RANGER—Old French: Ranger. "Forest keeper."
English variation: Rainger.

RANKIN—Old English: Rand-kin. "Little shield. Engraved shields were great protection in battle.

RANSFORD—Old English: Hraefn-ford. "From the raven's ford." In ancient days the raven symbolized great bravery when applied as a warrior-name.

RANSLEY—Old English: Hraefn-leah. "From the raven's meadow."

RANSOM—Old English: Rand-son. "Son of Shield." The son of an armored warrior.

RAOUL—See Ralph.

RAPHAEL—Hebrew: R'phael. "Healed by God." Cured in body and in mind, was this believer. Raphael, Italian "old master" painter; Rafael Sabatini, novelist.
Foreign variations: Rafaelle, Rafaello (Italian), Rafael (Spanish).

RAWLINS—Old Anglo-French: Raoulin-sone. "Son of little counsel-wolf." A brave small man who gave wise instructions.

RAWSON—Old English: Raed-wulf-sone. "Son of little counsel-wolf."

RAY—Old French: Ray. An honored title given to a sovereign. Ray Bolger, actor, dancer; Ray Milland, actor; Ray Lyman Wilbur, former U.S. Secretary of the Interior.

RAYBURN—Old English: Raburne. "From the roe-deer brook."

RAYMOND—Old German: Ragin-mund. "Mighty or wise protector." Protection by divinity. Raymond Massey, actor; Ramón Magsaysay, Philippine statesman.
English nickname: Ray.
Foreign variations: Ramon, Raimundo (Spanish), Raimondo (Italian), Raimund (German), Reamonn (Irish).

RAYNOR—Old Norse: Ragnar. "Mighty army." A leader of protective armed forces.
Foreign variation: Rainer (German).

READ—Old English: Read. "Red-haired or red-complexioned." Reed Hadley, actor; Reid Milner, educator.

READING—Old English: Reading. "Son of the red-haired one." Rufus Reading, Chief Justice of England (1860-1935).
English variation: Redding.

REDFORD—Read-ford. "From the red ford."

REDLEY—Old English: Readleah. "Dweller at the red meadow."

REDMAN—Old English: Raedman. "Counsel-man," or Old English: Raede-man. "Horseman."

REDMOND—Old English: Raed-mund. "Counsel-protector." English variations: Redmund, Radmund.

REDWALD—Old English: Raed-weald. "Counsel-mighty."

REECE—Old Welsh: Rhys. "Ardent one." A happy man who loved life and people.
English variations: Reese, Rees, Rice.

REED—See Read.

REEVE—Middle English: Reve. "Steward, bailiff." The high steward of the king.
English variations: Reave, Reeves.

REGAN—Irish Gaelic: Riagan. "Little king." A youth who had a regal bearing.
English variations: Reagan, Reagen, Regen.

REGINALD—Old English: Regen-weald. "Mighty and powerful." Reignald Denny, Reginald Gardiner, actors.
English nicknames: Reg, Reggie, Reggy, Rene.

English variations: Reynold, Reynolds, Ronald.
Foreign variations: Reinwald Reinald (German), Regnauld, Renault, René (French), Rinaldo (Italian), Reinaldo, Reinaldos, Renato, Naldo (Spanish), Reinold (Dutch), Reinhold (Swedish, Danish), Raghnall (Irish).

REID—See Read.

REMINGTON—Old English: Hremm-ing-tun. "From the raven-family estate." Where these black birds vocalized.

REMUS—Latin: Remus. "Speedy motion; fast rower of a boat." Remus and Romulus were the legendary founders of the city of Rome.

RENAULT—See Reginald.

RENE—See Reginald.

RENFRED—Old English: Regen-frithu. "Mighty and peaceful." A quiet hero who felt kindred with all men.

RENFREW—Old Welsh: Rhinffrew. "From the still river or channel."

RENNY—Irish Gaelic: Raighne. "Little, mighty, and powerful."

RENSHAW—Old English: Hraefn-scaga. "From the raven forest." Trees black with watchful ravens.

RENTON—Old English: Rantun. "Roebuck-deer estate." A sanctuary from hunters.

REUBEN—Hebrew: R'ubhen. "Behold a son." A reward of love and prayer. Rube Goldberg, cartoonist; Rubén Dario, noted Nicaraguan poet.
English nickname: Rube.
Foreign variation: Rubén (Spanish).

REX—Latin: Rex. "King." All-powerful in his majesty. Rex Harrison, Rex Reason, actors.
Foreign variations: Rey (Spanish), Roi (French).

REXFORD—Old English: Rexford. "Dweller at the king's ford." Rexford Tugwell, political writer.

REYNARD—Old German: Regin-hard. "Mighty-brave."
English variations: Renard, Rennard, Raynard.
Foreign variations: Reinhard (German), Renard, Renaud (French).

REYNOLD—See Reginald.

RHODES—Middle English: Rodes. "Dweller at the crucifixes," or Greek: Rhodeos. "Place of the roses."

RICH—Old English: Rice. "Powerful, wealthy one." See Richard.

RICHARD—Old German: Richhart. "Powerful ruler," or Old English: Ric-hard. "Powerful-brave." A keeper of the peoples' welfare. Famous from the 12th-century English King Richard the Lion-Hearted; Richard Wagner, German composer; Richard Nixon, former U.S. Vice-President; Richard E. Byrd, explorer; actors Richard Widmark, Ricardo Montalban, Ricky Nelson.
English nicknames: Dick, Dicky, Rick, Ricky, Richie, Ritchie, Rich, Ritch.
English variations: Ricard, Richerd, Rickert.
Foreign variations: Riccardo, (Italian), Ricardo (Spanish), Richart (Dutch), Riocard (Irish).

RICHMAN—Old English: Ricman. "Powerful man."

RICHMOND—Old German: Rich-mund. "Powerful protector." A helper of the unfortunate.

RICKER—Old English: Richere. "Powerful army."

RICKWARD—Old English: Ric-weard. "Powerful guardian."
English variation: Rickwood.

RIDDOCK—Irish Gaelic: Reidh-achadh. "From the smooth field." Meadowland cleared of trees and bushes.

RIDER—Old English: Ridere: "Knight or horseman." Rider Haggard, English novelist (1856-1925).
English variation: Ryder.

RIDGE—Old English: Hrycg. "From the ridge."

RIDGEWAY—Old English: Hrycg-weg. "From the ridge road."

RIDGLEY—Old English: Hrycg-leah. "Dweller at the ridge meadow." A little green mountain meadow.

RIDLEY—Old English: Read-leah. "From the red meadow."

RIDPATH—Old English: Read-paeth. "Dweller on the red path."

RIGBY—Old English: Rica-dene. "Ruler's valley."

RIGG—Old English: Hrycg. "From the ridge."

RILEY—Irish Gaelic: Raghallach. "Valiant, warlike one."
English variations: Reilly, Ryley.

RING—Old English: Hring. "A ring." His heirloom made this individual distinctive. Ring Lardner, writer.

RIORDAN—Irish Gaelic: Rioghbhardan. "Royal poet or bard." A singer children adored and women admired.

RIPLEY—Old English: Hrypan-leah. "Dweller at the shouter's meadow." A man who seemed to yell against the wind. Famed from Robert Ripley, author of *Believe It or Not*.

RISLEY—Old English: Hrisleah. "From the brushwood meadow." A place where man or beast could hide.

RISTON—Old English: Hristun. "From the brushwood estate or town."

RITCHIE—See Richard.

RITTER—North German: Ritter. "A knight." A handsome man in armor, protecting his king and country. Tex Ritter, actor.

ROALD—Old German: Hrodowald. "Famous ruler." Roald Amundsen, Norwegian polar explorer (1872-1928).

ROAN—North English: Rowan. "Dweller by the rowan-tree." Named for the rowan tree filled with bright red cherries. Alternate, Spanish: Roano. "Reddish-brown colored."

ROARKE—Irish Gaelic: Ruarc; Old Norse: Hroth-rekr. "Famous ruler." A sovereign whom the people eulogized. Noted from Robert Ruark, columnist.
English variations: **Ruark, Rourke, Rorke.**

ROBERT—Old English: Hrothbeorht. "Bright or shining with fame." Made world renowned by Robert the Bruce, King of Scotland (1306-1329), who preserved his country's independence. Robert Burns, Scotch poet; Robert Benchley, humorist; Robert C. Rule, Montana uranium discoverer; actors Robert Montgomery, Robert Taylor, Robert Mitchum, Bobby Clark, Bob Hope.
English nicknames: **Bob, Bobby, Rob, Robb, Robby, Robin, Bert, Rab**

English variations: **Rupert, Robertson, Robinson.**
Foreign variations: **Ruprecht** (German), **Roberto** (Italian, Spanish), **Riobard** (Irish).

ROBIN—See Robert.

ROBINSON—See Robert. Robinson Jeffers, American poet.

ROCHESTER—Old English: Roche-ceaster. "Rocky fortress," or Old English: Hrof-ceaster. "Sky-fortress." A fortress silhouetted against the sky. Rochester, comedian, entertainer.

ROCK—Old English: Roc. "From the rock." Rock Hudson, actor.

ROCKLEY—Old English: Rocleah. "From the rocky meadow."

ROCKWELL—Old English: Roc-wiella. "From the rocky spring." Rockwell Kent, painter.

RODD—Old German: Ruod. "Famous one." See Roderick.

RODEN—Old English: Hreoddene. "From the reed valley." Named for red brown reeds growing in the meadow.

RODERICK—Old German: Ruod-rik. "Famous ruler," or "Rich in fame." Rod Cameron, Rod Steiger, Rod Taylor, Roddy McDowall, actors; Roderick the Great, ancient Welsh ruler; Roderick, 8th-century Visigothic Spanish king.
English nicknames: **Rod, Roddie, Roddy, Rick, Ricky.**
English variations: **Broderick, Rodrick.**
Foreign variations: **Roderich** (German), **Rodrigue** (French), **Rodrigo** (Italian), **Rodrigo, Ruy** (Spanish), **Ruaidhri** (Irish), **Rurik** (Slavik).

RODGER—See Roger.

RODMAN—Old German: Ruod-mann. "Famous man or hero."

RODMOND—Old German: Ruod-munt. "Famous protector." English variation: Rodmund.

RODNEY—Old English: Rodan-ig. "Famous one's island."

RODOLPH—See Rudolph.

RODWELL—Old English: Rod-wiella. "Dweller at the crucifix-spring." Where a Christian long ago became a martyr.

ROE—Middle English: Roe. "Roe-deer." Named for the small, agile European deer.

ROGAN—Irish Gaelic: Ruad-hagen. "Red-haired."

ROGER—Old German: Ruod-ger. "Famous spearman." Famed from Roger Bacon, 13th-century English philosopher; Roger Maris, baseball star; Roger Moore, actor. English nicknames: Rog, Rodge. English variation: Rodger. Foreign variations: Ruggiero (Italian), Rogerio (Spanish), Rüdiger (German), Rutger (Dutch).

ROLAND—Old German: Ruod-lant. "From the famous land." Roland, the hero-nephew of the Emperor Charlemagne, died in battle against the Saracens in A.D. 778. Roland Young, Roland Winters, actors; Orlando Cepeda, baseball star. English nicknames: Rollo, Rolly, Rowe. English variations: Rollin, Rowland, Rolland, Rollins. Foreign variations: Orlando (Italian), Rolando, Roldan (Spanish), Roland (French, German), Rodhlann (Irish), Roeland (Dutch).

ROLF—See Rudolph.

ROLLINS—See Roland.

ROLLO—See Rudolph. Rollo or Rolf, A.D. 860-931, a Norwegian Viking leader, conquered western France and became the first duke of Normandy. Rollo Maitland, famous organist.

ROLPH—See Rudolph.

ROLT—Old German: Ruod-walt. "Famous power." The power of persuasion is often undefinable. Francis Rolt Wheeler, American writer.

ROMEO—Italian: Romeo. "Pilgrim to Rome." Romeo was the Italian hero of the Shakespearean play, *Romeo and Juliet*.

ROMNEY—Old Welsh: Rumenea. "Curving river." George Romney, English painter (1734-1802); Romney Brent, actor.

RONALD—Old Norse: Rognuald. "Mighty power." See Reginald. Actors Ronald Colman, Ronald Reagan. English nicknames: Ron, Ronnie, Ronny. Foreign variations: Renaldo (Spanish), Raghnall (Irish).

RONAN—Irish Gaelic: Ronan. "Little seal." A nobleman whose finger-ring bore the coat-of-arms of his ancestors.

RONSON—Old English: Ronald-sone. "Son of mighty-power."

ROONEY—Irish Gaelic: Ruanaidh. "Red one." English variation: Rowney.

ROPER—Old English: Rapere. "Rope maker." An artisan who twisted and braided long strand of flax or hemp.

RORKE—See Roarke.

RORY—Irish Gaelic: Ruaidhri. "Red king." A man whose spirit was as flamboyant as his hair. Alternate, Old German: Ruodrik. "Famous ruler." Rory Calhoun, actor.
Foreign variations: **Ruaidhri** (Irish), **Rurik** (Slavic).

ROSCOE—Old Norse: Raskog-r. "From the roe-deer forest." Roscoe Drummond, columnist; Roscoe Ates, actor.

ROSLIN—Old French: Ros-elin. "Little red-haired one."
English variations: **Rosselin, Rosslyn.**

ROSS—Scotch Gaelic: Ros. "From the peninsula." The Scotch clan Ross are famous in history. Ross Rizley, U.S. Congressman; Ross Hunter, motion picture producer.

ROSWALD—Old German: Roswalt. "Horse-mighty, or mighty with a horse." A man whose equestrian skill brought him fame.
English variation: **Roswell.**

ROSWELL—See Roswald.

ROTHWELL—Old Norse: Rauth-uell. "From the red spring."

ROURKE—See Roarke.

ROVER—Middle English: Rovere: "Wanderer, rambler." A restless one, constantly seeking new places and people.

ROWAN—Irish Gaelic: Ruadhan. "Red-haired."
English variations: **Rowen, Rowe.**

ROWE—See Rowan.

ROWELL—Old English: Rawiella. "From the roe-deer spring." At night when all was still, deer came there to drink their fill.

ROWLAND—See Roland.

ROWLEY—Old English: Ruhleah. "Dweller at the rough meadow." Where rocks and stubble made foot travel hazardous.

ROWSON—Anglo-Irish: Ruadh-son. "Son of the red-haired one."

ROXBURY—Old English: Hroces-burh. "From Rook's fortress." Old and mighty was this fortress, a discouragement to enemies.

ROY—French: Roi. "King." A medieval actor who portrayed a king in a historical pageant. Roy Woodruff, U.S. Congressman; Roy West, former U.S. Secretary of the Interior; Roy Campanella, baseball star; actors Roy Atwell, Roy Rogers.
Foreign variations: **Roi** (French), **Rey** (Spanish).

ROYAL—Old French: Roial. "Regal one." Royal Dano, actor; Royal W. Weiler, linguist, educator.

ROYCE—Old English: Royse. "Son of the king." Son of a pageant player. Josiah Royce, educator, philosopher (1855-1916).

ROYD—Old Norse: Riodh-r. "From the clearing in the forest."

ROYDON—Old English: Rygedun. "Dweller at the rye-hill."

RUBEN—See Reuben.

RUCK—Old English: Hroc. "Rook-bird." Named for his hair that was as black as the European crow.

RUDD—Old English: Reod. "Ruddy complexioned."

RUDOLPH—Old German: Ruod-wolf. "Famous wolf." A complimentary name for great daring. Famous from Rudolf of Hapsburg. 13th-century Holy Roman Emperor. Rudolf Friml, composer; Rudolph Valentino, silent screen actor.
English nicknames: Rudie, Rudy, Rolf, Rolph, Rollo, Dolf.
English variations: Rodolf, Rodolph, Rudolf.
Foreign variations: Rodolphe, Raoul (French), Rodolfo (Italian, Spanish), Rudolf (German, Danish, Swedish, Dutch).

RUDYARD—Old English: Rudu-geard. "From the red enclosure." Fenced-in, red loam pasture land. Rudyard Kipling, English author (1865-1936).

RUFF—French: Ruffe. "Red-haired."

RUFFORD—Old English: Ruhford. "From the rough ford."

RUFUS—Latin: Rufus. "Red-haired one." Famous from William Rufus, king of England, 1087-1100. Rufus Peckham, U.S. Supreme Court Justice, 1895-1910; Rufus King, author.
English nicknames: Rufe, Ruff.

RUGBY—Old English: Hroc-by. "Rook-estate." Where European crows came to eat and gossip.

RULE—Latin: Regulus. "Ruler." Saint Richard de Rule or Regulus famous for bringing relics of St. Andrew to Scotland in th 4th century. Alternate origin Old French: Ruelle. "Famous wolf."

RUMFORD—Old English: Rum-ford. "From the wide ford." Wide and shallow, a place on the river where people came to cross.

RUPERT—See Robert. Namesakes: Rupert Brooke, English poet; Rupert Hughes, author.

RURIK—See Roderick, Rory. Rurik, 9th-century Scandinavian leader, founded the Russian Empire.

RUSH—French: Rousse. "Red-haired." A Frenchman whose hair was like a torch.

RUSHFORD—Old English: Rysc-ford. "From the rush-ford." Where wild reeds looked like nodding sentinels.

RUSKIN—Franco-German: Rousse-kin. "Little red-head." John Ruskin, 19th-century English author.

RUSSELL—Old French: Roussel. "Red-haired one." Russell Sage, financier (1816-1906).
English nicknames: Rus, Russ, Rusty.

RUST—Old French: Rousset. "Red-haired." Hair like old iron rusted by wind and weather.
English nickname: Rusty.

RUTHERFORD—Old English: Hryther-ford. "From the cattleford." Rutherford Hayes, 19th U.S. President.

RUTLAND—Old Norse: Rotland. "From the root or stump land." Stumps left standing in cleared forest land.

RUTLEDGE—Old English: Reod-laec. "From the red pool." Clear, sweet water resting on a bed of red clay.

RUTLEY—Old English: Rote-leah. "From the root or stump meadow." A memento to man's struggle for subsistence.

RYAN—Irish Gaelic: Ri-an. "Little king." A prince with a king's potentials. Robert Ryan, actor.

RYCROFT—Old English: Ryge-croft. "From the rye field."

RYDER—See Rider.

RYE—Old French: Rie. "From the riverbank."

RYLAN—Old English: Ryge-land. "Dweller at the rye land." Where wild rye ripened in the summer sun.
English variation: Ryland.

RYLE—Old English: Ryge-hyll. "From the rye hill." Grain growing up to feed a multitude.

RYLEY—See Riley.

RYMAN—Old English: Ryge-man. "Rye seller."

RYTON—Old English: Ryge-tun. "From the rye enclosure."

S

SABER—French: Saber: "A sword."

SABIN—Latin: Sabinus. "A man of the Sabine people." Sabinus, planter of vines, gave his name to the ancient Sabini people, conquered by the Romans in 290 B.C.

SAFFORD—Old English: Salh-ford. "From the willow ford."

SALTON—Old English: Sael-tun. "From the manor-hall town," or Old English: Salh-tun. "From the willow enclosure."

SALVADOR—Spanish: Salva-dor. "The Savior." One who saves, rescues, frees, or teaches. Salvador Dali, Spanish painter; Salvatore Baccaloni, singer.
Foreign variations: Sauveur (French), Salvatore (Italian), Xavier, Salvador (Spanish).

SAM—Hebrew: Shama. "To hear." See Samuel, Sampson. Sam Rayburn, U.S. Speaker of House of Representatives.

SAMPSON—Hebrew: Shim-shon. "Sun's man or splendid man." A man of light and wisdom. Samson of the Bible was an Israelite judge noted for his great strength.
English nicknames: Sam, Sam-mie, Sammy.

English variations: Samson, San-som.
Foreign variations: Sansón (Spanish), Sansone (Italian), Samson (French, Danish, Dutch, Swedish).

SAMUEL—Hebrew: Shemuel. "His name is God," or "Heard or asked of God." A famous Biblical judge and prophet. Notables: Samuel Adams, American patriot; Samuel Johnson, English writer (1709-1784); Samuel Goldwyn, pioneer film producer.
English nicknames: Sammie, Sammy, Sam.
Foreign variations: Samuele (Italian), Samuel (French, German, Spanish), Somhairle (Irish).

SANBORN—Old English: Sand-burne. "Dweller at the sandy brook." Sparkling water filtered through white sand.

SANCHO—Spanish: Sancho; Latin: Sanctius. "Sanctified; truthful, sincere." Sancho Panza, famous character in Cervantes' *Don Quixote.*

SANDERS—Middle English: Sander-sone. "Son of Alexander." George Sanders, actor.
English nicknames: Sandie, Sandy.
English variations: Sanderson, Saunders, Saunderson.

SANFORD—Old English: Sandford. "Dweller at the sandy ford."

SANSOM—See Sampson.

SANTO—Italian, Spanish: Santo. "Saintly; holy; sacred." Familiar Spanish usage: Santo Domingo (St. Dominic), Santo Tomas (St. Thomas), Espiritu-Santo (Holy Spirit).

SANTON—Old English: Sandtun. "Sandy enclosure or town." A place washed white by an ancient sea."

SARGENT—Old French: Sergent. "Officer; attendant." "A sergeant of the law, war (wary) and wyse (wise)."—Chaucer, 13th century. John Singer Sargent, noted portrait painter (1856-1925).
English nicknames: Sarge, Sargie.
English variations: Sergeant, Sergent.

SAUL—Hebrew: Sha'ul. "Asked for." Called by God to fulfill his designated mission. "Saul of Tarsus," the original name of the Apostle St. Paul. Saul Lieberman, noted theologian.
English nicknames: Sol, Solly.

SAVILLE—North French: Sauville. "Willow estate." Where yellow pussy willows bloomed in the spring. Saville is a noted English family name, often used as a given name.

SAWYER—Middle English: Sawyere. "A sawer of wood." Famed from Tom Sawyer, Mark Twain's youthful hero of his novel.

SAXE—See Saxon.

SAXON—Old English: Saxan. "Of the Saxons or sword-people." Saxon was the designation used by the Roman conquerors for Germans who used short swords in war. John Saxon, actor.

SAYER—Welsh; Cornish: Saer. "Carpenter." An artisan in wood. Saer Bude is listed in the English Hundred Rolls, A.D. 1273.
English variations: Sayre, Sayers, Sayres.

SCANLON—Irish Gaelic: Scannalan. "A little scandal or snarer." A boy who captivated peoples' hearts.
English and Irish variation: Scanlan.

SCHUYLER—Dutch: Schuyler. "Shield," or "To hide." Schuyler Bland, U.S. Congressman; Schuyler Colfax, 17th U.S. Vice-President.

SCOTT—Old English: Scottas. "From Scotland." The source of "Scot" is the Early Irish word Scothaim meaning "Tattooed," referring to the appearance of the ancient Pictish-Scotch people. Scott Corbett, author.
English Nicknames: Scottie, Scotty.
Foreign variation: Scotti (Italian).

SCOVILLE—Old French: Escotville. "From the Scotchman's estate." (Meaning doubtful.)

SCULLY—Irish Gaelic: Scolaighe. "Town crier or herald." An announcer of news before newspapers were printed. Scolaighe or Scully was the grandson of the ancient Irish King Aedhacan of Dartry.

SEABERT—Old English: Saebeorht. "Sea-glorious." A hero of the sea.
English variations: Seabright, Sebert.

SEABROOK—Old English: Saebroc. "From the brook by the sea." A place where a small stream joined the sea.

SEAMUS—See James.

SEAN—See John.

SEARLE—Old German: Saerle. "Armor; armed one." A man in armor equipped for war.

SEATON—Old Anglo-French: Sai-tun. "From Sai's estate or town." The Norman French Baron Saher de Sai entered England with William the Conqueror in 1066; he later founded a town called Seaton in southern Scotland.
English variations: Seton, Seeton, Seetin.

SEBASTIAN—Latin: Sebastianus. "August one; reverenced one." St. Sebastian was a renowned 3rd-century Roman martyr; Sebastian Cabot, Italian explorer (1476-1557).
Foreign variations: Sébastien (French), Sebastiano (Italian).

SEDGLEY—Old English: Secgleah. "From the sword-grass meadow or swordsman's meadow."

SEDGWICK—Old English: Secg-wic. "Dweller at the sword-grass place."

SEELEY—Old English: Saelig. "Happy; blessed." Sir John Seeley, 19th-century English historian.
English variations: Seelye, Sealey.

SEGER—Old English: Sae-gar. "Sea-spear; sea-warrior," or Old English: Sige-here. "Victorious army." Sigehere was a 7th-century king of the East Saxons in England.
English variations: Seager, Segar.

SELBY—Old English: Sele-by. "From the manor-house farm." William Selby, 18th-century English musician.

SELDEN—Old English: Salhdene. "From the willow-tree valley."

SELIG—Old German: Saelec. "Blessed, happy one."

SELWYN—Old English: Selewine. "Manor-house friend," or Old English: Sel-wine. "Good friend." Selwyn Lloyd, English diplomat.
English variation: Selwin.

SENIOR—Old French: Seignour. "Lord of the manor or estate."

SENNETT—French: Senet. "Old, wise one." Mack Sennett, pioneer motion picture producer.

SEPTIMUS—Latin: Septimus. "Seventh son."

SERENO—Latin: Serenus. "Calm, tranquil one."

SERGE—Latin: Sergius. "The attendant." St. Sergius was a pope in the 7th century; Sergei Rachmaninoff, pianist, composer.

SERGEANT—See Sargent.

SETH—Hebrew: Sheth. "Appointed." Seth was the third son of Adam.

SETON—See Seaton. Ernest Thompson Seton, author.

SEVERN—Old English: Saefren. "Boundary." The River Severn flows from north Wales to the Atlantic through southwest England.

SEWARD—Old English: Saeweard. "Sea-guardian." William H. Seward, American statesman (1801-1872).

SEWELL—Old English: Saewald. "Sea-powerful."
English variations: Sewald, Sewall.

SEXTON—Middle English: Sextein. "Church official or sacristan."

SEXTUS—Latin: Sextus. "Sixth son." Sextus Empiricus, 3rd-century philosopher.

SEYMOUR—Old French: St. Maur. "From the town of St. Maur, Normandy, France." Seymour Berkson, publisher (1905-1959); Seymour Harris, noted educator.

SHADWELL—Old English: Schad-wiella. "From the shed-spring or arbor-spring." Where cream and butter were kept cool in summer.

SHAMUS—An Irish form of Seamus. See James.

SHANAHAN—Irish Gaelic: Seanachan. "Wise, sagacious one." An adviser with unexcelled comprehension.

SHANDY—Old English: Scandy. "Little boisterous one." A boy with great energy and zest.

SHANE—An Irish form of Sean. See John.

SHANLEY—Irish Gaelic: Seanlaoch. "Old hero."

SHANNON—Irish Gaelic: Seanan. "Little old wise one." A disburser of knowledge.

SHATTUCK—Middle English: Schaddoc. "Little shad-fish."

SHAW—Old English: Scaga. "Dweller at a grove of trees.

SHEA—Irish Gaelic. Seaghda. "Majestic, courteous, scientific, ingenious one."

SHEEHAN—Irish Gaelic: Siodhachan. "Little peaceful one."

SHEFFIELD—Old English: Scaffeld. "From the crooked field."

SHELBY—Old English: Scelfby. "From the ledge estate." Isaac Shelby, American frontiersman (1750-1826).

SHELDON—Old English: Scelfdun. "From the ledge-hill." Sheldon Cheney, writer; Shelley Berman, comedian.
English nickname: Shelley.

SHELLEY—Old English: Scelfleah. "Dweller at the ledge-meadow." A field banked by steep cliffs.

SHELTON—Old English: Scelftun. "From the ledge farm or town." "Shelton of Tibet," noted American missionary.

SHEPHERD—Old English: Sceap-hierde. "Shepherd." Shepperd Strudwick, actor; Shepherd Mead, writer.
English nicknames: Shep, Shepp, Sheppy.
English variations: Shepard, Sheppard, Shepperd.

SHEPLEY—Old English: Sceapleah. "From the sheep meadow."

SHERBORNE—Old English: Scir-burne. "From the clear brook."
English variations: Sherbourn, Sherbourne, Sherburne.

SHERIDAN—Irish Gaelic: Seireadan. "Wild man or satyr." Sheridan Downey, U.S. Senator.

SHERLOCK—Old English: Scirlocc. "Fair or white haired." Famous from Sherlock Holmes, detective in Sir Arthur Conan Doyle's stories.

SHERMAN—Old English: Sceran-man. "Wool cutter." An occupational name for a sheep shearer in medieval England. Sherman Minton U.S. Supreme Court Justice, 1949-1956; Sherman Adams, New Hampshire governor; Sherman Billingsley, restaurateur.

SHERWIN—Middle English: Sherwynd. "Swift runner," or Old English: Scir-wine. "Splendid friend."

SHERWOOD—Old English: Scir-wode. "Bright forest." Sherwood Forest was the home of Robin Hood in old England. Robert Sherwood, American dramatist.

SHIPLEY—Old English: Sceapleah. "Dweller at the sheep meadow."

SHIPTON—Old English: Sceaptun. "Dweller at the sheep estate."

SHOLTO—Irish Gaelic: Siolta. "Teal or merganser duck." Named for a place abounding in wild ducks.

SIDDELL—Old English: Siddael. "From the wide valley."

SIDNEY—Old English: Sydney, from Old French: Saint-Denis. "From St. Denis." Alternate, Phoenician: Sidon. "From the city of Sidon." Sydney Harris, columnist; Sid Caesar, comedian, actor; Sidney Blackmer, actor. English nickname: Sid. English variation: Sydney.

SIEGFRIED—Old German: Sigi-frith. "Victorious, peaceful." The hero of the Nibelungenlied, old German legends, a prince of the lower Rhine Valley who captured a treasure, killed a dragon and won Brunhild for King Gunther. Foreign variations: Sigfrid (German), Siffre (French), Sigvard (Norwegian).

SIGMUND—Old German: Sigimund. "Victorious protector." In Norse myths Siegmund was the father of Siegfriend. Sigmund

Freud, famous neurologist; Sigmund Romberg, composer; Sigmund Spaeth, music critic. Foreign variations: Sigismond (French), Sigismondo (Italian), Sigismundo (Spanish), Sigmund, Sigismund (German), Sigismundus (Dutch).

SIGURD—Old Norse: Sigurdhr. "Victorious guardian." In Norse myths Sigurd was the son of Sigmund.

SIGWALD—Old German: Sigiwald. "Victorious ruler or governor."

SILAS—See Silvanus. Silas was a companion of St. Paul in the Bible.

SILVANUS—Latin: Silvanus. "Forest dweller." There are over 14 Saints Silvanus; Silvanus Morley, Yucatan archaeologist. English variations: Sylvanus, Silas. Foreign variations: Silvain (French), Silvano, Silvio (Italian, Spanish).

SILVESTER—Latin: Silvester. "From the forest." St. Silvester was a pope from A.D. 314 to 335. English variation: Sylvester. Foreign variations: Silvestre (French, Spanish), Silvestro (Italian), Sailbheastar (Irish).

SIMEON—See Simon.

SIMON—Hebrew: Shim'on. "Hearing: one who hears." "And . . . Leah bare a son, and said, because the Lord hath heard . . ." —Gen. 29:32-3. St. Simeon the son of Cleophas, was crucified in A.D. 107; Simon Bolivar, South American liberator (1783-1830). English variation: Simeon. Foreign variations: Siméon (French), Simone (Italian), Siomonn (Irish), Sim (Scotch).

SINCLAIR—French: St: Clair. "From the town of St. Clair, Normandy." An English dialectical contraction of St. Clair. Sinclair Lewis, American novelist (1885-1951).

SKEET—Middle English: Skete. "Swift one." Great activity and speed were his motivation. Skeets Gallagher, entertainer.
English variations: Skeat, Skeets, Skeeter.

SKELLY—Irish Gaelic: Sgeulaiche. "Historian, storyteller."

SKELTON—Old English: Scelftun. "From the estate or town on the ledge." Red Skelton, noted comedian, actor.

SKERRY—Old Norse: Sker-eye. "From the rocky island." An island that was hard to cultivate.

SKIPP—Old Norse: Skip. "Ship owner." Skip Homeier, actor.
English nicknames: Skip, Skippy.

SKIPPER—Middle English: Skippere. "Ship-master." The master of his ship, the captain of his crew.
English nicknames: Skip, Skippy.

SKIPTON—Old English: Sciptun. " From the sheep-estate."

SLADE—Old English: Slaed. "Dweller in the valley.

SLEVIN—Irish Gaelic: Sliabhin. "Mountaineer."
English variations: Slavin, Slaven, Sleven.

SLOAN—Irish Gaelic: Sluaghan. "Warrior." A man in the service of his country. Sloan Wilson, American novelist.
English variation: Sloane.

SMEDLEY—Old English: Smethe-leah. "From the flat meadow." Smedley D. Butler, U.S. Marine Corps general.

SMITH—Old English: Smith. "Blacksmith; worker with a hammer." An artisan in metal craft. Smith Thompson, U.S. Secretary of the Navy under President Monroe.
English nickname: Smitty.

SNOWDEN—Old English: Snaw-dun. "From the snowy hill." A snow-capped mountain was this mountaineer's home.

SOL—Latin: Sol. "The sun." One who had the light of great wisdom. See Solomon.

SOLOMON—Hebrew: Shelomon. "Peaceful." A tranquil man untroubled by the petty things of life. King Solomon of Israel was famous for his wisdom. English nicknames: Sol, Sollie, Solly.
English variations: Solaman, Soloman, Salomon.
Foreign variations: Salomon (French), Salomone (Italian), Salomón (Spanish), Salomo (German, Dutch), Solamh (Irish).

SOLON—Greek: Solon. "Wise man." Solon was a 6th century B.C. Athenian Greek lawgiver noted for his wisdom.

SOMERSET—Old English: Sumer-saete. "From the place of the summer settlers." Somerset Maugham, English novelist.

SOMERTON—Old English: Sumer-tun. "From the summer estate." Somerton in the English county of Somerset was the summer home of the Saxon kings.

SOMERVILLE—Old Franco-German: Sumar-ville. "From the summer estate."

SORRELL—Old French: Sorel. "Reddish-brown hair."

SOUTHWELL—Old English: Suth-wiella. "From the south spring."

Robert Southwell, 16th-century English poet.

SPALDING—Old English: Speld-ing. "From the split meadow." A field divided by a river, fence or hedge. Albert Spalding, violinist.
English variation: Spaulding.

SPANGLER—South German: Spengler. "Tinsmith."

SPARK—Middle English: Sparke. "Gay, gallant one." A gentleman, elegant in dress and manners, a gay contender for a woman's hand.

SPAULDING—See Spalding.

SPEAR—Old English: Spere. "Spearman."

SPEED—Old English: Sped. "Success, prosperity." James Speed, American statesman (1812-1887).

SPENCER—Middle English: Spencer. "Dispenser of provisions." A man in charge of the village or manor house provisions. H. Spencer Lewis, historian, archaeologist; Spencer Tracy, actor.

SPROULE—Middle English: Sproul. "Energetic, active one." Animated, a man forever gay. English variation: Sprowle.

SQUIRE—Middle English: Squier. "Knight's attendant; shield-bearer." Sir Squire Bancroft, famous English actor.

STACEY—Middle Latin: Stacius. "Stable; prosperous." Robert Stacy-Judd, noted architect, writer, archaeologist.

STAFFORD—Old English: Staeth-ford. "From the landing-place ford."

STAMFORD—Old English: Stan-ford. "From the stony-ford."

Where men and beasts could cross in safety.

STANBURY—Old English: Stan-burh. "From the stone fortress." A stronghold clothed in memories, ivy, and wild roses. English variation: Stanberry.

STANCLIFF—Old English: Stan-clif. "From the rocky cliff."

STANDISH—Old English: Stan-edisc. "From the rocky park or enclosure." Land uncultivated, home of rabbits, deer and grouse. Celebrated from Miles Standish, New England founding settler.

STANFIELD—Old English: Stan-feld. "From the rocky field."

STANFORD—Old English: Stan-ford. "From the rocky ford." Shallow, clear water tumbling over boulders. Stanford White, famous American architect (1853-1906).

STANHOPE—Old English: Stan-hop. "From the rocky hollow." A valley almost filled with rocks.

STANISLAUS—Slavic: Stanislav. "Stand of glory; glorious position." Without fear or wavering, the hero stood firm against his enemies. St. Stanislaus was the patron of Poland.
English nickname: Stan.
Foreign variations: Stanislav (German), Stanislas (French), Aineislis (Irish).

STANLEY—Old English: Stan-leah. "Dweller at the rocky meadow." Stanley Matthews, U.S. Supreme Court Justice, 1881-1889; Stanley Kramer, motion picture producer; Stanley Holloway, actor.
English nicknames: Stan, Stannie.
English variations: Stanleigh, Stanly.

STANMORE—Old English: Stan-mere. "From the rocky lake."

STANTON—Old English: Stan-tun. "From the stony estate." The manor house was on a rock-strewn hill. Edwin M. Stanton, U.S. Secretary of War under President Abraham Lincoln. English variation: **Staunton.**

STANWAY—Old English: Stan-weg. "Dweller on the paved stone road."

STANWICK—Old English: Stan-wic. "Dweller at the rocky village."

STANWOOD—Old English: Stan-wode. "Dweller at the rocky forest."

STARLING—Old English: Staer-ling. "Starling-bird."

STARR—Middle English: Sterre. "Star."

STEDMAN—Old English: Stede-man. "Farmstead owner."

STEIN—German: Stein. "Stone."

STEPHEN—Greek: Stephanos. "Crowned one." Honoring St. Stephen, the first Christian martyr and St. Stephen, 10th-century king of Hungary. Stephen Decatur, U.S. Naval Commodore (1779-1820); Stephen Vincent Bénet, writer; Stephen Foster, composer; actors Steve Allen, Steve McQueen, Stephen Boyd. English nicknames: Steve, Stevie. English variations: **Steven, Stevenson, Stephenson.** Foreign variations: **Etienne** (French), Estevan, **Esteban** (Spanish), **Stefan** (German, Danish), **Stefano** (Italian), **Stephanus** (Swedish), **Steaphan** (Scotch).

STERLING—Middle English: Sterling. A nickname from an old English coin, or Old Welsh: Ystrefelyn. "From the yellow house." Sterling Holloway, Sterling Hayden, actors. English variation: **Stirling.**

STERNE—Middle English: Sterne. "Austere one." English variations: **Stern, Stearn, Stearne.**

STEVEN—See Stephen.

STEWART—Old English: Sti-ward. "Bailiff or steward of a manorial estate." Stewart or Stuart was the surname of a long line of Scotch and English rulers. Notables: Stuart Chase, writer; Stewart Alsop, journalist; actors Stewart Grainger, Stuart Holmes, Stuart Whitman. English nicknames: Stu, Stew. English variations: **Stuart, Steward.**

STILLMAN—Old English: Stille-man. "Quiet man." A man whose mind is free from troubled thoughts.

STINSON—Old English: Staen-sone. "Son of stone."

STIRLING—See Sterling.

STOCKLEY—Old English: Stoc-leah. "From the tree-stump meadow." A cleared forest, a memorial to man's progressiveness.

STOCKTON—Old English: Stoc-tun. "From the tree-stump estate or town." Frank Stockton, American writer (1834-1902).

STOCKWELL—Old English: Stoc-wiella. "From the tree-stump spring." Where men had hewn a path to a small stream.

STODDARD—Old English: Stod-hierde. "Horse-keeper." A caretaker of the villagers' horses in the Middle Ages.

STOKE—Middle English: Stoke. "Village."

STORM—Old English: Storm. "Tempest; storm." A turbulent person who raged at opposition.

STORR—Old Norse: Stor-r. "Great one." "Some are born great, some achieve greatness, and some have greatness thrust upon them."—Shakespeare.

STOWE—Old English: Stowe. "From the place."

STRAHAN—Irish Gaelic: Sruth-an. "Poet, wise man."

STRATFORD—Old English: Straet-ford. "River-ford on the street." Famous from Shakespeare's birthplace, Stratford-on-Avon, in Warwickshire. Stratford Canning, English diplomat (1786-1880).

STRONG—Old English: Strang. "Powerful one."

STROUD—Old English: Strod. "From the thicket."

STRUTHERS—Irish Gaelic: Sruthair. "From the stream." Struthers Burt, author.

STUART—See Stewart.

STYLES—Old English: Stigols. "Dweller by the stiles." An old enclosure or stockade. Styles Bridges, U.S. Senator.

SUFFIELD—Old English: Suthfeld. "From the south field."

SULLIVAN—Irish Gaelic: Suileabhan. "Black-eyed one." Sir Arthur Sullivan, English composer (1842-1900).
English nicknames: Sullie, Sully.

SULLY—Old English: Suthleah. "From the south meadow." See Sullivan.

SUMNER—Middle English: Sumenor. "Summoner; church legal officer." Sumner Welles, U.S. statesman; Sumner Whittier, U.S. Veterans Administrater.

SUTCLIFF—Old English: Suthclif. "From the south cliff."

SUTHERLAND—Old Norse: Suthrland. "From the southern land." In the time of the Vikings this was a name for the Shetland Islands and north Scotland.

SUTTON—Old English: Suthtun. "From the south estate."

SWAIN—Middle English: Swayn. "Herdsman; knight's attendant." King Sweyn Forkbeard of Denmark, died A.D. 1014, was the father of England's famous King Canute.
English variation: Swayne.

SWEENEY—Irish Gaelic: Suidhne. "Little hero."

SWINTON—Old English: Swintun. "Dweller at the swine-farm."

SYDNEY—See Sidney.

SYLVESTER—See Silvester.

SYMINGTON—Old English: Symon-tun. "Dweller at Simon's estate." Stuart Symington, U.S. Senator.

Tab 192

T

TAB—Old German: Tabbert. "Brilliant among the people," or Middle English: Taburer. "Drummer." Tab Hunter, actor.
English nicknames: Tab, Tabby.

TADD—Old Welsh: Tad. "Father."
English variation: Tad.

TAFFY—Old Welsh: Taffy. "Beloved one." A Welsh form of David.

TAGGART—Irish Gaelic: Mac-an-T-sagairt. "Son of the prelate."

TALBOT—Old French: Talebot. "Pillager." A man given booty or reward from war gains. Alternate, Old English: Talbot. An extinct type of dog, the ancestor of the bloodhound. Talebotus Talebot is recorded in Lancashire, England in A.D. 1284. Lyle Talbot, actor.

TANNER—Old English: Tannere. "Leather maker." The tanner was held in high esteem in ancient times.

TANTON—Old English: Tamtun. "From the quiet-river estate or town."

TARLETON—Old English: Thorald-tun. "Thunder-ruler's estate."

TARRANT—Old Welsh: Taran. "Thunder." A man turbulent and vehement in his likes and dislikes.

TATE—Middle English: Tayt. "Cheerful one."
English variation: Tait.

TAVIS—Scotch Gaelic. Tamnais. "Twin." A Scotch form of Thomas.

English variations: Tavish, Tevis.

TAYLOR—Middle English: Taylour. "A tailor." A profession as popular in the Middle Ages as it is today. Taylor Holmes, actor.
English variation. Tailor.

TEAGUE—Irish Gaelic: Taidhg; Tadhg. "Poet." A man who made rhythm out of words.

TEARLE—Old English: Thearl. "Stern, severe one." Conway and Godfrey Tearle, noted actors.

TEDMOND—Old English: Theod-mund. "National protector." An officer appointed by his king.

TELFORD—Old French: Taillefer. "Iron-hewer or cutter." An ancient French occupational title for a miner or metal worker.
English variations: Telfer, Telfor, Telfour.

TEMPLETON—Old English: Tempel-tun. "Temple or religious edifice-town."

TENNYSON—Middle English: Dennyson. "Son of Dennis." See Dennis. Alfred, Lord Tennyson, 19th-century English poet laureate.

TERENCE—Latin: Terentius. "Smooth, polished one," or Irish Gaelic: Toirdealbhach. "Shaped like the god Thor." Terence Rattigan, English dramatist.
English nickname: Terry.
Foreign variation: Terencio (Spanish).

TERRELL—Old English: Tirell. "Thunder ruler." A man compared to Thor, the old Norse god.

Terrell O. Morse, motion picture director.
English variations: **Terrill, Tirrell.**

TERRIS—Old English: Terrysone. "Son of Terrell or Terence."

TEVIS—See Tavis.

THADDEUS—Latin: Thaddeus. "Praiser," or Greek: Thaddaios. "Stout-hearted, courageous." Thaddeus was one of the twelve Apostles. Thaddeus Kosciusko, Polish military leader (1746-1817); Thaddeus Stevens, American statesman.
English nicknames: **Thad, Tad, Taddy.**
Foreign variations: **Thaddäus** (Germas), **Taddeo** (Italian), **Tadeo** (Spanish), **Tadhg** (Irish).

THAINE—See Thane.

THANE—Old English: Thegn. "Follower or warrior attendant."
English variations: **Thaine, Thayne.**

THATCHER—Middle English: Thackere. "Roof-thatcher."
English nickname: **Thatch.**

THAW—Old English: Thawian. "Ice thaw." A diplomat who could sway the sternest opponent.

THAYER—Old Frankish: Thiad-here. "National army." A man in the service of his country.

THAYNE—See Thane.

THEOBALD—Old German: Theudo-bald. "Boldest of the people." Theodbald was a 7th-century brother of Athelfrith, English king of Northumbria.
English variation: **Tybalt.**
Foreign variations: **Thebault, Thibaut, Thibaud** (French), **Dietbold, Tibold** (German), **Teobaldo** (Spanish, Italian), **Tiebout** (Dutch), **Tioboid** (Irish).

THEODORE—Greek: Theodoros. "Gift of God." Theodore Roosevelt, 26th U.S. President; Theodore Dreiser, novelist (1871-1945).
English nicknames: **Ted, Teddie, Teddy.**
Foreign variations: **Théodore** (French), **Teodoro** (Spanish, Italian), **Theodor** (German, Danish, Swedish), **Theodorus** (Dutch), **Feodor** (Slavic).

THEODORIC—Old German: Theudo-ric. "Ruler of the people."
English nicknames: **Ted, Teddie, Teddy, Rick, Derek, Derk, Derrick.**
Foreign variations: **Dietrich** (German), **Teodorico** (Spanish).

THEON—Greek: Theon. "Godly." A man who kept God's precepts or laws.

THERON—Greek: Theron. "A hunter." A man woh shot wild game to help feed the people.

THOMAS—Greek: Thomas; Aramaic: Teoma. "A twin." St. Thomas was one of the twelve Apostles. Namesakes: Thomas Jefferson, 3rd U.S. President; Thomas A. Edison, American inventor; Thomas Wolfe, Thomas Carlyle, writers; Thomas Dewey, U.S. statesman; Thomas Mitchell, actor.
English nicknames: **Tom, Tommie, Tommy, Tam, Tammy, Massey.**
Foreign variations: **Tomaso** (Italian), **Tomás** (Spanish), **Tomas** (Irish).

THOR—Old Norse: Thor-i-r. "Thunder." Thor was the ancient Norse god of thunder. This name became well-established in England. Thor Heyerdahl, Norwegian author, explorer.
English and Scandinavian variation: **Tor.**

THORALD—Old Norse: Thor-uald-r. "Thor-ruler; thunder-ruler."
English variations: Torald, Thorold, Terrell, Tyrell.

THORBERT—Old Norse: Thor-biart-r. "Brilliance of Thor or thunder-glorious."
English variation: Torbert.

THORBURN—Old Norse: Thor-biorn. "Thor's bear or thunder-bear."

THORLEY—Old English: Thur-leah. "Thor's meadow."
English variation: Torley.

THORMOND—Old English: Thur-mund "Thor's protection." Protected by the old Norse god of thunder.
English variations: Thormund, Thurmond.

THORNDYKE—Old English: Thorn-dic. "From the thorny dike or embankment." Thorndike Saville, American educator in engineering.

THORNE—Old English: Thorn. "Dweller by a thorn tree." A common English place name. Thorne Smith, American novelist.

THORNLEY—Old English: Thornig-leah. "From the thorny meadow."

THORNTON—Old English: Thorn-tun. "From the thorny estate." Thornton Wilder, Thornton W. Burgess, writers.

THORPE—Old English: Thorp. "From the village."

THURLOW—Old English: Thur-hloew. "From Thor's hill." Where thunder clouds gathered and lightning flashed before a storm.

THURSTAN—Old English: Thur-stan. "Thor's stone." A prehistoric monument to the god Thor. This name was introduced in England by the Danes before the Norman conquest in 1066.

TIERNAN—Irish Gaelic: Tighearnan. "Lord or master."

TIERNEY—Irish Gaelic: Tighearnach. "Lordly one."

TIFFANY—Old French: Tiphanie; Latin: Theophania. "Divine showing, appearance of God." Theophania was an ancient Greek spring festival celebrating the appearance of Apollo, the sun. Tiffany Thayer, novelist.

TILDEN—Old English: Tila-dene. "From the good, liberal one's valley."

TILFORD—Old English: Tila-ford. "From the good, liberal one's ford."

TILTON—Old English: Tila-tun. "From the good, liberal one's estate."

TIMON—Greek: Timun. "Honor, reward, value." Timon of Athens, vitalized by Shakespeare's play of that name, was a Greek skeptic philosopher.

TIMOTHY—Greek: Timotheos. "Honoring God." St. Timothy was a colleague of St. Paul.
English nicknames: Tim, Timmie, Timmy.
Foreign variations: Timothée (French), Timoteo (Italian, Spanish), Timotheus (German), Tiomoid (Irish).

TIRRELL—See Terrell.

TITUS—Greek: Titos. "Of the giants." "There were giants in the earth in those days." Genesis 6:4. Titus was a giant slain by Apollo in Greek myths. Tito Schipa, noted opera singer.
Foreign variations: Tite (French), Tito (Italian, Spanish).

TOBIAS—Hebrew: Tobhiyah. "The Lord is good." An acknowledgment or testimony. Tobias Asser, Dutch Nobel Peace Prize winner.
English nicknames: Tobe, Toby.
Foreign variations: Tobie (French), Tobia (Italian), Tobías (Spanish), Tioboid (Irish).

TODD—North-English: Tod. "A fox." An ancestor named after the sly and wise red fox. Robert Todd Lincoln, son of President Abraham Lincoln.

TOFT—Old English: Toft. "A small farm."

TOLAND—Old English: Tollland. "Owner of taxed land."

TOMKIN—Old English: Tomkin. "Little Tom." Named for his father Thomas.
English variation: Tomlin.

TORBERT—See Thorbert.

TORLEY—See Thorley.

TORMEY—Irish Gaelic: Tormaigh; Old German: Thor-mod. "Thor or thunder spirit." A name for a stormy, impetuous son.

TORR—Old English: Torr. "From the tower." Nickname for a man who lived in a medieval castle.

TORRANCE—Anglo-Irish: Torrans. "From the knolls." From a place of little hills.
English nicknames: Torey, Torrey, Torry.

TOWNLEY—Old English: Tunleah. "From the town-meadow."

TOWNSEND—Old English: Tunes-ende. "From the end of town."

TRACY—Latin: Thrasius. "Bold, courageous one," or Irish Gaelic: Treasach. "Battler."

TRAHERN—Old Welsh: Trahayarn. "Super-iron, super-strength." A man with unusual physical endurance.

TRAVERS—Old French: Traverse. "From the ossroads."
English variation: Travis.

TREDWAY—Old English: Thryth-wig. "Mighty warrior."

TREMAYNE—Old Cornish: Tre-men. "Dweller in the house at the rock." A home near a stone circle or ancient place of worship.

TRENT—Latin: Torrentem; Welsh: Trent. "Torrent, rapid stream." A river rushing to keep an appointment with the sea.

TREVELYAN—Old Cornish: Trev-elian. "From Elian's homestead."

TREVOR—Irish Gaelic: Treabhar. "Prudent, discreet, wise." Trevor Howard, actor.

TRIGG—Old Norse: Trygg-r. "True, trusty one."

TRIPP—Old English: Trip. "Traveler."

TRISTAN—Old Welsh: Trystan. "Noisy one." Tristan, whose name was confused with Tristram, was a famous knight of King Arthur's Round Table in old English legends.

TRISTRAM—Latin-Welsh: Tris-tram. "Sorrowful labor." Work disliked by the workman. Tristram Speaker, baseball star.

TROWBRIDGE—Old English: Treow-brycg. "Dweller by the tree-bridge."

TROY—Old French: Troyes. "At the place of the curly-haired people. Troy Donahue, actor.

TRUE—Old English: Treowe. "Faithful, loyal, true one."

TRUESDALE—Old English: Truite-stall. "From the beloved one's farmstead."

TRUMAN—Old English: Treowe-man. "Faithful one's adherent." Harry Truman, 33rd U.S. President; Truman Newberry, U.S. Secretary of the Navy, 1908; Truman Capote, author.

TRUMBLE—Old English: Trum-bald. "Strong, bold one."

TUCKER—Middle English: Toukere. "A tucker or fuller of cloth." See Fuller.

TUDOR—Old Welsh: Tewdwr. A Welsh variation of Theodore.

TULLY—Irish Gaelic: Tuathal; Maoltuile; Taithleach. "People-mighty," or "Devoted to the will of God," or "Quiet, peaceful one." Tully Marshall, silent screen actor.

TUPPER—Old English: Tuppere. "Ram raiser." A sheep raiser of old England.

TURNER—Middle English: Tournour. "Lathe-worker." Named for his specialized profession.

TURPIN—Old Norse: Thorfinn. "Thunder-Finn." This man from Finland was named for Thor, the god of thunder. A "Turpin" was Archbishop of Rheims, France, in the 10th century.

TUXFORD—Old Norse-English: Thiod-geir-ford. "Ford of the national spearman." A champion spearman who lived by a river crossing.

TWAIN—Middle English: Twein. "Cut apart or cut in two." An heir named for his divided estate or farm that was in two parts.

TWITCHELL—Old English: Twitchell. "Dweller on a narrow passage."

TWYFORD—Old English: Twiford. "From the double river-ford."

TYE—Old English: Tyg. "From the enclosure," or Middle English: Teyen. "Tied or bound."

TYLER—Middle English: Tylere. "Tile maker and roofer." A skilled potter and tiler of the Middle Ages.

TYNAN—Irish Gaelic: Teimhnean. "Dark or gray."

TYRONE—Greek: Turannos. "Sovereign." Famous from Tyrone Power, actor.

TYSON—Old French: Tyeis-; English: Son. "Son of the Teuton or German."

U

UDELL—Old English: Iw-dael. "From the yew-tree valley." English variations: Udale, Udall.

UDOLF—Old English: Od-wulf. "Prosperous wolf." The wolf names depicted courage.

ULFRED—Old English: Wulf-frith. "Wolf-peace." A warrior unafraid, who wanted peace, but not at any price.

ULGER—Old English: Wulf-gar. "Wolf-spear." A courageous man in war.

ULLOCK—Old English: Ulve-laik. "Wolf-sport." A challenger who competed with others.

ULMER—Old Norse: Ulf-maerr. "Wolf-famous."
English variation: Ulmar.

ULRIC—Old German: Wolf-rik. "Wolf-ruler," or Old German: Alh-rik. "All-ruler." A strong, courageous governor of the people.

ULYSSES—Greek: Odysseus. "Hater." One who detested deceit and injustice. Ulysses is a Latin form of the Greek hero-name Odysseus. Ulysses S. Grant, 18th U.S. President.
Foreign variations: Ulises (Spanish), Uillioc (Irish).

UNWIN—Old English: Un-wine. "Not a friend." One who thought of himself first.

UPTON—Old English: Up-tun. "Upper estate or town." Upton Sinclair, author.

UPWOOD—Old English: Up-wode. "From the upper forest."

URBAN—Latin: Urbanus. "From the city." Eight Popes of the Roman Catholic Church were named Urban.
Foreign variations: Urbano (Spanish, Italian), Urbanus (German), Urbaine (French).

URIAH—Hebrew: Uriyah. "Flame of Jehovah; My Light is Jehovah."

URSON—See Orson.

V

VACHEL—Old French: Vachel. "Little cow." Nickname for a cow owner. Vachel Lindsay, poet.

VAIL—Middle English: Vale. "Valley dweller."
English variation: Vale.

VAL—Latin: Valentis. "Strong." Power and strength. See Valentine.

VALDEMAR—Old German: Waldo-mar. "Famous ruler."

VALENTINE—Latin: Valentinus. "Strong, valorous, healthy." St. Valentine was a famous Roman martyr; his feast day is celebrated in many countries on February 14.
Foreign variations: Valentín (Spanish), Valentin (French, German, Danish, Swedish), Valentijn (Dutch), Valentino (Italian), Bailintin (Irish).

VALERIAN—Late Latin: Valerianus. "Strong, healthy, powerful." Valerian was a 3rd-century A.D. Roman emperor; St. Valerianus, Bishop of Auxerre, 4th century.

VALLIS—Old French: Vallois. "Welshman."

VAN—Dutch: Van. "From or of." A nickname from many Dutch surnames, used as a given name. Van Cliburn, concert pianist; actors Van Johnson, Van Heflin.

VANCE—Middle English: Vannes. "Resident at the grain-winnowing fans."

VARDEN—Old French: Verd-dun. "From the green hill."
English variations: Vardon, Verdon.

VARIAN—Latin: Variantia. "Variable." Man can be as changeable as the wind in spring.

VAUGHN—Old Welsh: Vychan. "Small one." One can be small in stature but great of soul and mind. Vaughn Monroe, orchestra leader; Vaughn Taylor, actor.

VERGE—Anglo-French: Verge. "Owner of a quarter-acre."

VERNE—Latin: Vernus. "Springlike, youthful." A youth fresh and strong as a young colt.

VERNER—See Werner.

VERNEY—Old French: Vernay. "From the alder grove."

VERNON—Latin: Vernum. "Springlike, youthful," or Old French: Vernon. "Little alder grove." A name given boys born in the spring. Vernon Castle, dancer; Vernon Duke, composer.

VERRILL—Old French: Verel. "True one." An honest man who searched for facts and told them truthfully.
English variations: **Verrall, Verrell.**

VICK—Old French: Vicq. "From the village." See Victor.

VICTOR—Latin: Victor. "Conqueror." Namesakes: Victor Hugo, French author (1802-1885); Victor Herbert, composer (1859-1924); Victor Borge, musician, entertainer; Victor McLaglen, Victor Mature, actors.
English nicknames: **Vic, Vick.**

Foreign variations: **Vittorio** (Italian), **Vitorio** (Spanish), **Buadhach** (Irish).

VINCENT—Latin: Vincentius. "Conquering one." Honoring St. Vincent de Paul, French priest (1576-1660). Vincent X. Flaherty, columnist; Vicente Blasco Ibañez, novelist; Vincent Price, actor.
English nicknames: **Vin, Vince.**
Foreign variations: **Vincente** (Italian), **Vincenz** (German), **Vincentius** (Dutch), **Vicente** (Spanish), **Uinsionn** (Irish).

VINSON—Old English: Vinsone. "Son of Vincent."

VIRGIL—Latin: Virgula. "Rod or staff bearer." The staff was used to designate authority or an official. Virgil Chapman, U.S. Senator; Virgil Grissom, U.S. astronaut.
English nickname: **Virge.**
Foreign variation: **Virgilio** (Spanish, Italian).

VITO—Latin: Vitus. "Live; living; alive." The animation that imbues all living things. Vito Marcantonio, U.S. Congressman; Vito "Vic" Damone, singer, actor.

VLADIMIR—Old Slavic: Vladimiru. "Royally peaceful or famous." St. Vladimir, Russian prince, died A.D. 1018; Vladimir Horowitz, pianist; Vladimir Sokoloff, actor.

VLADISLAV—Old Slavic: Vladi-slava. "Glorious ruler, royal glory."

VOLNEY—Old German: Vollmy. "People's or national spirit."

W

WACE—Old English: Wace. "Vassal; feudal tenant." A name taken in the days of manorial lords and tenant workers. Wace was a famous 12th-century Anglo-Norman poet.

WADE—Old English: Wada. "The advancer," or Old English: Waed. "Dweller at the river crossing."

WADLEY—Old English: Wada-leah. "The advancer's meadow."

WADSWORTH—Old English: Wades-weorth. "From the advancer's estate." Henry Wadsworth Longfellow, American poet. English nicknames: **Waddie, Waddy.**

WAGNER—German: Wagner. "A wagoner or wagon-maker."

WAINWRIGHT—Old English: Waen-wryhta. "Wagon-maker."

WAITE—Middle English: Wayte. "Guard, watchman." A trusted employee.

WAKE—Old English: Wacian. "Alert, watchful one."

WAKEFIELD—Old English: Wac-feld. "Dweller at the wet field." Charles Wakefield Cadman, American composer.

WAKELEY—Old English: Wac-leah. "From the wet meadow."

WAKEMAN—Old English: Wacu-man. "Watchman."

WALBY—Old English: Wal-by. "From the walled-dwellings" or "Home by an ancient Roman wall in England."

WALCOTT—Old English: Weall-cot. "Dweller at the wall-enclosed cottage."

WALDEMAR—Old German: Waldo-mar. "Famous ruler," or Old English: Weald-maer. "Powerful, famous." Waldemar the Great was a 12th-century Danish king.
English and Scandinavian variation: **Valdemar.**

WALDEN—Old English: Weal-dene. "From the forest valley," or Old German: Walten. "Ruler."

WALDO—Old German: Waldo. "Ruler," or Old English: Weald. "Mighty." Waldo Frank, author.

WALDRON—Old German: Wald-hramn. "Ruling raven." This raven depicted strength and authority.

WALFORD—Old English: Weala-ford. "From the Welshman's ford."

WALFRED—Old German: Waldi-frid. "Peaceful ruler."

WALKER—Middle English: Walkere. "Thickener of cloth, or 'fuller'."

WALLACE—Old English: Waleis. "Man from Wales; Welshman." Sir William Wallace, famous Scotch hero, died 1305; Wallace Reid, silent screen actor; Wally Cox, entertainer.
English nicknames: **Wallie, Wally.**
English variations: **Wallis, Walsh, Welch, Welsh.**
Foreign variation: **Wallache (German).**

WALLER—Old English: Weall-ere. "Wall-builder; mason." A master in masonry. Alternate, Old German: Walt-hari. "Army ruler."

WALLIS—See Wallace.

WALMOND—Old German: Wald-munt. "Mighty or ruling protector."

WALSH—See Wallace.

WALTER—Old German: Walt-hari. "Powerful warrior, army ruler." Namesakes: Sir Walter Raleigh, 16th-century English navigator; Sir Walter Scott, author; Walt Whitman, poet; Walt Disney, motion picture producer; actors Walter Huston, Walter Brennan, Walter Abel. English nicknames: Walt, Wat. Foreign variations: Gauthier, Gautier (French), Gualtiero (Italian), Gualterio (Spanish), Walther (German), Ualtar (Irish), Bhaltair (Scotch).

WALTON—Old English: Weall-tun. "Dweller at the town near a ruined Roman wall," or Old English: Wald-tun. "Dweller at the forest town."

WALWORTH—Old English: Weala-worth. "From the Welshman's farm."

WALWYN—Old English: Wealh-wine. "Welsh friend." A stranger once, but now a friend.

WARBURTON—Old English: Warburh-tun. "From the enduring castle town."

WARD—Old English: Weard. "Watchman, guardian." Ward Hunt, U.S. Supreme Court Justice, 1873-1882; Ward Bond, actor.
English variations: Warde, Warden, Worden.

WARDELL—Old English: Weard-hyll. "From the watch-hill." Where guards keep constant vigilance for the protection of the town.

WARDEN—See Ward.

WARDLEY—Old English: Weard-leah. "From the guardian's meadow."

WARE—Old English: Waer. "Wary, astute, prudent one," or Old German: Ware. "Defender."

WARFIELD—Middle English: Ware-feld. "Dweller at the weir-field." A weir was a dam across a small stream.

WARFORD—Middle English: Ware-ford. "From the weir-ford."

WARING—See Warren.

WARLEY—Middle English: Ware-ley. "From the weir-meadow."

WARMOND—Old English: Waer-mund. "True protector."

WARNER—Old German: Waren-hari. "Defending army or warrior." Warner Baxter, actor. Foreign variation: Werner (German).

WARREN—Old German: Waren. "Watchman, defender or true-man," or Middle English: Wareine. "Game-preserve keeper." Warin or Guarin was among the heroes of the medieval ballad, *Chanson de Roland,* the story of the nephew of the Emperor Charlemagne. Warren G. Harding, 28th U.S. President; actors Warren William, Warren Beatty.

WARTON—Old English: Ware-tun. "From the weir-dam town or estate."

WARWICK—Old English: Waeringawicum. "Fortress of the defender's family." English variation: **Warrick**.

WASHBURN—Old English: Waesc-burne. "Dweller at the flooding-brook." A small stream running wild in spring.

WASHINGTON—Old English: Hwaesinga-tun. "From the estate of the keen-one's family." George Washington, 1st U.S. President; Washington Irving, American writer (1783-1859); Washington Allston, painter (1779-1843).

WATFORD—Old English: Watel-ford. "From the hurdle-ford." A hurdle for fine jumping horses.

WATKINS—Old English: Watte-kin-sone. "Son of Walter."

WATSON—Old English: Watte-sone. "Son of Walter."

WAVERLY—Old English: Waefre-leah. "Quaking-aspen tree meadow."

WAYLAND—Old English: Weg-land. "From the pathway land or property."

WAYNE—Old English: Waen-man. "Wagoner or wagon-maker." Wayne Morse, U.S. Senator; Wayne Morris, actor.

WEBB—Old English: Webbe. "A weaver." A professional weaver of wool cloth.

WEBER—German: Weber. "A weaver."

WEBLEY—Old English: Webbe-leah. "From the weaver's meadow."

WEBSTER—Old English: Webbestre. "A weaver."

WEDDELL—Old English: Wadan-hyll. "Dweller at the ad-

vancer's hill." A man who was progressive in life.

WELBORNE—Old English: Wiella-burna. "Dweller at the spring-brook."

WELBY—Old English: Wiella-by. "Dweller at the spring-farm."

WELDON—Old English: Wiella-dun. "From the spring-hill."

WELFORD—Old English: Wiella-ford. "From the spring-ford."

WELLINGTON—Old English: Weolingtun. "From the prosperous one's family estate."

WELLS—Old English: Wiellas. "From the springs."

WELSH—See Wallace.

WELTON—Old English: Wiella-tun. "Dweller at the spring-town or estate." Welton Becket, noted architect.

WENCESLAUS—Old Slavic: Wenceslava. "Wreath or garland of glory." St. Wenceslaus was a 10th-century king of Bohemia.

WENDELL—Old German: Wendel. "Wanderer," or Old English: Wend-el. "Boundary-dweller." A man who lived on the boundary of two counties. Wendell Willkie, U.S. attorney, statesman; Wendell Corey, actor.

WENTWORTH—Old English: Wintan-weorth. "White one's estate." A descriptive characterization of a white-haired man.

WERNER—Old German: Warin-hari. "Defending warrior or army." Wernher Von Braun, U.S. space engineer.

WESLEY—Old English: West-leah. "From the west meadow." English variation: **Westleigh**.

WEST—Old English: West. "Man from the west." Directional names were popular in medieval England.

WESTBROOK—Old English: West-broc. "From the west-brook." Westbrook Pegler, journalist, columnist.

WESTBY—Old English: West-by. "From the west-farmstead."

WESTCOTT—Old English: West-cot. "From the west cottage."

WESTON—Old English: West-tun. "From the west estate."

WETHERBY—Old English: Wethr-by. "From the wether-sheep farm."

WETHERELL—Old English: Wethr-healh. "From the wether-sheep corner." Where white sheep grazed in deep green pastures.

WETHERLY—Old English: Wethr-leah. "Dweller at the wether-sheep meadow."

WHARTON—Old English: Hwer-tun. "Estate at the hollow, or embankment."

WHEATLEY—Old English: Hwaete-leah. "Wheat meadow."

WHEATON—Old English: Hwaete-tun. "Wheat estate or town."

WHEELER—Old English: Hweol-ere. "Wheel-maker." This man earned the respect of the people for his profession.

WHISTLER—Old English: Hwistlere. "Whistler or piper." A man popular at festive affairs and pageants. James McNeill Whistler, painter (1834-1903).

WHITBY—Old English: Hwit-by. "From the white farmstead."

WHITCOMB—Old English: Hwit-cumb. "From the white hollow." A valley named for its prevailing white clay soil. James Whitcomb Riley, poet (1853-1916).

WHITELAW—Old English: Hwit-hloew. "From the white hill." Whitelaw Reid, journalist, diplomat (1837-1912).

WHITFIELD—Old English: Hwit-feld. "From the white field."

WHITFORD—Old English: Hwit-ford. "From the white ford." A ford where a river ran over white clay. Whitford Kane, actor.

WHITLEY—Old English: Hwit-leah. "From the white meadow."

WHITLOCK—Old English: Hwit-locc. "Man with a white lock of hair," or Old English: Hwit-loc. "From the white stronghold."

WHITMAN—Old English: Hwit-man. "White-haired man."

WHITMORE—Old English: Hwit-mor. "From the white moor."

WHITNEY—Old English: Hwitan-ig. "From the white-haired one's island."

WHITTAKER—Old English: Hwit-acer. "Dweller at the white field."

WICKHAM—Old English: Wic-hamm. "From the village meadow or enclosure."

WICKLEY—Old English: Wic-leah. "Village meadow."

WILBUR—Old German: Willa-perht. "Resolute-brilliant one," or Old English: Willa-burh. "From the firm fortress." Wilbur Wright, aviation pioneer (1867-1912).

WILEY—See William. Wiley Post, aviator (1900-1935).

WILFORD—Old English: Wylig-ford. "Dweller at the willow-ford.

WILFRED—Old German: Willi-frid. "Resolute-peaceful one." St. Wilfrid, 8th-century English prelate; Wilfrid Hyde White, actor.
English variation: **Wilfrid.**

WILL—Old English: Willa. "Determined, firm, resolute." See **William.**

WILLARD—Old English: Willhard. "Resolute and brave." Willard F. Libby, U.S. atomic scientist; Willard Parker, actor.

WILLIAM—Old German: Willihelm. "Resolute protector." Notables: William the Conqueror, Norman subjugator of England in 1066; William Randolph Hearst, publisher; William Shakespeare, dramatist; William C. Menninger, psychiatrist; William Beebe, scientist; Willie Mays, baseball star; Will Rogers, actor.
English nicknames: **Will, Willie, Willy, Bill, Billy.**
English variations: **Wiley, Wilkie, Wilkes, Wilson, Williamson, Willis.**
Foreign variations: **Wilhelm** (German), **Guillaume** (French), **Guglielmo** (Italian), **Guillermo** (Spanish), **Vilhelm** (Swedish), **Willem** (Dutch), **Uilleam** (Scotch), **Uilliam** (Irish).

WILLOUGHBY—Old English: Wylig-by. "From the willow farm."

WILMER—Old German: Willamar. "Resolute, famous one."

WILMOT—Old German: Willimod. "Resolute spirit or mind." An endearing name for a kindly, wise, firm man.

WILSON—Old English: Willesone. "Son of William or Will." See **William.** Wilson Bissel, U.S. Postmaster General (1893-1894).

WILTON—Old English: Wylltun. "From the spring farm."

WINCHELL—Old English: Wincel. "From a corner or bend in a piece of land or a road." Walter Winchell, columnist, commentator; Winchell Smith, American playwright.

WINDSOR—Old English: Wendles-ora. "Boundary bank." A riverbank used for a land division.

WINFIELD—Old English: Wine-feld. "From the friend's field." Winfield Scott, U.S. Army general (1786-1866).

WINFRED—Old English: Wine-frith. "Peaceful friend." English variation: **Winifred.**

WINGATE—Old English: Wine-god. "Divine protection," or Old English: Windan-geat. "From the winding-gate," a gate on a turn-screw.

WINSLOW—Old English: Wines-hloew. "From the friend's hill." Winslow Homer, American painter (1836-1910).

WINSTON—Old English: Windes-tun. "From the friend's estate or town." Winston Churchill, English statesman; Winston Graham, author.

WINTER—Old English: Winter. "Born in the wintertime." When winter snows obscured the land, a son was born.

WINTHROP—Old English: Wine-torp. "Dweller at the friend's estate." Winthrop Rockefeller, business executive; Winthrop Ames, American theatrical producer.

WINTON—Old English: Wine-tun. "From the friend's estate."

WINWARD—Old English: Wine-wode. "Friend's forest," or Old English: Wine-weard. "Friend-guardian."

WIRT—German: Wirt. "Master," or Old English: Wyrthig. "Worthy one."

WITT—Old English: Witta. "Wise man." A man the townsmen sought for solace and advice.

WITTER—Old English: Witta-here. "Wise warrior." Witter Bynner, poet.

WITTON—Old English: Witta-tun. "From the wise man's estate."

WOLCOTT—Old English: Wulf-cot. "From Wolf's cottage." Wolf names were only applied to men of outstanding courage and bravery.

WOLFE—Old English: Wulf. "A wolf." L. Wolfe Gilbert, composer.

WOLFGANG—Old German: Wolf-gang. "Advancing wolf." Leader of an advancing army, or a progressive man. Wolfgang Mozart, famous composer; Johann Wolfgang Goethe, German author.

WOODROW—Old English: Wudo-roew. "Dweller at the hedge by the forest."

WOODRUFF—Old English: Wudo-raefa. "Forest-warden or bailiff."

WOODWARD—Old English: Wudo-weard. "Forest-warden; forester."

WOOLSEY—Old English: Wulf-sige. "Victorious wolf." A name given for a man of courage. Cardinal Woolsey, famous English prelate under King Henry VIII.

WORCESTER—Old English: Wire-ceaster. "Alder-forest army camp."

WORDSWORTH—Old English: Wulfweards-weorth. "Wolf-guardian's farm." William Wordsworth, famous English poet.

WORRELL—Old English: Waer-heall. "Dweller at the trueman's manor."

WORTH—Old English: Weorth. "Farmstead."

WORTON—Old English: Wyrt-tun. "Dweller at the vegetable enclosure." A man who lived where vegetables were grown for the market.

WRAY—Old Norse: Ura. "From the corner property."

WREN—Old Welsh: Ren. "Chief or ruler," or Old English: Wrenna. "Wren-bird." Christopher Wren, architect of St. Paul's Cathedral, London (1632-1723).

WRIGHT—Old English: Wryhta. "Carpenter." Wright Patman, U.S. Congressman.

WYATT—Old French: Guyot. "Little warrior." Wyatt Earp, famous American lawman, frontiersman.

WYBORN—Old Norse: Uig-biorn. "War-bear." An outstanding man, brave as a bear in battle."

WYCLIFF—Old English: Hwit-clif. "From the white cliff."

WYMAN—Old English: Wigman. "Warrior."

WYMER—Old English: Wigmaere. "Famous in battle."

WYNDHAM—Old English: Windham. "From the enclosure with the winding path."

WYNN—Old Welsh: Wyn. "Fair; white one." English variation: Winn.

WYTHE—Middle English: Wyth. "Dweller by a willowtree." George Wythe, a signer of Declaration of Independence (1726-1806).

X

XAVIER—Spanish Basque: Javerri; Xaver. "Owner of the new house." Honoring St. Francis de Xavier or Javier, born at his family's castle of Javier in Navarra, Spain; he was a missionary known as the "Apostle of the Indies." Foreign variations: Javier, Xever (Spanish).

XENOS—Greek: Xenos. "Stranger or guest."

XERXES—Persian: Ksathra. "Ruler; royal prince." Xerxes, King of Persia, B.C. 486-465, known in the Bible as Ahasuerus, was the husband of Esther in the Book of Esther.

XYLON—Greek: Xylon. "From the forest."

Y

YALE—Old English: Healh. "From the slope or corner of land." Elihu Yale, founder of Yale University (1648-1721).

YANCY—American Indian: Yankee. "Englishman." Seventeenth-century New England Indians distorted "English" to "Yankee," it is stated.

YATES—Middle English: Yates. "Dweller at the gates." A man who lived at the city gates.

YEHUDI—Hebrew: Jehujidah. "The praise of the Lord." Yehudi Menuhin, violinist.

YEOMAN—Middle English: Yoman. "Retainer." A man attached to the staff of a manorial estate who owed it occasional service.

YORK—Old English: Eofor-wic. "Boar-estate," or Old Celtic: Eburacon. "Yew-tree estate."

YULE—Old English: Geol. "Born at Christmas."

YVES—See Ives. St. Yves or Yvo Helory, 13th-century Breton, is patron saint of lawyers. Yves Montand, actor.

Z

ZACHARY—Hebrew: Zekharyah. "Jehovah hath remembered." The modern form of Zachariah, from the Bible. St. Zachary, a Pope, died in 752; Zachary Taylor, 12th U.S. President; Zachary Scott, actor. Foreign variations: **Zacharias** (German), **Zacarías** (Spanish), **Zacharie** (French), **Zakarias** (Swedish), **Zaccaria** (Italian), **Zakarij** (South Slavic).

ZADOK—Hebrew: Tsadhoq. "Just, righteous one." Foreign variation: **Zadoc.** (French).

ZANE—See John.. Zane Grey, American author.

ZARED—Hebrew: Zared. "Ambush."

ZEBULON—Hebrew: Zebulon. "Dwelling place." Zebulon was one of Jacob's sons in the Bible. Zebulon Weaver, U.S. Congressman; Zebulon Pike, U.S. Army officer and explorer.

ZEDEKIAH—Hebrew: Tsidhqiyah. "Justice of the Lord."

ZEEMAN—Dutch: Zeeman. "Seaman." Peter Zeeman, Dutch physicist.

ZELOTES—Greek: Zelotes. "Zealous one." A person diligent and enthused with life and responsibilities.

ZENAS—Greek: Zenas. "Living."

ZEUS—Greek: Zeus. "Living one," or "Father of gods and men." Zeus was the ancient Greek ruler of heaven.

ZIV—Old Slavic: Zivu. "Living one."

ZURIEL—Hebrew: Zur-iyel. "God; my stone or rock." God is the Creator or Foundation of all things.

Congratulations— But...

What about all those questions and problems that arrive with a new addition to the family? Here are several invaluable books for any new or expectant mother. They are filled with helpful hints for raising healthy children in a happy home. Best of luck and may all your problems be little ones!

☐ 24642	HAVING A BABY AFTER 30 by Bing & Colman	$3.95
☐ 23821	BH&G NEW BABY BOOK	$3.95
☐ 23659	THE BABY CHECKUP BOOK: A Parent Guide to Well Baby Care by Sheila Hillman	$3.95
☐ 01409	INFANT MASSAGE: A Handbook for Loving Parents by Vimala Schneider	$4.95
☐ 24412	CARING FOR YOUR UNBORN CHILD by Gots, M.D.'s	$3.95
☐ 23934	UNDERSTANDING PREGNANCY AND CHILDBIRTH by Sheldon H. Cherry, M.D.	$3.95
☐ 23122	NINE MONTHS READING by Robert E. Hall, M.D.	$3.95
☐ 22721	FEED ME! I'M YOURS by Vicki Lansky	$2.95
☐ 24973	SIX PRACTICAL LESSONS FOR AN EASIER CHILDBIRTH by Elisabeth Bing	$3.50
☐ 23407	NAME YOUR BABY by Lareina Rule	$2.95
☐ 24496	THE EARLY CHILDHOOD YEARS: THE 2 TO 6 YEAR OLD by Theresa & Frank Caplan	$3.95
☐ 24233	THE FIRST TWELVE MONTHS OF LIFE by Frank Caplan, ed.	$4.95
☐ 23249	SECOND TWELVE MONTHS OF LIFE by Frank Caplan	$4.95
☐ 25444	COMPLETE BOOK OF BREASTFEEDING by M. Eiger, M.D. & S. Olds	$3.95

Prices and availability subject to change without notice.

Buy them at your local bookstore or use this handy coupon for ordering:

THE FAMILY—TOGETHER AND APART

Choose from this potpourri of titles for the information you need on the many facets of family living.

SPECIAL MONEY SAVING OFFER

Now you can have an up-to-date listing of Bantam's hundreds of titles plus take advantage of our unique and exciting bonus book offer. A special offer which gives you the opportunity to purchase a Bantam book for only 50¢. Here's how!

By ordering any five books at the regular price per order, you can also choose any other single book listed (up to a $4.95 value) for just 50¢. Some restrictions do apply, but for further details why not send for Bantam's listing of titles today!

Just send us your name and address plus 50¢ to defray the postage and handling costs.